From Silo to Spoon

From Silo to Spoon

Local and Global Food Ethics

PAUL B. THOMPSON

OXFORD
UNIVERSITY PRESS

Oxford University Press is a department of the University of Oxford. It furthers the University's objective of excellence in research, scholarship, and education by publishing worldwide. Oxford is a registered trade mark of Oxford University Press in the UK and certain other countries.

Published in the United States of America by Oxford University Press
198 Madison Avenue, New York, NY 10016, United States of America.

Library of Congress Cataloging-in-Publication Data
Names: Thompson, Paul B., 1951– author.
Title: From silo to spoon : local and global food ethics / Paul B. Thompson.
Description: New York, NY : Oxford University Press, [2024] |
Includes bibliographical references and index.
Identifiers: LCCN 2023032633 (print) | LCCN 2023032634 (ebook) |
ISBN 9780197744734 (paperback) | ISBN 9780197744727 (hardback) |
ISBN 9780197744741 (epub)
Subjects: LCSH: Food supply—Moral and ethical aspects.
Classification: LCC HD9000.5 .T456 2023 (print) | LCC HD9000.5 (ebook) |
DDC 363.8—dc23/eng/20230714
LC record available at https://lccn.loc.gov/2023032633
LC ebook record available at https://lccn.loc.gov/2023032634

DOI: 10.1093/oso/9780197744727.001.0001

Paperback printed by Marquis Book Printing, Canada
Hardback printed by Bridgeport National Bindery, Inc., United States of America

Dedicated to Walker L. Thompson

Contents

Acknowledgments

This book is a successor to *From Field to Fork: Food Ethics for Everyone*. As I said there, my writing turned toward new audiences around 2012, shifting from a focus on scientists and other professionals within food systems to non-specialists interested in the production, processing, distribution, and consumption of food. Other philosophers were a prominent part of my new audience, and the earlier book was written with an eye to the possibility that they would use it for their teaching. The earlier book received the North American Society for Social Philosophy's (NASSP) Book of the Year Award for 2015. That award encouraged me to follow up with this sequel, and I would like to thank the NASSP for their recognition of my work. Perhaps more than anything, the appreciation I received from this group of philosophers validated my turn toward a philosophical readership.

This book is not simply a continuation of *From Field to Fork*, however. That book adopted an introductory and pedagogical standpoint in a specific sense. I was communicating what I had learned from three decades of interaction with scientifically trained food system specialists to readers with an interest in food ethics but with little familiarity with the received views of food system experts. At the same time, I took pains to introduce ideas from philosophical ethics in a rudimentary fashion. The book addressed general areas of food ethics rather than specific problems. Although I did not shy away from advocating my own views altogether, I downplayed the general philosophical perspective from which I have done my work. In this book, I develop that perspective by considering a series of more focused philosophical problems, including the rationale for food aid, the quandaries of locavorism, and the ethical justification of food labels. These essays lead into chapters where I draw a contrast between my own approach and that of other environmental philosophers. The book culminates with one chapter introducing my brand of agrarian philosophy and a sequel that brings this philosophy to issues that are being raised in the philosophy of race. I hope that readers who enjoyed *From Field to Fork* will find this book a worthy successor, but I also hope that this book draws in new readers with a general interest in philosophy.

My turn to a new type of reader would not have been possible were it not for my move to Michigan State University (MSU) in 2003. The W. K. Kellogg Professorship in Agricultural, Food, and Community Ethics provided very generous financial support for my work, but I am thinking of the intellectual community at Michigan State when I write this. I had a long-standing relationship with rural sociologist Lawrence Busch that dated back to his years at the University of Kentucky and my years at Texas A&M. I had good colleagues on MSU's agricultural economics group long before joining the faculty. Glenn Johnson, in particular, had taken me aside and given me a patient education in the economics of the food system, and James Bonnen was an early supporter of bringing philosophers into the sometimes insular network of agricultural specialists. They were retired by the time I joined the faculty in East Lansing, but Sandra Batie, Al Schmid, John Staatz, and Dave Schweikardt were there and continued to shape my thinking. Later, my teaching and writing collaboration with Patricia Norris became one of the most profound influences on my thought.

Sandra Batie was operating a project to coordinate activity among the endowed chairs in MSU's College of Agriculture and Natural Resources (CANR). It became an important source of intellectual growth for me, reconnecting me with old friends such as Richard Bawden, James Tiedje, and Michael Hamm, and introducing me to Christopher Peterson, Joan Rose, Dave Beede, Jim Detjen, Tom Dietz, Soji Adelaja, and Jianguo "Jack" Liu. This was the Sustainable Michigan Endowed Project (SMEP), which later involved Mark Skidmore, David Hennesy, Felicia Wu, Jinhua Zhao, Bill Porter, Eric Freedman, and Rick Foster. SMEP was a laboratory for trying out ideas on food ethics and the philosophy of sustainability. The list of other CANR colleagues who have played formative roles in my thinking is too long to recount, but I would single out Rebecca Grumet, with whom I taught a course on social and ethical issues in agricultural biotechnology; Laurie Thorp, an innovator in adult natural resource education; and Janice Swanson, an animal scientist that I had been working with long before either of us came to MSU.

This powerhouse lineup of agricultural scientists notwithstanding, it was the MSU philosophers who had the biggest influence on my subsequent work. When I appeared as a candidate for the newly created W. K. Kellogg Chair in Agricultural, Food, and Community Ethics before a polite but skeptical faculty in the philosophy department, I was quizzed on my engagement with feminism. I think they were more interested in my attitude than my facility. I answered that although I did not feel like I had a grasp of what feminist philosophers were up to, I had been attentive to the food-related work of Susan Bordo (who was my colleague in graduate school) and Lisa Heldke. This satisfied them for the time being, but it was two feminists in the MSU department, Marilyn Frye and Hilde Lindemann, who taught me that there *was* no single thing that feminist philosophers were up to. Kristi Dotson, Kyle Whyte, Elena Ruíz, Tacuma Peters, and John McClendon, all of whom joined the Michigan State department after me, were crucial for opening me to the philosophical dimensions of race. I was recruited by then department head Steve Esquith, who helped me reinvigorate my interest in development ethics. Debra Nails, Richard Peterson, Michael O'Rourke, and Catherine Kendig are among the other MSU philosophers who deserve special note for shaping my thinking over the years, but, in truth, all the MSU philosophers have been sensational colleagues. I am also indebted to my Purdue philosophy colleague Leonard Harris for my first introduction to the philosophy of race and to one of my Purdue students, Debra Jackson, for making me think hard about gender in the courses I was teaching.

Turning specifically to the preparation of this manuscript, I was fortunate to have the most careful cadre of readers and critics that I have ever enjoyed in my career. They include Lee McBride III, whom I met when he was a PhD student under Harris's supervision at Purdue, and Lisa Heldke, with whom I have developed a long-standing friendship. Joining them were a number of my former doctoral students from MSU: Danielle Lake, Ian Werkheiser, Samantha Noll, Zachary Piso, Monica List, and Jared Talley. Blake Ginsberg was still completing his graduate studies at the time he read the text. Other readers include Anne Portman, Joey Tuminello, Patricia Norris, Robbie Richardson, and Tom Dietz. There was also Jennifer Welchman, the external reviewer for Oxford University Press, as well as Lucy Randall, Oxford University Press's amazing philosophy editor. Lucy also helped with *From Field to Fork* and *Sustainability: What Everyone Needs to Know*, my book with Pat Norris. All of these readers made important comments that have improved the book immensely.

Erin Anderson contributed the drawing that appears in the Introduction. Ken Marable has done indexing for several of my books. Thank-you, Ken. I would also like to acknowledge Lauralee Yeary, who supervised much of the review process for Oxford, and Egle Zigaite, my OUP project editor. Staff at Newgen Knowledge Works contributed copy editing and production assistance, for which I express my gratitude.

Some of the chapters in this book reprise themes from earlier publications and probably cannibalize a few sentences or paragraphs. Others are entirely new areas of inquiry for me. However, even where I am revisiting themes like food aid, labeling, sustainability, or agrarianism (Chapters 2, 4, 6, and 7) the treatment in this book goes substantially beyond what has appeared in previous works. What is more, the topical chapters have been revised to support the marriage of agrarian and pragmatist philosophy that is made in Chapter 7, providing a meta-ethical envelope that situates my overall philosophical project. Against the background of obvious problems with any view that calls itself "agrarian," the concluding chapter sketches my ideas on rapprochement between environmental philosophy and the philosophy of race, the two crucial philosophical themes of my lifetime.

Some readers are annoyed by footnotes and references to other writers. I have chosen to include them, leaving clues for readers who want to follow-up. I also want to acknowledge the scholarship of others that has informed my work. Some footnotes amplify points in the text, especially when a longer discussion is ancillary to the topic at hand. I have also adopted some conventions intended to help readers. Acronyms are pervasive in the field of food and agriculture. In every chapter where I refer to USDA or FAO, you will see the full name spelled out (e.g., US Department of Agriculture or Food and Agricultural Organization of the United Nations) prior to my subsequent use of the acronym. In addition, pegging ideas to a human being improves the flow of a text and helps us keep track of where the inquiry is going. I like to use both first and last names for that purpose and will include a person's full name the first time I refer to him or her in any given chapter. With the exception of these acknowledgments, which mention several friends who have passed, I will also include the years of their birth and death the first time their name appears in the book. This will give you a way to put them into a historical narrative and to see the history of philosophical thinking as a developing a continuous storyline. If a name isn't followed by a parenthetical birth and death indication, the person was still living in 2022, when this book was written.

Introduction

León is a software engineer who works for a well-known IT firm in California. His brother Milo runs an art supply store nearby. The two are very close. They describe their parents as former hippies who fed their children on brown rice and organic vegetables. Milo still maintains a mostly vegetarian diet, though he eats eggs and dairy products. He occasionally consumes fish and enjoys a celebratory hot dog once a year. León drifted further from his parents' principles, and he gave up any pretense of dietary ethics as he began to socialize over steak dinners with clients of his company. Both of them have started to wonder about bringing up children they might someday have in the same way they were raised.

There is not one single thing that troubles them, but they are rethinking their diets along different pathways. León thinks that his parents were a bit obsessive. Their focus on a healthful diet made him jealous of friends who enjoyed candy and sodas or collected the toys in drive-through kids' meals with burgers and chicken nuggets. Although he thinks anyone is fully entitled to choose whatever it is that they want to eat, he thinks dietary choice is purely a matter of aesthetics and personal taste. Milo also takes joy in little vacations from the dietary ascetics of his parents, but he is asking himself whether his parents failed to appreciate the challenges that less well-off families and working mothers face in feeding their families. The inexpensive and ready-to-eat meal is a boon to working mothers, he thinks. While both of them are revising their parents' dietary puritanism, León is coming to see a person's diet is their own business, while Milo is starting to understand dietary responsibilities in terms of the overall social context.

In one sense, León's perspective would probably have been taken for granted in his grandparents' generation. Very few people would have thought about dietary choice in ethical terms throughout the first half of the 20th century. However, hippies or not, León and Milo's parents were early converts to the idea that what they choose to eat has ethical implications. In one respect, they were simply following a commonsense principle of prudence to live a healthful life. They would have been among the first to suspect that many

From Silo to Spoon. Paul B. Thompson, Oxford University Press. © Oxford University Press 2024.
DOI: 10.1093/oso/9780197744727.003.0001

of the items in the supermarket could harm them. Like Milo, they were also thinking about the broader impact of the foods they eat and beginning to rethink their diets in moral terms. Many present-day vegans and vegetarians who started with a focus on animals have themselves become more expansive, incorporating concern for social justice into their diets. The tension between viewpoints that stress individual choice or personal values and those that see many of the things we do as involving social duties is a frequent topic in philosophical ethics.

Everett works for a charitable nongovernmental organization (NGO) with a strong religious affiliation. The NGO conducts a broad range of humanitarian activities, including disaster relief and community development among impoverished communities all over the world. Everett works in the fund-raising side of the organization, making appeals through pamphlets, television commercials, a website, and other types of social media. Everett knows that pictures of hungry children accompanied by short bios are very effective fund-raising techniques. People who make donations are told that their contribution will provide food for this child for a week, a month, or a year, depending on how much they give.

Although Everett is reconciled to making these appeals, they trouble his conscience. To actually link one person's gift to another specific individual's need consumes too much money, though some NGOs do it. Others fake it, which is also troubling on ethical grounds. However, Everett also finds the message of feeding hungry people through charity itself problematic. He worries that gifts of food promote a permanent dependency relationship among recipients who frequent food banks or who get food deliveries from internationally oriented charities. There are also ethical problems for the people who make these gifts. When his organization appeals to their sympathy, it distracts them from more complex issues that reproduce the conditions of poverty and deprivation. What is more, many of the individuals his organization helps face food insecurity on a short-term basis—after a hurricane or late in the year where the crops they grew earlier are starting to run short. They do need food, but the images used to convince people to contribute portrays these people in a way that is both misleading and not properly respectful of the agency food recipients possess in normal circumstances. Everett is thankful their problems are not endemic, but he worries that his organization has oversimplified its messaging and may not deserve the trust of its donors.

Food systems are complex, yet just as it is possible to be over-individualistic in thinking about one's diet, many people maintain an overly individualized picture of food security. As Everett's concern illustrates, understanding the moral imperatives of food in terms of feeding hungry individuals is not entirely bad. People who see the hungry person as a worthy beneficiary of our charity enable organizations like his to do a world of good things. Perhaps we should not try to disabuse people of this image. Nevertheless, the public's ignorance of systemic processes that create food deficits makes thorough reform of the food system more difficult. There are ethical questions at every level. How should we understand our obligation to help the hungry? How should our response be implemented? Then, as Everett's worries show, how should we even communicate about our moral obligations in ways that both motivate action and also increase everyone's sophistication?

Xiaojing is pursuing an advanced degree in geography at a European university. Her father, who lives in Nanjing, China, comes from a small farming village in Jiangsu Province. He lived through the Great Famine years of 1959–1961 and vowed to escape the poverty of Chinese farming. Though he is reluctant to speak of a time when he was reduced to begging (some desperate people ate their children),[1] Xiaojing knows the shame her father felt and the pride he now takes in having a daughter who is able to pursue research. She has an uncle and a great aunt who still farm the family plots, but the village population has collapsed. Where forty or fifty families, each with several children, once farmed the patchwork of uneven fields tailored for race, maize, and other food crops, there are now a dozen households. Although these rural villages were excepted from the most onerous applications of China's one-child policy, no one under the age of fifty lives in the village today. It is not clear what will happen after her father's generation passes.

The Chinese government has undertaken agricultural modernization policies that consolidate these traditional farms, encouraging the use of Western technology and farming methods. However, Xiaojing's professors are promoting the preservation of smallholder farms like the one her uncle runs. Xiaojing is not so sure. Her aunt and uncle live in a small walled compound with two enclosed rooms, only one of which has electricity. There is no running water in the house. There is a shared facility where everyone in the village can get water, bathe, and use the toilet, but their water has to be boiled before they can drink it. Xiaojing's teachers promote food sovereignty and worry that that the industrialization of farming weakens community ties. Her father says that, along with a nearby stream where they could fish, strong community ties helped them survive the famine years. However, he

also pities his brother and has never encouraged anyone in Xiaojing's generation to consider farming the family homestead.

Xiaojing has a personal view on one of the most difficult issues in food
ethics. In Western countries, the industrialization of the agricultural sector
was accompanied by waves of farm bankruptcy and the consolidation of
many small, family farms into larger operations that could take advantage
of equipment and modern business practices. Now a large segment of the
public has grown suspicious of agribusiness. They worry about the environmental impact of chemicals and genetically engineered crops. They do not
trust either farmers or farm supply companies that seem to be motivated
solely by the desire to maximize profits. And, indeed, in China as in many
rapidly developing economies, the profit motive has led to crises in the safety
of food. Yet it seems unjust to expect the next generation of farmers to en-
dure the hardships experienced by her father's generation. Xiaojing shares
the view of many food system professionals: new technologies are necessary
to feed the world.

The individuals I have just discussed are not real people. They are philosophical thought experiments, devised to illustrate ethical quandaries in
food ethics. All of us need to eat, and most people in industrial societies eat
several times a day. An upswing in reflection on the typical diet has been
going on since the 1960s, the time of León and Milo's parents.[2] If some diets
are better than others, we should be able to identify some normative principles that explain why that is the case. Food ethics would then be a philosophical reflection on the reasons that people have for choosing to eat one thing
rather than another, as well as for organizing the production, processing,
and distribution of food in one configuration rather than another. However,
there are subtleties that this picture overlooks. I think of this book as a philosophical inquiry. My goal is to reconsider some familiar questions in food
ethics, revealing their complexities and placing them in greater philosophical depth. Our collective thinking on food has yet to address many of the
important philosophical puzzles in food ethics, and each chapter in this book
will demonstrate what some of these puzzles are.

Some of the philosophical issues that create controversy in the food system
have very little to do with ethics, as philosophers understand it. Some are issues in social theory and power, while others have to do with the management of uncertainty or inequality in the distribution of knowledge—topics
that philosophers associate with epistemology. This suggests that food ethics
is a doorway into broader philosophical understandings of the world and

humanity's place in it. In this respect, food ethics can serve as an introduction to philosophy itself. In fact, I do not assume that readers have much background in philosophy as it is taught in universities today. The chapters in this book have been written so that readers with a minimal grasp of ethics and social theory can pick and choose without reading them in order. Nevertheless, the order is not arbitrary, and readers who do go from cover to cover will be led down a path that moves steadily into more comprehensive philosophical questions.

There are still more reasons to think philosophically about food. One is reflected in most philosophers' neglect of the topic. Philosophical attention to the production and consumption of food has waned steadily for centuries. Many readers well-read in philosophy will assume that food and agriculture have *never* played an important role in philosophical thought, but this presumption is a cultural artifact of industrial society. The challenges of the current era call for an awakening of environmental consciousness. Unlike many environmental philosophers, I think that this awakening must take account of food. On the one hand, reflecting on food should lead us into a more sensitive understanding of our place within the environment. On the other hand, an environmental ethic that fails to consider food is unlikely to answer the call for an awakened outlook on humanity's place in nature. Thus, in this book I am also developing the rationale for a particular philosophical approach to environmental ethics and an alternative understanding of the human condition.

How Philosophers Think of Ethics

My book *From Field to Fork* summarized the ways that philosophers approach ethics with a graphic image of a decision-maker. It illustrates how both people and groups make choices under three kinds of constraint. First, there is what is technically possible. Second, there is what is legally admissible. Finally, there are informal norms and expectations that derive from culture. One form of philosophical ethics emphasizes critical evaluation of formal and informal rules, policies and institutions that constrain our behavior. Some philosophers who take this approach derive their understanding of what we are allowed to do from detailed inquiry into the nature of human freedom: Are we really free when we act in ways that fail to respect others? Others view both legal and customary norms as a sort of contract or bargain that has been negotiated implicitly among everyone in society (Figure I.1). Both views are often called *rights-theories*.

While some think of ethics in terms of rules that constrain our choices, others focus entirely on the consequences: the outcome that our behavior causes. Outcomes measure impact in terms of increases and decreases in the health, wealth, and well-being of ourselves and the others affected by our action. One answer to the ethical questions being pondered by León, Milo, Everett, and Xiaojing can be found in determining which of our options leads to the best consequences and presuming that one acts with moral justification when one chooses that option. *Utilitarianism* is the most influential version of this focus on consequences. Yet there are still other ways to think of ethics. They might start by imagining a person of impeccable moral character, someone who is sensitive to the thick structure of interpersonal relationships in which he or she is embedded. Such a person may be more attentive to the disciplines of virtuous conduct than to any particular decision-making situation. Philosophers call this approach *virtue theory*.

The thought experiments I have presented might be analyzed in terms of these three different ways that philosophers approach ethics. For example, Everett is tormented by the way good outcomes from charitable gifts rationalize acts that do not respect the recipients of these gifts. He might find support for these feelings in an ethical framework that stresses rights and duties: even if his organization is promoting the health, wealth and well-being of people, its way of doing it neglects a duty to recognize their right to decide for themselves what is good for them. Xiaojing's teachers may be thinking of the smallholding farmer as a paragon of virtue, as someone coming very close to living the kind of life that everyone should live, in spite of their poverty. Then Xiaojing would be taking a consequentialist/utilitarian line in emphasizing the difficulties that smallholding farmers (like her aunt and uncle) face.

Although every chapter will draw upon the ideas of rights theory, utilitarianism, and character ethics, I do not take any of these approaches to provide a universal, one-size-fits-all method for evaluating human action in ethical terms. In addition to going more deeply into a few interesting cases that involve food, the book gradually develops an alternative way to understand what moral philosophy is about. This aspect of the book makes it relevant to readers who are not especially interested in food but who follow work in ethics more generally, or who have an interest in ethics or pragmatist

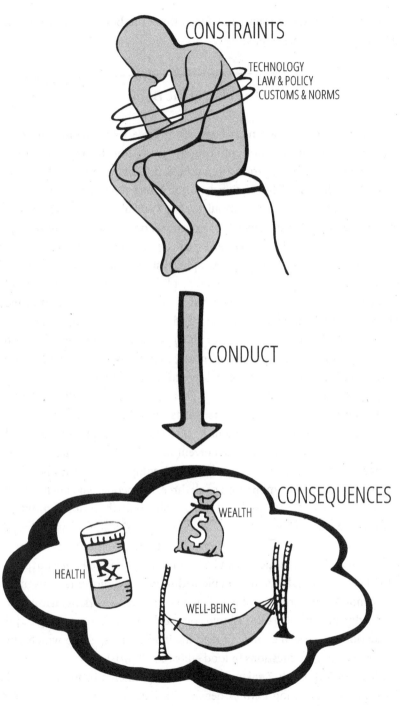

Figure I.1

philosophy. So there is a sense in which I think this book is a contribution to ethics in a more general sense.

The Plan of the Book

My earlier book examined how this three-way picture of rights/ consequences/virtues moral philosophy plays out through a series of questions relating to the production, processing, distribution, and consumption of food. It was a self-consciously introductory treatment of these issues.[3] This book also utilizes this vocabulary, but I will also use a different three-fold model, one that classifies types of moral discourse, to analyze important issues in food ethics. Chapter 1 provides an outline of that model and explains how it contributes to philosophical studies of practical importance. Chapter 1 also explains how I situate my philosophical approach within the tradition of pragmatism. A pragmatist approach differs from that of many philosophers who use moral theories to address practical issues. Their vision of applied ethics holds that we literally *apply* theories developed on purely abstract grounds. These philosophers are, in my view, insufficiently curious about the contour of situations that seem to call for ethics.

Chapter 2 starts with the food movement. Some readers will wonder what the food movement is, while others will assume that food ethics is all about furthering it. The food movement is composed of people who think that there are deep problems with the current food system. They are working to change it, either through policy shifts, technological innovations, cultural adaptations or some combination of all three. For people who are part of this social movement, the phrase "food ethics" congers up the moral commitment to making a change. The idea that there could be ethical reasons for keeping the food system just as it is seems absurd. Although I agree that there needs to be change, this standpoint can block inquiries into the larger purpose of a food system. It makes some people within the food movement insensitive to the moral commitments of people who continue to work in farming or in food industry firms. Chapter 1 builds on the distinctions separating inquiry, persuasion, and social control to map the intellectual space in which open-minded inquiry on questions in food ethics can flourish.

Chapters 3 through 7 take up a series of problems in food ethics. For some philosophers, food ethics began with Peter Singer's article "Famine, Affluence, and Morality," from 1972. Singer couched his argument for the moral duty to aid hungry people against the backdrop of a recent famine on the Indian Subcontinent.[4] Chapter 2 revisits the moral perplexities of food security and famine relief by taking a closer look at the reasons why people need food assistance, and comparing those reasons to the way that food aid has actually worked. Chapter 3 turns toward alleged tensions between global impacts of the food system and the recommendation to eat foods grown near one's home. Here, I defend a modified version of the ethic advocated by the local food movement. Chapter 4 takes up the ethics of food labeling, asking what venders must provide in the way of information, and what it is reasonable for consumers to demand on moral grounds. Framing the answer to this question in terms of a "consumer right to know" becomes problematic, and I argue that it is better to think of this as a right of exit. The debate over labeling of genetically engineered foods provides a context for examining this ethical issue.

Chapters 6 and 7 discuss topics that I have covered at greater length in other places, so readers who want more detail should look to the footnotes. Chapter 6 takes up environmental pollution from industrial agriculture, noting the difference between toxic effects and a broader, more aesthetic or spiritual understanding of pollution as defilement of a natural order. The idea of genetic pollution is used as a test case for the distinction. I defend the idea that although gene technologies do not introduce conceptually novel forms of toxicity (to humans or other species), it is plausible to view some forms of gene technology as having polluting effects in the sense of violating the natural order. Chapter 7 is a discussion of sustainability. It develops the idea that we must make a distinction between sustainable development and sustainability as such. Importing too much development theory into our understanding of sustainability defeats the attempt to make improvements in the sustainability of our food systems.

Chapters 2 through 7 can be characterized as practical ethics: philosophical concepts and methods of analysis are used to analyze and explore moral issues that various actors in the food system face (including eating). However, the discussion of sustainability in Chapter 7 marks a transition to the final two chapters, where I take up questions of a more purely philosophical bent. The very idea of sustainable food systems implies both descriptive and normative content. As a descriptor of some process or practice, sustainability is referencing whether or to what extent that process or practice can be expected to continue. Specification of that description draws one into debates on the definition and context of the process or practice as well as stipulating the relevant time frame. Yet, when that work is done, claims about whether the process or practice is sustainable or not appear to be matters of fact. However difficult it might be to model a process or practice, the model will either generate accurate predictions or make unreliable forecasts. In that sense, sustainability estimates can be either true or false.

Nevertheless, when people use the word "sustainability," they often mean to say that the process or practice in question *should* be sustained. In this sense, talk about achieving sustainability functions very much like the way that people talk about progress, democracy, or social justice. The word is naming a normative ideal, and if there is any sense in which one could be right or wrong about sustainability, it is with respect to whether one has been properly inclusive and reflective in the way that one understands this ideal. Chapter 7 explores this tension by comparing my own thinking on sustainable food systems with that of others who have framed the concept in idealized terms. I take a more persuasive standpoint as I recount reasons to support my own approach. However, in the spirit of inquiry, I also note reasons to emphasize the normative dimensions of sustainability and conclude the discussion by asking whether there is a path forward that could resolve the tensions between these two ways of thinking about sustainability.

The emphasis on concepts appears again in Chapter 8, where I discuss two philosophically distinct ways in which we might understand the food system. The dominant perspective starts with an understanding of "the economy" as the sphere of production, employment and exchange. Twentieth-century debates in social and political philosophy reflect different ways to evaluate the performance of government, private firms, and social relations within this sphere. One school of thought has placed priority on the overall impact of the economy on welfare, that is, the health, wealth, and well-being of the population. There are debates within this school about how welfare can be aggregated: How far can one go in totalizing benefits and costs to come up with an overall assessment of welfare for the population as a whole? A somewhat different school has emphasized entitlements and constraints intended to protect individuals from ethically unacceptable compromises to their personhood, their autonomy, and their freedom. However, *everyone* who has participated in this philosophical debate appears to have accepted the assumption that agriculture, food processing, and food retailing are simply sectors or industries within this larger entity they call "the economy."

This assumption is a two-edged sword. On the one hand, it helps us think about the food system with a set of ethical and political concepts that emerged out of 19th and early 20th century critiques of abuse, oppression and dispossession in manufacturing. The Industrial Revolution sparked a massive increase in the output of goods (and a corresponding reduction in their price for household consumers), but it also created labor markets that drove wages below the level at which workers could survive. Meanwhile, factory jobs ruined the health of low-wage workers and harmed the community with polluted air and water. Social theorists sought ways to retain the industrial revolution's productivity while reining in its morally objectionable excesses. Utilitarianism, libertarianism, contractualism, egalitarianism, liberalism, capitalism, socialism, and Marxism have populated our vocabulary with concepts that allow us to debate the structure of "the economy." A 19th-century debate focused primarily on manufacturing has yielded ideas that we now apply to every sector in the industrial economy. The food sector is no exception, and this trend has yielded important ways to conceptualize ongoing forms of injustice in the production, processing, distribution, and consumption of food.

On the other hand, this way of conceptualizing the food system has become so pervasive that most of us have lost track of how things could be different, how a different world is possible. Prior to 1800 (indeed well into the 19th century), people did *not* think of agriculture and food as mere sectors of "the economy." Indeed, it is questionable when the very idea of an economy emerged in the sense we have today. When early political economists like Adam Smith (1723–1790) spoke of "economy," it was something people did; they husbanded their resources and economized on both productive and consumptive activity. Along with work by French physiocrats, Smith's *The Wealth of Nations* laid the conceptual groundwork for thinking in terms of "the economy," but it would not be until economists such as Simon Kuznets (1901–1985) developed a framework for computing gross domestic product (GDP) that a unity (e.g., "the economy") comprising distinct industrial sectors could be conceptualized as such.[5] More pertinent to the theme of Chapter 7, this philosophy for understanding agriculture and food as one industry among many prevents us from understanding the wisdom (as well as the madness and cruelty) in earlier ways of thinking about food systems. Chapter 8 synthesizes and condenses themes on agrarian philosophies of agriculture that I have been exploring my entire adult life, and it emphasizes the sources that brought me around to this way of thinking during the last two decades of the 20th century.

Nonetheless, pre-industrial modes of thinking about agriculture and food systems have not disappeared altogether. Among other sites, they live on in images of the *paysanne*, the *campesino*, or the family farm. European and North American cultures delineate these images in terms of race and gender. The family that farms is stereotypically white, and the farmer is male. The systems of property rights and entitlements that accompany them were imposed upon indigenous peoples through conquest and colonization. Native and enslaved peoples were limited to fieldwork in these food systems and prevented from participating as farmers, ranchers or landowners. These unjust practices were later applied to racially identified immigrants. White men deployed agrarian rhetoric to assert their supremacy as the most powerful actors within Western food systems. In most cases, I would regard the victims of this oppression as the ones who most faithfully continue to embody agrarian ideals, yet the urbanization of industrial society has so thoroughly dissociated people from the agrarian world that agrarianism has itself come to be viewed as a white supremacist philosophy. With that thought, it becomes imperative to close the book in Chapter 9 with some thoughts on food justice and structural racism.

Food Justice and Racism: A Prolegomena

The final chapter of this book was a challenge for me. Writing on Mexican immigrants who have started small diversified farms in the United States, Laura-Anne Minkoff-Zern notes that they are stigmatized as unskilled field laborers who have no long-term commitment to land or community within U.S. borders. This has prevented them from getting loans and accessing the services they need to run their farms. The white male stereotype excludes farmers of color, and Minkoff-Zern writes that "white farmers and consumers will . . . have to face the exclusionary nature of alternative food movements."[6] Later she notes, " an overwhelming trend among alternative food activists and actors to disregard race and racial politics in their spaces as well as narratives, including farmers markets, community-supported agriculture boosters, student activists, food security groups, food purchasing coops, and alternative farming coalitions."[7] Given this circumstance, a book on food ethics needs to confront issues of race more squarely than I have done in previous efforts.

However, I had mixed feelings on how to do that. First, I have regarded my position as a white male as disqualifying. Although I have participated in some of the most degrading work in contemporary food systems, I am not situated to speak on issues of dispossession or oppression based on race. I have been leery of the white savior complex, where white men write or speak as if they *could* represent the experience of persons of color or, worse, actually step in and resolve their problems.[8] Since adolescence, I have thought of myself as someone who maintains implicitly racist attitudes of which I am probably unaware. My privilege blinds me to vices others see in my personality traits, despite my efforts to shed them. Even as a young man I also presumed that bias was a built-in feature of policy and procedure. My untutored understanding of culture suggested past injustices would resonate well into the future. I have not been one of those white Americans who is surprised to learn that blacks and whites see things differently.

I also spent enough time in the American South during the 1960s to have encountered vicious and vituperative hatred of blacks by other whites. Even if I cannot fully empathize with a racially identified person (much less speak for them), I nonetheless know how unsettling it is to encounter an angry white supremacist, and I have seen how prone many are to violence. Unlike some of my Northern friends and colleagues, I have feared for my own safety at the hands of misanthropes. I feel continuing shame following such encounters, because I have rarely summoned the courage or wit to respond as I subsequently felt I should. Addressing the issue of race required me to face some of my own demons and to do so in public.

Ironically, my consciousness of personal complicity in racisms of all sorts has prevented me from appreciating how blithely *unaware* many other whites are. Most significantly, I have not seen how directly confronting the legacy of race-based exclusion and oppression could have an edifying impact on my students or my readers. "Isn't all this just too *obvious* to warrant mentioning?" I have thought to myself. Later in life, I have come to understand how unobvious it was for many of the people I was supposed to teach. Some of the racial affronts I catalog in this book's Chapter 9 could well have been included in *From Field to Fork*, a book that I wrote with the goal of introducing readers to the complexity of food ethics. At the same time, when others take it upon themselves to undertake *my* edification, I have felt patronized and resented someone pointing out something that was obvious to me. As G. W. F. Hegel (1770–1831) taught in his *Phänomenologie des Geistes* (1807), efforts to oppose a given force or trend directly often have the opposite of their intended effect. The only satisfactory option is to transcend or move beyond the opposing dichotomy.

However, Hegel was more optimistic about *Aufhebung* than I am. I remain caught within the contradictions of racism and racial identity formation. In writing Chapter 9, I have been especially troubled by the gap between authors like Minkoff-Zern, who document oppression within the industrial food system, and the growing number of philosophers who have explored the conceptual, historical, and experiential foundations of the racial dialectic. They are not speaking to one another. For reasons already stated, I do not imagine myself to be someone who could bridge this gap.[9] As such, I have framed the inquiry in Chapter 9 as a conversation hoping to bring the philosophy of race into a deeper engagement with agrarian and embodied eater perspectives as well as the history of agriculture. I respect the complexity of the philosophical discourse on race and acknowledge that I cannot fail to err, both by oversight and through misunderstanding. I hope that future exchanges can be constructive.

And, Finally, Some Lingering Concerns

The issues covered in this book span a wide range of topics in agriculture, but I have not made an effort to represent the full breath of the field. *From Field to Fork* (2015) did strive to be somewhat representative, but you do not need to read *From Field to Fork* first. *From Silo to Spoon* stands on its own. As indicated above, I do not assume that my readers will be conversant in philosophical terminology, so there is some overlap with the earlier book with passages that orient readers to important concepts. In a few cases, topics in this book do represent a more detailed discussion of issues from the previous one, and it has been important to summarize elements of those issues for readers who come to this book first. Other topics are omitted from this book altogether. In the case of nutrition, I do not feel like I have anything new to say. In the case of animals, I have so much to say that I hope to put that all together in some future book. Many philosophers teach courses on food ethics that are dedicated entirely to the question of whether we should all be vegetarians. Needless to say, they will be disappointed with this book. If you cannot wait for the next one, here is a footnote that explains some of my thinking on the animals issue.[10] No one should complain that I have dodged the questions of animal ethics, even if I have not put much on those questions between the covers of this particular book.

Two key issues lie in the background of topics covered in the book, receiving very little explicit acknowledgment and no sustained inquiry. One is climate change, which is already having dramatic effects on food production. The Intergovernmental Panel on Climate Change (IPCC) predicts that some important food producing regions will have lost 50% of their capacity by 2050, and will be completely unable to sustain any agriculture by the end of the 21st century.[11] Many of the most severely affected areas are places where smallholder and subsistence farming still dominates. As such, getting a grip on these issues requires that one realize the tension between ethical values that prioritize total global food production and those that emphasize the plight of small and resource-deprived farmers attempting to survive in a global food system dominated by well-capitalized agribusiness operations. Chapter 3 provides an entrée into the imperatives relating to small farmers outside the most industrially developed countries, but more could be said about how climate change exacerbates the issues described there.[12]

The other issue is the effect of the COVID-19 pandemic on the food system. Both the lockdown and the virus itself have had dramatic effects on the food sector. Early in the pandemic, workers in slaughterhouses were reported to be especially vulnerable to the virus and to spread it to the surrounding community. A study published in *Food Policy* confirms that U.S. counties with meatpacking plants had, on average, more than double the number of reported COVID cases as counties without them.[13] Furthermore, as public health authorities enforced restrictions on indoor behavior, restaurants were among the firms most dramatically affected, while grocery stores and delivery services experienced a boom.[14] There is little doubt that these perturbations to the food system will have long-range effects. They may be indicators of unsustainability in the global food system. However, it may still be a bit early to philosophize about COVID-19 and food ethics. There are reasons why Hegel wrote that the owl of Minerva flies only at dusk.

1

A Little Throat-Clearing Before Dinner

In daily life, people think of ethics in fairly straightforward terms. We know what we should do, and we know that temptation, self-interest, and our vulnerability to those who have power over us can sometimes prevent us from doing it. We also know that there are differences of opinion on some issues. Some see government as a legitimate agent for achieving morally justified ends; others do not. Some see the morality of abortion in terms of the pregnant woman's right to control what happens to her body, others see it in terms of the rights of unborn children. I think there is also some appreciation of the way even *describing* these issues can spark moral debate. Some readers may already be pushing back on my approach.

At the same time, too much focus on divisive topics distracts us from fact that there is tremendous agreement on most moral norms, even as we move from culture to culture. Many philosophers would be comfortable with the way that R. M. Hare (1919–2002) described this territory of agreed upon norms, calling it *common morality*. However, inside the university, philosophers tend to think of ethics as their turf, and Hare was no exception. Although he wrote that common morality provides adequate moral guidance in the majority of circumstances, Hare also developed a philosophical approach for cases where common morality fails us. Thus, we can ask, where does common morality fail us with respect to food? This question opens one of the doors into a more philosophically oriented inquiry into the production and consumption of what we eat.

Noticing a curious bit of English grammar helps make the point: the same word *ethics* functions as both a singular and a plural term. Ethics *are* the rules and norms that govern conduct; ethics *is* the activity of sorting out disagreements. Not many English words can take singular and plural forms so easily. If you ask what ethics *are*, the answer generally refers to Hare's common morality. If you ask what ethics *is*, you will often be referred to the philosophy department at your local university. And when philosophers talk about the common morality, it is usually to criticize it. Peter Singer developed Hare's approach by arguing that the common morality fails to appreciate the

From Silo to Spoon. Paul B. Thompson, Oxford University Press. © Oxford University Press 2024.
DOI: 10.1093/oso/9780197744727.003.0002

moral significance of sentient beings—animals capable of experiencing pain. He said patterns in the human use of animals exhibit prejudicial habits in the common morality that do not stand up to critical reflection.[1] Although I will not engage with questions about the ethics of eating animals in this book, the questions that ethical vegetarians have raised about eating meat or other animal products show the difference between common morality—what many people have in mind when they hear the word *ethics*—and the reflective, questioning approach of philosophical ethics.

In fact, this chapter will hardly touch on food topics at all. Instead, I want to explore the difference between common morality and philosophical ethics in a bit more detail. The chapter oscillates between explanations for readers new to philosophy and passages spelling out how my approach differs from the kind applied ethics specialists have come to expect. I will introduce some historical background and define some terminology. These ideas will not come up in every chapter. Although the chapter provides background for what I regard as philosophically innovative about my approach, feel free to skip ahead if you get bored.

How Philosophers Think of Ethics (Again)

The Introduction mentions how philosophers often classify according to the framework of consequentialism, rights/duties and character ethics. These are *ethical theories*. They provide general principles for determine how one should act in any situation. To use them, one must fill in important details and matters of fact in order to reach a prescription. This work of filling in is sometimes called *applied ethics*, or *practical ethics*. In addition, it is possible to step back from the work of actually thinking about what is right and wrong in order to better understand ethical situations, or circumstances where individuals or groups are called upon to act in prescribed ways. Hare's distinction between common morality and philosophical ethics is an example of just such "stepping back" in order to be clear about what it is that we think we are doing. The jargon term "metaethics" names this kind of philosophizing. I will revisit the distinctions that define ethical theory, applied or practical ethics, and metaethics presently, but for now the point is just to provide a very general orientation to the territory we are entering in this chapter.

If your eyes started to roll when you saw the word "metaethics," I feel your pain; I'm with you. In fact, I don't need to drag most readers through this material in order to address food aid and international development (Chapter 3), the locavore ethic (Chapter 4), or food labeling (Chapter 5). However, other chapters take up tensions between the ways people understand the very idea of ethics, itself. Indeed, Chapter 2 explores the role (and limits) of philosophical ethics in food activism, and food activism is exactly what some people think that food ethics is all about. So putting some context in front of that discussion (which crops up more frequently in later chapters) is probably a good idea.

I take a nonstandard approach to metaethics. I will not claim to have invented it because there is seldom anything truly new in philosophy. Nevertheless, I am not aware of anyone who approaches the work of ethics in quite the same way I do. The traditional topics in metaethics include *agency*: How do we distinguish the features of *action* as opposed to doings that we would see as morally significant? If someone takes a sledgehammer and smashes your antique Japanese ceramic vase, we see it as an action. There are reasons behind it, and the perpetrator is morally accountable. If he or she slips on a banana peel and damages your antique, it's a different story. We might look to whoever it was that left the banana peel for someone to slip on. Now, as interesting as such matters are, I'm not going to go on about them because it is often easy to address them in context rather than dragging readers through a lot of rigmarole. What is more, these are matters that other philosophers have addressed quite adequately, from my perspective.

The thing that philosophers have not addressed, at least in so far as I'm aware of, is the interactivity among three types of discourse. "Discourse" may sound pretentious but it is just a term to classify many different forms of expression and communicative exchange. The most straightforward examples are written and spoken language that purport to establish a basis for action: newspaper articles and opinion pieces, political speeches, and non-fiction essays are forms of discourse. More generally, films, fiction, journalism, and conversation join books and articles in literary, historical, or philosophical fields. Furthermore, I am not thinking only of writing and speech when I talk about discourse; we can even understand things like advertising, art, or even architecture as playing a discursive role. Discourses can have many different purposes, but in this book I focus on three. Sometimes the point of a discourse is to pose questions and pursue answers that are not known with the discourse begins. Other times, it is to persuade. At still other times, a discourse constrains or licenses certain types of action without necessarily engaging the people it affects in any thought process at all.

All three types of discourse have ethical implications and significance. In the balance of this short chapter, I will clarify the aims and function of each type, and say why anyone working in ethics should be attentive to the differences.

Metaethics and Three Types of Discourse

I once heard Richard Rorty (1931–2007) describe philosophy as a genre—a distinctive type or style of writing. Although many philosophers were irritated, it is a useful way to help shape a reader's expectations. We have a sense of genres like fantasy, humor, European history, lyric poetry, or science fiction. We also recognize musical genres: hip-hop, heavy metal, country, light opera, and jazz. It would be difficult to define any of the genres definitively, and there will be cases that overlap genres or challenge their boundaries. Yet readers and listeners develop a taste for works in a particular genre. It is helpful to think of philosophy as one genre among many. Rorty made this remark in part to pop the academic discipline's balloon of self-importance. Philosophy professors once thought of their discipline as the queen of the sciences and themselves as sovereigns of university faculties. Some have thought that great philosophers have the power to change culture. I think of philosophy as a kind of writing aimed at truth but never failing to consider challenges to the assumptions made in following that path. Not everyone has a taste for this kind of writing.

Following Rorty on this point, ethics is a subgenre of philosophy in much the same way that bebop or fusion are subgenres of jazz. Hare's distinction between common morality and philosophical ethics explains how the reflective, questioning standpoint of philosophy differs from other forms of writing or speech that might appear under the banner of food ethics. Rorty's notion of philosophy as a genre underlines the way that philosophical ethics is a *discourse*. It is domain where participants have some notion that they are exchanging ideas with one another. This is one more feature that distinguishes it from common morality. When people use the word *ethics*, they might be referring to the rules, practices, constraints, and forms of discipline that constrain our activity, but, as a discourse, food ethics takes those rules, practices, constraints, and forms of discipline as part of its subject matter. Philosophical food ethics is *moral discourse*.

A fair amount of the moral discourse we encounter in our daily lives simply reinforces prevailing notions of what is right and good. It helps to gird against temptation and self-interest, or it attempts to guard us from those who would use their power to make us do wrong. In some cases, it does this by assembling allies or identifying enemies. I classify these important functions as forms of *social control*. In the social sciences, social control is the study of

> mechanisms, in the form of patterns of pressure, through which society maintains social order and cohesion. These mechanisms establish and enforce a standard of behavior for members of a society and include a variety of components, such as shame, coercion, force, restraint, and persuasion. Social control is exercised through individuals and institutions, ranging from the family, to peers, and to organizations such as the state, religious organizations, schools, and the workplace. Regardless of its source, the goal of social control is to maintain conformity to established norms and rules.[2]

Notice, however, a tendency to push back against the very idea of social control when it comes to ethics. Coercion, force, and patterns of pressure do not sound very ethical. When someone is described as controlling, that is not a favorable attribute. Here, control is manipulative and underhanded. What is more, most of us rebel against some aspect the social order and society's means of enforcing it. However, I do not want readers to understand my use of the word *control* in this nefarious way. As a general form discourse, social control is not inherently malicious. Some amount of social control is needed simply to reproduce the expectations that support common morality.

In fact, simple repetition and juxtaposition of words, gestures, and physical acts establish and reinforce habituated patterns of conduct. Much as infants learn to speak by immersion in the constant speech patterns of their family household, people acquire the rudiments of common morality through their absorption in the nexus of rewards and penalties (perhaps as simple as facial expressions) and expressions of praise or blame. Any one household is situated within a more comprehensive expressive environment of reciprocal smiles, frowns, curses, and courtesies. I will often speak broadly of social control as a discursive practice or simply as a type or kind of discourse. However, social control clearly encompasses many things that we do not normally think of as forms of discourse.

What is more, these mechanisms of social control may not—usually do not—involve a conscious or deliberate attempt to constrain behavior. We *may* think of social control in terms of more devious and power-seeking methods, and I am not excluding strategic or cynical means of pressure or compulsion when I refer to social control.[3] I include the techniques of propaganda, deception, and political manipulation in my conception of social control, but I also include habituation that occurs in the day-to-day process of living. While social control incorporates bits of speech and writing that are clearly examples of discourse, these unspoken elements may be more influential in affecting behavior. I am lumping a number of distinguishable things together here, but my point is simply to differentiate practices that serve to maintain conformity and social cohesion from what philosophers do when they contribute to the genre of ethics.

The philosophical discourses I have in mind are more reflective. They attempt to take a step back from the active give and take that constrains behavior. They engage one's rational capacities. However, there are different ways to do this even within the philosophical standpoint. One type of philosophical discourse asks a person to think about what is right and what is good. In this approach, the questioning attitude is directed toward a general and theoretic understanding of what acting rightly requires. After establishing a view on these matters, philosophers working in this genre ask how they apply to a particular situation and then take up the task of encouraging their listeners or readers to act in whatever manner the theory says that they should. Philosophers who take this approach assume that these theories provide the moral direction or normative content for food ethics. For them, *food ethics* involves prescriptions or dictates on how to produce or consume food. Food ethics is different from *ethical theory* that tells us how to act in *any* situation. Ethical theory should be directive or action-guiding in every situation, including (but not limited to) situations that involve food. This makes food ethics quite literally an *applied ethics*, where a theoretical standpoint is applied to food.

Other philosophers (and I am one) prefer the term *practical ethics* to applied ethics. Explaining their reasons would take this introductory discussion too far off course, but here is one of them: when it comes to food, the most common type of applied ethics is *persuasive*. In this way of doing ethics, the philosophical questioning has been settled at the level of theory, and the philosopher's role shifts toward persuading us that the action indicated by theory is what they should do. Philosophically persuasive writing or speech addresses the belief system of readers (or listeners). It presumes that action follows from belief and that exposing reasons for acting one way, rather than another, will motivate a person to behave in conformity with the recommended course of action. A persuasive moral discourse might aim to correct faulty beliefs, or it might make the implications of beliefs already held more obvious. Persuasion thus adopts a rhetorical standpoint which presumes that the speaker (or writer) knew what the listener (or reader) should do even before starting to speak (or write).

Philosophical persuasion differs from that third type of moral discourse about food, which I will call *inquiry*. Moral inquiries occur when a speaker does not already know what is right and good or how to move from norms to action. Perhaps the most common type of moral inquiry is the inner conversation that people have with themselves, with the demons and angels that live inside their head. Yet it is possible to engage with others in a joint exploration where we trade reasons and challenges one another's hypotheses. Inquiry is rhetorically structured by the presumption that moral discourse is purposive, it has a point. The point is to lead inquirers toward the right or best thing to do. Inquiry is thus open to the arguments of persuaders, but to have an answer in hand at the outset means that one is not actually engaged in inquiry at all. What is more, inquiry is open to the possibility that the questions themselves should be susceptible to challenge.

Succinctly, the rough classification into categories of social control, persuasion, and inquiry allows us to see three different ways in which someone might approach food ethics as a practice. Whether as persuaders or inquirers, philosophers generally understand themselves as rejecting the discourses of social control. Up to a point, I agree: philosophical ethics can be either persuasive or inquisitive, but it is never satisfied with producing behavior that simply conforms. Philosophers are committed to getting it right, and not simply in terms of conduct. Philosophers are trying for accurate speech and writing, as well. It would not be amiss to say that even in ethics, *truth* is the guiding norm for philosophy. My approach also aims to get things right. In this sense, my work is in the mainstream of philosophical ethics. Yet I also strive to take discourses of social control seriously. I am mindful of social control even as I engage in inquiry. In fact, philosophers are deceiving themselves if they think that they can remove themselves from discourses of social control. Isn't it just obvious that however much philosophers protest to the contrary, their writing and teaching function within the wider sphere of "coercion, force, restraint, and persuasion" that constitutes social control?

Spirals, Twists, and Tangents *or* the Discursive Limits of Ethics

But there is more. Formulations such as "getting it right" and "truth" invite spirals of clarification, qualification, definition, and redefinition. Soon philosophers are talking about their talk—a practice that is sometimes called "going meta." "Meta" is derived from a Greek word meaning "about," so metaethics is talking about ethics. As already discussed, it is a discourse that takes the aims, structure, and methods of ethics as its subject matter. However, someone who has turned to food ethics hoping for practical advice is going to get hungry long before the spirals of metatheory and metaphysics reach their conclusion (if, indeed, they ever do). Later in the book, I will use the MEGO acronym (my eyes glaze over) when my inquiry threatens to move so far into meta discourses that I expect even the most patient reader to lose track. We can keep these meta discourses going indefinitely inside the university, but we only do that by pausing them when it comes time to eat. If I can indulge my reader's patience for just a few more paragraphs while I talk to my fellow philosophers, I can bring the present meta discourse to a hiatus, if not a conclusion.

There are reasons to cut the spirals of endless philosophical exchange short, especially in the context of ethics. The moral discourse of social control is inherently performative, even when it is not intentionally or consciously directed to achieve a specific purpose. *Performative* writing or speech is like making a promise where the act of promising *creates* the listener's expectation of your future conduct, and simultaneously *creates* the speaker's moral obligation to engage in a specific form of future conduct. Discourses of social control create expectations, too. They are performative in at least this minimal sense: in making normative claims—even in a discourse of social control—a group of human beings create a nexus of mutual assumptions and prospects. They do so in an environment that creates demands on everyone's actual conduct. Even those who chafe at these demands perceive the power, the force, or demandingness implicit within them. From this demand, the experience of normativity, of responsibility to others, arises. Again, I am not saying that this is *all* that morality involves. I believe that there are also emotional groundings for morality, for example. Nevertheless, this performative dimension of moral discourse should press philosophers of ethics to think differently about the spirals, twists, and tangents we pursue in academic settings.

Here is why: the very idea of discourse implies a group of speakers and hearers, readers and writers, performers and watchers. When moral discourses (again, including social control) succeed in setting expectations and obligations within some vaguely defined group, I will refer to this group as a *community*. In moral communities, discursive performance has simultaneously created expectations, and established boundaries in which those expectations prevail. However, there will be turbulence. Not everyone agrees, not everyone feels bound and members of any community will have disgruntlements and reasons to resist or question the prevailing expectations. Such disgruntlements and reasons are, of course, a prod to persuasion and inquiry. They provoke creative development of discourses to challenge mechanisms of social control. Persuasion and inquiry challenge discursive practices that function to create the very community in which normative expectations flourish, but they also interact with less reflective elements of social control. When that happens, these philosophical discourses are performative in the exact same way described above. A challenge to prevailing patterns within a community can revise, reform, and even invent new expectations. These new expectations, in turn, help reproduce and reestablish the community of discursive practice.

Now, academic philosophers are aware of all this, and the typical response is to reject discourses of social control on the ground that they are relativistic: they abandon philosophy's commitment to a style of discourse that pursues the truth. However (and we are finally getting to the hiatus), there is another response that philosophers might make. Very few communities will tolerate incessant tangents, spirals of deeper questioning, endless clarification, or meta-discourse. People get tired (or hungry). They have other things to do. Then there is a schism: the community divides into those who are willing to go meta and those who are not. When that happens, the cross-talk may continue to have meaning for the subcommunity, but it has no impact on the community as a whole. It ceases to have the socially performative ability to interact with other cultural forces shaping behavior. Philosophical ethics is not like high-energy physics, where a small community of insiders develop vocabulary tailored to their special needs, then go off and build amazing things. Linguistic or theoretical innovation in physics affects non-physicists when it leads to technology. The cathode ray tube gave us television (I'm not saying this is necessarily a good thing). Absent a self-imposed discipline that I hope to model throughout this book, there is nothing comparable that brings far-flung academic conversations in ethical theory back to the lives of non-philosophers.

To put this point differently, if philosophers are not in some sense using the mechanisms and vocabulary of controlling discourses in the larger community, they are not doing ethics. The impact of ethics, if there is one, has to occur within the formation of expectations and norms for the community at large. When the pundits or professors become totally disconnected from the discourse of social control, they are no longer doing ethics at all.[4] This does not mean that we should never talk *about* those mechanisms and their consequences. Failing to do that would be failing to do philosophy. Perhaps ethics is a special subgenre that calls for its practitioners to perform a delicate balancing act, teetering between two performative failures. On one side we fail to execute a discourse that is ethical, while on the other side we fail to be philosophical. The focus on food is useful because it helps keep philosophical discourse grounded; it is interesting because it crosses the territory between these extremes.

Skepticism Versus Fallibilism *or* How to Stay Focused on Inquiry

My intention is to conduct an open-ended inquiry that exposes ethical commitments embedded within the food system and releases us to consider alternatives. You may have already noticed that I do not forego persuasion in doing so. Why do I insist that my approach differs from the persuasive discourse of most applied ethics? First, I am very far from having convinced myself that I am right. I *am* persuaded that a form of group-think blocks us from seeing the flaws in our way of life—including our food system—and prevents us from considering alternatives. When I say "we" I mean human beings generally, though people whose normative presumptions are most closely aligned with patterns reinforced by the mechanisms of social control are especially liable to group-think.[5] My own bias toward inquiry comes from observing what I take to be forms of group-think among both establishment figures like corporate executives, agriculture and food scientists, and, indeed, many farmers, as well as among activists advocating for particular alternatives.

More philosophically, my bias toward inquiry derives from the pragmatist commitment to *fallibilism*. Explaining this will involve another one of those annoying MEGO tangents, but bear with me. For 500 years, and some would say longer, European philosophy has been obsessed with the problems of skepticism. Stated baldly, skepticism is the view that knowledge is impossible. We human beings cannot really know anything. Of course, stating the case baldly underplays the nuance that makes skepticism both interesting and culturally important. There is, on the one hand, an interplay with key notions in Judeo-Christian or Islamic theology and religion. Perhaps humanity's inability to know reflects our dependence on an omniscient God. We humans do not know, but our faith in God provides a warrant for our entire system of beliefs. Readers who know a little philosophy will recall that René Descartes (1596–1650) produced an elegant version of this view in his *Meditations on First Philosophy* (1641). On the other hand, Descartes also wrote that there are some things that we do know with certainty. In his *Meditations*, he argued that even when we try to doubt our own existence, we know with confidence that we are doubting. Hence, we know that we exist. In his equally influential *Discourse on Method* (1637), he claimed that whatever we cannot doubt without contradicting ourselves, we know with certainty. We can build the edifice of true knowledge by paying close attention to the logical and mathematical relationships with which we assemble indubitable simples into a complex whole.

Cartesian rationalism was opposed by empiricists who argued that everything we know derives from our five senses. We observe patterns in what we see, hear, touch, taste, and smell. Our confidence in the existence of objects beyond our sensory perceptions is a presumption rather than something that we can observe directly. You can know that you sense a given odor associated with fresh-baked chocolate chip cookies, and your subsequent taste of the cookie and its feel in your mouth reinforces the supposition that there is an object beyond your mind responsible for all these percepts. Yet all this doesn't add up to knowledge of things beyond the perceptual realm. The Scottish philosopher David Hume (1711–1776) produced some of the most persuasive versions of this skeptical philosophy. Immanuel Kant (1724–1806) developed a synthesis of rationalism and empiricism holding that we do have knowledge about the structure of our concepts, as Descartes thought. Nevertheless, Kant agreed with Hume: we cannot have certain knowledge of anything lying beyond our experience, including even the mere existence of ordinary objects. Aside from their historical importance, the arguments of these thinkers played an important role in the rise of modern science.

Readers new to these philosophical ideas need to understand that this two-paragraph gloss obscures far more about the history of modern philosophy than it reveals. It is intended merely to introduce the pathway that led philosophers and social scientists to struggle with skepticism. This has had a powerful influence on social scientists that study culture. Although it may not have occurred to him, Kant's picture of the human condition suggested the possibility that not everyone's conceptual map is the same. If people cannot appeal to any independent reality to resolve philosophical differences, it begins to look as if Daniel Patrick Moynihan (1927–2003) was wrong: everyone *is* entitled to their own facts.[6] It is not clear that this form of skepticism ever bothered ordinary folk, but perhaps it should. As I write in the third decade of the 21st century, many are sounding alarms about the erosion of respect for truth. A plethora of theories for coping with skepticism emerged in the 20th century, but this plethora itself became part of the problem.

In 1877 and 1878, Charles Sanders Peirce (1839–1914) launched a revolutionary philosophical program that challenged skepticism at the core. According to Peirce, while we can challenge any element of our belief systems, is impossible to throw one's entire belief system into doubt because one must use the experience and understanding one has in the very act of making a skeptical challenge. As such, Peirce argued, Descartes's emphasis on hypothetical certainty was misplaced. We should instead examine the methods people exercise to fix or stabilize their beliefs when they are in a circumstance of actual doubt. For Peirce, the problem that initiates a philosophical inquiry is not the certainty or contingency of beliefs but the warrant or reason for basing one's actions on one proposal rather than another. Peirce notes strengths and weaknesses in each of the methods he considers, though he also concludes that an approach similar to experimental science conducted among a community of inquirers holds the greatest promise. This form of empiricism demands that we do not elevate any proposition to the status of absolute certainty. Any given idea or proposition, even those that seem most secure, *might* be wrong. Nevertheless, the sheer fact that our inherited system of habits, thought patterns, and tendencies has gotten us to a point at which puzzles emerge provides the basis for posing and researching the questions that trouble us. The pragmatist sees fallibilism where others have seen skepticism.

If all this strikes you as mere common sense, great! However, for most people, quite a bit of common sense *does* get exempted from all possibility of questioning or criticism. Philosophical pragmatism commits one to remain open to the possibility that virtually *any* element of our cognitive commitments might, on further experience and examination, turn out to be mistaken. Nevertheless, it rejects the core tenet of skepticism, the possibility that *every* element is wrong. That would leave us entirely without resources for future action. At the same time, reasoned challenges to any specific idea are fair game. Peirce's fallibilism retains what is correct about skepticism, namely, its openness to alternatives and its power to resist group-think. Yet it resists the idea that since we can't really know anything, one belief system is just as good as any other.

While I am happy to leave my reader with the thought that there is nothing very exceptional about the pragmatist view, I will insist that it puts us at odds with philosophies that place emphasis on persuasion, as opposed to inquiry. There will be times in our lives where the attempt to persuade others is fully appropriate. There are times when it is important to decide an issue collectively or to mobilize cooperative action. When the matter is urgent, we may not be able to indulge the tangents and side questions that arise in a truly open-ended inquiry. Yet, for the pragmatist, we might be wrong, even in our judgment of urgency. When we find ourselves in disagreement, the response should be to initiate a joint inquiry rather than to engage in persuasion. When there is a rationale for reconsidering commitments that provoke persuasive discourse, we should turn to inquiry. Whether these commitments are revised or reinforced depends on the inquiry we conduct in that particular situation.

The final point to stress is that fallibilism poises us for cooperative inquiry. In Perice's preferred approach, we become resolute in our view of things through participating in a community of people dedicated to the norms of inquiry. While these norms stipulate many things that people can do when they are by themselves—forming a hypothesis, running an experiment, then checking to see whether the results are consistent—performing these activities within a community that shares and carefully considers each other's results is transformative. The communicative, intersubjective experience of joint inquiry changes the picture imagined by Hume and the other empiricists. Experience is social, and so is knowledge. Knowledge subsists less in the mind or perceptual field of the individual as in the collective capacity for action, interaction, and transaction. The philosophical project launched by Descartes imagines the human being to be a solitary creature, but human development is inherently social. Indeed, the ability to entertain a philosophical question presupposes the acquisition of a language with complex grammatical capacity. It is difficult to imagine how any creature could do that, apart from long practice in communicative interaction with others.

So, What's on the Menu?

How does all of this set the table for food ethics? Chapter 2 introduces us to the food movement, which consists of loosely coordinated activities intended to change the way that food is produced, processed, distributed, and consumed in the 21st century. It consists of people who are pursuing centuries-long efforts to more fairly allocate the burdens involved in growing, transporting, and preparing food as well as access to food itself. The movement also includes people who have some new concerns: the health and environmental costs of industrial farming, impacts on farmed animals, or fears about the sustainability of the food system as a totality. While later chapters will delve into a few of these worries in some detail, Chapter 2 examines how people in the food movement understand ethics as a solution rather than an activity. In a nutshell, they say everyone should tailor their dietary choices so that the power of the dollar is wielded as the change-agent that will resolve each of these problems in the food system. That, for them, is what food ethics is.

Perhaps some readers have already guessed why that understanding of food ethics threatens to derail the whole point of this book. To use the ideas developed in this chapter, food activists envision food ethics as a means for exerting social control. Consumer spending power, properly channeled, will bring about the changes they are working toward. Their outlook sees some role for persuasion, to be sure. Perhaps philosophically sophisticated arguments will convince people to adopt the consumption practices that, they say, will bring about a better world. Yet the activists' criterion seems to judge the value of philosophy solely in terms of its ability to motivate behavior. That is quite different from an ethics of inquiry. A purely persuasive discourse fails to ask what we are entitled to expect from our food system, or how humanity's collective methods for producing and distributing foods figure in the way we understand progressive change.

This chapter has laid out a metaethical framework organized around three broadly defined categories of discourse. In addition to the food movement's engagement with social control, there are persuasive philosophical discourses intended to influence dietary choice. In contrast, inquiry is a discourse that asks "What should I or we do? What *is* the right way to think about issues involving food?" But the level of abstraction in these questions should make us cautions. In fact, truly meaningful inquiries are more concrete: Should I adopt a locavore diet? What kinds of product claims should be allowed? A pragmatist approach to inquiry will use ideas from all the major philosophical traditions in pursing these questions, but it will focus on particular cases. With a particular case, we face genuine doubts. We do not know what to do. Attempts to answer all our ethical questions with a general theory reflect a quest for certainty based on sham doubts. They philosophize as if, without philosophers, people would be without recourse for thinking about their moral responsibilities.

In a word, the chapter has set the stage for an argument (or maybe it's only a vision) that develops continuously throughout the book. The three-discourse metaethics and pragmatist fallibilism are iterated through a series of ethical inquiries on familiar topics. In the final two chapters, the theme of pragmatism is revisited as a more comprehensive framework for understanding the topical inquiries that have gone before.

2

Food Ethics Arrives (or Does It?)

Philosophical food ethics is a deliberative inquiry[1] into the reasons and rationales that people associate with food. It encompasses debates over the production, consumption, and cultural significance of the human diet. My interest is in the organization and performance of the food system rather than an individual's personal choices. However, the aggregated effect of many individual choices is part of the system. The idea of a food system includes the distribution of edible goods and the technological apparatus to produce them, prepare them, and dispose of waste. It also includes complex structures like markets, along with government regulations and social norms that structure markets. All of these activities and processes presuppose ethical commitments, and philosophical food ethics (as I do it) aims to expose and discuss them. For me, food ethics is a component of social philosophy.

However, the expression "food ethics" is also used to describe a person's orientation to food and dietary choice. For many people, food ethics is about making dietary choices that have desirable consequences. To choose ethically is to choose the option that produces the best effects. Others similarly focused on their own behavior might evaluate their diets in terms of rights or duties. They might see some of the options available on grocery shelves as off-limits in virtue of the way that humans, animals, or ecosystems were exploited in the productive and distributive processes that brought a given product to those shelves. Still others may see their food choices as components in a network of interpersonal relations. These relations themselves may serve as the focus for deciding whether eating a given item is morally acceptable or not. These three ways that people see their food choices reflect the utilitarian-rights-virtues breakdown of applied ethics.

There is, however, a third way to think about food ethics. Associating food consumption with ethics and morality can be a form of social control. Here, when someone mentions ethics in connection to food, they are effectively saying, "Do this!" Perhaps they express this command explicitly, but it is more likely that they are signaling how a person's diet will contribute to their acceptance and reputation in a given group. Here, moral

From Silo to Spoon. Paul B. Thompson, Oxford University Press. © Oxford University Press 2024.
DOI: 10.1093/oso/9780197744727.003.0003

language—the language of good and bad, right and wrong, justice and exploitation—is being used to underline or reinforce certain expectations while discouraging others. Pointing out the philosophical presumptions on which expectations rest usually weakens the sense that one must comply with them, and this is the tension on which the reflections in this chapter hinge. Eaters who already know what goals they hope to achieve, who already know what duties they must fulfill, or what virtues they hope to embody are likely to think that philosophical food ethics is a waste of time. At best, what these eaters want is factual information about the dietary options they have and the consequences of each. At worst, they will see philosophical questioning as opposing the realization of those goals and a counter to their efforts to enlist others in their cause. The apparent antagonism of philosophers' questioning and an activists' goal of just doing the right thing is the focus of this chapter.

The chapter begins with two sections that set the stage. Although there have long been disputes and even battles over food and agriculture, it is helpful to see how food ethics took its present shape over a period of about 100 years. It arose in part from technological transformation of the food system, but also from changes in the personality of eaters. Given this background, we shift to consider the meaning of ethics as that concept might be applied to food. The balance of the chapter explores, extends, and amplifies the way in which food ethics can be construed as a philosophical activity, as a discipline of personal comportment, and as a form of social control.

How Food Ethics Became a Thing

Starting in the 1970s, a new set of ethical issues started to be associated with food. The palate of people of the industrialized world expanded gradually and unevenly over a longer time frame, with relatively little variety in the cooking of working-class households well into the 20th century. Growing up in the 1950s and 1960s, I witnessed steady growth in the types of food that my family cooked at home and brought in or ate at restaurants. Growth in middle-class tastes set the stage for a shift in the valence and receptivity toward social and ethical dimensions of the food system. Someone might claim that food ethics—philosophical *or* activist—is just a product of wealthy people looking for something to do.[2] However, 1970s style food ethics was also responding to the technological and political restructuring of food production throughout earlier decades. My version of this story emphasizes its philosophical impact.

If we look back 200 years, people would have tended to see their food choices as matters of prudence rather than ethics.[3] This began to change during the 20th century for a number of reasons. Helen Zoe Veit traces the early history of campaigns to encourage American citizens to see wasting food as a moral problem, underlining the idea that American farmers have a responsibility to feed the world.[4] For another thing, the emergence of national healthcare systems meant that unhealthy diets create social as well as personal costs. Most significantly, however, the food system itself changed. Already by the end of the 19th century, urbanization had made lack of food access more visible, if not also worse. Food processing opened the door to adulteration and contamination. The industrialization of production caused harmful environmental impacts. The growing influence of multinational corporations created a global marketplace, where pursuit of profit created crushing burdens on small-scale players such as farmers, workers, and consumers. These insults accumulated over the course of the 20th century, and, by the dawn of third millennium, a new social movement was on the horizon.[5]

Ronald Sandler's overview of food ethics points us toward social activists who resist something they call "the global food system." I am not sure their sense of the food system is quite the same as mine. The object of their resistance is serviceably indicated by a network of major corporations, the farmers that buy from and sell to them, and government agencies that support their activity. First are companies that manufacture farm inputs such as seeds, chemical fertilizers and pesticides, and machinery. Then there are companies that source and manufacture foods distributed through grocery stores and restaurants. The grocery stores and restaurants themselves have become multinationals or franchise operations. Conglomerates that control the processing, trade, and distribution of farm commodities sit in the middle. A more detailed description would include agencies within national and local governments as well as the international organizations that regulate global trade. Finally, there are also farmers, who are seen as both victims of this system and also as players within it, especially to the extent that they are themselves well-capitalized and represented by politically powerful organizations such as various commodity-based lobbying groups.[6]

This global food movement builds on sources of discontent that existed for decades, if not longer. Perhaps the most obvious complaint is the impact of agricultural chemicals on human and ecosystem health. *Silent Spring*, by Rachel Carson (1907–1964), came out in 1962. Many scholars call it the beginning of environmental consciousness in the United States. The title of Carson's book calls attention to the bioaccumulation of toxic chemicals in the environment and their impact on songbirds. The immediate effect of the book was the passage of laws like the Clean Water Act, the creation of the Environmental Protection Agency, and the ban on the chemical pesticide DDT.[7] DDT was not used solely for agricultural purposes. It was developed for controlling insect vectors of infectious disease. Nevertheless, *Silent Spring* had the effect of raising questions about the use of chemical pesticides in food production, and these questions have continued to be a primary motivation for North American environmental and consumer groups who advocate for change in farming practice.[8] Concerns about food and health continue to be an important in the food movement, but *Silent Spring* was also instrumental in the formation of academic environmental science programs in North American universities.

Colleagues from the United Kingdom have told me that it was *Animal Machines: The New Factory Farming* by Ruth Harrison (1920–2000) that had an impact on public opinion comparable to Carson's *Silent Spring* in the United States. Published in 1964, with a foreword by Carson, Harrison's book sparked a new interest in the treatment of animals generally. Like *Silent Spring*, many of the book's political targets have very little to do with food production. Reforms in animal testing and sport hunting are examples. Nevertheless, like *Silent Spring*, *Animal Machines* raised the public's awareness of problems with agricultural technology. Harrison criticized the crowded conditions in which livestock were raised. Campaigns against factory farms (or concentrated animal feeding operations [CAFOs]) have been of particular interest to philosophers persuaded by ethical arguments for vegetarianism. As the controversy over pollution spurred philosophers to take up environmental ethics, concern for animal ethics led to programs in many European veterinary colleges. Carson and Harrison each raised concerns that found a home in higher education.

The parallel influence of Carson and Harrison points to the fact that there are local, national, and regional versions of the food ethics story. I will stress the U.S. version, where there was a history of concern with social issues associated with agriculture and agricultural production long before Carson's work on environmental impact. From this vantage point, perceived unfairness to economically vulnerable farm producers goes back at least to the last quarter of the 19th century.[9] For example, the National Grange of the Order of Patrons of Husbandry (better known simply as The Grange) is an advocacy group founded after the Civil War that lobbies in support of farming communities. A series of farm-oriented populist parties emerged in the 1890s. The rural impact of the Great Depression, which saw a wave of farm bankruptcies, was chronicled by John Steinbeck (1902–1968) in his 1939 novel *The Grapes of Wrath*. While Steinbeck followed a lower-class white family to the orchards of California, the injustices to other laborers in American agriculture were worse. These include the exploitation of Chinese, Japanese, Philippine, and Mexican field workers, not to mention the enforced servitude of several million African slaves prior to the Civil War. Socioeconomic injustices include collusive acts to disenfranchise free black farmers after the war and the genocide and removal of Native Americans from their ancestral access to land, fisheries and other natural resources.[10]

This history is the backstory for food ethics. Nevertheless, my suggestion is that something new was afoot was beginning in the 1960s, and it continued through the 1970s on to the end of the 20th century. The grave wrongs in the history of American food production did not register very much in the conscience of white, middle-class Americans until then. The average citizen might have known about the hardships of smallholders and farm labor, but it is questionable whether they would have viewed them as injustices. Even if they did, these average citizens would not have imagined themselves as having any particular responsibility to redress them. The CBS network's 1960 television documentary *Harvest of Shame* and the United Farm Workers of America (UFWA)'s grape strike on behalf of California migrant labor told a different story. Between 1966 and 1970, the UFWA mobilized consumers into a boycott of table grapes that placed responsibility on the dinner table of the American consumer. This primed the pump for a coalition that bound growing environmental consciousness to the labor movement and to the public's sympathy for the plight of the family farm. Warren Belasco's history of the food movement finds its origin in the counterculture of the 1960s, when mimeographed newsletters and hand-circulated flyers promoted brown rice and other plant-based dishes.[11]

Events continued to propel the narrative right to the end of the 20th century. Organic food production and consumer food co-ops had origins in the counterculture of the early 1970s. The social unrest associated with a spate of U.S. farm bankruptcies during the 1980s was brought to the attention of a wider audience by Farm Aid benefit concerts organized by Willie Nelson,

John Mellencamp, and Neil Young. It might be an exaggeration to characterize these early forms of activism and discontent as a social movement. Nevertheless, they did attract attention from the media as well as a small cadre of academics. North American philosophers began to undertake new scholarship and teaching on both environmental and social justice issues within the food system in the 1970s. The W. K. Kellogg Foundation, the U.S. Department of Agriculture Office of Higher Education, and the U.S. National Science Foundation supported individual scholars who contributed to this renaissance in food ethics. The Agriculture, Food, and Human Values Society was founded in 1988, and three of its first five Presidents were philosophers.[12]

My career as an observer and analyst of dissent in the U.S. food system began in 1981. There has scarcely been a year go by without the publication of some book or prominent media event attempting to expose sources of trouble and injustice in the food system.[13] During the last twenty years of the 20th century, none of them had anything like the impact of Carson's *Silent Spring* or Harrison's *Animal Machines*. Suddenly, in 2001, Eric Schlosser's book *Fast Food Nation: The Dark Side of the All-American Meal*, broke like a firestorm over the American cultural landscape. Schlosser's book was followed in 2002 by Marion Nestle's *Food Politics* and in 2006 by Michael Pollan's *The Omnivore's Dilemma*.[14] Pollan's book was especially significant for the emergence of food ethics because Pollan styled himself as an affable naïf trying to express his environmentally oriented ethical values through his dietary choices. Peter Singer and Jim Mason also hit the bookstores in 2006, with *The Ethics of What We Eat: Why Our Food Choices Matter*.

The Aesthetic Dimension

Although social issues are the driving concern of the food movement, the aesthetics of food consumption have also contributed to the emergence of food ethics. The gourmet's appreciation of fine food and wine plays a role in the discourse of social control. Growing aesthetic appreciation of food can be seen in the popularity of food magazines, television programs, and especially in the international celebrity of chefs: Gordon Ramsey, Jamie Oliver, Wolfgang Puck, and many others. Julia Child (1912–2004) starred in a series of cooking programs that moved the trend beyond cookbooks with her 1963 television program *The French Chef*. Technological advances in film dating back to the 1970s allowed foods to be represented with eye-catching detail and clarity. Arguably beginning with the 1987 film *Babette's Feast*, by director Gabriel Axel (1918–2014), the preparation and consumption of food itself began to be thematized cinematically. Most of the film's 102-minute running time is dedicated to Babette's loving and meticulous orchestration of the meal and to the sumptuousness of the title feast itself. Based on a story by Isak Dinesen (1885–1962), Babette is a chambermaid at a monastery, and her meal evokes pleasure from the monks, who are members of an abstemious religious sect that offered her asylum. As the story winds up, we learn that, in Babette's former life, she was a great chef. Now exiled, she has come into money. Having spent her fortune on the meal, she will be remaining among the sect as a servant dedicated to their austere way of life. Babette reveals that her artistry in cooking is her true wealth, presumably a point against the somber asceticism of the religious sect. *Babette's Feast* is Pope Francis's favorite film.[15] There are now hundreds of films that celebrate cooking and the life of the chef.

The growth in visual media's attention to food was preceded by an expansion of the palate, especially in North America. So-called ethnic cuisine restaurants are ubiquitous everywhere in the 21st century, and many people will not appreciate how dramatically different today's foodscape is when compared to the dining choices of the generation that fought World War II. Ettore Boiardi (1897–1985) came to the United States in 1914, eventually becoming head chef at the Plaza Hotel in New York City. After successfully operating his own restaurant, he created the national brand we know as Chef Boyardee, which he sold to American Home Foods in 1946.[16] People in today's food movement mock "Beefaroni" and do not appreciate Ettore Boiardi's role in establishing Americans' taste for Italian food. Similarly, Asian food was not widely available outside Asian enclaves until the 1970s. Although Asian style cooking first came to the Americas with Chinese immigrants in the 19th century, Westerners are only recently learning to appreciate the diversity and variety of cooking styles that co-exist within Asian traditions. The big three are Chinese, Japanese, and Thai cuisines, though Korean, Philippine, Malaysian, and Indonesian restaurants are becoming increasingly common in North American or European cities.

Like Ettore Boiardi's canned sauces, Chinese food was immediately adapted to Western tastes. It began to spread beyond urban "Chinatowns" in the 1950s. There is no such thing as "Chinese food" from a Chinese perspective, of course. There are instead numerous regional cuisines that are seen as totally distinct and recognizable. Meanwhile, Chinese expatriate cooks are supporting thriving businesses in every corner of the world by adapting basic methods of Chinese cooking to local tastes. In the documentary film *The Search for General Tso*, filmmakers discovered that the popular dish General Tso's Chicken does not exist in Hunan Province, homeland of the real General Tso (1812–1855).[17] The Americanization of tastes notwithstanding, growth in the aesthetic appreciation of foods from other cultures opened a door to ethics. Lisa Heldke worries that the tendency to create stereotyped dishes that have no authentic connection to the homeland invites us to adopt stereotyped viewpoints not only of Asian cultures, but also of individual representatives of Asian culture. She notices, in short, the way that an aesthetically inspired appreciation of foods from any culture other than one's own can rapidly take on ethical significance.[18] Food aesthetics inevitably gives rise to food ethics.

The moralization of food aesthetics can also be seen in the Slow Food Movement, founded by Carlo Petrini as an act of aesthetically based resistance to fast food. Slow Food is now embracing the social justice and environmental sustainability goals of food ethics. The celebration of fine dining, elegantly prepared and leisurely consumed artisanal foods certainly complicates and challenges some thrusts of food ethics. Along with the three celebrity chefs already mentioned, Petrini has attempted to resolve the tensions in favor of an integrated social movement that would add beauty and delight to the overarching goal set for food ethics without sacrificing the commitment to right conduct, social justice, and sustainability.[19] Seen as a social phenomenon, food ethics arises from social activism to promote organic farming, consumption of local or artisanal food, and as a call to appreciate careful selection and preparation of meals that represent both innovative and traditional cuisines. In the latter sense, especially, food ethics advocates attention to food as an expression of cultural identity. It suggests that through the aesthetic appreciation of food, individuals can undertake a spiritual practice that will connect them to their own culture as well as to cultural traditions and ways of being that originate in the far-flung comers of the globe.

Perhaps inevitably, the food movement has stumbled over identity politics. A. Breeze Harper criticizes the way that food activism was (and perhaps still is) dominated by whites. She notes how black vegans report feeling marginalized within activities organized to support plant-based diets, calling out whites who reproduce the pattern of marginalization by performing stereotypical rituals of welcome and forced inclusion when met by non-white participants. Harper sees a connection between the way that non-whites are estranged from the core identity of food movement participants and the white, middle-class fascination with ethnic foods. Harper writes that foods normal for members of a given group are viewed as exotic and sought-after among whites, and especially so among young whites who identify with the food movement. Harper is dissatisfied with Heldke's treatment of exotic appetites, arguing that even the *worry* that there might be colonizing aspects to seeking unusual ethnic foods repeats a pattern that places a white identity at the center, relegating non-whites to the periphery.[20]

Aesthetic appreciation of food plays into a politics of insiders and outsiders. "Insiders" are people who have somewhat detailed knowledge of how the food system works. They may be employed professionally within the food system, or, like me, they may work in non-profit organizations (universities or advocacy groups) where they have direct experience of problems. Everyone else is an outsider. The gourmet becomes an insider through study and devotion to the art and appreciation of cooking. Food media enhances this appreciation through building insight first into the machinations of food retailing (restaurants and high-end groceries), then extending backward into the food chain.

"Outsiders" may have personal tastes and ethical commitments, but they have at best casual knowledge of how the food system functions. This makes them easy marks for activists who hope to enroll them in support of a social cause as well as for corporations and other businesses who are focused solely on their pocketbooks. At the same time, insiders are very far from being in agreement with one another. Indeed, insider disagreements energize the movement for change, on the one hand, or for maintaining the status quo, on the other. Whichever perspective an insider takes, the goal is to enlist outsiders. Although aesthetes may not adopt a missionary standpoint (differentiating themselves from the masses is important), they have often allied with other types of insider in formulating their criteria for taste. At the same time, all insiders may be uncomfortable with anyone who encourages outsiders to think too deeply about the ethics of food. That might involve raising questions about issues that they have already settled among themselves.

I do not pretend to offer a thorough sociological analysis of the food movement, nor do I say that a few ethnic restaurants or even widely read books caused it. My overall point is simple: today's food ethics grew out of events within intersecting discourses that altered expectations, especially in the decades following World War II. Although explicit advocacy was a component of this discourse, expectations were also being reconfigured by more subtle mechanisms of social control.

Ethics—As Philosophers Do It

Before getting into philosophers' version of food ethics, consider ethics itself. At the beginning of *The Republic*, Socrates (c. 470–399 BCE) and his friends are hanging out down at the Piraeus, the fortified port area just outside of Athens. Today, it is an urban area with a population approaching half a million people, depending on how one defines the boundary. In Socrates' day, it was outside the borders of the Athenian state. As such, it was a place where men of Athens could explore ideas that would be regarded as heretical, irresponsible, or disloyal if uttered in quarters where every act of speech was presumed to be both sincere and interpreted literally. It was a place for bullshitting, in the best sense of that word—a sense that is very close to that of *philosophizing*. By loosening the expectation that whatever one says is what one takes to a sincere expression of what thinks, people open a space for creatively playing with ideas. By doing that, they might learn something.

On this particular day, Socrates and friends are shooting the breeze about *dikaiosynē*, which we usually translate as *justice*. There are good reasons why Socrates and his friends went out of the city to philosophize about justice.[21] Unlike bullshitting with your friends about flute playing or the latest play by Euripides (c. 480–c. 486 BCE), philosophizing about morals can be easily misunderstood. People might think you are disrespecting sacred principles or encouraging others to revolt against them. Ideas floated as part of a philosophical inquiry might be heard as serious proposals. Moreover, if one's philosophizing leads to change or growth in the way one understands morality, the fear that philosophy could have some destabilizing or corrupting influence would appear to have some merit. It would certainly seem that way from the perspective of anyone deeply invested in and utterly convinced of the morality of the status quo. Thus, it is better to ensure that this particular philosophical activity is performed outside the sphere in which genuine moral exhortations are expected to be asserted. To put the point differently, it is important to distinguish philosophizing from social control.

Socrates and his friends are doing ethics. This might seem like a strange thing to say because in colloquial 21st-century English you might be said to *have* ethics or to act in accordance with or contrary to ethics, but ethics would not be something that you *do*. The word "ethics" is commonly understood to have two related meanings. First, ethics are moral principles that govern a person or group's conduct. Second, ethics is a branch of knowledge that concerns moral principles. The second definition gets us closer to what Socrates and his friends were doing down at the Piraeus, but, as philosophers, their concern was not simply to list or catalog these principles. Philosophy is an activity in which one plays with words and ideas with the aim of extracting their deepest significance and uncovering their connections to other practices and ways of life. Ethics, then, is the activity of philosophizing about morality and considering moral ideas (like justice) in an open-ended, critical spirit.

As it happens, Socrates winds up at the home of Polemarchus (d. 404 BCE), where he and his friends ask Polemarchus's father, Cephalus of Syracuse (5th century BCE), about justice. Perhaps it would help to know what Plato (428–348 BCE) knew when he recounted this story some years after Socrates had been sentenced to death for corrupting the youth of Athens. Polemarchus was also forced to drink hemlock and preceded Socrates in death by five years. Events that occurred years after the story that Plato is telling highlight the risk that Socrates and his friends were taking. Cephalus is a wise old man, but he is not a philosopher. He tells it straight out: justice is telling the truth and keeping your promises, nothing more. Socrates objects, though not directly to Cephalus who has religious duties to which he must attend. Polemarchus takes over the defense, and the philosophical game is on. *The Republic* goes on for another 300 pages or so, but the primary difficulty we encounter in understanding the emergence of food ethics is illustrated by this simple exchange between Cephalus and Socrates. Cephalus wants some rules to live by, while Socrates wants to engage in a philosophical inquiry. You have probably guessed that my aims in this book are closer to those of Socrates than Cephalus. No one who was aiming to offer helpful dietary advice would take readers on a detour through Plato's *Republic* before getting down to brass tacks. At the same time, many philosophers seem to have gotten out of the habit of taking people like Cephalus seriously and that, too, is a mistake.

Ethics, Diet, and the Rediscovery of Food Ethics

Philosophical inquiries on food are rare, but they became vanishingly so during the 20th century. This started to change in the 1970s, when Peter

Singer published two of his earliest works. The article, "Famine, Affluence, and Morality" used the backdrop of food shortages to make a philosophical argument that Singer would later generalize to a broader set of issues. He argued that virtually all members of industrialized democracies had wealth that they should use to relieve the suffering of people undergoing the trauma of famine. This prescription follows, he said, from a very simple moral principle: if it is in your power to prevent something bad without sacrificing anything of equal value, you should do it.[22] Singer revisited this line of reasoning many times, giving its fullest articulation in his 2009 book *The Life You Can Save*.[23] Although Singer argued that his reasoning could be applied across the spectrum of moral theories, it caught other philosophers' attention as a peculiar implication of utilitarianism. If you can do more good by letting someone else have your money than by using it to do what you want, then you should, on moral grounds, give it to them. *Utilitarianism* is a moral theory that recommends acting to achieve the best outcome, understood in terms of impact on the welfare of everyone affected by your action. This suggests that there really is no such thing as charity that goes beyond what is morally required since doing the greater good simply *is* what is morally required. These implications have struck many as quite implausible.

As with the debate over justice in *The Republic*, this is a philosophical conversation that can continue at length. This is the point to notice: if Singer is simply saying that when we *can* do some significant amount of good at little cost to ourselves, we are morally obligated to do so, then nothing in this principle ties it narrowly to food. We could make the same point about resource-poor people who need a scarce medication or vaccine, or who need a winter coat or a warm place to sleep. Nevertheless, food has a special emotional resonance that may be philosophically significant. By presenting his arguments against the backdrop of famine, Singer reminded everyone that lack of access to food is a very precarious position to be in and that many of those who find themselves in that position do so through no fault of their own. I return to Singer's paper and to food's ability to engage our emotions in the next chapter. For now, it is important to see how Singer put the rationale for institutions built to address hunger through governments, international charitable organizations, and local food pantries on academic philosophers' radar screen. His writings have arguably sparked several decades of reflection on these efforts and their effectiveness.

Singer's second effort arose from his call to reconsider the way that humans are treating animals. An early article in the *New York Review of Books* and

message implying that this is a morally good thing to do. The point is to harness the buying power of consumers to influence the practice of for-profit firms. Loyalty to labor was the most prominent 20th-century example. People were encouraged to "look for the union label" and avoid purchasing clothing, automobiles, and household goods produced by a non-unionized workforce. This form of consumption ethics stressed solidarity with the workers. It made the transition to "fair trade" during the last quarter of the 20th century as people were encouraged to purchase goods made by self-employed artisans (sometimes working in co-ops). Civil society groups made special arrangements to ensure that these artisans received a fair share of the final price. Fair trade movements took up food goods, especially coffee, but they also they also included clothing. Garment and textile workers were a long-standing concern of the labor movement, but the move toward foods allowed for the inclusion of farmers who do not work for wages. Although the small coffee growers supported by fair trade are not employees, they are still vulnerable to exploitation. Certification schemes and purchasing co-ops for tea and coffee were well established by the time that *The Omnivore's Dilemma* and *The Ethics of What We Eat* appeared in 2006.

How do books like *The Omnivore's Dilemma* or *The Ethics of What We Eat* relate to Socrates' debating justice in ancient Athens? The standard philosophical answer is that, after quite a bit of wrangling with his friends, Socrates finally comes up with the answer. He proposes a *theory* of justice. Philosophers who follow this tack have been cooking up theories of ethics for centuries, and Peter Singer follows the tradition. Figuring out the theory that should guide or conduct is the philosophical part, while telling us what to eat is an application of the theory. Singer works in the tradition of moral theories that define the right thing to do in terms of what results or consequences that follow from our actions; his view is a form of *consequentialism*. Consequentialist theories that understand outcomes in terms of an action's impact on welfare and that call for choosing options expected to maximize welfare are *utilitarian*.[28]

Singer claims that a sophisticated form of utilitarianism is the correct moral theory. He recognizes two levels of moral deliberation. In saying that justice consists in telling the truth and keeping one's promises, Cephalus exhibits a form of common morality—a set of rules to live by that has been handed down from generation to generation. The rules of common morality don't necessarily require us to estimate the impact our actions on others' welfare or choose the option that maximizes welfare. They are more like shortcuts that work for us most of the time. Yet sometimes they fail to provide guidance, and, at other times, they go astray, leading us toward choices that not only fail to produce the greater good but do so in a disastrous fashion. At such points, we need critical morality, and it is at this point, Singer claims, that a formal version of utilitarianism can step in. At the level of critical morality, we pause and consider the costs and benefits of our action, and we revise or augment our common morality with a careful analysis intended to produce consequences that have the greatest good for the greatest number.[29]

We should notice what two-level utilitarianism implies for the persuasive dimension of Singer's thought. It is not obvious that arguments capable of persuading individuals to change their personal behavior would also be effective in changing public policy or altering traditional patterns of behavior, but traditional utilitarians argued as if this were the case.[30] With two-level utilitarianism, the shift from personal to political becomes subtle. Status quo social policies and practices correspond to common morality. A two-level utilitarian can consistently argue that many (arguably most) of these practices do not need a detailed evaluation of their impact on social welfare. In fact, a two-level utilitarian can use non-utilitarian arguments drawn from common morality. Our food system is the agglomeration of decision-making by many individuals, but if the collective result is not achieving the greatest good, there is reason to change others' behavior. However, there is a dilemma for Singer's approach. People make food choices every day, often several times a day, and they make a lot of their consumption choices out of habit. The costs of trying to reform habitual behavior can exceed the benefits of doing so.

In fact, thoroughgoing two-level utilitarians might reconcile themselves to the common morality of many food practices, even when the performance of the food system is suboptimal. At a minimum, they will be mindful of the costs that efforts to change the system entail. One implication of all this is that although Singer believes that utilitarian reasoning is the best reasoning, he need not also believe that he should try to convince everyone to think like a utilitarian. What matters is whether or not your conversation partner is persuaded to adopt the course of action that maximizes utility (e.g., net welfare), not whether or not their reasoning is philosophically sound. We should notice how far this thinking is from the Socratic ideal, but Singer has done this frequently. Singer tries to establish his prescriptions for helping the poor and reforming human use of animals on principles that people like Cephalus can accept.[31]

Utilitarians also have to face a more general problem. There can be cases where it seems that simply manipulating other people is the surest path to the greatest good. Singer is not spouting things he does not believe in simply to persuade someone else, as Socrates' opponent in *The Republic*, Thrasymachus (c. 459–c. 400 BCE),[32] might. He can regard the claims of his conversation partners simply as statements of first-level common morality. Singer is thus sincere when he constructs arguments that rely on common moral beliefs. Nevertheless, this feature of two-level utilitarianism makes social morality quite different from personal morality. At the personal level, one does many things from habit, and the two-level theorists' acceptance of common morality excuses one from worrying about that. Yet when one does ask oneself, "What should I do; how should I act?" a suspicion that one could produce more good by abandoning common morality will trigger tactical considerations about persuading and manipulating others. Only when two-level utilitarians have convinced themselves that further inquiry will not be repaid by an improvement in social welfare do those considerations cease.

Here is the point I want readers to notice: in the transition to a political context, the mode of discourse shifts. In effect, the two-level utilitarian already knows what should be done based on a critical inquiry they have conducted in private. The public, political discourse then shifts from query to persuasion and, possibly, social control. A two-level utilitarian is using the language of common morality to persuade others, but do they actually believe what they say? He or she is trying to change the status quo by deploying the rhetorical skills of the sophist. The logical (i.e., modal) form of the discourse shifts. Rather than, "What should *we* do; how should *we* act?" it becomes, "Given that you believe X, here is why you should do Y." This is a significant alteration from the perspective of public philosophy. The point of the conversation has ceased to be one of reasoning together and has become a contest in which one party seeks to influence the behavior of another.[33]

The tension between query and persuasion has a long history in philosophy. Citizens of Athens in Socrates' day assembled on a hillside called the Pynx to decide important issues for the city. They listened as fellow citizens made speeches to convince them of one course of action or another. The city soon attracted foreigners called *sophists* who offered to train potential leaders in the skills of persuasion as well as more general knowledge of how to live. Socrates himself was viewed as a sophist, but he distanced himself from other sophists by insisting that he knew almost nothing. I view this tactic as Socrates' attempt to maintain the discursive standpoint of inquiry (though other philosophers view it as a very effective technique for persuading others). Similarly, Socrates' retreat to the Piraeus was a way to escape the political milieu of the city, where he would have been seen as just another sophist attempting to persuade the rich and powerful that his services were valuable. Far from the Pynx or the Agora (another hillside where smaller groups assembled to debate matters of politics), Socrates and his friends could carry out an inquiry into the nature of justice. Rather than being presumed to already have answered the moral questions, they distanced themselves from the effort to persuade others.

I could be wrong about Socrates, but I am guided by the thought that inquiry and persuasion model the activity of ethics in importantly different ways. The distinction does not imply that persuaders are themselves incapable of being persuaded differently. Attempts to persuade are often met with reasons to reject the conclusion that is the object of a persuasive argument. Sometimes a speaker is faced with counterarguments that are themselves persuasive. Persuasive speakers working within the spirit of philosophy may find themselves forced to change their mind. There is certainly a place for persuasion in philosophy, as well as in institutions like elections or the adversarial judiciary. Yet there is still this important difference between persuasion and query: persuaders insist that opponents prove them wrong; inquirers are always open to consider an alternative path, if only to see where it might lead. This difference is critical to the way we understand food ethics.

Food Ethics as Political Economy

The Omnivore's Dilemma sparked an uptick in morally tinged dietetics. However, a small number of people deciding to eat according to the dictates Singer and Mason recommended could not achieve most of the objectives sought by *The Ethics of What We Eat*. An individual might *feel* better about themselves, but impacts on farmed animals or on smallholding food producers in less industrialized economies cannot be achieved unless the number of people changing their food purchases rises to the level that they affect markets. However, this might not require as many like-minded people as one might think. A shift in the shopping preferences of only 2–3% of the public at large will attract the attention of the food industry, especially when shoppers are willing to pay a premium to get what they want. As people start to recognize their power to move markets, further shifts in the nature of food ethics occur.

First, shopping itself becomes a political act. One may buy a cage free egg out of solidarity with laying hens, but one *also* buys it because one sees that act as "shifting the demand curve." This arcane bit of economic jargon demands a little explanation. Economists draw a line on a graph estimating how many eggs would be purchased as prices go up or down, and they call that the *demand curve*. There is a corresponding *supply curve* that reflects how many eggs the industry is willing to produce at a given price. That magic point at which these curves intersect is the *market price*. If enough people become willing to buy more expensive eggs on moral grounds (e.g., because the hens suffer less), then the entire demand curve is going to change. Specifically, it will shift so that it intersects with the supply curve at a point where producers are willing to produce more of these humanely produced eggs. There are philosophers who doubt the efficacy of these market mechanisms, but I am not one of them. Changing your pattern of food purchasing has consequences for other people's behavior, and, in this case, it can encourage producers to do things that you want them to do. That is politics.

Even if it is doubtful that a single individual's purchasing power can move markets, as moral reasoning sways more and more consumers, a shift in their market behavior stimulates producers to respond. The fact that many people must change their behavior points us to the importance of provoking others to act in the political dimensions of food ethics. The role of persuasion is the philosophically significant difference between a purely personal consumption ethic and a political one. At a personal level, one is asking oneself, "How should I act?" At the political level, one is trying to persuade others to act in a specified way. This politically motivated emphasis on persuasion introduces a strategic dimension into ethics. One is less concerned with the considerations that informed one's own choice than with identifying reasons that will affect the behavior of others. The political activist makes a guess as to what those reasons might be. Whether or not they are good reasons matters less than whether they are effective in motivating behavior. (The debate over the efficacy of market power is discussed at more length in Chapter 4).

What is more, the potential for affecting others (in this case, egg producers) raises questions about social institutions and the role of government. For example, one might think that there should just be a law that achieves better animal welfare directly by regulating egg production. This is, in fact, the tack taken with respect to eggs in Europe, where laws were enacted to eliminate certain objectionable forms of egg production in the 1990s.[34] Arguments for passing laws to govern the food system will borrow a lot from the persuasive style of food ethics, but they will also have to interact with a long-standing philosophical tradition of thinking on the nature and point of governments, politics, and the overall shape of society. Someone who is happy to alter their diet voluntarily may be quite *un*happy to have government step in and do it for them. Proposals for legislation also attract the attention of seemingly unrelated interests. An energy company or a manufacturer may be interested in laws to regulate the food industry because they imagine that similar regulations may be enacted in ways that affect them. Third parties may have little interest in the underlying dynamics of how *food* is produced, processed, or distributed, but they are very interested in how production, processing, and distribution are regulated in general.

If you are an activist, the point of all this starts with assembling enough political momentum to get your objectives realized. This shapes both the way that an ethically motivated activist relates to market behavior as well as to the political process of getting support for government action. In either case, it is now about increasing the number of people engaged in the effort. Whether the goal is to motivate enough consumers to shift the demand curve or to convince enough voters to voice concerns to their government officials, the *discourse*—the talk and writing that is the stuff of food ethics—is geared toward enrolling people into the movement. Members of a social movement practice ethics less by soul-searching than by searching for whatever it is that will align others with their objectives or will put those opposed to their objectives on the defensive.

All this means that food ethics moves even more decisively into the persuasive domain. As this occurs, two things are antithetical to philosophical thinking. First, anything that retards enrollment in the movement becomes a problem. Persuasion seeks to overcome any differing point of view because the persuader already knows what is right. The work of discovering what is right is over, if it ever began. Disagreement in social persuasion and social control is different from disagreement in inquiry. From the standpoint of inquiry, people who hold opposing views are *agonists*: they speak for two distinct ends, but both of them might be right. One possible goal for inquiry is to discover how a larger truth or a broader framework might incorporate the wisdom from each. From the standpoint of persuasion, they are *antagonists*. They are enemies, and only one of them can win the argumentative showdown.

Second, the persuasive standpoint incorporates armor. It develops a defensive posture to ensure that no opposing point of view can dislodge it from its political, action-oriented objective. The defensive posture has both philosophical and psychological dimensions. The philosophical aspect is the just-mentioned difference between agonists and antagonists. Agonists recognize that they are seeking different priorities but should be open to alliances with others who are not directly opposed to their goals. They are ready to listen, but the bulletproof vest of the antagonist blocks conversation. It is as if there is not enough air in the room to allow breath to any but one's own point of view. Many people in the food movement that I would like to call my friends have landed in this mindset.

A Little Ethics Before Dinner—or Afterward

Of course, it is entirely possible to persuade someone by engaging them in a little soul-searching. That is arguably what Peter Singer has been doing for his entire career. However, it is also necessary to build social movements by finding alliances and refining objectives so that unnecessary conflicts are avoided. I am not saying that doing any of this is unethical; it is a necessary aspect of living in a democratic society. Yet the point of talking, reading, and writing has moved very far from the Piraeus by now. In this kind of political discourse, the movement's objectives dominate the meaning and activity of food ethics. Movement objectives might change, to be sure. However, anyone who calls participants in a social movement to reflect philosophically on their objectives is plausibly seen as an enemy. I am sure that this chapter has already bored some of the food activists out there to tears. Others are enraged, sure that I'm a tool of the food industry. Participants in the social movement for food ethics align along vague and shifting objectives, but time is short and the battle is long. Philosophical conversations must be moved far from the Pynx and conducted in quarters (like the Piraeus) where the give and take will not be mistaken as a sign of weakness.

Are there other ways to think about food ethics and social change? In fact, I think that efforts to build solidarity with farmers or create cooperative networks function as alternatives to consumption ethics and Singer's style of advocacy for it. That is why this book will *not* tell you what to eat. It won't tell you how to farm or garden, either. There are many other possibilities in food ethics, and each of them has its own form of politics and advocacy.

Developing an appreciation of these possibilities presupposes some understanding of the insider's perspective, a theme that we will take up in the next chapter by asking "What makes food special?" Succeeding chapters will explore issues that arise from the model of consumption ethics as well as some of the alternatives to it, but I will rarely find a reason to go all the way back to Socrates at the Piraeus. I will strive to model inquiry rather than persuasion, and I am sincere in saying that we must inquire together.

3

The Ethics of Food Aid and Famine Relief

Food ethics must include the ethical analysis of food systems in less industrialized parts of the world. When viewed from a naïve consumption ethic, one thinks of contributing to programs that feed the poor, who are often imagined as beggars living in urban slums. I do not want to be read as opposing this kind of charitable action. There *are* beggars in urban slums who need to be fed, as well as working poor who struggle with food access. Yet the focus on urban hunger may be a misdiagnosis of the appropriate focus for moral concern. Food producers, be they farmers, fishers, herders, hunters, or foragers, should be a focal point in discussing the food systems of countries that receive food aid. While it is both natural (and often appropriate) to understand global food issues through the interpretive frameworks of hunger, food security, and the right to food, these approaches can obscure the ways in which well-motivated attempts to address problems make the situation worse.

The fundamental problem in food ethics can be stated in just a few sentences. Programs intended to feed hungry people with food grown in the industrialized world can hurt food producers in the region where food is being distributed. When gifts of food undermine the role that food production plays in these local economies, the people harmed are among the poorest of the poor. There are, indeed, urban poor who benefit from gifts of food, but statistics indicate that between 50% and 75% of people at the World Bank standard for extreme poverty (income of about $2.15 per day in October 2022) live in rural areas. Over half of them are household farmers, and many of the rest depend on food production for employment. Smallholding farmers and herders can and do produce a significant portion of what they eat, but they also need income from their food production to supplement their diets and other elements of the household budget. When staple foods donated from exporting countries undercut the livelihood of these rural residents, their welfare is compromised. Therefore, we should not be sanguine in our support of moral injunctions to support food aid.[1]

From Silo to Spoon. Paul B. Thompson, Oxford University Press. © Oxford University Press 2024.
DOI: 10.1093/oso/9780197744727.003.0004

Given this, readers may be surprised that I end the chapter by presenting arguments in favor of certain types of food aid. The recent history of moral debate over giving food to distant peoples is reviewed before arriving at the following conclusion: food aid delivered as emergency assistance is ethically defensible, but food-based forms of ongoing development aid are complex issues requiring both economic sophistication and insights from mainstream development ethics. Almost as an adjunct to this argument, the chapter develops a root ethic for food aid based on sharing. This ethic *would* apply to issues of hunger in your neighborhood, but we should be careful about metaphorical extensions to non-food goods. An appreciation of how food differs from other goods that contribute to a person's quality of life helps us understand the difference between two forms of international assistance.

Food and Famine in Applied Ethics

Published originally in 1972, "Famine, Affluence and Morality" was one of several early papers that established the reputation of a young Australian philosopher named Peter Singer. Singer's paper appeared at time when devastating famines were making headlines, and it is not surprising that it was taken up quickly. Allowing populations or individuals to go hungry is universally regarded as a moral evil. The series of internationally endorsed declarations supporting individual rights to adequate food begins with the 1945 UN Charter and the 1948 Universal Declaration of Human Rights. The 1966 International Covenant on Economic, Social, and Cultural Rights; the 1974 Universal Declaration on the Eradication of Hunger and Malnutrition; and the 1996 Rome Declaration on Food Security reaffirmed and sharpened international cooperation for ensuring sustenance. Goal number one of the 2000 Millennium Development Goals calls for the eradication of hunger. Throughout this history, agencies charged with eradicating hunger have recognized complexities, ironies, and unintended consequences issuing from measures taken to achieve that objective.

This complexity has not always been appreciated in philosophy settings where Singer's paper was paired with "Lifeboat Ethics: The Case against Helping the Poor," by the ecologist Garrett Hardin (1915–2003). Crushing food emergencies were making headlines in the 1960s, and population ecologists were predicting global food shortages throughout the last quarter of the twentieth century. Singer argued for a moral obligation to feed starving people, while Hardin argued against it.[2] Hardin's paper was published two years after Singer's, but he was already famous for "The Tragedy of the Commons," which discussed how food production could deplete fragile environments. This straightforward opposition in their points of view resulted in these papers being reproduced in anthologies designed for teaching. It would seemingly have been difficult for any student of these subjects in the 1970s or 1980s to avoid the "Singer/ Hardin debate." The pairing surfaced again in the 2008 collection *Global Ethics: Seminal Essays*.[3]

In addition to their pedagogical usefulness as a ready-made debate, both papers generated significant commentary and criticism. Singer's paper was praised for cutting through a great deal of jargon and bypassing technical debates in moral theory to establish a straightforward rationale for addressing compelling needs. Citations to the paper continue in this vein. At the same time, Singer's overall conclusion was viewed as surprisingly contrary to common sense. Singer relied on a thought experiment involving a small child drowning in public view to establish the principle that if one can save the life of another without sacrificing anything of significant moral value, then one ought to do it. Readers were shocked by the recognition that most of us violate this principle all the time. When we make purchases of a less than strictly necessary nature, we could be using that money to aid victims of famine.[4] To some critics, Singer's principle creates moral burdens that exceed human cognitive capacities. Alternatively it undercuts reasonable tendencies to value the morally less compelling needs of those close to us over the subsistence needs of distant others.[5] Although these are genuinely interesting philosophical questions, they are quite far from the food security issues that are the focus of this chapter.

In "The Tragedy of the Commons," Hardin argued that when everyone has access to a renewable resource, it is sure to be depleted because the combined effect of many users will exceed the resource's ability to renew itself (e.g., carrying capacity).[6] In the "Lifeboat Ethics" article, Hardin applied a utilitarian ethic to the problem of carrying capacity. Removing constraints on human population growth associated with famine and hunger would only result in a total population that exceeds the carrying capacity of the global environmental commons. When that happens, more suffer from starvation than would have suffered if well-intentioned people resist the temptation to feed those starving in the present. If one's ethic requires choosing the course of action that produces the greatest good for the greatest number, the suffering of starving masses in the future more than offsets the lives saved by feeding people in the present.[7]

However, Hardin's side of the debate has come to be seen as deeply problematic. The analysis succumbed to both empirical and ethical pitfalls. Empirically, Hardin's analysis fails to conform to what is now known about human population ecology. Given the findings of demographers even at the time he was writing in the 1970s, Hardin should have known that letting people starve is an unreliable check on population numbers. Improving women's literacy, for one thing, is more effective. More significantly, Hardin's "Tragedy of the Commons" paper was followed by four decades of research on open-access resources like pastures or fisheries (called *common pool resources*). The present consensus is that Hardin's assumptions about the potential for cooperation in pursuit of ecological objectives were overly pessimistic. In addition, his recommendations overstated the role that private control of ecosystems could play in maintaining their productivity.[8]

A full accounting of the ethical critiques that have been mounted against Hardin would consume the balance of this chapter, if not the entire book. Hardin portrayed the issue as a conflict between rich and poor nations and described the poor as unable to control their rates of reproduction. This argument mobilizes racial prejudices and depicts people living in Africa, Asia, and Latin America as threats. Recent analysts of the debate between Singer and Hardin claim that whether Hardin's intent was racist or not, his argument plays upon an ideology of white racial superiority: The people he is allowing to starve are implicitly black and brown. Their implied inability to control their own reproductive activity or to manage their resources echoes a stereotype that must be expunged from contemporary thinking. Commentators also note Hardin's favorable statements regarding eugenics.[9]

Hardin-style arguments combining utilitarian ethics with population ecology thus appear to have run their course, at least in the form in which they were originally formulated.[10] As for Singer, passages in *Practical Ethics* suggested that he was willing to temper the extreme burdens to bring aid implied by his 1972 analysis on the ground that maintaining minimal social bonds among family and neighbors limits one's ability to divert one's wealth to people who need it more. He has stuck to his guns, however, in claiming that most of us neglect a duty to do more for the needy than we usually do.[11] One might well ask where this leaves the Singer–Hardin debate in the world of the twenty-first century.

Food and Famine in Development Ethics

David Crocker introduces the Singer–Hardin debate as a key framing device for his own theory of development ethics.[12] Crocker is a "capability theorist." This means that he is working in a philosophical tradition most famously associated with Amartya Sen and Martha Nussbaum. The key ethical claim is that development should seek to enhance people's power or ability to achieve aspects of personal welfare (i.e., their capabilities). The capabilities approach situates the problems of food access in an importantly different philosophical tradition from that of Singer or Hardin. Sen argues that some people realize the capability relevant to food by having the income to buy it, while others can produce food themselves. Still others may depend on gifts or government entitlements.[13] Although Crocker uses the Singer–Hardin debate as the launching pad for his adaptation of the capabilities approach, "famine relief" is actually a proxy for broad questions in the theory and practice of international development. Crocker's specific contribution to capability theory is to emphasize economic or political opportunities as crucial elements of a person's capability set.[14] His shift from hunger and famine to multilateral efforts toward poverty relief and political empowerment makes an important philosophical turn.

Hugh Lafollette classifies those who address hunger and food security from the more encompassing framework of economic growth and civil rights as advocating a *developmental perspective*.[15] Capability theorists see their approach as an alternative to the methods and goals of international assistance programs as they were understood in the decades immediately following World War II, but they do not reject the developmental perspective.[16] Other philosophers have also raised similar questions without resorting to the idea of capabilities. For example, Henry Shue's book *Basic Rights* discusses the role of food in development planning. Shue's point is that people who lack basic rights cannot meaningfully exercise civil liberties. Hungry people are vulnerable to quiet forms of coercion that undermine civil protection of rights to free expression and ownership of property. Shue concludes that food security exemplifies a positive freedom that must be guaranteed by society before negative liberties (such as freedom of speech or the right to enter into economic exchanges) become meaningful.[17] Whether articulated in terms of rights or capabilities, the developmental perspective argues that the moral dimensions of hunger should be understood in terms of underdevelopment or maldevelopment.

Jean Drèze and Amartya Sen assembled the key economic arguments for incorporating the phenomenon of hunger under the developmental perspective. Contrary to assumptions implicit in the Singer–Hardin debate, they argue that lack of food was not the root cause of starvation and food deprivation in the twentieth century. Instead, a breakdown in entitlement systems had left poor people without secure access to food, even when adequate supplies of food were available locally.[18] Their empirical observations were widely interpreted as meaning that the moral imperatives of development have little to do with gifts of food and a great deal to do with promoting political solutions that would enable poor people to resist forms of exploitation and economic vulnerability. Thus, while Crocker emphasizes the compelling nature of food needs, duties to give aid in response to the problems of hunger become incorporated into a more comprehensive package of capabilities (or basic rights) under the developmental perspective. These subsistence rights also include personal security and healthcare. Sen has gone on to argue that if basic political rights are respected, hunger is unlikely to be a problem anywhere.[19]

One can trace a trajectory that moves further and further from Singer's original focus on food. While Singer's 1972 article can be read as a treatment of ethical obligations to aid starving people, Shue's basic right to food is articulated within the context of the role that food plays within more comprehensive goals of economic and social development. Crocker and Sen continue the developmental trend, and other influential philosophers have followed suit. John Rawls (1921–2002) proposed a law of peoples that understands hunger and famine as problems for government to address, rather than calling on charitable acts by individuals. Rawls subsumes the significance of food within a more comprehensive set of basic needs that are consistent with his idea of "primary goods" (e.g., goods that support any of many sets of values and life goals). While Shue characterizes food security as one of several positive rights, Thomas Pogge emphasizes how food insecurity is the consequence of inadequate safeguards to protect against exploitation by elites. Extreme poverty is a form of harm that violates individual liberty.[20]

In fact, the shift away from famine relief is almost total in contemporary development ethics. Elizabeth Ashford writes that "lack of secure access to basic necessities results principally not from famine or other natural disasters, but from . . . coming to be deprived of any realistic chance of earning a subsistence income."[21] Ashford takes this as the starting point for the ethics of food security rather than as a result derived from an analysis of famine or food deprivation. Silvia Berryman argues that a focus on famine distracts our attention from the more serious ethical problems of poverty. She writes that Singer's emphasis on rescue—evident in the famous "drowning child" example and reiterated in the very title of his book *The Life You Can Save*—diverts attention away from the mechanisms that reproduce poverty and structural injustice. Berryman goes on to note institutional and organizational features of developmental assistance programs that can be implicated in this process.[22] Ashford and Berryman both claim that the ethical issues raised by famine can be subsumed under an approach addressed toward poverty. From this vantage point, the emphasis on famine is actually a distraction.

In sum, the developmental perspective implies that embedding food security within a more comprehensive set of fundamental human interests sidelines the central question that motivated Singer's 1972 paper. Hunger becomes a metaphor, albeit one with a significant emotional punch. From the developmental perspective, Singer's advocacy of famine assistance becomes a proxy for a more general argument in support of development assistance. *The Life You Can Save* makes this move explicitly, using the issue of hunger as the launching point for much more extensive obligations to support development assistance. Thus, Singer himself appears to have embraced the developmental perspective in his recent work. Perhaps he always viewed hunger and famine merely as entry points for a broader perspective on the moral imperatives to support economic development but that would not have been obvious in the 1972 article.

Treating food as an emblematic exemplar for a more comprehensive class of basic needs broadens the discussion in a natural manner that I do not intend to contest. Nevertheless, this virtually ubiquitous trend in development ethics also has the effect of diverting attention from whether giving aid in the form of food is indeed an actionable moral obligation or whether it hurts more than it helps. The continuing relevance of Hardin's side in the debate hangs on the fact that his observations do not have obvious bearing on broader imperatives of development, questions such as whether people in less industrialized regions should enjoy civil rights, access to education, or even basic healthcare. While I reject Hardin's version of the "it hurts more than it helps" conclusion, I will argue that our evaluation of food aid should retain a focus on hunger, as opposed to the broader imperatives of development.

Food Aid as a Moral Imperative

It will prove helpful to trace how the very idea of a duty to feed poor people in foreign lands came about. Helen Veit argues that food-oriented development ethics has origins in the two World Wars. For Americans, this ethic begins with propaganda campaigns promulgated by the US Food Administration (USFA) during World War I. The agency's primary responsibility was to channel grain to US allies in Europe, where the war had severely disrupted local grain production. Under the leadership of Herbert Hoover (1874–1964), this logistical work was coupled with a massive public education effort intended to increase political support. Hoover asked Americans to limit their own consumption and, above all, to curtail the waste of staple grains so that food could be sent to hungry women and children in France and the Netherlands, as well as to troops engaged against the Central Powers. Veit argues that this campaign fixed the idea of a moral obligation to share bounteous American harvests in the mind of the American public.[23]

The message was revitalized during World War II, and afterward during the execution of the Marshall Plan to rebuild Europe. The US Congress authorized P.L. 480, the "Food for Peace" program in 1954. The rationale proposed by the Dwight D. Eisenhower (1890–1969) administration was to use surplus production by US farmers for Marshall fund–style development assistance. The image of using unneeded American food to prevent hunger in the developing world appealed to the American public. Farmers anxious to find markets for excess production also supported the Food for Peace program. P.L. 480 funds thus were a significant source of both political and monetary support for foreign assistance in the United States. This rhetorical framing for aid had a disproportionate impact on the way everyone, including academic philosophers, understood famine relief during the era when Singer wrote.[24]

Yet, as early as 1960, conservative agricultural economist (and Nobel laureate) Theodore Schultz (1902–1998) was arguing against the creation of large-scale programs to divert US farm surpluses to feed hungry people in the developing world. Schultz believed that the policy-driven surpluses were costly and inefficient. Schultz was not against foreign aid, but he felt that relying on the P.L. 480 programs to support foreign aid embedded a hidden cost structure into US foreign assistance programs. He also noted that programs anchored in food aid were very likely to distort local markets for agricultural commodities in recipient countries. This, in turn, would have adverse effects on local farmers in these countries.[25] Schultz's way of thinking eventually became part of the argument for policies of "structural adjustment" in the 1980s. Schultz had laid down the reasons for thinking that low food prices create disincentives for production by local farmers. As a result, investments were not being made in land improvements or new technology, and rural producers were falling ever further behind in their ability to be competitive within world commodity markets.[26] While philosophers were worrying over the demandingness of Singer's moral principle, the mantra of "getting prices right" became associated with the neoliberal Washington Consensus on development policy. Conservatives with a bias toward market solutions became broadly suspicious of aid programs and condoned them only when coupled with stringent programs to integrate developing country agricultures more fully into the global economy.[27]

Either selling or donating grain and dairy products became the chief mechanism for funding all non-military forms of US foreign aid for several decades. Eventually the "Food for Peace" program became widely favored by US farm organizations, and political support for food-based forms of international assistance became widespread among farm-state congressional representatives. Vernon Ruttan (1924–2008) finds that the rationale for government food aid programs in the United States had more to do with keeping domestic prices high for American farmers than it did with beneficence to the poor of developing countries.[28] Thus, even while philosophers like Lafollette were becoming more confident in rebutting the population-based arguments of Hardin, economists were calling for an elimination of food aid programs being operated by the US government. However, Ruttan also notes that whatever failings might be associated with government food aid, these programs represented a substantial resource commitment to the poor in developing countries. He was willing to forgive the selfish political motives for food aid in light of the fact that its halo of humanitarianism made it more palatable to the public than other forms of foreign aid.[29]

By the 1990s, critics of its unintended consequences were more inclined to manage food aid than to eliminate it. The goal was to bring P.L. 480 programs more squarely in line with the development paradigm being advocated by Sen and Drèze.[30] Chief among these are programs that convert donated food to cash on world markets and the subsequent purchase of food needed on a local basis from local farmers.[31] Writing in 1991, Edward Clay concludes, "If food aid is provided in increasingly flexible ways, with purchases in developing countries and monetization rather than direct distribution, then . . . the food aid debate would no longer need to be distinct from the overall debate about the magnitude and effectiveness of development aid in general."[32] In point of fact, America's unsalable food surplus has declined steadily ever since this early-1990s discussion. While the Food for Peace program still continues to supply US grain for foreign aid, it does not currently serve as a mechanism for domestic price supports. Food aid programming described in US government sources now emphasizes developmental objectives rather than feeding hungry people.[33]

Food as a Moral Good

Given the shift away from famine relief and toward development ethics, it is worth asking whether Singer's original focus on famine has lost all relevance whatsoever. I think not. In this section, I explain how food assumes a special significance in moral terms. In the following section, I show how the implementation of food aid betrayed those terms. The chapter concludes by identifying circumstances in which deliveries of food aid *are* morally justified. When these circumstances are satisfied, the developmental perspective on food security—the idea that it is just one component of a more comprehensive moral imperative for development—is mistaken. This is not a thoroughgoing refutation of Shue or of capabilities theorists like Sen and Crocker, though it *is* possible to go too far in sweeping food needs under the umbrella of poverty and development. As such, Singer's initial focus on food emergencies has enduring merit.

Food needs differ from other basic needs. As common sense knows and all theories of development presume, food is a biological necessity for the short-term survival of human beings. This fact alone distinguishes food and water from most of the other basic needs typically included in the accounts of development ethics. While individuals may find themselves in specific circumstances where access to shelter or medical care is critical to avoiding death, total loss of access to food usually results in death over a period measured in weeks. This biological vulnerability is universal for all human beings at all times. Food-secure individuals undoubtedly fail to grasp the full reality of this vulnerability as it is experienced by anyone who has involuntarily gone without food for even a matter of days. Yet even the abstract possibility of severe hunger is sufficient to gain a purchase on the moral imagination that risks of extended homelessness or inadequate medical care simply do not have. Lafollette and Larry May emphasize the way that children are among the most vulnerable and innocent victims of chronic hunger. As innocent victims, hungry children make a claim upon us that adults, who may have some complicity in their plight, lack.[34]

It is important not to overstate the singularity of food among basic needs. Death from starvation occurs, but food deprivations that do not reach starvation levels exacerbate the risk of debilitating disease. In that circumstance, food security intertwines with inadequate housing or healthcare, and, here again, children will be among the most vulnerable. This helps explain why Sen and Dreze emphasize the means for realizing nutritional well-being as one aspect of a person's capabilities among others. It is appropriate to regard these needs as organically interrelated when examining the ethical significance of poverty and underdevelopment. Yet this does not negate the fact that the specter of extended or pervasive hunger has compelling moral significance in its own terms. The human body signals the need for sustenance through pangs of hunger. The word "pangs" is apt, but not a term that is in common use among moral theorists. *Pangs* are sudden physical or emotional pains that intrude upon one's conscious life. They are not willful. The subjective experience of hunger pangs is available to anyone who skips a meal or two. This gives hunger a moral resonance that poverty lacks. It is, again, proper to note that food-secure people who undertake a voluntary fast do not approximate the subjective experience of chronic or severe hunger. Yet while we should not overstate the singular experience of short-term food deprivation, we should not understate it, either.

In sum, even mild hunger pangs experienced by well-fed people provide a grounding for the moral significance of food that is less strongly felt in the case of most other basic needs. The initial claim is not that hunger and thirst are more significant on ethical grounds, but rather that they are *felt* in a way that differs from lack in other basic needs. Combined with the fact that even well-off people are likely to experience mild hunger from time, the quality of feeling hungry motivates an empathetic response that may be weaker—indeed much weaker—in the case of capabilities. Any ethical theory that recognizes empathy and emotion as components in generating moral feeling or sustaining moral commitment will surely acknowledge that hunger and thirst are especially significant for generating an empathetic (as opposed to sympathetic) response.

Food also has objective characteristics that distinguish it from the goods and services that must be provided to address other basic needs. Food

commodities have low exclusion costs: it is relatively easy to constrain physical access to grains, beans, eggs, milk, and other foodstuffs. It is more difficult to keep fresh air, solar energy, and water under lock and key, especially
in regions that do not already have an industrial infrastructure. It is also difficult to control access to the benefits of a police presence or a health service.
Both have value for people who do not make direct use of it and who have not
borne some of the cost of maintaining it.[35] Low exclusion cost implies that
the person who has food is in a position to prevent someone else from getting
it, and this puts the owner in the position to require compensation for access.
However, foodstuffs may have relatively *high* exclusion costs prior to harvest.
Fences will keep some people out, but others can breach them (and fences
are notoriously ineffective against deer). Scavenging or poaching creates vulnerability for the farmer. It may also serve as a food source that retards the
development of markets and mitigates the need for formal programs of food
aid in rural areas.

Classic food commodities are also alienable goods. They are readily
removed from the site of primary production and can pass through many
hands prior to their final consumption. The extent of alienability is limited
primarily by infrastructure. Historically, foodstuffs were consumed relatively
near the site of production. E. P. Thompson (1924–1993) argued that many
local communities presumed the existence of a localized moral economy
that gave villagers a moral claim on the grain growing in the fields of local
farmers. As roads and canals developed in post-medieval Europe, farmers
exercised a legal right to seek better prices by trading in other locales. Doing
so provoked riots and unrest.[36] Given modern transportation networks and
understandings of property rights, grains produced in Iowa or Kansas can
be alienated from nature and pass through a series of trades before being
consumed in China or the Sudan.

The combination of alienability and low exclusion cost means that food
commodities move much more fluidly through international markets and
trading channels than the goods needed to satisfy virtually all other basic
needs. Housing, personal security, and medical care must be produced at
the site where they are consumed (though there are, of course, supplies that
enable such production that are amenable to commodity exchange). Like
shiploads of rice or maize, pharmaceuticals are both alienable and have low
exclusion cost. Yet drugs do not become converted into effective medical
care without some active expenditure of medical expertise on the receiving
end. In contrast, the knowledge needed to convert dry food commodities

into a sustaining meal is virtually ubiquitous.[37] It is, therefore, possible to see aid delivered in the form of foodstuffs as having more completely satisfied its respective need provided, of course, that it actually *is* delivered. Goods delivered to supply other basic needs require a more developed institutional framework on the receiving end before they can become relevant to capabilities.

Two features of what economists call *rivalry* complete this picture of food's place in the institutional structure of distributive goods. First, commodities delivered as food aid are consumed when they are eaten. Unlike education, housing, or even medical care, when grains, beans, and other foodstuffs are used for food, it means using them up. The goods are no longer there to be used again, and new goods will have to be supplied in relatively short order to meet the persistent biological need for food. Second, many grains and beans amenable to use as food can also be used as seeds. While this will not be the fate of milled commodities delivered as food aid, it does mean that there is a rival relationship between the portion of a crop that farmers are saving for seed and the portion that they are eating or selling for food. Food is consumed in use, but seed is not (though, of course, the good becomes temporarily unavailable while the crop is in the ground). Although these characteristics of food commodities will not figure prominently in the discussion below, they do interpenetrate the moral significance of food in sometimes rather complex ways. For example, several African countries rejected US food aid coming in the form of unmilled maize in 2002 because they feared that farmers would save some to plant as seed. Such a possibility threatened their access to European markets where genetically modified (GM) crops are not accepted, or at least that is what they believed.[38]

The peculiar moral dimensions of food are coupled with characteristics that, given legal conventions and trade agreements, fix the institutional structure for economic exchange. These peculiar characteristics of food then become peculiar to food *aid*. Food needs are constant and require frequent resupply. While this supply can to some degree be sourced from local production, it can also be derived from distant sources, given reasonable notice. What is more, the additional fact that any individual's immediate need for food can be satiated means that once a foreseeable supply is secured, additional quantities can be seen as surplus. It is thus somewhat reasonable for wealthy people who have food to conceptualize food needs as amenable to a moral practice of sharing. The experiential quality of one's own need to eat provides a unique basis for empathetic grounding of food's moral significance. It is difficult to imagine how one might share other basic needs—one's personal security, one's healthcare, or even one's home—with needy people in distant locales.

Now, one can share one's wealth as well, to be sure. My point is not to undercut the arguments for redistributing wealth that has become commonplace in development ethics. I mean to show how the moral appeal to aid the hungry stands on a different ground. Scripting the appeal as one of sharing, as Veit suggests in her history of food assistance, ties it to a basic cultural form.[39] Fulfillment of the script through the sharing of food that will be eaten also limits the social domain of the script. Because food is a rival good consumed in use, potential for diversion to uses not envisioned in the act of sharing does not loom large in the mind of one who shares. More subtle and tendentious elements of sociality associated with the acquisition, retention, and redistribution of wealth need not become activated. It thus may be plausible to understand the check that one writes to Oxfam or even the letter one writes in support of government food aid by analogy to the can of peas or chili that one donates to the local food drive. The emotive dimension of hunger may override offsetting complexities that arise in the attempt to secure food-related capabilities.

Other basic needs—shelter, bodily security, healthcare—require much more complex interventions that unfold over an extended period of time. It is more difficult to imagine how a simple act of sharing could address these needs fully. These considerations distinguish food needs from other basic needs and indicate how the ethics of food must also be disambiguated from a general argument for capabilities in development ethics. In sum, material differences in the very nature of food differentiate initiatives to address hunger from other types of development assistance. In addition, providing food differs from poverty alleviation because food emergencies affect people who are not poor. Noticing these distinctions is not intended to undercut or refute the moral or political argument for addressing food security as one component in an interlocking nexus of needs, each of which is implicated with others in the reality of extreme poverty, exploitation, and global injustice. Nevertheless, food does differ from other goods (including cash) that might be offered to the needy both in the way that it registers emotionally for donors and in its immediate criticality for participants in need. The distinctive character of food needs, on the one hand, and of assistance programs specifically conceptualized as food aid, on the other, suggests that questions central to the famine relief argument may be of continuing interest.

However, it is also important to discipline the moral imagination by recognizing that food has its own complexities. As noted at the beginning of the chapter, delivering food to hungry people can damage the prospects of poor farmers. Furthermore, in many parts of the world, poor farmers are both more numerous and worse off than the people who would be helped by donations of food from countries with an agricultural surplus. It is the impact on smallholding farmers, rather than worries about population growth, that explains why food aid hurts, rather than helps. This fundamental problem in food ethics introduces one final way in which food aid differs from other forms of development assistance: food aid can undercut the economic agency (e.g., capability) of poor people that assistance programs are intended to help. It is less likely that programs to address other basic needs would harm a large indigenous population of people living in extreme poverty in a similar way.

Why Food Aid Became Contentious

Although food is different from healthcare, housing, and education distributed through development assistance, it is still not obvious why food aid became the subject of moral condemnation among development specialists. Here, it helps to appreciate the categories that specialists use to classify aid. The international development establishment uses jargon terms "program aid," "project aid," and "humanitarian aid" to categorize the main forms of foreign assistance. *Program aid* is generally bilateral assistance offered by one government to another. *Project aid* is often supervised by charitable agencies or other non-profits pursuing development activities, even if the money comes from government sources. Project aid is usually organized as a scheme or activity with a limited time horizon and explicitly articulated ends in view. Project aid might support programs to improving schools, promote new agricultural techniques, or establish clinics. Government grants, private foundation funding, or contributions individuals make to charitable organizations might pay for these programs. As discussed later, food aid has played a role in government funding of development projects. In contrast to these two categories, *humanitarian aid* is offered in response to acute needs, and it may consist of blankets, temporary shelter, medical supplies, or food.[40]

A slightly different typology is more intuitive, and especially so with respect to the moral rationale for aid. *Security assistance* is offered primarily as a component in a bilateral agreement (formal or informal) binding parties into a military or political alliance. *Development assistance* aims at long-term improvement in recipients' quality of life. It is intended to encourage economic growth and the creation of both physical and institutional capabilities that will eventually allow people to attain the ability to participate as full partners in the modern global economy. *Emergency assistance* is short-term aid offered in response to what can be regarded as temporary shortfalls arising from natural disasters (such as flood or famine) or human catastrophes (warfare or severe economic dislocations).[41] While the categories may overlap in ways that make classifying the nature of any specific gift difficult, these terms accurately reflect three distinct types of ethical rationale. My terminology stresses the way aid is justified, but the categories also map on to the categories of program, project, and humanitarian aid in the majority of cases.

Security assistance congers images of jet airplanes and shoulder-mounted missile systems. That is exactly what program aid consists in, much of the time. One might wonder how the category could even be relevant to food aid, but, for several decades, the so-called Great Powers utilized grants of food both to cement strategic alliances and to fund outright purchases of military hardware. Although this practice has declined markedly, Christopher Barrett and Daniel Maxwell show how the United States continued to funnel significant portions of bilateral assistance to Afghanistan through the food aid mechanism well into the twenty-first century. They provide data showing how aid flows rose sharply after US military action displaced the Taliban in 2001. Although there were genuine food needs in the wake of the war, Barrett and Maxwell conclude that US food aid "plainly had far more to do with the politics and public relations of war than with food security in a land of intense and widespread suffering."[42] In the category of security assistance, the fact that food is an instrumentality of aid becomes secondary to moral considerations that center on the justifiability of the security arrangement itself.[43]

The ethical rationale for gifts of food in the domain of development assistance (or "project aid") differs from security assistance, but the way that food is used in these projects is surprisingly similar. As with security assistance, it may be possible to fund projects intended to promote long-term development through gifts or concessional sales of food commodities. The United States did this for several decades under P.L. 480, the "Food for Peace" program. The very title of the program suggests the way programs of development aid can be seen to converge with self-serving strategic rationales for security assistance. The gift of food is expected to be rewarded through the establishment of peaceful relations. Such gifts differ from security assistance in one morally important respect, however. Development aid intends to promote the capability for participating in reciprocal transactions and social engagement on an equal basis. Security assistance demands that client groups remain dependent on their more powerful and advanced benefactors. Only eternal vigilance prevents the elision of the ethically laudable intention into its less savory cousin.[44]

The machinations of aid funding are so complex that it is impossible to be accurate without burying a reader under tedious detail and qualification. Stated baldly, food figures in the process like this: countries like the United States buy commodities from their farmers. They put these commodities on a boat and send it to a recipient nation where it is then sold for less than the donor country paid for it (not to mention shipping costs), and the money is then used for either security measures or development projects. The recipient country would get more bang for the buck if the donor country would just give them the money they spent on farm commodities (e.g., corn [maize], soybeans, wheat, rice, sugar, or possibly milk products) in the first place. This is the sense in which Schultz found the scheme to be inefficient. However crazy it sounds from an economics perspective, it works politically for two reasons. First, buying from your own farmers helps support the domestic price of these farm commodities, which is something that many governments (and especially the United States) are doing anyway. Second, food aid is more popular than other foreign aid because it can be presented to the public as fulfilling a moral responsibility by helping the nation's farmers "feed the world." If this is the only way to make foreign assistance palatable to a skeptical public, then perhaps we should just swallow our pride and do it, as Ruttan suggests.

Such uses of food aid are indefensible unless the security and developmental goals they are being used to support are themselves defensible. This is questionable in many cases, and the emotional attraction of food aid distracts attention from careful scrutiny of the purposes that aid is actually going to support. Furthermore, even when security or development objectives are justified, questions about the efficiency and politics of using farm surpluses to fund them counts against this approach to foreign assistance. In addition, to the points noted just now, there are the knock-on impacts on the recipient economy noted by Schultz and Ruttan. Even if recipient governments distribute food aid in urban centers, there are still likely to be negative impacts on the price that farmers receive for their products. Some economists believe that since many farmers are themselves net consumers of food (e.g., they spend more on food than they make from selling it), there may actually be some benefit from lower food prices, even to rural smallholders who derive a significant portion of their cash income from farming.[45]

In contrast to security and development assistance, humanitarian forms of food aid are specifically intended to feed people during or after a food crisis. Emergency assistance offers goods that will alleviate immediate human needs, including medical assistance, shelter, and clothing, as well as food. In many cases, recipients of emergency assistance will recover from the circumstances that placed them in need. They will replant crops, rebuild fishing boats, or do whatever is needed to bounce back from the catastrophe that put them in a position of need in the first place. Although the recipients of emergency assistance are often less well-off than middle-class Americans or Europeans, they may not be poor, especially in the context of their local society. However, lest I be accused of misleading my readers, it is important to note that recovery takes time in the best of cases, and there are many emergencies that extend over years and even decades. The Intergovernmental Panel on Climate Change (IPCC) predicts that we will see more food emergencies in the future, with some of the most currently food-challenged areas of the globe losing most of their ability to produce food altogether by the end of the century. The rationale for emergency assistance bleeds over into development assistance in cases like this where there is, in fact, no actual recovery. What is needed is a substantially reconstituted food system.

Food Aid That Really Helps

My view is that the moral case for emergency food assistance is both secure and significant. The case for using food as a form of development aid is more complex. Let us start with the reasons why emergency assistance is warranted in ethical terms, though in truth this is really a no-brainer. Emergency food shortages have many distinct causes: war, natural disasters, and economic disruptions. In 2017, Hurricane Maria struck the islands of Dominica, St. Croix, and Puerto Rico. One of the immediate effects was lack of access to food. The flooding associated with hurricanes can destroy both stored food and crops in the field, but, in this case, the food shortage was due to the storm's impact on infrastructure, especially roads and the electrical grid. The international relief organization Oxfam sent volunteers to address emergency food and water shortages, and celebrity chef José Andrés organized an effort that marshalled existing food resources in a major feeding operation.[46] In 2020, the United Nations World Food Programme announced that 16 million people in Yemen were on the brink of famine and could not be sure whether they would eat another meal. The food shortage in famine was the combined result of an extended war and the COVID-19 pandemic, which further damaged local food systems.[47] Surely, these are cases where one does not need a philosopher to endorse the acts of Oxfam, Andrés, or the United Nations in moral terms.

In a food crisis, catastrophic events have caused a shortfall of food. The catastrophe may be a natural disaster, or it may be the result of war or political oppression. Like the passerby who saves Singer's drowning child, we in rich countries have the wealth to do something about it. Singer's paper articulates the moral obligation to feed the poor squarely as a response to hunger, and, like that of the drowning child, this situation calls for immediate action with a presumption of closure. The child pulled from the pool is saved and will presumably be returned to the care of a loving family. In the same way, the starving hordes are fed for a season, after which they return to whatever pursuits occupied them before this catastrophe. However, Singer's argument was made at a time when many assumed that persistent famine would be the reality for the foreseeable future, and the denial of closure was a critical component in Hardin's opposing argument.

In fact, famines were conspicuously absent during the last three decades of the twentieth century. Although a dictionary definition of "famine" states that it is simply an extreme shortage of food, a famine is not declared unless at least a third of the population in a region are suffering from acute malnutrition. Cormac Ó Gráda reviews famine throughout recorded time from the perspective of economic and ecological history, arguing that, in the twentieth century, periods of food deprivation became shorter and less uniformly distributed across the populations they affected. He notes that there are no universally accepted criteria for determining whether a famine has occurred. Nevertheless, some food crises fall short of meeting famine conditions even when lack of food causes damage to health and even death. For example, a partial crop failure can cause these outcomes throughout a region, but ancient sources on famine more typically discuss multiyear periods of food deprivation. By this standard, the food crisis that follows a hurricane, a swarm of locusts, or a volcanic eruption would not automatically qualify as a famine. In addition, famines are implicitly understood to involve disruptions in a regional food system. We do not classify policy failure to provide food for a subset of the population as a famine. Ó Gráda's analysis suggests that, over time, better transportation and communication technology, agricultural improvements, and democratically responsive governments combine to prevent food crises from becoming famines. He notes that some theorists believe famine is a thing of the past.[48]

In this light, Singer's use of the word "famine" seems problematic. Singer's 1972 article begins,

As I write this, in November 1971, people are dying in East Bengal from lack of food, shelter, and medical care. The suffering and death that are occurring there now are not inevitable, not unavoidable in any fatalistic sense of the term. Constant poverty, a cyclone, and a civil war have turned at least nine million people into destitute refugees; nevertheless, it is not beyond the capacity of the richer nations to give enough assistance to reduce any further suffering to very small proportions.[49]

The statement is not supported with any citations, so it is difficult to know exactly what events Singer had in mind. Singer would have been writing just a few months after George Harrison (1943–2001) and Ravi Shankar (1920–2012) organized the Concert for Bangladesh. Proceeds from the concert and sales of the recording released afterward were dedicated to Bangladeshi relief. The Wikipedia article on the concert quotes a number of music industry sources on current events in Bangladesh, including atrocities of the Bangladesh Liberation War and a cyclone in 1970.[50] The situation in West Bengal would have been widely known by readers of Rolling Stone magazine in 1972. In retrospect, it seems clear that there was a food emergency among refugees from these events, but it is not clear that there was a famine, as economic historians typically define that term.

The Bengal food crisis that Singer discussed in "Famine, Affluence, and Morality," turns out to be linked by geography with one of the more complex food crises in history. Amartya Sen's book Poverty and Famines includes a detailed retrospective analysis claiming that food availability decline (or FAD)—clearly the problem in Puerto Rico and Yemen—had nothing to do with the situation in Bengal in the 1940s. Rather, an inflationary surge put the price of food out of reach for Bengalese living in extreme poverty. Given his finding that an adequate supply of food was available in the shops, Sen argued that an immediate government purchase and distribution of locally available food would have resolved the problem, rather than an international emergency assistance effort such as described above. Sen also discusses a regional famine in Ethiopia that *was* caused by a crop failure, but here he argued that supplies were available elsewhere in the country. Hence, again, an emergency humanitarian effort was unnecessary.[51] *Poverty and Famines* occupies a significant place in capability theory, as well as the argument for focusing on poverty, rather than food, in contemporary development theory.

Sen's recommendation for 1943 would appear to imply that Singer was wrong in 1972, when he called upon readers to support a food relief effort. However, Peter Bowbrick has published an analysis disputing Sen's interpretation of the Bengal famine, citing evidence of FAD resulting from the combined effects of a bad crop year, a cyclone, and a downturn in imports. Bowbrick is vehement in his insistence that a government purchase of locally available food (e.g., Sen's recommended remedy) would only exacerbate the spike in food costs under such circumstances, and he cites statistics and government documents to indicate that the primary failing of British administrators in Bengal was to presume, as Sen does, that food supplies were adequate. He concludes, "The only way to be sure of curing a famine, however caused, is to import more food."[52]

I have no wish to implicate myself (or my readers) more deeply in this dispute between economists. I have already provided an argument for interpreting the ethics of an emergency food shortage differently from the problems of poverty. This argument emphasizes the immediacy with which food shortages affect survival, as well as ways in which physical characteristics of food differ from those of education, healthcare, housing, and other basic needs. I repeat that this argument should *not* be taken to imply that the problems of hunger are unrelated to the conditions of poverty. Indeed, *chronic* hunger, as distinct from famine or a food emergency, is yet a different problem, and one for which the capabilities remedy would appear to be more adequate than Bowbrick's. However, the Bangladeshis that Singer had in mind in 1972 were experiencing a food emergency caused by the combined impact of warfare, genocide, and a typical FAD type of natural disaster. Given the immediacy of their situation, the moral salience of emergency food assistance can and should be distinguished from supplementing their opportunity set with capabilities for education, long-term healthcare, fair labor contracts, or the right to organize politically. They might need all these things, but it is not as if a program to build clinics or schools could substitute for food assistance in such circumstances.

Given this analysis, Singer's mobilization of intuitions supporting aid in the form of food is apt. His statement that richer nations have it within their means to eliminate the suffering from the food emergency is accurate, and the moral argument he marshals in favor of doing so is compelling. However, it is not so clear that richer nations had a clear path for intervention in the suffering associated with Operation Searchlight, the military operation organized in Pakistan that drove people from their homes in the early 1970s and accounted for a significant portion of the deaths.[53] How or even whether Western-style economic development projects led by nongovernmental organizations (NGOs) based in richer countries should play a role in Bangladesh's governance cannot be assessed without engaging substantially more complex issues. Bangladesh's agricultural development trajectory is intertwined with the history of colonialist exploitation, followed by decades of international market distortion by Western democracy's agricultural subsidies. It is thus unfortunate that Singer moves so rapidly from the position staked out in "Famine, Affluence, and Morality" to the perspective of *The Life You Can Save*, where the famine relief argument is proxy or metaphor for much broader poverty relief initiatives. I am not saying that poverty relief is a bad thing, or even denying that everyone who has the means to promote it should do so. I am saying that economic development is an exercise fraught with moral complexity. It demands inquiry, rather than persuasion. Some of the moral issues associated with development ethics are revisited in Chapter 7.

Food Aid and the Fundamental Problem in Food Ethics

Although I have stated that inquiry withdraws from advocacy, this does not imply that one must refrain from drawing conclusions. This chapter makes substantive ethical claims in food ethics. First, development ethicists' tendency to sublimate hunger and food assistance under a rubric of poverty relief and economic development assistance is a moral mistake. Insecure access to food is certainly a problem associated with poverty, and this is true within industrialized richer countries as well as the former colonial states struggling to recover from the richer world's exploitation of their people and natural resources. All this implies that capability theory may not do a good job of identifying the moral imperatives in food emergencies.

At the same time, I do not mean this weakness as an argument against the capabilities approach as a theory of economic and political development. In *From Field to Fork*, I argued that the role of the food sector in development is one of the big questions in development ethics. Although I shrank from endorsing a strong view, I surveyed some reasons why resisting the West's model of industrial agriculture might be a good idea. I offered words in support of the smallholder, suggesting that less industrialized regions have reasons to retain a larger portion in primary food production (e.g., farming, herding, fishing) than the single-digit percentages we see in the West. However, these are complex issues, and the complexity of the issues is itself a reason why we should not burden the ethics of offering emergency food assistance with all the complications of economic development.

Second, I have laid out a framework for understanding why food is different from other goods that might be in the package of primary goods or basic rights that every human being needs. To say that they are different is not to make a statement about the priority of food with respect to other subsistence rights. My sense is that priorities will depend a great deal on circumstances. Nevertheless, foods are alienable goods that are consumed in use, needed on a regular basis, and exchangeable to a degree that is highly determined by the available infrastructure. They are perishable, but variably so. Foods are renewable resources, but only with great planning and effort, and the base for renewing food resources is itself subject to damage or depletion. What is more, food commodities have competing or rival uses that are morally significant. The phrase, "eating the seed corn" points us to a morally significant feature that foods do not share with many other primary goods. All these features make food amenable to a moral practice of sharing, though other institutions can and do disrupt that social form. And most obviously, human beings are vulnerable to hunger in a unique and compelling way. These aspects of food explain a lot about the nature of food ethics, and they should not be neglected in favor of a capabilities ethic that subsumes food under the rubric of health.[54]

There is an enduring tension between supporting the rural poor of less-developed regions—overwhelmingly involved in food production—and making food cheap for the urban poor. This is "the fundamental problem in food ethics." A naïve view of food aid could undercut a poor farmer's livelihood. The tension is morally problematic precisely because it is unclear how to address it. Do the reasons for supporting a rural population of economically vulnerable food producers outweigh the compelling reasons for feeding the urban poor? I am not sure.[55] However, in this chapter, I have made the distinction between development-oriented food aid and emergency assistance and concluded that this fundamental problem is *not* a reason to resist emergency food aid. Famine, or more accurately a food emergency, should compel us to act for the reasons that Singer noted in the 1970s. Whether implemented through international agencies such as the World Food Program, religious and civil society groups, or direct government action, food aid will raise further ethical issues in conceptualizing and bringing about the organization needed to carry out emergency assistance.[56] However, that should not surprise us. Life is complex.

4

Local Food

The Moral Case Reconsidered

Buying locally produced food is a mainstay for participants in the food movement, but many arguments have been leveled in opposition to it. This chapter begins with a brief discussion of *locavorism*: the food ethic that recommends sourcing one's diet primarily (or as much as is feasible) from foods grown or produced within roughly a hundred miles of where one lives. My interest is in a specifically philosophical interpretation of the ethic. Many criticisms of locavorism point to unwanted consequences that would ensue if the ethic were practiced by a significant number of people. I agree. Widespread, overly literalistic adoption of the locavore ethic would have negative impacts.[1] However, the arguments mounted in favor of the locavore ethic merit consideration even if following its recommendations would have consequences that some of its advocates do not suspect. Authors who claim that locavores would do more harm than good seldom broach the philosophical questions at work in the local food debate. Readers interested in the reasons why a locavore ethic might fail will find more help in the footnotes to this chapter than in the main text.

Nevertheless, there have been philosophical evaluations of the local food ethic that go well beyond the claim that it just won't work. Philosophical criticisms help further the inquiry into to food ethics in three ways. First, the critiques I examine make a positive contribution to the goal announced in this chapter's title: an evaluation of the moral case for locavorism. Second, they model a standard of applied ethics that can itself be evaluated from the standpoint of food ethics. Finally, I argue that this approach to applied ethics has led the authors I discuss to overlook the most persuasive arguments for locavorism. In this, I will be introducing some philosophical themes that tend toward a particular interpretation of virtue ethics. These themes will be developed further in later chapters. In short, the most obvious ways to interpret locavorism according to the standard model of applied ethics are likely

From Silo to Spoon. Paul B. Thompson, Oxford University Press. © Oxford University Press 2024.
DOI: 10.1093/oso/9780197744727.003.0005

to misunderstand what the more powerful arguments for locavorism are intended to support.

Locavorism

It should not be necessary to offer an extended introduction to the locavore ideal. As defined by Samantha Noll, the goal is to "minimize the distance between production, processing and consumption of products in food systems," especially in comparison to current practice.[2] Reducing energy use in the food system was a primary rationale in early statements of the locavore ethic, though Noll mentions added health benefits from eating less processed food and economic benefits to local economies. The idea of evaluating the energy footprint of a food system through the concept of "food miles" has been discussed in the United Kingdom at least since the 1990s. Jules Pretty, Andy Ball, Tim Lang, and James Morison applied the concept in a "total costs assessment" made of the typical United Kingdom food basket.[3] Lang endorsed the concept of a local diet more widely (though never in the sense of extreme locavorism) in his influential work on food policy.[4] The concept began to circulate in the United States after a 2001 white paper by a group at Iowa State University's Leopold Center for Sustainable Agriculture.[5] The locavore idea was popularized by Bill McKibben, followed by Alisa Smith and J. B. MacKinnen, and then by Barbara Kingsolver.[6]

Noll merges the local food ethic with *food sovereignty*. The idea of food sovereignty was introduced as a counter to development economists' concern with food security. Food security means simply having access to food, wherever it came from. Conceptually, one might be food secure because some charitable organization is shipping in food grown in some industrialized nation. Yet there are obvious vulnerabilities in such an approach. In contrast, food sovereignty arose out of smallholding farmers' resistance to forces that would have either deprived them of their access to land or markets, thus extending the reach of the corporate-dominated food system that prevails in much of the industrialized world. Noll argues that participating in locavorism promotes solidarity with these resistance movements. The argument *for* eating local rests on alleged transformative effects that it has on the developed-world consumer's social identity, of who and what they experience themselves to be.[7]

The link between locavorism and social identity formation introduces themes that I will take up only in the closing sections of the chapter. Many philosophers would try to show that moderate locavore diets are morally required by producing a formally structured argument that ends with the conclusion "We are morally required to buy local food in preference to non-local food." On my reading, Noll does not take this tack. However, the stylized construction of an argument for locavorism does provide a basis for critical evaluation of specific claims that locavores make. In the classic style of analytic ethics, an applied ethics argument contains both empirical premises—factual statements about buying local food and the causal connection between doing so and other states of affairs—and at least one premise that states what anyone is morally required to do in general terms. The argument is refuted either by showing that one of these premises is false or by demonstrating a flaw in the logic. The anti-locavore articles by Helen De Bres and Carson Young do both of these things.

De Bres and Young exemplify a general approach to analysis in applied ethics with a consequentialist orientation to moral decision-making. Consequentialists understand food ethics in broadly utilitarian terms: what you eat should produce a good outcome, and the outcome it produces is the standard for deciding whether your choice is morally justified. The consequentialist approach brings the clarity and rigor of analytic philosophy to many moral questions. It exemplifies one model of the way that academic philosophy can contribute to food studies. Analytic philosophy progresses through the give and take of carefully structured arguments and through critique of the premises or the inferential structure of those arguments. The analytic style of applied ethics requires one to begin with a plausible reconstruction of the position one intends to critique, in this case, the pro-locavore argument. The next section summarizes De Bres's and Young's characterization of the case for eating local and then follows the logic of their refutations. Only in the closing sections of the chapter will we return the question of whether the version of locavorism that De Bres and Carson challenge is the same as the one that Noll defends.

De Bres and Young on Locavores

Stated simply, locavorism is the injunction to eat foods that are locally grown (perhaps within 100 miles of one's residence). When the command is advanced on ethical grounds, people who do not practice locavorism are acting contrary to the dictates of morality. However, linking this simple statement of locavorism to morality is not as straightforward as it might seem. The first interpretive task is to define the scope of the claim: What, exactly, does this directive tell us to do? De Bres and Young both specify the scope of a local food ethic by distinguishing it from related questions such as the rationale for organic production or small-scale polycultures. A discourse of social control might blur these themes, but it is important to start by focusing on the considerations militating for the central locavore principle. Once these have been identified it might be appropriate to ask how locavorism supports or overlaps with other moral considerations.

De Bres also interprets the locavore ethic as advocating a norm applicable to relatively affluent people who purchase their food. It does not apply to those who produce food themselves, nor is it intended to prescribe dietary choices for individuals whose poverty dictates an overriding attention to price. De Bres then recognizes that the locavore principle can be applied with different degrees of tolerance or consistency. *Extreme* locavorism would be the claim that literally everything one eats must be locally grown. She rightly sets this aside as unrealistic, unworkable, and quite likely to have adverse environmental consequences were it to be taken seriously.[8] This cannot be what locavores intend to advocate. Carson Young's analysis is less detailed, but his approach is similar to De Bres in each of these respects. Like De Bres, he sets aside the thought that the extreme view is what proponents of locavorism could have intended to advocate.[9]

A fair summary of De Bres's analysis is that many arguments *against* the locavore at best apply only to extreme locavorism. They do not advance a compelling reason for rejecting the claim that local foods should be preferred at least for some items in the consumer's grocery basket. This is an important component of De Bres's interpretation of the pro-locavore argument. Although she intends to argue against the claim that locavorism is morally obligatory, she presents a more accurate representation of the case *for* locavorism than studies attempting to refute the local food ethic by showing how it leads to a bad outcome.[10] De Bres thus concludes that there *are* cases where purchase of locally grown food promotes certain moral goods. Such behavior can be a component of building relational ties among community members; it can cultivate a sense of local place; buying local can be a political statement that signals resistance to dominant social actors. Again, Young devotes less attention to the positive aspects of locavorism, but his analysis is consistent with De Bres.

In summary, these applied ethicists refine the interpretation of the locavore 100-mile diet in two ways. First, they distinguish the implications of the rule from other norms, such as eating organic food or buying from small-scale farmers. Second, they show that an extreme or literal translation of the rule results in absurdity. Both refinements counter the way that injunctions to eat local function for some food movement activists. As a practice of social control, injunctions to buy food from one's region, to buy organic food, and to buy from small-scale farmers all function as invitations to enroll in the social movement against. . . . Against what? Against industrial agriculture? Against corporate power? Against capitalism? It is the nature of social control to influence habits of thought by blurring these distinctions. By insisting on the distinctness of these recommendations, De Bres and Young open a space for inquiry. However, we should also notice how their refinements also distinguish the version of locavorism that they will critique from Noll's claim that locavorism includes a commitment to food sovereignty.

De Bres develops a pluralistic account of the goods that might be supported by locavorism. She does not go on to argue for a procedure that would allow one to rank the value that each of these goods contributes to the overall well-being of society. However, she also denies purchasing local food either a necessary or sufficient role in *causing* the desirable outcomes she lists. Hence, while moderate locavorism is permissible (within some limits), it is *not* morally required. It is worth taking pains to clarify exactly what De Bres is accomplishing with this move. De Bres does not deny that the locavore's food purchases help to bring about certain outcomes, nor does she deny that these outcomes are morally significant. Nevertheless, the connection between action and consequence is not strong enough to support the judgment that someone who fails to follow locavorism acts immorally. De Bres is challenging the inference that moves one from the list of good outcomes that are reasonably pursued by buying local to understanding locavorism as a moral obligation.

The style of analytic applied ethics often presumes that some sort of formal argument lies behind any moral commandment. Important premises may not be explicitly articulated. They may not be front of mind or something that a person who is persuaded by the argument is consciously thinking about. The good outcomes from locavorism will not justify the conclusion that it is morally obligatory unless there are also reasons to think buying local is better than anything else a person might do. One might reconstruct the argument by explicitly claiming a locavore ethic is the singular or overridingly effective way to build community relationships, promote a sense of place, or resist the economic power of dominant actors, but De Bres thinks this is not plausible. People might choose to pursue these morally beneficial ends in other ways.

Arguments in applied ethics can also fail if moral premises contradict principles that have a stronger grounding in morality. In this connection, De Bres says people cannot be held morally accountable for failing to purchase locally grown foods, even when doing so does promote or contribute to bringing about these ethically desirable outcomes. In this aspect of her argument, she appeals to a moral premise that is widely accepted in democratic societies: people should be free to organize their lives in pursuit of any bundle of goods, so long as their pursuit does not involve activities that are morally proscribed because they harm third parties. While much of De Bres analysis is consequentialist, the argument for this form of liberalism might be made by a rights theorist. Rights are often justified as constraints that protect the freedom or interests of others. Yet it is also important to note that consequentialists defend individual liberties on the ground that they maximizes the total amount of good that can be realized across society. Indeed, the strength of this principle derives in part from being supported on both rights-based and consequentialist reasoning.[11]

Young's analysis similarly considers general types of argument to support locavorism, but all four of the cases he considers emphasize alleged benefits. First are benefits to the environment. Some local products could actually be more harmful. Second are benefits to community cohesion. Like De Bres, Young sees many ways to promote cohesion and no reason to favor locavorism over other ways. Young also considers whether a bias for locally produced food would tend to support small business, concluding that it would not because many (in fact arguably most) locales contain local producers that are giant corporations, as well as small farmers and independent grocers. Finally, he echoes De Bres in arguing that any benefits to merchants or workers within local economies would be more than offset by making purchases that economize on food expenditures, leaving room in a consumer's budget for other purchases (music, art, home improvements?) that return benefits to one's neighbors.[12]

There are two significant differences between De Bres and Young. First, Young is more explicitly consequentialist. His arguments concentrate narrowly on the outcome of following a locavore ethic, and they contest empirical claims about its alleged benefits. Although I also read De Bres as working within a consequentialist framework, her concern with a consumer's freedom resonates with non-consequentialist principles. As discussed later in the chapter, she is also willing to give serious consideration to themes that many consequentialists would dismiss out of hand. Second, while De Bres's analysis is specifically targeted against the claim that locavorism is morally obligatory, Young's arguments provide reasons to think local purchases actually do not achieve the good outcomes that they are alleged to produce. Young's argument could therefore be understood as a philosophically more explicit version of anti-locavore arguments made by critics such as James McWilliams or Pierre Desrochers and Hiroku Shimizu. Their books conclude that we have good reasons to *avoid* doing what the local food ethic recommends.[13] Nevertheless, Young is like DeBres in recognizing the economic nostrum *De gustibus non est disputandum*. Those who have a taste for the local are permitted to exercise it; the error lies in generalizing this to others whose tastes differ. Thus, Young also concludes that locavorism is morally permissible.

Other Criticisms of the Locavore Ethic

In fact, I think that de Bres and Young reach the most defensible conclusion that can be mounted on consequentialist grounds: there are ethically desirable goods that can be pursued through localism, but people who choose not to practice a locavore diet violate no moral principle. Philosophers contributing to the growing literature on the ethics of locavorism have reached similar conclusions.[14] Other philosophers have complained that locavorism neglects ethical issues such as the treatment of animals in intensive production systems.[15]

Importantly, enthusiasm for eating local diets began to provoke a counter discourse well before philosophers entered the fray. Mostly, that discourse has attacked empirical premises in the locavore ethic. Christopher Weber and Scott Matthews produced a study of climate impacts that weighed the putative environmental impact of local diets more carefully.[16] By the 2010s, the literature poking holes in the locavore case began to be as extensive as the earlier literature that had attempted to use the food miles concept as a heuristic for considering the broader environmental costs of dietary choices. The aforementioned study by Desrochers and Shimizu, a geographer and an economist, respectively, runs to nearly 200 pages and debunks claims that local diets build social capital, that they have environmentally beneficial outcomes, and that they have a positive impact on food security.

Neither De Bres nor Young reviews Desrochers and Shimizu's arguments in detail. Nevertheless, both of these philosophers are certainly right to note that such criticisms of the locavore diet are most pertinent to an extreme interpretation. As a response to this overheated literature, the analysis of these philosophers presents a welcome breath of moderation. It is also important to note that their treatment emphasizes whether or not there are overriding moral reasons to follow a locavore ethic. "Overriding" means that these reasons would require someone to be a locavore, as opposed to simply permitting someone to exercise local preferences for moral reasons. The focus on overridingness allows De Bres and Young to arrive at the nuanced position that moderate locavorism is morally permissible but not morally required.

However we should also notice that popular treatments by McKibben, Kingsolver, or Smith and MacKinnen were never represented as serious attempts to measure the impact of the locavore diet, nor did they claim that extreme *or* moderate locavorism was morally required. There is thus a gap of sorts between these influential treatments and De Bres's and Young's emphasis on moral obligatoriness. Applied ethics provides no basis for supporting either extreme or moderate versions of the locavore diet as morally obligatory, but that conclusion is entirely consistent with the advocacy we find in McKibben, Kingsolver, and many other locavores. Locavorism is something people are permitted to do, but this is a very weak statement, as we generally allow individuals quite a bit of latitude in what they eat. Does this mean that I am in perfect agreement with other philosophers writing on the locavore ethic? Actually not. In the following section, I expose some problems in the analyses of De Bres and Young, problems that also apply to other applied ethicists that I have not analyzed in detail. In the balance of the chapter, I explain why I would not adopt a consequentialist applied ethics to interpret the moral case for locavorism.

Estimating Outcomes for the Local Diet

As social science refutations of locavorism show, the connection between buying local and the putative benefits of doing so is limited. The cause-effect relationship is weaker that the locavore thinks. These arguments have ethical significance because utilitarianism assumes that one's conduct will have outcomes for health, wealth, and well-being. One can refute a consequentialist argument by showing the action won't produce the outcome it has been alleged to bring about. De Bres and Young have demonstrated that much of the anti-locavorism literature overplays this strategy because no one would have been tempted by the extreme interpretation of locavorism in the first place. A more subtle type of criticism emphasizes completeness: you have not made a convincing consequentialist argument if important elements have been left out of the calculation.

Virtually all of the philosophers writing on locavorism have used a version of this incompleteness critique. To their credit, De Bres and Young take up some potential benefits that are not reflected in the refutations made by many critics. De Bres' evaluates the claim that "Buying local food supports one's local community better than buying non-local food."[17] Young considers whether owners and employees of firms selling local food derive benefits not achieved by other local merchants. In evaluating this aspect of their analyses, recall that neither of them understands the locavore ethic as a test of every item that winds up one's plate; that would be extreme locavorism. The locavore's claim is only that there are *some* foods whose purchase supports the local community. De Bres and Young each claim that there are other ways to achieve these ends, ways that are not discussed in the reconstruction of the locavore ethic they critique. In the absence of clear evidence that locavorism is the optimal way to achieve these ends, the inference from the social benefits of locavorism to the claim that it is required on moral grounds fails.

But have De Bres and Young themselves given a complete account of the ways the buying local achieves socially worthy ends? Significantly for the locavore argument, there *are* reasons to think that purchasing locally produced goods supports the local community, even when support is interpreted strictly in economic terms. They are reasons that neither De Bres. Young nor any of the other philosophers writing on locavorism consider. The argument turns on the *velocity of money*, which can be defined succinctly as the number of times one dollar is spent to buy goods and services per unit of time. An economist would explain why it matters by introducing a model, but here, an anecdote will suffice. Consider two cases: A: Leticia makes a dollar by selling some zucchini from her garden. She stuffs it under her mattress for a rainy day. B: Marguerite makes a dollar from *her* garden and buys lemonade from Adzuki who then pays her babysitter who in turn goes down to the hardware store to buy a screwdriver. The owner of the hardware store pays an employee and had to buy the screwdriver from the manufacturer, so someone benefits there, too. Much of magic in trading societies comes from the fact that, as money moves from one exchange to another, the benefits multiply. In A, only Leticia is better off (the fact that the purchaser also enjoyed her zucchini to the side). In B, Marguerite, Adzuki, her babysitter, and several folk down at the hardware store have all benefited from Marguerite's productive activity. That is the root idea behind the velocity of money.

Benefits from these exchanges stay within the local community only so long as the money does. If the owner of the hardware store buys the screwdriver that she sells to Adzuki's babysitter from a national or global firm, the benefits continue but they do not facilitate yet another exchange within the local economy constituted by Marguerite, Adzuki, the babysitter, and the folks at the hardware store. Keeping money circulating within a local economy a little longer is indeed a significant factor in local economic development. However, you don't want to go crazy with velocity of money arguments. If the only local screwdriver is a hand-forged boutique model that costs $100 and breaks easily, not many people are going to be able to own screwdrivers. That is where the germ of truth behind de Bres's or Young's argument comes in. Furthermore, we might consider case C: Tanya takes the dollar she made from selling zucchini and immediately uses it to pay for cloud storage of photographs. This expense may have velocity, but the people at the cloud service who can spend the dollar they got from Tanya's purchases are probably living on another continent. The benefits will be accruing far from Tanya's garden. Perhaps it doesn't matter; perhaps the geeks selling the cloud storage are spending Tanya's dollar on something that is produced by people who live in Tanya's neighborhood. Maybe they want a boutique screwdriver.

The point is that benefits can circle, and one can ask whether it matters much whether the circles are big or small. Like virtually everything in economics, there are debates about how velocity affects development both locally and economy wide. Yet, unlike electronic file storage or many manufactured goods, the food economy is a place where the velocity of money can grow without that dollar having to leave the local area.[18] It would be misleading to suggest that economists are unanimous in this opinion. One can produce reasons to think that money has more social utility when it ends up in the pocket of someone quite far from one's local community. In *The Ethics of What We Eat*, Peter Singer and Jim Mason argue that you can do more good by buying food grown by poor farmers in less-developed regions than by buying local. Their argument hangs on the plausible thought that putting one's dollar in the pocket of a poor person has more value (more social utility) than putting it into the pocket of a better-off person nearby.[19] The fact that a resource-challenged farmer is more likely to spend their recently earned dollar than save it amplifies social utility even more.

Although philosophers writing on the local food ethic ignore the velocity of money, De Bres and Young do not neglect economic considerations entirely. De Bres engages Singer and Mason directly when she questions the value of local spending in comparison to that of purchasing food from poor farmers in distant parts of the world. De Bres presumes that the benefits of local spending go to comparatively better-off neighbors. "In short, the line goes, when you purchase that local tomato from a relatively affluent local farmer, what you are *not* doing is purchasing a tomato from a much poorer farmer in a developing country. You are thereby harming—or at least, not helping—some of the world's most vulnerable people."[20] de Bres does discuss a possible reply that questions the benefits of trade, but she ends by citing Peter Singer in support of the claim that we should take obligations to buy from the poor much more seriously than we usually do.

Once again, however, one can question the completeness of the analysis. It is certainly true that U.S. consumers might find themselves purchasing a tomato grown in Mexico, but we should not imagine ourselves benefiting a poor farmer when we buy one. Mexican tomato exporters are large-scale, well-capitalized farms that employ low-wage farm labor, often in conditions that are even worse than those of undocumented farmworkers north of the Rio Grande.[21] Perhaps I am nitpicking here, but the point I would stress is that the particular consumption decision at issue actually makes quite a bit of difference in these calculations. De Bres was off base in picking tomatoes but would have been on firmer ground if she had chosen to make her point in reference to rice or coffee, commodities that *are* grown by impoverished farmers and imported into wealthy nations. For all their problems, fair trade supply chains do present opportunities to help the poor.[22]

The more general point to notice, however, is that the moderate locavore might not face the tension described by Singer and de Bres very frequently. Local producers in places like Europe, North America, and Australia or New Zealand are unlikely to be growing coffee. Even when producers local to consumers in industrialized economies *do* produce fruits or vegetables that are also grown by poor farmers from faraway places, they are less likely to be appearing in markets at the same time. Moderate locavorism implies selective application of the "eat local" rule. It presumes some knowledge of the local food system, but beyond buying directly from producers at the local farmers' market, that knowledge is likely to be incomplete.

Consequentialism and Food Ethics

The economic points just considered qualify de Bres's and Young's analysis of the moral case against local food, but they do not contradict their general conclusion. Eating local is, in some cases, justifiable and supportable on ethical grounds but cannot be judged morally mandatory. What then, is the point of carping about the completeness of their analyses? My answer is that these quibbles illustrate a broader problem with consequentialism in food ethics. De Bres's and Young's model of applied ethics reflects the influence of Peter Singer, who has used it to argue for generalized obligations (e.g., duties that would apply to almost everyone) with respect to victims of famine and to agricultural animals. Singer's argument for vegetarianism implies that the meat eater's purchase is causally linked to the suffering of animals, and his book with Jim Mason broadened this pattern to other concerns in food production and distribution. The suggestion that we can identify the morally significant consequences of what we eat (or more precisely, what we buy) is the linchpin underlying this particular conception of food ethics.

However, the causal connection between a consumer purchase and the economic demand that in turn stimulates one type of food production rather than another is exceedingly complex. As a new generation of young philosophers have begun to analyze putative impacts from purchasing one kind of food rather than another, the simplistic causal linkage implied by Singer's approach has been brought into question. They ask whether a given individual's choices really can be said to have causal efficacy in circumstances where the link between action and outcome is not only mediated by a number of other actors, but may, in fact, only attain causal significance once a threshold of collective action has been breached.[23] This work in food ethics addresses the question as if it raised issues in ethical theory, but the underlying problem cannot be addressed without considering a nexus of questions about social causality, leading directly into metaphysics, epistemology, and the philosophy of science.

Many of these difficult problems with local food are problems in the philosophy of economics and social behavior. Economists do not spend much time worrying about causal efficacy, but they differ over the implications of phenomena like velocity for economic development. Milton Friedman (1912–2006) hypothesized that economic development would slow the velocity of money because (to paraphrase a bit) rich people would be more likely to stuff a dollar under the mattress or delay their consumptive activity. However, participants in some very old debates in agricultural economics claim that development in the local food economy would be less prone to this tendency than development in manufacturing or heavy industry.[24] There are also philosophical differences among economists about the scale at which economic activity attains significance. At one extreme, there is really only one global economy and any attempt to apply economic theory at regional or municipal scales is an invitation to fallacy. Yet the notion that there is no such thing as "the market" and that market processes operate within institutional parameters that dramatically shape economic performance also has its advocates. These are just a few of the open questions in the economics of the food system. I would argue that it is at least reasonable for planners in local or regional economic development to consider policies that promote local food systems as a way to accelerate the velocity of money *within* their regional economies.[25]

In a similar vein, global trade in agricultural commodities mediates the influence that consumer demand in the developed world retail food sector has on very poor farmers. Smallholding farmers still constitute as much as half of the world's population living on one Euro per day, the World Bank standard for extreme poverty. Impacts on smallholders are important issues in food ethics. Yet the complications just mentioned make reckoning the consequences of one's food purchases for poor farmers in faraway places a doubtful vantage point from which to launch an ethical inquiry.[26] Provoking casual readers to consider the causative impact of their food choices may encourage them to reflect on the structure of the food system. However, it is questionable whether probing deeper and deeper into the complexities connecting phenomena at one order of system organization to system behavior at a different order will result in an ethics of consumer choice. The questions in food ethics are frequently questions in social theory, not individual consumer choice. Social scientists make philosophically based choices about how they will treat social causality, but consumers who rely on their findings are generally acting on blind faith.

The problems I am describing here may not matter much to the type of ethical theorist typical of 20th-century analytic philosophy. Whether focused on maximizing social welfare or respecting rights, an ethical theorist can still say that what we *should* do is make choices that advance these goals even if we can't be sure how the options before us do that. In other words, some ethical theorists are just not troubled by lacunae in our knowledge of facts; that's not their job. Utilitarians also have some elaborate ways to incorporate measurements of uncertainty into the calculation of benefit and cost. I ask, what happens when those appropriately discounted evaluations of net utility are introduced into public discourse? What happens when they are bandied about as strategies for social control? My answer is, they will be countered by an endless stream of objections noting points that have been left out, just as I have done here. Discourses on topics like the velocity of money rapidly turn on technicalities that are only meaningful within highly constrained expert contexts. This observation does not *refute* a consequentialist. Nothing I have said here shows that the consequentialist's view is false. One could, in fact, argue my point on consequentialist grounds: unending controversy and extreme technical complexity limit the social utility of consequentialist argumentation in practical contexts.[27]

The Agrarian Question

De Bres also asks how agrarian arguments figure in arguing for a moral requirement to eat local food. The agrarian tradition presents a challenge to mainstream approaches in ethics and political theory. De Bres introduces a useful scheme for interpreting agrarian claims. One type of agrarian argument is Aristotelean: "By engaging us in intimate contact with the land and climate, farming focuses our attention on the natural forces that shape our lives, encouraging us to work patiently with these forces rather than against them." She also associates a form of agrarianism that stresses how human flourishing requires a historically deep understanding of belonging to "a concrete location and a particular lineage"[28] with the Danish existentialist Søren Kierkegaard (1813–1855). In addition, she sees arguments that stress the farmer's control over productive activity as owing a debt to Marxism. The discussion of these perspectives is limited to a few paragraphs and is not sufficient to indicate the exact sense in which De Bres connects recent work by Wendell Berry or Norman Wirzba, as well as Lisa Heldke, Brian Donahue, and David Orr (the authors she discusses by name) to the writings of these figures from the history of philosophy.[29]

The merits of her foray into agrarian philosophy of agriculture and food systems notwithstanding, the structure of De Bres's approach to food ethics requires her to hold these arguments to the standard of whether or not they present a convincing reason to think that anyone has something like a moral duty to purchase local food. There is really only one conclusion that she *could* reach, given that criterion:

> In short, there are many ways, other than engagement with farming, for communities to flourish and be virtuous, some of which have worked, do work, and will work better for some people than farming ever did, does or will. For this reason, the empirical connection that agrarians attempt to draw between traditional agriculture, well-being and morality is too weak to shore up the community support argument, our initial motivation for turning to agrarian ideas. . . . Our duty to support our community is arguably "imperfect" in nature, allowing us discretion over which specific means of support, including locavorism, to adopt.[30]

Young does not even consider this pattern of argument.

Yet surely, if there is one theme that could tie Kierkegaard to other figures DeBres mentions, it would be the rejection of decisionism: the assumption that the subject matter of moral philosophy is to identify criteria for making choices. As different as Aristotelianism, Existentialism, and Marxism are, they all argue that one's environment—and in this case we mean much more than the natural or biological environment—plays a fundamental role in shaping one's mentality. The mind exhibits a certain plasticity that responds to the rhythms and patterns of one's day-to-day activity, establishing for each person a sense not only of their own possibilities but also of the human condition itself. Kierkegaard, Aristotle (384–322 BCE), and Karl Marx (1818–1883) each experienced their own sociocultural environment as exhibiting the signs of decay and corruption. The notion that an individual could combat these forces of decline simply by choosing actions with better consequences (or choosing to eat local food) contradicts the main thrust of moral philosophies that stress character formation. For Marx and Kierkegaard (though possibly not for Aristotle) the social ideology of the choice-making subject was a prominent indicator of the debauched state into which their worlds had fallen.

Like these great philosophers, Berry and Wirzba (though possibly not Heldke, Donahue, or Orr) tie moral decline to the rise of a particular understanding of the human condition. Now a thorough discussion of these five writers would become tedious. Heldke is a feminist philosopher who might be surprised to find herself being classified as an agrarian. Donohue is a historian whose study of the community farm in a New England village is the basis for his thinking on alternative food systems. Orr is a well-known educator and prolific writer who has weighed in on many topics in environmentalism. Wirzba is a Protestant theologian who has also edited many of Berry's works. I interpret him as emphasizing the lived experience of the body in opposition to theologies that understand spirituality in the form of a disembodied mind. Berry, of course, is a poet, essayist, and novelist whose creative works revolve around his fictionalized versions of friends and neighbors in Port Royal, Kentucky, and the farm he has operated with his wife, Tanya, for over forty years.[31] Berry's name will come up at several points in this book.

On my reading, Berry, Wirzba, and I all agree that consumerism is a moral problem. I suspect these two might also agree that placing the decision-making feature of the mind at the heart of morality is the symptom of a more fundamental philosophical mistake. On this faulty view, the mind ponders alternative courses of action. The choice among possible actions might be evaluated with respect to an outcome, as they are for utilitarians, or according to some alternative decision principle, such as the Categorical Imperative. In either case, the mind is an instrument of scission, eliminating possibilities in selecting the favored alternative. For decisionism, the *cut*—the decisive moment at which the will opts one way rather than any other—is the action that determines the morality of the choice-making subject, whether it be through a calculation of outcomes or a determination of duty. Both Berry and Wirzba diagnose the present age as intoxicated by a spirit of excess and ultimately illusory freedom. They diagnose the error as humanity's denial of our embodied and earthbound being. Berry and Wirzba do advocate a therapy that reconnects body and earth through farming and through a deeper understanding of food.[32] It is, in this sense, fair to characterize them as agrarians. However, there is thus a profound sense in which the disciplined analysis that De Bres imposes on the five figures she names as agrarian misrepresents the criticism they are trying to raise.

De Bres rejects the agrarian view because choosing local food fails to be efficacious for bringing about the close-knit community values and the tie to the land that Berry and Wirzba celebrate. But if I am understanding them correctly, the problem Berry and Wirzba are addressing could never be resolved by making better consumption choices. In fact, the problem consists in thinking that better choices *could* have a salvific nature. By "salvific" I mean something like morally therapeutic. If consumerism is the curse of "the Present Age" (to quote Kierkegaard), the dissolute condition that people have fallen into, the driving philosophical problem is to reverse the corrupting influences that encourage people to think that they can achieve rectitude through better shopping. In effect, De Bres's reason for rejecting Wirzba and Berry is simply a restatement of the very proposition that their philosophy is geared to reject.

In sum, De Bres is right to say that agrarianism provides no reason to believe that, standing there at the grocery store in front of an array of food options, we should select the locally produced artisanal cheese instead of the individually wrapped slices. However, Berry and Wirzba are also right to call the portrayal of humanity's ideal as being "the reflective shopper" into question at the deepest possible level. To translate agrarian philosophy into a viewpoint that could help us decide what to eat is to miss the way that agrarians reject choice-making as the appropriate target for ethical analysis. Berry and Wirzba do not advocate for decision-making that more efficaciously causes economically good outcomes. Their advocacy should be viewed more like the famous wager of Blaise Pascal (1623–1662). Speaking to the debauched person, Pascal says, yes, accept God because the risk of rejecting him looks like a bad bet: you might end up in hell. Perhaps later a true faith will arise, but it would only arise through a transformation of character. Pascal endorses the argument not because he thinks the wager itself is a good moral argument. He hopes the attitude of the payoff-evaluating gambler will eventually recede, opening to the person of faith.

If what I am suggesting stands, Berry, Wirzba, and Pascal all recognize that their advice is an inauspicious basis for the transformation of a person's moral character, but they also think that a corrupt mind is unlikely to be responsive to the philosophical considerations they deem appropriate. Their advice is geared to a person who lives by evaluating the payoff of their opportunities then makes a choice. However, as someone undertakes the practices of virtue, or "goes through the motions," so to speak, perhaps genuine virtue will follow. Even if the chances are slim, the moral payoff is so large that it's worth a shot.[33] The agrarian vision lies beyond the reach of anyone who would evaluate it on decisionistic criteria, but perhaps the adoption of agrarian practice will bring about the transformation that allows us to leave the choice-making shopper behind, once and for all.

But Again, There Is More

Of course, perhaps not as well. To grasp the import of an agrarian argument is not necessarily to be entirely convinced by it. That is why we need food ethics, and it is why impatient readers looking to save the world with better shopping are going to be as disappointed by my book as De Bres was by Wendell Berry. As is often the case, I am ambivalent: De Bres's analysis is important on many levels, not the least of which is that it provokes a wider reflection on the rationales for supporting local food. However, many of the rationales she discusses operate well beyond the boundaries of her framing assumptions: they have very little to do with whether moderate locavores have a moral responsibility to choose local food. This is not simply a conceptual mistake. It reflects and reinforces a certain type of narrowness in the social imagination, as I will now try to demonstrate. Nevertheless, De Bres is within her rights to define a narrow question and explore how various rationales do or do not answer it. Along with many of the applied ethicists that I have not discussed at length in this chapter, I fault Young for considering a much narrower breadth of philosophical considerations that bear on diet and food production. All the same, both De Bres and Young model a reflective and deliberative approach to a consumption-oriented food ethics. If you are looking for philosophically grounded consumer advice, they serve well.

My goal is to press the inquiry beyond the limits of a consumption ethic but there is little doubt that many participants in the food movement are indeed looking for what Singer, De Bres, and Young have on offer. Contrarily, the history of advocacy for locavorism shows that it was always intended as a heuristic that could ease consumers into a more rewarding relationship with their food. Analytic philosophers' fascination with definitions has never coped well with heuristic thinking. De Bres and Young both fall into the trap. When De Bres and Young define locavorism as a morally grounded injunction to prefer locally produced food, they imbue even mild locavorism with literalism that was never intended by its advocates. (Of course, the literalism of extreme locavorism is even worse.) This kind of literalism is not atypical among those who hope to manipulate food consumers. I recall one large

university food service that attempted to fulfill its pledge to include more locally produced food on the plates served in student dining halls by counting
the corn chips manufactured by a national brand. The company did, in truth,
source from local (as well as distant) farmers for its factory, which was just
a few miles from the campus. Young calls out this type of reasoning in his
article, but rather than interpreting it as an abuse of locavorism, he straight-
facedly cites it as an argument against it. Young writes as if food activists
would have endorsed factory-produced corn chips under their intended
interpretation of the locavore ideal. This kind of philosophical analysis can
make reasonable people roll their eyes in frustration.

We should reconvene the philosophical analysis by asking what it means to
see locavorism as a heuristic rather than a decision rule. A heuristic enables
learning by giving someone a framework for considering his or her actions,
in this case food purchases. The heuristic is eventually replaced by deep
knowledge or expertise, but this is not a rule-determined algorithm. A mature consumer-oriented food ethics would reflect a myriad of considerations
as well as the gaps and uncertainties that plague even the most sophisticated
food buyer's knowledge base. It is not as if the causal nexus between producer
and purchaser has disappeared, but instead calculative rationality is applied
only to sharpen evaluation of options in specific situations rather than as a
comprehensive decision strategy. The expert is relying on intuitions that reflect learning through trial and error.[34] What is more, as an expression of a
food *movement*, the locavore heuristic has a social dimension intended to
indicate a direction for progressive change. It is in this sense an ethos rather
than a rule for action.[35]

What would a more reasonable account of the locavore ethos include?
Before answering that question, it is important to repeat what has already
been said. *Unreasonable* interpretations of locavorism are out there, and both
De Bres and Young have produced studies that counter them. Their work also
goes some distance toward countering naïve interpretations made with good
intentions. Indeed, locavorism came under fire from within the food movement for its insensitivity to matters of food justice. De Bres and Young expose
gaps in the locavore ethic, but we can react in one of two different ways. On
the one hand, we can discard the local food ideal altogether, seeing it as inadequate in virtue of its implicit elitism, its environmental deficiencies, and
its failure to confront distributive and structural injustice in the food system.
We might explain this rejection philosophically as a deficit with respect to
liberal conceptions of justice inherited from Kant. On the other hand, we

might respond by asking how the local food ethic needs to be fleshed out to more adequately realize relational norms, community building, and the agrarian ideal. That is the path that Noll has followed. Let us see where that second path leads.

As recounted already, the measurement of food miles began in the United Kingdom as an indicator for energy consumption in the distribution component of the food system. Broccoli eaten out of season in London might have been grown in Spain or Africa. Hothouse tomatoes eaten in Houston may have been flown in from the Netherlands. The food miles rubric indicates the energy these two types of consumption use in getting the product from a farmer's field to that produce section in your local market. Since transporting foods burns fossil fuel, food miles also indicate a consumer's contribution to climate change. An ecological consumption ethic requires one to choose products with lower environmental impacts, and food miles function as a metric for estimating these impacts. Yet how are consumers standing in the produce section of their market to know? "Eat local" is a heuristic that functions as a stand-in or estimate for full knowledge of the environmental costs. Since locally produced foods travel shorter distances, there are fewer fossil fuel costs embedded in them, or so one supposes. The supposition is probably right for out-of-season broccoli or tomatoes, but estimating the actual amount of energy embedded in a tomato or a broccoli floret requires one to consider not only the fuel that powered the airplane to import them, but also the gasoline from dozens of smaller vehicles moving about the countryside. There is also energy used in producing the food. The energy costs of building and operating a greenhouse to grow bananas in Norway (thereby lowering food miles) also need to be part of the calculation. This means, as Webber and Mathews showed, that the locavore heuristic is an imperfect indicator of environmental impact.

The extreme locavore ethic is going to result in bad choices. On that, all the philosophers agree. Nevertheless, a food miles rubric has alerted the ethical consumer to the fact that food has embedded environmental costs, and that is a good thing. So what *should* a food shopper standing in the produce section do? Alerted to the embedded environmental cost, reasonable shoppers might reduce the amount of produce they buy out of season. This was, in fact, a central message in Barbara Kingsolver's paean to local food. At this point, the locavore ethic makes a pivot. No longer focused exclusively on limiting the environmental impact of food consumption, the decision to avoid eating fresh produce out of season leads to unexpected benefits to the consumers themselves. They rediscover the taste of fresh food and varieties of fruits and vegetables not bred to withstand the insults of storage and transport. They have to expand their gastronomic repertoire and learn to cook new foods. Eating becomes more meaningful, as seeking and preparing fresh fruits and vegetables, and maybe even meats and cheeses, becomes a way of flourishing, self-expression, and, with one's dining partners, a form of bonding.

Imbued with a new appreciation for freshness and variety, the ethical (but reasonable) food consumer might visit the local farmer's market. This will be an especially useful strategy for obtaining produce that is in season. Farmer's markets are, for the most part, venues where food producers sell very recently harvested foods. They will be local in virtue of the fact that very few farmers will find it useful to travel very far from their fields to sell their crops. The locavore ethic then makes a further pivot. The ethical but reasonable shopper discovers new pleasures in meeting and talking with the venders in the market, building relationships wholly distinct from the automated scanning of barcodes they experience in their local grocery store. Perhaps the consumer will graduate to participation in community supported agriculture (CSA), where members agree to share some risk with farmers by signing up for a subscription of food products that will become available as each ripens throughout the growing season. The relationship between an eater and his or her farmer deepens further with the CSA. The locavore ethic is now into the territory of relationship building and the creation of community bonds. Some will go even more local by becoming gardeners; they become producers rather than consumers. At this juncture, Kingsolver also closes the circle by returning to the environment. Food connects people back to nature. At the farmer's market and the CSA, connection runs through the farmer. Patrons of the market learn some of what the farmer knows: the fragility and risk of food production, the need to conserve soil fertility, and perhaps even a vicarious experience of the difficulties and rewards of working daily in commerce with the natural world. The gardener gets these experiences firsthand.[36] These ties to farming also resonate with Noll's advocacy for food sovereignty.

The Locavore and the Citizen

A theorist of the public sphere (that vague domain where the discourse of social control plays out) might describe these pivots in the locavore ethic in terms of dissociation, counterpublics, and articulation. As people move through these phases in a discourse, the simple practice of shopping is transformed well beyond the naïve formulation of a consumption ethic, where a consumer simply tries to spend their money in ways that harness market forces in support of better outcomes. First, the ethical (but reasonable) consumer's pivot from a literalistic concern with food miles toward seasonality and diversifying their diet dissociates the *meaning* of locavorism. No longer cashed out through an environmental life cycle analysis, "eating local" translated as eating in season is now associated with practices of food preparation and communal eating. That's what dissociation means. In this context, the consumer is not just a shopper executing a decisionistic program. Elements of production, of active fabrication in materials of one's daily life are coming into play. This agency becomes political with the next pivot, which takes the ethical (but reasonable) consumer beyond the household and back into the quasi-public sphere of economic exchange.

The farmer's market, co-op, or CSA facilitates the coalescence of a counterpublic comprising people at differing stages along locavore journey. For starters, a *counterpublic* is a group of people who share intersecting self-understandings (e.g., social identities). For a counterpublic, the social identity includes markers of solidarity that oppose, reject, or resist elements of the dominant group. In this case, members of the dominant group understand themselves as consumers. In the context of a counterpublic, the locavore ethic transforms the social identity of parties to a food exchange. Venders are identified through the practices of their productive agency, practices such as farming, cooking, and all the minute doings that go into these activities. The social dimension of vender identities is articulated by the agency of the buyer, who negotiates the transaction by enunciating its significance for the forward-looking consequences within both the household and the broader environment. Articulation means the household, the marketplace, and the farmer's fields reconfigure as connected places. In political respects, this reconnected locus of identities functions as a unified locus of civic voice. This new sphere of activity creates the opportunity for emergence of a new public, a new community, one taking an interest in the structure and maintenance of their potential for mutual interaction.

A mainstream vision of the food system locates it primarily within the private sphere and defines the private sphere as the relative absence of state intervention into the transactions of private citizens and for-profit actors. Such interventions are thought to be legitimate to the extent that they preserve the private property relationships that are necessary for exchange or promote the production of goods that are inherently public in virtue of structural characteristics that disincentive their production by for-profit (e.g., private) firms. The locavore heuristic counters this vision by moving food into a domain—the public sphere—that is inherently political.[37] This is especially significant for individuals. Although for-profit firms' primary activity is in the private sphere, the mainstream vision gives them a voice—a discursively effective mode of action for arguing in the public sphere, the domain of government activity and of citizen participation. In the public sphere, they argue against regulation and oppose government involvement in their business activity. They represent a public, a congregation of actors organized around an interest in shaping state action. Who will oppose them?

Jürgen Habermas described "new social movements" that contrast with the classic social movements of the 19th and 20th centuries. The labor movement or the civil rights movement created publics with claims on the state because members had social identities that defined criteria of state intervention necessary for enactment. Workers demanded intervention in labor markets; racial groups demanded protection from cooperative strategies intended to deprive them of constitutionally guaranteed rights. Yet no unified social identity is challenged by damage to the environment, loss of aesthetic possibilities, or declines in community solidarity. These interests require discursive innovation—new ways of talking and enrolling individuals into a counterpublic opposing the interests of profit-seeking firms. Lacking these discursive resources, advocates of these interests fail to attain effectiveness in democratic societies.[38] And that is where food sovereignty comes in.

The formation of a counterpublic is not easy. Dissociation and articulation are rhetorical strategies that redefine or alter tropes toward new or more inclusive ends. They function to broaden a movement, bringing more people in, or to reorient the buzzwords that signal participants in a movement toward goals that are politically achievable at a given moment in time. The processes of formation that mobilize language or thought operate within the discourse of social control, though non-discursive forms of power will almost certainly be operative, as well. At the same time, one should not expect publics with opposite interests to remain silent. They may respond with arguments to defend the priority of their own interest, but they may also adopt a surreptitious strategy to undercut the rhetorical moves of their opponents. One way food industry firms might try to defeat the formation of a food movement is to reinforce the notion that participants in this movement occupy the social identity of consumers. With this thought, the argument circles back to Samantha Noll's claims about local food as a justifiable form of identity politics.

Food ethicist Michiel Korthals describes the politics of the food movement as a contest between the social identities of consumer and citizen. The social identity of the consumer has been defined by economists and consolidated by political theorists over a period of 200 years. The consumer has preferences, a ranked set of outcomes or states-of-the world. As a matter of fact, consumers rank their preferences however they want (e.g., *de gustibus non est disputandum*). Such consumers will order their preferences to get as much of what they like in states-of-the-world that follow from their actions, given the amount of what they have had to give up in order to get it. They are economizers. In contrast to consumers, when we act as citizens we take a more idealistic standpoint. We evaluate political choices not so much in what they have for ourselves as in whether they lead to a better world. Replicating an argument made by Mark Sagoff, Korthals says that while it is true that we act as economizing citizens in the private sphere, once we enter the public sphere, prepared to debate the functions of government, we understand ourselves as citizens.[39] One could go further. Does the citizen model limit the boundaries of a person's social imagination to the geographical boundaries of their city or state? Can the food movement make a further pivot to a cosmopolitan worldview? These questions show that the inquiry remains open.

Given what has been argued in this chapter, the locavore ethic can be understood as a discursive strategy that addresses people first in their identity as consumers, inviting them to incorporate their preferences for environmental quality into their food purchases. Perhaps things end there, but Barbara Kingsolver's version of the ethic dissociates locality from the standard of food miles, articulating it as seasonality. This articulation takes a step beyond the consumer's fixation on exchange. As the ethic pivots further toward engagements with farmers or growing food oneself, one is invited to consider localness through a different mentality, the perspective of Korthal's citizen. Here, one may see oneself as part of a new public making new claims upon public life. With Noll's move to food sovereignty, one enrolls in the food movement. One no longer defines the locavore ethic simply by looking at a map while trolling the aisles in the grocery store. For Noll the locavore ethic stakes its claim in the public sphere rather than the private sphere where *de gustibus non est disputandum* reigns. This is just the kind of identity transformation that theorists of the public sphere see as crucial for resisting profit-seeking actors' subversion of democratic governance.

Then Finally . . .

Does anything is this talk of dissociation and counterpublics make locavorism morally mandatory? Obviously not, no more than Pascal would have said his gamblers' argument makes belief in Christian theism ethically mandatory. Yet it is possible for locavorism to be addressing ethical issues without also implying that it is the only morally acceptable dietary practice. Food ethics should recognize the inevitability of the food movement's subversive character. The locavore ethic seduces people who are very comfortable in understanding their relationship to food through the purchases they make at stores and restaurants. It hopes to hook them with new delights and better-tasting food. New recipes and expanded tastes put them on the road to political engagement. That road takes them to farmer's markets and CSAs and makes them appreciate the many forms of abuse inflicted by the current food system. The practicing locavore may not even realize that he or she has accepted a veiled invitation to become enrolled in the food movement, a counterpublic opposing a food industry intent on maintaining the governance institutions that have given us the industrial food system.

Of course, the public constituted by the food industry and its partners in government and universities is equally cunning. This mainstream group already holds many levers of power. It opposes every attempt to construct food identities that empower ordinary people. Citizens who see themselves as having a legitimate interest in the structures governing the production, processing, and distribution of food are not likely to be their friends: better to reinforce the notion that food purchases are ordinary transactions in which buyers' only legitimate interest lies in getting what they want at the lowest possible price. Government documents and peer-reviewed studies that insist upon casting subjects as consumers are evidence of the subversive strategies pursued by those enriched by the industrial food system. People who read such prose (as well as many people who write it) will never realize that the script they perform casts them as passive recipients of benefits or bearers of cost. The consumer's agency ends when the cut is made and the bill is paid.

Are analytic ethicists who work in utilitarian or neo-Kantian traditions guilty of complicity with the food industry? I think that goes much too far. Neither De Bres nor Young insists on a strictly economizing image of the person standing in front of his or her local produce section. As a matter of utilitarian ethics, they *should* rank their choices in terms of social utility, but it is not at all clear that this is an approach that favors industry interests. Something like the Categorical Imperative provides another approach: a decision rule that cannot be universalized as applicable to everyone is eliminated from consideration entirely. In every case, the ethic being applied by De Bres and Young understands the consumer as a decision-maker who is advised and/or constrained by normative standards that make significantly greater demands than simple preference satisfaction. Yet the retreat to a decisionist standpoint does appear to block the emergence of a reflective stance in which one sees oneself engaged with political agency, with the formation of a counterpublic.

In concluding, it is also important to notice that the pivots I have noted in the expanded version of locavorism do nothing to address distributive inequalities, food insecurity, or structural injustice in the food system. That does not mean that I intend to dismiss such issues; some of them are discussed in other chapters. There are no magic incantations or simple rules that will solve every ethical problem in food. We may hope that, once enrolled in the food movement, our ethical (but reasonable) locavore will encounter further opportunities to pivot toward norms and identities that are responsive to food justice. The community-building aspect of the locavore ethic could be just such a path. Yet, without active pursuit of those norms, it will remain just a hope. Members of the food movement should not think they can dispense with philosophical inquiry. Perhaps a narrowly justice-oriented food ethics falls short on ethical responsibilities in the environmental and aesthetic domains? The work of displacement and articulation is never done. It is in that sense that food democracy is always "to come."[40]

5

The Ethics of Food Labels

Product information is a critical piece of infrastructure for any kind of consumeroriented food ethics. You cannot choose foods that promote ethical ideals in the absence of information about where those foods came from or how and by whom they were produced. In this chapter, we will encounter some of the philosophical puzzles that arise in providing that information. My analysis suggests that food labels are frequently evaluated in terms of their ability to further social outcomes, but product information is interpreted better through ethical and political principles of religious tolerance and liberty of conscious. Even when people do hope to further social change through their food purchases, labels do much more than simply facilitating consumer choice. They function as institutions that support a citizen's opportunity to participate in the public sphere.

My discussion of food labels connects to the previous chapter's discussion of local food by showing how the information infrastructure of the food system either frustrates or facilitates a person's ability to express an identity as citizen versus consumer. I provide a brief orientation to the way that our current food system frustrates consumer voice as well as show how the proliferation of traits sought by ethical consumers has complicated things. My endpoint is the view that what matters ethically is exit, rather than choice. Just as people in political democracies should not be coerced into any specific religious practice, the food system should be organized so that people are never forced into objectionable consumption. We begin with a philosophical thought experiment.

Aunt Orva

I would like to introduce you to my Aunt Orva. Over ninety, Aunt Orva grew up in small-town rural Indiana during the Great Depression (1929–1939). Orva's parents took food very seriously. They were not farmers, but farming was the economic basis of their community. Their sheer proximity

From Silo to Spoon. Paul B. Thompson, Oxford University Press. © Oxford University Press 2024.
DOI: 10.1093/oso/9780197744727.003.0006

to farming neighbors made them aware of where *food* came from, even if they were not always sure where their next meal might come from. Orva is deeply religious and takes each meal as a gift from God. Still today, Orva never takes a bite until the blessing of God has been asked. These pre-meal prayers or "saying grace" may have been more common in Orva's youth, yet many families continue this religious practice today. At Orva's table, the grace is never slighted or given a perfunctory manner. Every meal is a religious experience at Aunt Orva's house, and nothing is put on the table that is not worthy of her faith.

Aunt Orva has never taken to Hostess Twinkees, Hamburger Helper, frozen entrees, or any other prepackaged, precooked, or pre-anything product when it comes to food. She's never been to McDonald's or Pizza Hut. Orva eats green beans, tomatoes, and corn-off-the-cob in season. The rest of the year, she mostly eats what she was able to buy from local farmers or personally harvest out of the backyard garden the previous summer. She still "puts up" or cans the harvest in glass jars, which she stores in her basement. She occasionally buys whole fruits and vegetables[1] from the fresh produce, canned, and frozen sections of the supermarket, but never a can of soup or a frozen pie. I have occasionally seen a box of corn flakes or a loaf of store-bought bread in her cupboard, but whenever I am invited to eat at Orva's table, everything has been made fresh from scratch: oatmeal, biscuits, stews, or cake. Vegetables are fresh from the store or someone's garden and served with only salt, pepper, and a little butter on the side.

Orva complains about the quality of flour and yeast she gets these days. She would never consider a pre-packaged mix. She longs for the time when she could get fresh milk or eggs from nearby neighbors' farms. The one "new" product she has welcomed over the past decade is organic brown-shelled eggs. She doesn't know or care about the organic part, but these eggs remind her of what she used to eat in years gone by. Like many rural Hoosiers, Aunt Orva is a rock-ribbed Republican. Her conservative values come out most forcefully when anyone threatens to interfere with the rhythms of her daily life. Debates about immigration, trade with China and wars in Ukraine or the Middle East pretty much pass her by. However, the fact that she cannot get locally grown tomatoes from her IGA in the middle of August infuriates her.[2] It is a serious insult to her sensibilities, and fixing problems like that is what it would take to make America great again, as far as Orva is concerned. Fortunately, she is still well enough to grow a few tomatoes herself, and she can buy what she needs for canning at a local farmer's market.

Aunt Orva and her neighbors are pretty sure that all this interference in their day-to-day life is a sign of serious moral decay. She is not the type to write her local newspaper or speculate that liberals are child-molesting drug addicts. She does not have social media accounts or consult the Internet, in any case. Nevertheless, I can sense the resentment she feels. At no time is that resentment greater than when she suspects her religious faith is being disrespected. When her ability to practice the requirements of that faith are threatened by changes in her surroundings, she becomes angry. That happened twice in the time I've known her. Once was when the county commissioners threatened to discontinue the Christmas nativity displays at the courthouse on account of the First Amendment's prohibiting an established church. The more frequent occasion arises when her ability to praise God through cooking and eating is compromised by the shoddiness, impurity, and general unavailability of the food ingredients she knew in her younger days.

Now, I should confess that Aunt Orva is a fiction. I hope that she is plausible and that readers can imagine someone quite like her. I have spent a fair amount of time in the Southern and Midwestern United States, and I know many people like her in at least some respects. My own grandmother (I called her Nana) was a lot like Orva, save for the fact that she was born in 1910 and would be more than 110 years old as I write today. My Nana lived most of her life in deeply Republican Southwest Missouri, but her sense of indebtedness to New Deal programs in the 1930s made her into a lifelong Democrat. Like the fictional Orva, my real Nana never toyed with processed food or chain restaurants. The only place she would eat outside her home was a locally run cafeteria where the food looked familiar and where she could see it go from the chafing dish to her plate. She *did* complain about the quality of flour and yeast and she *did* say grace before every meal. I want readers to have someone like Orva or my Nana in mind as they read this chapter because I do not want you to imagine that the only people interested in the purity (or the story) of their food are left-leaning hippie granola-eaters.

Our Food System to 1990

Orva pines for the food of her past, but the systems people develop for producing, processing, distributing, and preparing food have undergone continuous evolutionary change throughout human history. The modifications that occurred during the 20th century differed from earlier times in several key respects. Already by 1900, people in cities were shopping at grocery stores, and even rural folk would have been buying canned goods, processed meats, and the raw ingredients for baking at a local market. Still, someone like Aunt Orva might well have milked a cow or wrung a chicken's neck with their own hands when they were younger. If, like Aunt Orva, they lived in a rural area, they would almost certainly have gotten some food directly from the farmers that grew it or raised the animals. Aside from the rich, American women of Orva's generation would have known their way around a kitchen when it came time to cook, and quite a few men could match them. At the same time, certain processed foods were fully integrated into their diets. Dr. John Harvey Kellogg (1852–1943) served corn flakes at his Battle Creek, Michigan, sanitarium in 1894. They were marketed by his brother, Will Keith Kellogg (1860–1951), in 1906. The entire Battle Creek area became a hotbed of processed food innovation, and W. K. Kellogg became one of the richest Americans by marketing his convenient breakfast food through novel approaches in brand-name labeling and advertising.[3]

It is possible that human beings have always experienced nostalgia for antiquated foodways as they get older, but the year 1900 is a good reference point for present purposes. The problems with prepared and packaged food were well known to people living at the turn of the century. They knew quite a bit about the chicken they bought from a cousin or a neighbor before they killed it, plucked the feathers, and cooked it, and they were concerned about the fact that they had no idea what was really inside that can of chicken soup. Stories of deceptive and disreputable contamination of foods and medicines circulated widely at the dawn of the 20th century. Government chemist Harvey C. Wiley (1844–1930) exposed adulteration of foods, eventually becoming the founding director of the U.S. Food and Drug Administration (FDA). Government regulation of food safety was one response to consumer's ignorance of food ingredients, but the other solution appeared right on the product itself. The brand names we still know today, Heinz ketchup, Campbell's soup, and Kellogg's cereals, arose because consumers could associate a brand name with consistent quality. A food industry firm could capture the loyalty of consumers who were concerned about what might be inside the package.[4]

Other changes in the food system would come to erode consumer confidence in later decades. Farmers were applying pesticides to their crops, with the annual tonnage increasing steadily after the introduction of new toxic agents during World War II. At the same time, the food industry itself was using non-nutritive extenders in processed food and increasing the shelf life of products through preservatives. The FDA was on hand to evaluate the safety of these products, but the scientific methods in use could overlook sensitivities that were present in a small percentage of the population. Food safety agencies were not always aware of the dangers associated with some ingredients. For example, trans-fats (partially hydrogenated vegetable oils) have been in use since the 19th century, with consumption increasing significantly in the 1950s, '60, and '70s. The first warnings about their health effects were sounded in 1981, but it took the FDA until 2015 to accumulate enough data to warrant banning them.[5] What is more, the FDA's focus on the toxicity of specific food ingredients meant that broader dietary effects, such as the increased use of sugars and fats, were entirely unregulated.

My fictional Aunt Orva would have observed many of these changes over the course of her lifetime. She might have countered worries over what was in the food she ate by sourcing as much of her food as possible from rural neighbors she felt she could trust and by refusing to eat foods from packages. Such an orientation might explain the impurity beliefs and the sense of moral decay that Aunt Orva (as well as my real Nana) associated with the foods she got from the grocery store. She could (she thought) be somewhat sure about the vegetables she got from neighbors, but she couldn't know what had been applied to items in the produce section of the grocery store. Any more thoroughly processed food was just beyond the pale. Yet, in attributing these worries to women like Orva, I do not imply that they would have actively complained about it. Warren Belasco has argued that demands for greater assurance about foods did not come from religiously conservative women in Indiana or Missouri. It came from pot-smoking, brown rice-cooking twenty-year-olds who were listening to Grateful Dead records and buying cookbooks by Adele Davis (1904–1974), Euell Gibbons (1911–1975) or Frances Moore Lappe. They were ditching their Kellogg's cereals and sprinkling granola they bought at the food co-op into yogurt (a combination my Nana almost certainly never tasted). Belasco says that discontent with the industrial food system begins with the counterculture movements of the 1960s and 1970s.[6]

As Belasco notes, the 20th century ends with a significant surge of interest in alternatives to the food available in the grocery stores of the 1950s, '60s, and '70s. As recounted in Chapter 2, the recognition of health and environmental risks combined with a growing appreciation of food's aesthetic quality to spark the food movement. The thought experiment I am proposing with Aunt Orva implicitly privileges a U.S. context, but the growth of an alternative food system was global, at least among the industrialized nations that had been so dramatically affected by the use of chemicals in farming and food processing. It led farmers and small, start-up food companies or markets to develop standards that would mark their products as free from chemical contamination. The 1980s and the 1990s saw a proliferation of these standards, and the International Federation of Organic Agriculture Movements (IFOAM) worked to unify them.[7] This resulted in a functionally equivalent set of international standards for food that could be labeled "organic" (or, in some places "*biologique*" or "ecological"). The multiplicity of standards in the United States led farmers to call upon the U.S. Department of Agriculture (USDA) to develop a marketing label for organic food that would have legal bite: producers that did not demonstrably meet this standard could be prosecuted.[8] The organic label marks a turning point in the ethics of food consumption.

The Moral Affront

As a thought experiment, my fictional Aunt Orva provides entry into the mindset of someone looking for more informative food labels, but it might not be clear why these concerns take on moral significance. In searching for a food ethic, someone might be tempted to stress the ways that changes in the food system affect a person's health. This would capture Orva's concern under a moral principle of nonmaleficence: acts or procedures that risk harm to others should not permitted, at least not in the absence of strict criteria for protecting informed consent. Furthermore, there is no doubt that safety concerns have long been prominent in criticisms of the industrial food system. In 1932, two engineers, Arthur Kallet (1902–1972) and Frederick Schlink (1891–1995), published *100,000,000 Guinea Pigs: Dangers in Everyday Foods, Drugs and Cosmetics*. The book gave rise to consumer protection organizations such as Consumer's Union.

Importantly, harm to health is exactly the problem that food safety regulation was created to address. No one is contesting the legitimacy of applying the non-maleficence principle to food, but the appropriate response is usually just to ban the offending product. That is what food safety regulatory agencies do. Kallet and Schlink were not calling for labels; they wanted the FDA to be even more aggressive in removing substances from the food system.[9] I am asking you to imagine my Aunt Orva because her concerns are both broader than and different from safety concerns. This will help us get to the heart of the moral concerns, but it is also true that *antinomian* safety concerns (e.g., worries that have little scientific underpinning) will have moral significance in much the same manner as Orva's religious objections.

I have foregrounded Aunt Orva's religious orientation in order to locate the philosophical problem apart from health and safety issues. For health, the principle of non-maleficence does all the philosophical work. However, people like my Aunt Orva might say that the act of eating unites their spirituality with the materiality of their earthly body. They might say that taking nourishment is a sacrament performed in accordance with religious law. Kosher and halal exemplify religious dietary codes, but I am imagining Orva as someone whose religious orientation to food may be quite personal, not sanctioned by a recognized faith tradition but nonetheless quite common among people in my grandmother's generation. Perhaps it is not so uncommon today. Someone taking such an attitude might also see little or no health benefits from observing religious dietary rules. Many practitioners of kosher or halal see things just that way; they do not observe their food codes because they think religiously sanctioned food is safer to eat.

Given all this, we can guess how Orva feels about unseen ingredients, and, in the 21st century, unseen ingredients include genes from other organisms, so-called GMOs.[10] She might not have been upset at first. She might have thought it would only affect packaged food she was not eating, anyway. That strategy had worked to give space for her peculiarly spiritual belief system as it related to dyes, preservatives, and other food ingredients, concerns that were in the newspapers during her childhood. Orva might have been less worried about her health. She had eaten worse things during those Depression years. However, the debate started by Harvey Wiley and carried on by Kallet and Schlink helped sear a concern about the purity of food into her brain. The 1906 law that established the FDA was not the *safe* food and drug, act; it was the *Pure* Food and Drug Act. Yet these undetectable contaminants—invisible chemicals or foreign genes—are an affront to the purity rules she has painstakingly developed over a lifetime of cooking and serving food. I imagine her muttering under her breath about the daily ritual of preparing, blessing, and consuming a meal shattered by the heedless acts of soulless corporations and godless bureaucrats!

People like my Aunt Orva may have rather vague worries that things have gotten out of control. Her belief system has been destabilized and her recognition of its fragility leads her to wonder where the evil will strike next. This will not end well, she thinks. I do not mean to suggest all such disruptive tendencies generate philosophically persuasive reasons to accommodate a person's attitudes in the public sphere. John Stuart Mill (1806–1873) provided important guidance on when a person's preferences should be indulged and when they shouldn't. Succinctly, we should tolerate belief systems up to the point that they would lead someone to engage in acts that harm others.[11] Orva's belief that foods should meet her standards of purity isn't harming anyone. That makes it very different from racial or gender-based prejudices. It is difficult to see why Aunt Orva must abandon her faith orientation in order for new agricultural and food technologies to come on line.

Yet, before rushing to the conclusion that Orva's spiritually based food beliefs are protected by something like a principle of religious liberty, it is important to ask whether protecting them could itself be interpreted as harming someone. I think that there are at least two ways in which institutions, laws, or policies to protect Orva's beliefs could be construed as harmful. First, if the government decides that venders are *required* to tell Orva about what she regards as impurities in her food, this can be understood as a form of compelled speech. Mill's principle protects inaction as well as action. We should tolerate someone's refusal to act (in this case to speak) up to the point that their refusal results in actual harm to others. Now, as we have seen, impurities in food can indeed be dangerous. However, food safety agencies generally respond to food safety risks by banning the offending substance altogether.[12] The impurities that are causing Orva fits have already been determined *not* to be causing harm. Therefore, requiring a vender to disclose information about them might count as an instance of compelled speech.

The other source of potential harm derives from the cost of labeling. The food industry has often protested against requirements to provide information about their products on the grounds that doing so will increase their costs, in turn increasing the price that consumers must pay. For example, in 2018, the U.S. FDA started requiring chain restaurants to post information on the calories and fat content of their menu items. The policy was adopted only after more than a decade of debate about the costs of ascertaining this information and making it available. The food industry also complained about the impact such labels might have on product sales, especially given the likelihood that consumers would misuse information on a label.[13] The food industry resisted GMO labeling on similar grounds.

There is also a corollary to this second argument: if there are enough people like Orva, the market will provide incentives for entrepreneurs to figure out how they can offer the kind of purity she wants. Eventually, the demand for foods made without GM grew to the point that it was profitable to develop a "non-GMO" label.[14] The food industry's argument includes the thought that markets have a built-in response to Orva-like concerns. When the costs of labeling are absorbed by the opportunity for profits, no one is worse off. What is more, the pressure from competitors will relieve the government from needing to compel speech.

Markets don't solve ethical problems, however. It is important to ask how much protection Mill's principle of toleration affords to religious, spiritual, or philosophical beliefs when they are held by a minority that is too small to mobilize market forces. Kosher and halal labels exist partly because there are plenty of people who will buy products labeled that way, but, viewed globally, governments have interpreted their responsibility to support these religiously based systems in different ways.[15] It is also important to frame this inquiry in light of social reality. The U.S. First Amendment asserts that *government* must not discriminate on the basis of religion, but it does not prohibit individuals or for-profit firms from doing so. In practice, principles of free speech and liberty of conscience have been extended into the private sphere. In some cases, extension has occurred through formal legislation. In the present age, the law prohibits discrimination on the basis of social identities including race, gender, sexual orientation, and religious affiliation in economic transactions. Other extensions are informal. It is difficult to imagine a firm of any size discriminating against employees on the basis of their political party affiliation, for example. Firms serving national markets routinely adopt non-discrimination policies that go well beyond legal requirements.

In sum, the practical scope that toleration of different belief systems takes is a function of both market forces and the discourse of social control. More accurately, market forces *are* a form of social control. An open society's toleration of alternative beliefs has a history, in other words, and future expansion or contraction in the scope of protection accorded to belief systems and social identities will be shaped by that history. Our inquiry into liberty of conscience's meaning for food labels will be furthered by a review of practice. At bottom, Orva's beliefs classify foods as pure or impure in much the same way religious dietary beliefs classify foods as permitted or prohibited.

Similarly, what one *may or may not* say about a food, as well as what one *must* say depends upon where a given food falls into a system of classification.

The Philosophy of Food Classification

Alexandra Pliakas provides a very helpful introduction to the philosophical problems raised by dividing the things we eat into a system of categories or kinds. Before thinking about organic foods or GMOs, we should understand that seemingly simple classifications are more convoluted than might be expected. Pliakas points out that we operate with a system of types and tokens: the individual florets of broccoli or cauliflower that we actually eat are tokens of the general type. The broccoli we ate yesterday is a token of the type (or kind) "broccoli." The broccoli on our plate today is a different token from the broccoli we ate yesterday, but they are both tokens of the same kind. Any general classification can constitute a type, while types that reflect the structure of the natural world are called *natural kinds*.[16] Now, my Aunt Orva thinks of broccoli, Brussels sprouts, and cauliflower as different kinds of vegetable, and so do I. For a botanist, however, they are different cultivars of *Brassica oleracea*. If we presume that genus and species mark the natural kind—the reality existing independently from human perception and use— then broccoli, Brussels sprouts, and cauliflower are all tokens of the same natural kind.

Pliakas argues we should think of food types as *functional kinds*. They reflect a system of categories we set up purely for our own convenience.[17] Of course, no one actually "set up" the distinction between cauliflower and broccoli. Most of these distinctions are created through cultural evolution, a (perhaps) benign discourse of social control. However, one generation will inherit the classification system of the previous one. For food kinds, classifications that go deep into history clash with the inventions of the present. Take margarine, for example. Oleomargarine was developed in France as a substitute for butter during the 19th century. The dairy industry did not want customers to be fooled into buying it. However, at the time, butter was routinely sold from a tub rather than a package, and this mode of sale continued until the mid-20th century. There was no place for a product label. Many potential customers were illiterate, in any case. So, many countries around the world adopted policies banning the use of yellow food coloring that would make margarine look like butter. By the 1960s, new technologies were altering the basic mix of ingredients in butter substitutes, many of which began to use hydrogenated plant oils instead of animal fat derivatives. At this point, the term "margarine" begins to fall out of use, and the less discriminating category of "spreads" begins to take its place. My 92-year-old mother-in-law still instructs her daughter to buy her some "oleo," but our daughter would have no idea what she is talking about.

There are circumstances that lead governments to make extensive change in the way that foods are classified for the purpose of regulation. During the 1990s, member states of the European Union worked to harmonize laws that defined a large number of common foods, including beer, wine, chocolate, and processed meats. Some of the old definitions had protectionist goals in mind: if beer has to be brewed from a very specific blend of ingredients to count as beer, only brewers from a specific region will be able sell their product under that designation. Other products claimed that unique regional features were crucial for their identity. Wines and cheeses are key examples, and the categorization of cured meats is also contested. On one hand, there is cured ham, while on the other there is prosciutto di Parma. Producers in the region of Parma feed their pigs on acorns and whey from Parmigiano-Reggiano, but it is the breezes of the Emilia Romagna hills that are said to give it its distinctive flavor. In between there is prosciutto itself: Does it have to come from Italy? These categories were carefully negotiated throughout the European Union in the 1990s. The European criteria are largely ignored elsewhere, and especially in the United States, where your champagne might come from California and your prosciutto might come from Iowa.[18]

My Aunt Orva would surely regard many of these disputes as rather insignificant, silly even. Yet, speaking philosophically, that simply reflects the sense in which Aunt Orva's metaphysical presumptions (her categories) reflect her personal experience. That, remember, is the experience of a religiously conservative Protestant who grew up in the American Midwest. A scientist might be more inclined to accept a Linnaean genus-species classification of ingredients: that's the one that makes broccoli and cauliflower tokens of the same kind. However, the scientists' system of kinds might be insensitive to the peculiar quality of the breezes blowing through the curing houses outside of Parma. I once toured the Bordeaux countryside with a vintner who showed me factories built on soils that, he told me, God had intended for wine production. Building factories there was a crime against nature, he thought. His food metaphysics might have been truly religious, but it differed from Aunt Orva (and my Nana). Neither of them ever took a drink.

In summary, the classification of different food types is more complex than people are initially inclined to think. At the same time, the categories that any given person uses to make sense of their plate are taken to be utterly obvious and non-controversial. Serious debates over which terms can be used to classify a food usually come down to money. Creameries did not want to lose any sales to butter substitutes, and they did not want their customers to be fooled into purchasing what they regarded as an inferior product. How should those debates be resolved on philosophical grounds? We have already seen why science is of limited application: broccoli, cauliflower, and Brussels sprouts are all members of the same natural kind. Tradition and common-sense experience play a large role in sorting out which category any given food token fits into, but different traditions will configure the common sense differently. Food kinds are functional kinds, but the functions that interest one group are not the functions that matter to another group. All this is pointing us toward the thought that the classification of food is culturally relative. Once again we are returned to Mill's *On Liberty*, the *locus classicus* for evaluating the ethical significance of culturally relative goods.

Food Labels and Liberty of Conscience

Mill spoke primarily about ethics: How should we regard the views of others, and how should we regulate our own conduct in a manner that respects difference? In contrast, public policy defines the problem in terms of government involvement: When is it appropriate for states to step in and enforce standards of conduct through legislation, the courts, and the power of the police? A less crisply definable level exists in between, where non-state actors govern. As already seen, brand names emerged as a partial solution to the quality, safety, and purity concerns of late 19th- and early 20th-century consumers. Kosher and halal standards are defined in part by rabbis and imams, but they are also shaped by the fact that people willing to buy such products have created a market demand for them. This domain of "soft law," emergent from patterns of communication and transaction, is where many ethical issues in food labeling are negotiated.

It may be helpful to start with state action. Mill's theory justifies state actions that protect people against injurious or deceptive trade practices. As already discussed, food safety agencies were created during the early decades of the 20th century to protect consumers from harmful and dishonest adulteration of foods.

This principle implies that states can act against product claims that are false and misleading. However, who is to say when a claim is false or misleading? The rough answer reflected in contemporary law distinguishes between misleading claims about health, on the one hand, and claims that have aesthetic or economic significance, on the other. Government agencies have been much more willing to take action against companies that claim dubious health benefits. When American companies claiming to offer champagne or prosciutto violate the French and Italian understanding of truthfulness, the U.S. Government has been more reluctant to intervene. The government might even see Mill's principle operating to prevent them from interfering in a company's right of free speech. If customers associate the words "champagne" and "prosciutto" with a generic kind of sparkling wine or cured ham, rather than a region of production, both they and the U.S. companies marketing these products would be harmed by a state action that prevents consumers from purchasing the product at a lower price than producers in the northeast of France or Parma are willing to offer.

Sometimes these standards change. Food safety agencies have attempted to maintain and even sharpen the distinction between product claims that have health and safety implications, and those that do not. They do this through a multipronged attack. First, many food authorities, including the FDA, have standardized rules for ingredient and nutrition labeling required on canned or packaged foods. Nutrition labels define a portion size and declare the number of calories, as well as the percent daily value of vitamins, fats, protein, sodium, and other nutrients in a serving of the product. These are *mandatory* labels. Second, food safety agencies regulate food producers' use of many terms, include "light," "reduced calorie," or "functional food" based on studies that combine nutrition science with social psychology and communications research to understand how consumers use these claims to pursue dietary goals. These labels involve *regulated language*. Finally, there are *warning* labels. Warning labels are used very sparingly in the United States, but are applied when there is scientific evidence of harmful consequences from consuming a food ingredient. Government agencies concluded that simply banning such substances would do more harm than good. Alcohol and tobacco warnings are the most prominent examples, with the United States' attempt to ban alcohol use in the 1930s serving as a prime indicator of how banning a product can fail to have the desired effects on public health.

Governments also step into the middle zone with what in the United States are called *marketing* labels. Marketing labels are developed for the promotion of trade. Here the examples are grades and standards for produce and meats.

USDA Prime, Choice, or Select are claims developed to indicate the marbling and fat content indicative of meat quality. Grades such as "Fancy," "No. 1," or "Utility" indicate the size, coloring, water content, and other quality features of apples. Marketing standards are created because they reduce costs and help exchanges between growers and the retailers or food manufacturers move smoothly. Apples fit for applesauce may be unfit for sale at a grocery store, for example. The ethical rationale for marketing standards has historically been purely utilitarian. These standards reduce costs for buyer and seller alike. When cost reductions are passed on to consumers they increase social welfare and are ethically justified for that reason. This kind of product label might emerge without government intervention at all, simply as conventions that get developed by producer organizations or by cooperation among buyers. However, the government gets involved when there is a worry that grades and standards will be developed as a way to distort or limit supply in order to increase profits. Such collusion harms consumers by raising prices. A state agency may step in to function on the public's behalf by facilitating classifications that serve the public interest while prohibiting those that thwart it.

As discussed already, product claims that constitute a dangerous or deceitful practice violate consumer rights in a straightforward manner. However, what about the person who *thinks* that a practice is dangerous, even if a food regulatory agency concludes that it is not? There are two lines of philosophical inquiry to follow in such cases. The question of who is right and who is wrong about the reality of risks take us into epistemology and philosophy of science. The questions are tortuous because no amount of scientific evidence can remove all doubt about the very possibility of harm.[19] In this chapter, I want to pursue the other line of inquiry. Can someone (Aunt Orva, say) assert the moral right to the information she needs to enact her spiritual practices? Can the person who suspects that a practice is dangerous assert a similar right, even when the preponderance of the evidence is against them? I will argue that both of them can draw upon the liberal tradition's liberty of conscience to insist that foods compatible with her belief system remain available to them but also that the right protecting this liberty is narrower than sometimes thought.

The Labeling Debate

Before getting into the ethical arguments, it is important to see how the need to assert such a right came to be a matter of debate. The current systems for organic labels were still being debated throughout the 1990s, and questions about labeling genetically engineered foods were on the horizon. As already noted, an internationally harmonious system for organic labels resulted from the coordinating activity of groups like IFOAM. The process would not have been so harmonious if organic advocates had insisted that the organic products are superior on food safety or nutritional health criteria. Instead, the organic label means simply that a list of specific farming practices (mostly involving synthetic fertilizers and pesticides) were not used. Buyers are free to apply their own beliefs about the healthfulness of organic food, but a merchant who makes such a claim is stating something that goes well beyond what the label itself declares. The organic label does not even imply that the product is chemical free.[20] As a marketing label making no health claims, the organic label is not reviewed or certified by food safety authorities such as the FDA.

The story for genetically engineered foods was markedly different. Japan and the European Union responded to general consumer reluctance about genetic engineering in agriculture by requiring a mandatory label for all foods derived with recombinant DNA. In the United States, the FDA concluded that such labels were misleading, implying a health risk where, in their judgment, none existed. From the late 1990s to the mid-2000s, FDA actively discouraged labels that claimed "no GMO" (or words to that effect). This decision sparked two decades of debate in the United States as advocacy groups pursued efforts to label products of biotechnology at the state level. Support for these ballot initiatives often argued that consumers have a right to choose whether gene technologies were used to produce their food. In 2017, the U.S. Congress passed legislation intended to end state-by-state labeling requirements, though the implementation of that legislation remains controversial.[21] By this time, the FDA had relented in their opposition to "non-GMO" product claims, and the USDA created a program for accrediting marketing labels that certify products as containing no GMOs.[22]

The U.S. debate provides a useful test of the way that liberty of conscience might be used to demand government involvement in food labeling. Those arguing against labeling for GMOs tended to portray the label as a decision-support mechanism evaluated in utilitarian terms. That is how regulated language developed for ingredient labels is viewed, for example. People with food allergies or dietary sensitivities use claims about ingredients or sodium levels to avoid health risks. Regulating terms like "reduced calorie" or "lite" help dieters achieve health goals by ensuring that this language has a consistent meaning. In contrast to these claims, the lack of any nutritional or food safety benefits means the GMO label could not deliver a scientifi- cally meaningful benefit to consumers. As such, if there were *any* costs as- sociated with the label, they would fail to be offset by benefits to consumers. Even worse, the label might be interpreted to imply a health or dietary benefit where none existed. The GMO label failed all these cost-benefit tests.[23]

However, it is not clear labels should be evaluated as decision-support tools in the first place.

Clearly, some believed that GMOs were risky to eat, and the debate over GMO labeling probably led others to worry about safety, too. However, what about people whose objection to gene technology rested on their concerns about its effect on the social practice of farming, or who saw gene technology in aesthetic or religious terms? They are not thinking that GMOs pose a risk to health, but they still might not want to eat them. For that matter, what about consumers who simply prefer non-GMOs on purely arbitrary grounds? For this segment of the public, the healthfulness is an irrelevant test. And, finally, don't nonconforming views on health and safety deserve respect in a liberal democracy, even when science provides no basis for them? For this ques- tion, it is important to determine whether nonconforming behavior places others at risk. In the case of dietary beliefs that lead people to avoid certain foods, it is hard to see how it could. Pro-labeling anti-GMO activists could have cited all these perspectives in support of their cause. In fact, activists calling for labels tended to assert that the appearance of unlabeled genetically engineered food was denying consumers' "right to choose." It is important to see why this argument was ethically problematic.

Problems with the Right to Choose

The "right to choose" argument has important philosophical weaknesses. It seems to say that people should be able to buy a food of a given type, in this case a type that is not genetically engineered. However, if "consumer choice" means that people have a moral right to options that will satisfy their die- tary desires, the claim cannot be supported on liberal grounds (the rationale articulated by Mill), no matter how much initial plausibility it might have. Certainly, all of us would like options when we make any kind of consumer purchase, but what we would like and what we can claim by right are two different things. If I walk into my local burger joint, Burger Totality, I might prefer to have an option to the single-, double-, or triple-patty combos I can order with or without cheese. I might prefer a soy or shrimp patty, instead. Indeed, I *can* get soy patties or fish sandwiches at many burger emporiums, but I would be mistaken if I thought I had a right to them. Having a right to soy or shrimp burgers would mean that there must be some grounds on which I could claim that the proprietor of Burger Totality is legally, morally, or at least customarily expected to provide these options to customers on demand. Rights implicate duties.

Rights imply that a valid claim can be made on behalf of the rights-holder. In my Burger Totality scenario, claiming that I have a right to choose means some good or service—a soy or shrimp burger—must be delivered to the rights holder, namely, me. However, claims can be asserted without being valid. Claims become *legal* rights when they are encoded in the laws of a community or state. Claims become *moral* rights when they are supported by some system of ethics. Claims become *customary* rights when the institutions or habits of a social group create reasonable expectations that they will be fulfilled. Someone at the head of the queue at Burger Totality does have the right to be served next (at least in the United States and Great Britain) because queueing for service is a well-established social institution. If I am next in line at Burger Totality, my expectation for next service is not only reasonable; it is likely that a counter attendant who served someone from the back of the queue would spark a minor revolution from the customers standing in line. I have no legal recourse in such a situation, though violators of robust customary rights might be prosecuted for creating a nuisance. In short, legal, moral, and customary rights become entangled in sometimes surprising ways. The right to merchantable goods (in this case burgers that fulfill the requirements of goods commonly advertised and sold as such) is actually a legal right.

Nevertheless, it is difficult to imagine why someone who arrives at Burger Totality expecting a soy or shrimp burger can claim anything more than disappointment when their desire is frustrated. One must either live with the proprietor's menu or walk away, hungry and unhappy, but not legally, morally, or even customarily wronged. In contrast, a potential customer's rights *would* be violated were he or she prevented from walking away and forced, either by coercion or deceit, to eat the standard single-, double-, or triple-patty burger that happens to be on the Burger Totality menu. It may be difficult to picture being forced to eat a hamburger at knifepoint, but being deceived about what is in that hamburger is not difficult to imagine. A vegetarian who requests a soy burger and is then knowingly served meat might legitimately claim to have his or her rights violated. Muslims who ask for halal but get haram have been disrespected. Some time back, a chain restaurant secretly added beef tallow to "improve" the flavor of their fries, upsetting the expectations of vegetarian customers.[24] Any of these cases can be understood as transgressing a customer's rights. Certainly, the seriousness of the transgression depends on many contingencies. We tend to be more forgiving of mistakes than intentional deception. But what about the guy who orders fish or shrimp and is told, "Sorry, not available"? He may leave dissatisfied, but he never had a right to a soy or shrimp patty in the first place. Given this, why would we think that shoppers have a right to other foods that satisfy their moral preferences? The more pertinent question is to determine whether the lack of a label forces people like Aunt Orva into a situation they find intolerable and from which they cannot escape.

Exiting the System

Let us return to Orva's case. Orva's rights are violated when she is deceived about what she bought or when she is actively prevented from exercising her values. You will recall that Orva has been avoiding industrially produced food for a long time. She has been doing this by growing her own or trading with individuals she feels that she can trust. In this behavior, Orva is exercising what Albert Hirschmann (1915–2012) called "exit" in his 1970 exploration of the tension between contrasting approaches to political agency. For Hirschmann, exit involves removing oneself from a transactional relationship altogether.[25] Having exit means that one can opt out of a given set of arrangements. Exit also figures prominently in the social contract theory of John Locke (1632–1704). For Locke, the legitimacy of government is thought to rest upon an implicit agreement, that is, on consent of the governed. Locke states that so long as people remain within a polity, they have agreed to be bound by its laws and authority, even when they do not agree in every particular. This form of implicit agreement depends on the ability to opt out of the social contract, even though in doing so people forfeit the benefits conferred by participation in the polity's arrangements for governance. Exit has practical implications for contemporary theories of democracy: Participation in the public sphere cannot be described as consensual if people have no possibility of exiting the polity and escaping the force of its laws.

Hirschmann expanded the scope of this idea, arguing that it describes the relationship between consumers and the firms offering goods and services in a modern industrial economy. As the quality or opportunity of goods and services on offer changes, the consumer might just suck it up, remaining loyal to a vender or brand. This version of loyalty is very close to Locke's vision of *implied consent*, a citizen's willingness to be bound by the laws of a state. Alternatively, they can opt out of the relationship, perhaps seeking a different vender or making other alterations in their lives so that they do not need to participate in the exchange relationship, at all. Short of exit but more active than loyalty, one exercises *voice* when one works to change the nature of the relationship. Hirshmann's study illustrates how these modes create a political economy. When exit has few costs, voice becomes less attractive, and the capacity for exercising voice may itself decline. Advocates of change may therefore discourage exit. Yet voice is always costly.[26]

At this juncture, the labeling debate begins to hook up with themes discussed in the previous chapter. The exercise of voice demands a communicative process—a form of discourse—that pushes participants toward shared meaning. Philosophers such as Nancy Fraser or Ernesto Leclau and Chantal Mouffe have argued this is an essential component of democracy.[27] Yet people like my Aunt Orva may find voice quite unattractive. They may view themselves (correctly or not) as fervently committed to a minority perspective. She may be correct in thinking there is little hope of convincing others through argument in the public sphere. To the extent that voice requires (or is judged to require) a sacrifice of meaning-generating commitments in a person's belief system, loyalty may be more attractive than voice, even when exit is their preferred strategy. I have imagined Orva as someone whose social identity includes a reluctance to "rock the boat." This explains why Aunt Orva might be disinclined to "take on the food system" in the sense explored in Warren Belasco's *Appetite for Change*. Philosophies of participatory democracy have made the case in favor of opportunities for voice, but the Aunt Orva thought experiment illustrates why it is also imperative to preserve opportunities for exit.

The first point to emphasize is that exit satisfies Orva's morally justifiable dietary demands even if asserting a "right to choose" is an overreach. People should not be forced into dietary choices that are contrary to their values, but this is a statement of negative liberty, or freedom from interference by others. Insisting that someone has an obligation to satisfy Orva's purity standards would violate *their* negative liberty. Now, it is important to recall that we have already reviewed situations where regulatory agencies should intervene in a vender's marketing behavior. But on what grounds could one argue that anyone is morally required to satisfy a mere dietary preference, however profoundly it might be felt? As long as Orva can walk away from situations where there is nothing on the menu she wants to eat, her negative liberty is assured. Now, there was a brief time when the right of exit from consumption of GMOs was threatened in the United States because there was no way that an ordinary consumer could tell the difference between a food that had been genetically engineered and one that had not. However, the creation of the process-based non-GMO marketing standard has remedied that.[28]

Interestingly, even Europe's mandatory GMO labeling would not protect exit if every product on offer was labeled as containing GMOs. This leads us toward a second point. Although the moral case for requiring any actor to offer products that allow Orva to pursue her social identity is weak, the claim that the food system should, indeed, present options that make exit possible is much stronger. This implies that, from a system perspective, options must, indeed, be available. From a practical standpoint, this means that firms should act cooperatively to maintain exit, at least when there is evidence that a significant number of consumers want it. Although it is far from perfect, the voluntary process-based marketing label declaring foods to be GMO free achieves this goal, but only if food producers take the trouble to offer these foods. It is important to notice that the organic label and the Fair Trade label function similarly. I think the question of when we should allow market forces to determine whether a given label is in use and when we should view a label as morally required to preserve exit is both open and interesting. I do not think that this chapter provides much guidance beyond the claim that minorities should be able to act on at least some quasi-religious or philosophical beliefs, even when the profit motive does not incentivize firms to offer alternatives.

Finally, the labeling debate qualifies some of the arguments on locavorism discussed in Chapter 4. I endorse the heuristic, quasi-Pascalian case for locavorism that was presented there. We may view the local foods diet as enrolling its practitioners into processes of identity formation that deepen their self-understanding and support ideals of environmental citizenship. However, a moral position that *required* participation in *any* practice of identity formation would be illiberal. People like my Aunt Orva should not be forced to participate in voice. They should not be coerced into dissociations that dislodge them from the possibility of loyalty, as Hirschmann defined it, and coerced into a counterpublic coalesced around articulation or voice. Opportunities for voice should certainly remain open, but, as Hirschmann noted, people may find participation in a counterpublic less attractive when exit is a meaningful alternative. If this is a retreat into a more libertarian approach to food ethics, so be it. With Mill, I would counter that a society which tolerates diverse identity-forming practices—that is, which does not view dietary choices in terms of universal moral requirements—provides the most conducive environment for the cultivation of virtue, in any case.

With that thought in mind, it is time to reconsider how the structure of the food system may evolve in the future.

Back to the Future

As noted already, Japan and the European Union required mandatory labels for GM foods quite early, while the United States eventually caved in to pressure for mandatory labeling with a confusing amendment to the Agricultural Marketing Act in 2016.[29] Other issues lie on the horizon. Cellular technologies for producing animal protein are under development, and cellular milk and eggs are being marketed already. These techniques use microbes or other organisms to "grow" the biochemical constituents of meat, milk, and eggs in a bath. In one sense, they are similar to age-old processes for brewing beer or making cheese, but the microbes they use have been genetically engineered. In the early going, such products will be labeled proudly in the attempt to lure customers opposed to the mistreatment of animals and the environmental impacts of dairy, meat, and egg production.

Should these technologies be mainstreamed as costs decline, as they are predicted to do? Or should everyone always know that no actual cow was involved in producing the milk your two-year-old is drinking? One can envision utilitarian/cost-benefit reasoning that would argue against any form of labeling for alternative animal proteins. There will be arguments from the scientific community claiming that these synthetically produced animal proteins are "chemically identical" to products produced on the hoof. People who have been critical of genetically engineered plant foods are already coming out in favor of this new biotechnology, mainly because it alleviates the need to keep animals in cages or, in the case of meats, kill them.[30] Yet, as

Cor van der Weele writes in her defense of cultured meats, the technology has generated criticism from others who see it as continuing the same disturbing trajectory that gave us GMOs.[31]

In the meantime, labels intended to help consumers support more humane farming practice have already emerged. Again, the European Union has enacted state-governed labeling policies, while the United States, Canada, and many other countries have relied upon third-party certification schemes. These humane animal farming labels reflect a core concern of ethical consumerism: shoppers are encouraged to buy products that promote better treatment of farm animals. Yet these labels are not without their ethical complications. There are, for example, immediate conflicts that arise in developing a strategy for voluntary labeling. One can set the standard of compliance high, so that one is confident that animals are living the best possible life, but there will be animal producers who are not interested in making such dramatic changes to their production system. Alternatively, one can improve the lives of many more animals if one entices more producers into the labeling scheme. Eliminating the most painful and distressing practices for a large number of animals may produce more total benefit than moving a smaller number to a near-optimal state of welfare.

Even more fundamentally, the procedures for establishing and certifying a food label are ethically vexed. The process criteria important for food ethics cannot be determined by inspecting the final product. Were workers fairly paid? Were animals humanely treated? Were milk cows fed on organically produced feed? Were genetically engineered plants used in a recipe? Third-party certifiers validate these claims (also referred to as *process-verified labeling* or *voluntary assurance schemes*). These systems operate in the gray zone between government activity and the private sphere. An organization develops a system to determine whether any given food meets certain value-based criteria. Theoretically, they could be anything, but they typically specify conditions or benchmarks that apply to the way that a food is produced, whether on the farm or after it leaves the farm gate. In the most typical model, other organizations are hired to inspect the production process, including records, to determine whether standards are being met. The process-verified label indicates that the producer has performed the process as specified by the standard. The standards developer and the certifier intervene in the transaction.

Their activity is intended to assure the buyer that the seller's claims about a given production process are true.

Product claims made through voluntary assurance schemes are marketing labels. They facilitate transactions that would otherwise be stifled by the buyer's difficulty in obtaining reliable information and the seller's difficulty in establishing trust. In most cases, the government's role lies in accrediting the scheme—ensuring that the certifiers are faithfully executing the intent of the original criteria. Yet there is one more wrinkle. Certifiers are usually paid for their activity by producers who hope to attract a better price if their products can be labeled "fair trade," "environmentally friendly," or "humanely produced." There is thus the potential for conflict of interest (or agency risk): a certifier who is lax in applying the criteria for these normative goals may be able to recruit more paying customers. In the United States, the USDA polices these standards with its process-verified program, assuring consumers that they can believe what a process-verified label says. Yet that kind of assurance requires trust in government.

The opportunity for cheating as well as more subtle questions in the ethics of auditing mean that voluntary assurance schemes are ripe for abuse and replete with opportunity for philosophical inquiry. We see, for example, that kosher and halal claims fall into the category, as well. Are fair trade, humanely produced, environmentally sustainable, or non-GMO labels a case where activities that *should* be taken over by government have been pushed into the private sector? Alternatively, does government involvement in developing these standards actually constitute an incursion on liberty of conscience? Americans would almost certainly think that the U.S. government has no role in determining the criteria for a kosher or halal food label, or even in inspecting the production process to see if the rules are followed. Is the answer different for Israel or an Islamic state? Is the answer different for determining what counts as fair treatment for workers or humane treatment of animals? Both domains are hotly contested on philosophical grounds. Perhaps governments should maintain a stance of neutrality with respect to the determination of these norms, much as they do when it comes to claims made on religious grounds. Unlike the assertive role of European states, government would step in only to maintain its traditional role of assuring that whatever is claimed about the product is actually true.

The Wrap Up

Like the discussion of local food, the story goes on, but the chapter must end. In general, philosophers writing on food have been very slow to take up the philosophical issues in food labeling.[32] I hope that I have shown that the traditions of free speech and liberty of conscience—what the U.S. tradition of constitutional law calls First Amendment concerns—provide the resources for thinking about these issues. Adapting that tradition, I have argued that people should be free to develop and apply a range of moral, religious, and spiritual norms in defining the standards that they think the production, distribution, and consumption of food should meet. The primary goal should be to develop a food system that is not coercive toward the standards that minority groups should be required to meet. At the same time, there will be some practices that cross the line drawn by Mill's version of "do no harm." (For example, religious liberty does not protect someone who genuinely believes in white supremacy when they violate basic human rights.) The question of where non-humans fit into the scheme is one where philosophers have been active for some time.

My Aunt Orva thought experiment is intended to evoke sympathy with an individual whose food metaphysics is plausibly consistent with the belief system of religiously conservative Americans. My guess is that more than a few people out there can identify with her. At the same time, her belief system is not encoded in the explicit tenets of any church that I am aware of. Does that vitiate her right of exit from a food system she finds intolerable? Conservative Protestants are not a majority of Americans, but they are a large and politically powerful group. As such, they exert enough economic power to provide merchants with an incentive to respect their values. What happens when the belief systems of smaller groups are challenged by the dominance of an increasingly integrated food system? What if they are minorities that have repeatedly suffered from oppression and systemic exclusion? We are increasingly hearing claims of food sovereignty defended in spiritual or religious terms. Does this elevate the food traditions of Native Americans or Latinx people from the Aymara regions or communally farmed *eijidos* to the status of protection under the First Amendment and similar religious liberty statutes? While I am sympathetic to this possibility, I do not think this chapter has addressed that question.

I have suggested that when it comes to food practices, the key rights at stake will be the right to avoid being placed in a position without options. In general, no one, not the state or the private sector, has a responsibility to satisfy religious or culturally based food preferences, no matter how sincerely they are held. Although this is a bold claim (and possibly mistaken) I hope that it will provoke deeper reflection and more writing by other philosophers. For their part, food system innovators and for-profit operators should undertake more care in considering how their activity can foreclose other people's opportunity to practice a spiritually meaningful life.

6

Pollution as a Moral Problem

This chapter explores the idea of pollution. How does the idea of pollution inform our understanding of what is good for the environment as well as what is bad for it? The question is clearly meaningful outside the food system: industrial manufacturing and transportation are major sources of environmental pollutants. However, there are reasons beyond the food sectors' contribution to ecological damage for a focus on agriculture. One reason is historical. Rachel Carson's *Silent Spring* (1962) brought pesticide pollution into the public consciousness. Although Carson's work on pollution from agricultural chemicals was extremely influential, the notion of pollution has received remarkably little discussion from philosophers. I begin the chapter with a context setting overview of events that helped to establish the importance of pollution within the public mind. One possible explanation for the lack of philosophical attention to pollution resides in the thought that it is just too obvious. We don't need a philosopher to explain what it means.

Yet theories of pollution from anthropology and religious studies challenge the assumption that the philosophical dimensions of pollution are quite so simple. These culturally oriented concepts of pollution stress their symbolic function in social control rather than focusing narrowly on biological harm. After exploring the ethical implications of these cultural approaches, I turn to the notion of pollution that has motivated scientific understanding of the risk from agricultural pesticides. Finally, I compare these two approaches to pollution with a case study on the speculative polluting impact from genetically engineered crops. I argue that implicit, group-level value commitments underlie contrasting views on genetic pollution. Although pesticide risks do provide a useful framework for evaluating the risks of genetic pollution, only a cultural theory of pollution can help us understand why this debate is so intractable.

From Silo to Spoon. Paul B. Thompson, Oxford University Press. © Oxford University Press 2024.
DOI: 10.1093/oso/9780197744727.003.0007

The Backstory

Farmers use chemical poisons to protect their crops from animals, including insects, that eat or otherwise damage plants and cause a significant loss in harvestable yield. Chemical agents can also be effective ways to control mold, fungi, and other organisms that damage crops. These organisms are collectively known as plant pests. The term "pesticide" covers chemicals that target insects, small mammals (rodents), and fungal pathogens. The use of such chemicals is old, but the chemical industry developed more effective forms of insecticide during World War II. After the war ended, the industrial capacity for producing pesticides used by the military was repurposed for agriculture. It is only a small exaggeration to say that the story of environmental and public health risks from toxic agricultural chemicals begins in the 1950s. The poster child for this story is the chemical DDT. DDT was relatively cheap to manufacture, transport, store, and apply. It was also the chemical that attracted Rachel Carson's attention in *Silent Spring*.

The initial toxicity tests on DDT suggested that it was lethal to insect pests but not harmful to vertebrates (including humans), at least at the amounts being used for pest control in both military and agricultural applications. The harmful effects from most toxins correspond to the dose, or level of exposure. In the case of food, the dose is the amount of the toxin consumed either through eating or by direct exposure in the field or greenhouse. The greater the exposure, the greater the effect. Very small amounts may have no effect at all. Furthermore, the amount of toxic exposure that would kill a very small organism (a bug, say) may have no effect on a larger organism, like a bird. Early studies on the toxicity of DDT showed no effect on vertebrate species, like birds or people. However, by the late 1950s, entomologists noticed a gradual increase in strange behavior and a decline in the population of small rodents (especially squirrels) and small birds. Carson's explanation of bioaccumulation in *Silent Spring* helped readers understand how a small *direct* exposure to a toxic substance can have serious health and environmental impact. As birds eat more and more insects killed by a toxin, the amount of the toxin they consume ultimately exceeds the "no effect" level. Exposure to DDT eventually accumulates to harmful levels. There is no reason why accumulation would be limited to birds. As humans accumulate larger and larger exposure through repeated consumption of miniscule amounts, the potential for a toxic impact grows. This is particularly the case for chemicals that stay in body tissue for long periods of time.[1]

There are, in fact, many forms of pollution associated with contemporary agriculture. Excess nitrogen from fertilization can contaminate water supplies and volatilizes as nitrous oxide, a potent greenhouse gas. Methane and carbon dioxide are emitted by animals in the process of producing meat, milk, and eggs. The Natural Resources Defense Council (NRDC) includes the creation of antibiotic-resistant bacteria among the polluting impacts of industrial animal production.[2] It is also important to remember that agriculture is itself an environmentally disruptive activity. Simply clearing land for crops or grazing reduces the habitat for wild plants and animals. That has negative effects on biodiversity. The idea of pollution might be stretched to include all these forms of environmental damage, but the cases that will be discussed later in the chapter reflect a fairly narrow range of the ways that agricultural production might harm the environment or public health. Even taken in this narrow sense, widespread recognition of these polluting impacts is limited to the past century. Some would argue that recognition is not widely appreciated even today.[3]

Carson's work sparked a social movement focused on controlling the environmental damage from insecticide use. In the United States, it led to a substantial revision of the Federal Insecticide, Fungicide, and Rodenticide Act (FIFRA) in 1972. This included the creation of a new government agency, the Environmental Protection Administration (EPA), to administer FIFRA. *Silent Spring* established the toxic environmental impact of agricultural chemical use as an issue for food ethics. At the same time, environmental philosophers and food ethicists have done surprisingly little work on the issues that Carson brought to light. Introductory textbooks bringing Carson's work to student's attention continue to include discussions of pollution from agricultural chemicals,[4] but they tend to presume that the moral dimensions of pesticide use are so obvious that they require no explication. Very few academically trained philosophers have addressed the topic. This chapter questions that neglect.

Pollution in Environmental and Food Ethics

Why do environmental philosophers skip over the problems of agricultural pollution? Here is one possible answer: although Carson's pioneering book focused on an agricultural chemical, industrial manufacturing arguably yields more poignant case studies for environmental ethics. The Love Canal is a waterway originally envisioned as a shipping lane to bypass Niagara Falls. As events transpired, only a short section of the canal was completed. Love Canal became the name of a working-class neighborhood in the city of Niagara Falls, New York, near the structure. The Hooker Chemical Company used the partially completed canal as a chemical waste disposal landfill in the 1940s. Later, the Niagara Falls School Board built a school on top of the site. Chemicals began to leak into the groundwater, causing human health effects that were not fully evident until the 1970s. The Love Canal became an emblematic industrial pollution event. The absence of forethought, evasions of responsibility for the human health consequences, and the vulnerability of uninformed or less politically influential populations are among the obvious moral problems evident in the Love Canal case study.[5]

Like dioxin, the main chemical at the root of the Love Canal incident, many industrial pollutants are byproducts of an industrial process. The primary products are intended for a specific purpose, but the toxic byproducts are not. Combustion of coal and gas to fuel the generation of electricity and other manufacturing practices emits sulfur oxides, volatile organic compounds (VOCs), and particulate matter into the air. Nuclear power produces radioactive wastes. In these cases, pollution is a cost, an unwanted output that puts a drain on the economic value of the production process. The situation in food and agriculture is both similar and different. Farmers apply chemical fertilizers and pesticides to crops to boost the harvestable yield. The unwanted health and environmental impact of these compounds can be viewed as a cost of production that must be deducted from the value of the food produced, just as dioxin, VOCs, or radioactive waste would be a cost to manufacturing. Absent some form of regulation, these are not costs that the producer (whether a farm or a factory) must bear. They are externalities: costs that are passed on to third parties, some unborn at the time that a pollution event occurs.[6] Environmental philosophers approach pollution as an ethics of externalized cost and impacts to future generations.

However, unlike the pollution at the Love Canal site, pesticides and fertilizers are not a byproduct. They are not a waste material. They do not enter the environment because people engaged in some otherwise valuable pursuit find themselves with a noxious and potentially hazardous substance that needs to be disposed of. Farmers spread chemicals on their fields deliberately. They purchase them from companies that intend for them to be applied in the environment. No one wanted the waste materials that went into the Love Canal, but farmers and their suppliers do want agricultural pesticides, and they are willing to pay for them. This does not mean that the logic of externalities is irrelevant to agricultural chemicals, but, contrary to other types of industrial pollution, the moral evaluation of agricultural chemicals emphasizes the rationale for using them in the first place. This frames the moral evaluation as the comparison of benefits and risks.[7]

The Pesticide Question: Environment, Economics and Ethics, edited by David Pimentel (1925–2019) and Hugh Lehman, is probably the most frequently cited source on pesticide ethics. Pimentel was a Cornell University entomologist and one of most persistent and effective critics of pesticide use for the past fifty years. Lehman is a Canadian philosopher who, with Frank Hurnik (1932–2018) founded *The Journal of Agricultural and Environmental Ethics*. Even as Carson was bringing the effect of DDT on songbirds to public attention, entomologists were recognizing that pesticides kill beneficial insects as well as those that are damaging their crops. When beneficial insects, birds, bats, and other predators decline, the population of surviving pest species explodes. To make matters worse, the individuals having genetically based immunity or resistance to the effects of the chemical toxin dominate this new population. Further use of the pesticide is less effective. This means that the benefit-risk calculation for agricultural pesticide use must extend well beyond the comparison of crop protection benefits and the risk of bioaccumulation. Pesticides also have ecological effects.

Ecological effects are regional: the phenomenon of resistant pests is not confined to the farms of producers who overuse pesticides. Resistant pests will attack the crops of a farmer who does not use pesticide, and they can inflict serious damages if the beneficial insects that would have controlled these pests have been killed by his or her neighbor's spraying. Entomologists such as Pimentel have stressed the need for an ethical response that goes beyond any individual farmer's economic self-interest. There is value in a balanced insect ecology, and it is a form of value that has payoffs for producers. Pimentel and Lehman explain how a well-functioning insect ecology can be viewed as a service that beneficial insects perform, but it can also be seen as an intrinsic value. On this latter view, which is characteristic of a main theme in environmental ethics, a balance among the organisms occupying an ecosystem is valuable in itself, beyond any use that human beings might see in it.[8]

Pimentel and Lehman also show that agricultural chemical use is an assurance problem. Many topics in environmental ethics arise because individuals cannot achieve an objective working alone. For example, reduction of greenhouse gases entering the atmosphere cannot be achieved without widespread reduction in the use of fossil fuels. At the same time, individuals who make sacrifices to achieve this goal see their effort wasted when others do not cooperate. Unless cooperative effort is assured, it may be irrational to impose costs on yourself. Ethics provides the rationale that opposes this purely self-regarding calculation of costs and benefits. Viewed as an assurance problem, the ethics of agricultural chemical use differs from the ethics of industrial pollution, where victims had no role in releasing the pollutant into the environment in the first place. However, it is not clear that ethics is *enough* to motivate individuals to sacrifice their personal interests, especially when they doubt that others will do the same thing.[9]

Pimentel and Lehman's approach to the ethics of agricultural chemical use remains relevant, but it does not address the sense in which pollution can be understood as a moral concept. Kevin Elliott's more recent work on pollution (discussed later in the chapter) provides an entrée into the philosophy linking pollution to toxicity. Pimentel and Lehman implicitly accept a notion of pollution that is quite similar to Elliott's. However, there are additional philosophical dimensions to pollution in the food system that are overlooked by these approaches. People like my Aunt Orva (introduced in Chapter 5) are attentive to the residue that chemicals leave on their food, but recall that Orva is not especially worried about food safety. For such people, chemical residues are impurities that make food distasteful and possibly dangerous, but dangerous in any specific sense may not be foregrounded in Orva's thinking. Additives and adulterants added to food in processing are also pollutants in this sense. From Aunt Orva's perspective, they are simply not supposed to be there. Before returning to the moral themes that connect pollutants to damaged health, a little detour connecting pollution to the idea of purity will prove helpful.

Pollution and Purity

Any philosophical inquiry into pollution would be well advised to begin with a review of work by Mary Douglas (1921–2007). Working originally toward an anthropological theory of religion and cosmology, Douglas developed an analysis of pollution and environmental risk that she eventually generalized and extended to contemporary society. "In essence," she writes, "pollution ideas are adaptive and protective.

They protect a social system from unpalatable knowledge. They protect a system of ideas from challenge."[10] Douglas's work in *Purity and Danger: An Analysis of Concepts of Pollution and Taboo* examines cultures in which demarcating the sacred and the profane is important. In such cultures, says Douglas, dangerous consequences are expected to follow from neglecting the rituals that separate the sacred from the profane. Douglas then generalizes this observation: pollution ideas play an important functional role in safeguarding a system of thought categories. Categories delimit classes or collections of things and do so in a manner that takes on importance for social coordination and the performance of socially essential tasks. They are often dichotomous or at least mutually exclusive classifications. Categorical systems of interest to philosophers, anthropologists, and linguists play a fundamental role in "sense-making" or meaning-generating processes. As such, some system of categories or another is thought to be both emblematic and enabling for communication, thinking, and perhaps also for perception.

Douglas grounds her argument on the role of pollution ideas in the psychology of learning. Perception and language alike depend on patterns of cognitive organization that structure sensory inputs. Learning involves assimilating new inputs into these patterns, but, in normal circumstances, the learning process conserves the existing scheme. What a person already knows permits at most minor modifications and adaptations in the overall structure of their cognitive architecture, their worldview. Culture for Douglas consists in shared patterns of behavior and cognition that arrange goals, meanings, and values into a hierarchy. The system of classification is adaptive in a double sense. First, a culture's categories affect biological reproduction. Human populations—the bearers of culture—reproduce themselves with varying degrees of success. This is a fairly complex process, but extreme examples illustrate the basic point: some factions of the Christian sect known as Shakers adopted the cultural norm of celibacy as a spiritual practice. This obviously reduced the biological reproduction of the group and is a contributing factor in the small number of practicing Shakers today.[11] We can imagine cultural norms with even more catastrophic consequences: the Jonestown cult of the 1970s engaged in mass murder/suicide. The nature of their shared cultural norms ensured that this particular population of human beings would *not* be repopulated by succeeding generations.[12] Norms for using or preserving natural resources will have less immediate impact, but they can be equally deadly.[13]

. The second sense in which culture can be adaptive may be of more relevance to Douglas's theory of pollution beliefs. The pattern of categorizations that constitute transmissible cognitive organization can be said to "survive" as it is transferred from one generation to the next. Here, it is not people or human populations that survive, but their culture. Systems of categories can also spread from one human population to another. Both of these processes involve learning. There are many ways in which one system of categories might "out compete" alternative configurations. At the most basic level, they might encourage more successful utilization of the environmentally available food or energy resources. They might support more effective forms of warfare against other cultural groups. They might simply be easier to remember or communicate. Douglas is directing our attention to the advantage pollution beliefs confer in comparison to competing cultures that lack these particular cognitive structures. Pollution beliefs protect the system of categories from erosion, decay, and cognitive drift. They support a cultural practice within the group that resists displacement by competing ideas from other groups. They support clarity and decisiveness in circumstances that were otherwise be shrouded in ambiguity.[14]

As mentioned much earlier in this book, I view the establishment of categories through habituation as a form of performativity. Thinking or talking in a way that implies or invokes categories is like promising: it functions as a normalizing activity that creates expectations for future action. In fact, I take Douglas's evolutionary approach to cultural formation to be deeply characteristic of pragmatism, though I would not characterize Douglas herself as a pragmatist. In this respect, it is important to see how Douglas's way of understanding the evolutionary role of pollution ideas differs from that of theorists who stress biological selection. On a typically biological understanding of evolution, pollution beliefs would be evolutionary because populations holding these beliefs would have reproductive fitness: they would be more successful in passing their genes on to successive generations. However, in stressing learning theory, Douglas is drawing attention to the way that belief systems are *themselves* reproduced by communicative and cooperative practices. A group of human beings will almost certainly have a plurality of beliefs circulating at any given time. Douglas is telling us that belief systems containing robust pollution ideas will have an advantage in the sense of being more communicable, more stable, and more likely to be sustained by social practice. As such, they have a greater probability of being faithfully reproduced from one generation to the next. Significantly, pollution ideas may or may not have any intrinsic biological function; they may not lend direct support to practices that contribute to survival. However, when they are conjoined (even by chance) with habits, practices, and ideational forms that do confer advantages, they help *those* cultural institutions pass from one generation to the next.

Given this epistemological framing, we can examine how Douglas thinks that these belief systems actually work. On the one hand, pollution is categorically opposed to purity. The purity of a sacred or sacrosanct domain is compromised by admixture or by contact with the secular or profane. Within religious practice, this form of pollution is not primarily an ethical concept. Among ancient Hebrew tribes the rites of purification are enacted in circumstances without regard to intention or volition. That means that one does not engage in a purifying ritual because one has knowingly or intentionally violated a moral or religious principle (e.g., willfully done something sinful). Ritual purification is thus not an act of expiation or reparation for violation of a moral code. Indeed, impurities can arise in connection with acts that are meritorious. Nonetheless, a person in a state of impurity must avoid contact with sacred objects or places. Once polluted, a person must undergo the restorative ritual before undertaking a sacrament.[15]

At the same time Douglas writes, "We would expect to find that the pollution beliefs of a culture are related to its moral values, since these form part of the structure of ideas for which pollution behavior is a protective device."[16] In other words, even if there is no logical or intrinsic connection between purification rituals and moral offenses, the protection that pollution beliefs afford against dissipation and decay assures the continuity of moral codes. What is more, some aspects of a moral code depend more heavily on the shelter provided by pollution beliefs than others. Moral offenses that prompt rapid and unpleasant punishment from other members of one's social group are less likely to need sanction from pollution beliefs than are those of a more ambiguous nature. Importantly, actions or events that appear to challenge or threaten the established moral order *without* any obvious or immediate adverse impact are precisely those that are most in need of extra sanctions. Pollution beliefs will prevent a lengthy period of uncertainty, ambiguity, and vagueness about what should be done or what kind of response is appropriate. This picture leads Douglas to conclude, "Pollution beliefs certainly derive from rational activity, from the process of classifying and ordering experience. They are, however, not produced by strictly rational or even conscious process but rather as a spontaneous by-product of these processes."[17]

This overall pattern is maintained when pollution beliefs are considered outside of a strictly religious context. Again, culture is (at least in part) a system of categorical distinctions. Douglas showed how categorical classification is especially evident with respect to food. Distinct cultures develop classification schemes that place potentially edible plants and animals into nested categories. The way in which food categories are nested within one another determines first whether a given substance is food or non-food. They go on to govern which foods are to be eaten in combination, at particular occasions, or during specific times of the day. Some of these practices may regulate the cultural group's use of natural resources and in this way play a role in securing the group's continuing ability to occupy a particular ecological niche.[18] More generally, the categorical classifications that make up the tacit knowledge of any cultural group facilitate everyday engagements and transactions. The system of categories enables communication and the coordination of behavior. Douglas's point in the above quote is that there is great deal of arbitrariness in the way that any given system of categories is constructed. Nevertheless, once a particular set of categories becomes operative within a social group, the coordination enabled by those categories provides a powerful rationale for maintaining them.

Even if the categories themselves have no rational basis, retaining practices based on categorical classifications (and thus the classifications themselves) is at some level functionally imperative for the continued social effectiveness and even survival of the cultural group. The question of which categories are critical may not be easy to answer, but the point crucial to Douglas's analysis of pollution is simple: the ensemble of classificatory categories enables social practice for any cultural group. It is precisely the lack of immediate feedback that makes a violation of any particular categorical classification more likely to require the additional symbolic apparatus of purity and pollution. In such instances, the potential threat to the overall system of classifying and ordering experience must be countered. The rational or ethical basis for belief that a particular form of activity or contact constitutes pollution does not reside either in the evidence for risk or even in the coherence or justifiability of categories themselves. Rather it lies in society's need to avoid constant revision, negotiation, and upheaval in a system of categories that is working serviceably well.

Although Douglas's theory of pollution was developed as an account of ritualized religious practice, it was clear at the outset that it is applicable to numerous secular aspects of contemporary culture. For example, dogs and cats are not classified as food within European cultures despite widespread recognition that flesh from these species is edible and indeed eaten in some Asian and Native American cultures. Clearly, contamination of a food product with dog or cat would be regarded as an impurity and a grave offense by the vast majority of Americans and Europeans. In fact, it violates U.S. law. However, there is no scientific basis to regard such contamination as a threat to public health, nor is there a scientific basis for the underlying categorical judgment that dogs and cats are not food. I have often enjoyed taunting conversation partners who proposed that the U.S. system for regulating food safety is "totally objective" and free of value judgments with the prospect of the "Real Dog Hot-dog." Needless to say, real dog hot-dogs are not even a remote possibility in the U.S. food system, but the rationale for this resides primarily in the way that our categorization of edible species meshes with countless other social practices. These include the keeping of companion species, expectations about merchantability of foods, and sheer prejudice. Our food beliefs derive from centuries of everyday practice extending back to the Western European cultures that are now pervasive throughout North America. Even if the traditional culture of Native Americans and many immigrant communities would have accepted that dogs *can* be food, the overwhelming majority of Americans (as well as Western Europeans) regard the suggestion with disgust.[19]

I hope readers are relating these ideas to the concerns of my fictional Aunt Orva. Yet, as a philosopher, I am compelled to ask whether there are any conceivable circumstances under which this largely arational categorization of edible species might be subjected to revision. The answer to this question is yes, but the circumstances under which revision might actually occur are complex. Diets are constantly changing. Americans are eating a wide variety of foods that were totally unknown in Midwestern households of my youth. They include sushi, pesto, acai, quinoa, and totally synthetic foods like plant-based meat substitutes. Chapter 2 discusses how these late 20th-century changes in diet arose in connection with a food movement. It is worth emphasizing that such changes have nothing to do with a rational or critical reevaluation of my grandmother's categorical belief that uncooked fish is not edible. Nevertheless, categorical beliefs sometimes do undergo revision through critique, debate, and the consideration of scientifically generated and validated evidence.

For example, racial and gender ideas supporting white supremacy and patriarchy were targeted by critics. Change in the institutions that encode and reproduce these ideas has been slow, but the moral debate has derived support from scientific studies that undercut faulty presumptions about the biological underpinnings of these ideas. Perhaps there needs to be something important at stake in order for rational argument to dislodge a system of categories. If so, the reason why it is difficult to imagine something that would shake our view that dogs and cats are not meat animals is simply that it is also difficult to imagine the circumstances in which something important would be accomplished by changing it. There is growing support for integrating insects into the Western diet, for example, rationalized by considering the nutritional and environmental benefits.[20] This is all entirely consistent with Douglas's claim that the function of pollution ideas is to guard a system of categories against instability, drift, and changes of meaning that introduce needless havoc and disruption in daily life.

Pollution and Environmental Science

In contrast to Douglas's subtle and convoluted theory of pollution, Kevin Elliott's article "Pollution" for the *Encyclopedia of Environmental Ethics and Philosophy* states that pollution is simply the release of harmful substances into the environment.[21] Elliott's approach to pollution combines ethics and science at a fundamental level. The role of ethics is to stipulate and, if necessary, defend a notion of harm, while the role of science is to determine the potential causes of harm as well as the circumstances in which harm is likely to materialize. In full-blown risk assessment, this determination can involve the detailed analysis of conditions in which individuals are exposed to the potential for harm, including the development of statistical or probabilistic measures that reflect the influence of intervening variables. Elliott's work on chemical hormesis illuminates additional value judgments interwoven in the methods and assumptions needed to move from data to a projection of risk. In particular, Elliott notes that evidence is unable to resolve an ongoing controversy over whether hormesis—the shift from beneficial to toxic effects as exposure varies—should be regarded as the default profile for chemical risk or whether it is a rare phenomenon.[22]

While Elliott's approach to pollution appears to provide a more straightforwardly rationalistic alternative to Douglas's, some qualifications need to be noted. First, we should recognize that Elliott's definition operates within some contextualizing assumptions that are not explicitly stated. Someone who fires a bullet from a speeding vehicle in the course of a drive-by shooting releases a potentially harmful substance into the environment, yet it seems clear that Elliott does not intend to include such acts under his account of pollution. Perhaps there is a presumption that release into the environment implies some minimal degree of spatial diffusion. Acts intended to cause harm or acts causing proximate, immediate, and targeted harm are more readily classified in alternative terms. It is not immediately clear that the contextualizing assumptions about what does and does not count as pollution in Elliott's sense can be specified in terms of necessary and sufficient conditions. The more general point to note is this: while Elliott's approach may appear to state what is important about some paradigmatic cases of pollution, he does not even attempt to state the considerations or qualifications that influence our collective sense of what counts as a paradigm case. Elliott is relying on a sense-making set of categories that support the mutual expectations of environmental scientists. Nevertheless, the fact that not *all* cases of releasing a harmful substance into the environment count as pollution seems beyond dispute.

Second, Elliott explicitly states that classifying a given act under the category of pollution is a normative judgment. This judgment identifies the *harm* done by the act. Viewed from a value-free perspective, injury and death are just events. They become morally significant when viewed as harms. Elliott's approach is open to the possibility that harms can be of multiple kinds and that there might be significant disagreement about whether to regard a given state of affairs as constituting harm. The cases considered in Elliott's book tend to involve non-controversial forms of mortality and morbidity among human beings. Yet economic loss might also constitute a form of harm, as would emotional damage experienced as the result of harm to friends and family and even harm suffered in response to insults to one's aesthetic sensibilities. Furthermore, it is entirely possible to endorse harm to non-human species or potentially even to non-living entities such as ecosystems or breeding populations. Although these putative harms are disputed, they are a prime subject matter for debates in environmental philosophy. If one turns to the practice of environmental scientists, mortality and morbidity among non-human species are routinely classified as harmful impacts of pollution. Even plants can be harmed in these classifications.[23] The categories deployed to define harm in the environmental sciences do not require sentience, much less reflective self-awareness.

Although the value judgments determining the scope of harms attributable to pollution in Elliott's approach are not limited to impacts on human health, they may be implicitly limited to the class of phenomena studied by biologically trained environmental scientists. I say "may be" because the classifications being deployed in environmental science as well as in common speech are vague and constantly changing. Suppose I own a piece of land, and my neighbor builds a concentrated animal feeding operation (CAFO) for pig production on his property. The stink (air pollution) and the potential for runoff from his manure pits (water pollution) reduce the value of my land. Many people would be willing to classify the economic loss I suffer as a harm and would see the introduction of air- and water-borne pollutants into the environment as the source of this harm. In short, these economic losses qualify under Elliott's definition. However, if my neighbor opens a massage parlor offering sexual services, I may suffer a similar loss in the value of my property. I do not think that we would see the massage parlor as a form of pollution. At a minimum, it seems unlikely that an economist studying the impact of a sex business on land value would be encouraged to publish in an environmental science outlet. Furthermore, if this massage parlor *were* described as pollution, as it well might be among people complaining to the county zoning authority, I think both speaker and hearer would understand this description as a metaphorical use of the word *pollution*. This suggests that the everyday grammar of pollution reflects the biologically oriented conventions of the environmental sciences. At the same time, it has become routine to speak of noise or light pollution in urban areas even in the absence of any documented impact on health. These usages do not seem metaphorical.

Further inquiry on these qualifying comments might plunge Elliott's approach into an extended philosophical controversy. They illustrate how usage of the word *pollution* exhibits flexibility and contextual dependency, as well as the possibility that it may be undergoing active shifts in its core meaning within ordinary language. Nevertheless, one cannot deny the appealing directness and simplicity of Elliott's approach when compared to Douglas. To the extent that agricultural chemicals or CAFOs would be the target of toxicologists, ecologists, or public health scientists, release of harmful substances in the environment is what they mean. The chief qualification is that the route entering the environment must involve biological mechanisms, or the harmful impacts must themselves be biological in nature. With this framework in mind, we can consider a class of potential pollutants that have been especially controversial in recent decades: genes.

Genetic Pollution and the Environmental Risks of GMOs

As with many issues in food ethics, the case of genetically engineered food crops or animals provides a case study that reveals important philosophical dimensions. Recall that the acronym "GMO" now functions as a purely conventional indicator for certain products of gene technology.[24] Like most classificatory nouns in ordinary language, it is vague. In my experience, the expression is not used in connection with microorganisms that have been genetically transformed to produce drugs. It is unclear if it implies transgenesis, or movement of a genetic construct from one species to another. On the one hand, there are still scientists who object to its use on the ground that "genetically modified" does not imply a meaningful distinction in the context of foods. On the other hand, the expression is handy and is in use by people who are fully cognizant of its limitations. There is probably a third hand as well: this usage may be fading away. I may already be out of touch in using it.

These observations about the meaning of the acronym testify to the way that GMOs are a boundary-crossing technology. The very idea of a GMO challenges fundamental cultural categories. The claim is often that moving genes from one species to another threatens implicit notions of purity and, by extension, the system of classification that undergirds a fair portion of social life.[25] Although boundary-crossing[26] evokes Douglas's view on purity and pollution, the thesis explains too much in the present context. Not only does it provide little reason to expect the widely noted difference in the public reception of so-called red (e.g., medical) and green (e.g., agricultural) biotechnology,[27] but it is also insensitive to the way that pollution ideas stress something that is happening in the environment. In fact, Douglas's original treatment of pollution shares one important feature with Elliott's. Both understand pollution as something that spreads through a mechanism of contagion or physical contact. Given contemporary theories of contagious disease, it may seem inaccurate to describe the transport of chemical contaminants through soil, water, or air as a form of contagion, but this notion of the potential for invasive movement into a clean, pure, or uncontaminated space is a component of pollution ideas that is especially germane in the present context. In short, it is important to distinguish the problem of genetic pollution from metaphoric, symbolic, and conceptual challenges to categorical stability.

Making such a distinction qualifies the sense in which an act can be coded as pollution in either Douglas's or Elliott's sense. Proposals to introduce human

genes into non-human animal species or to clone food animals trouble categorical classifications and provoke fear or disgust.[28] Nevertheless, it is not
until there is both physical contact and uncontrolled movement through the
environment that pollution occurs in the literal sense. My analysis of genetic
pollution will emphasize forms of contamination that operate through some
mechanism of contact, contagion, or spread, but this may not capture what is
most threatening about gene technology. The mere idea of gene transfer may
threaten conceptual categories. What is more, anything that merely *threatens*
conceptual categories may have already caused harm in a purely symbolic
or metaphorical sense.[29] As important as such considerations might be in
a different context, in this chapter, I am interested in pollution beliefs that
envision events transpiring in real physical space. With this important qualification in mind, it is possible to examine how each of these two contrasting
accounts of pollution makes an appearance in the consideration of genetically modified crops.

It is Elliott's theory of pollution that is followed in scientific studies. Reports
from the U.S. National Research Council (NRC) use a model common to
many environmental risk assessments. First, they identify forms of harm that
might occur as a result of genetic constructs moving through the environment. Then they use a variety of data sources to estimate the probability that
such harm will actually materialize. In early studies, the primary focus was
on antibiotic-resistant markers. The primary hazard of interest was increased
virulence of harmful bacteria owing to the transfer of resistance.[30] In the late
1990s, a new round of studies and committees were convened to examine
the potential for other types of environmental hazard. These include the potential for conventional types of impact associated with the use of toxins for
pest control, including the potential for increased resistance to toxins in pest
populations, impacts on non-target species that could trigger changes in the
composition of species, and other effects on ecosystem services. Studies on
the movement of genes into wild relatives investigated the possibility of un-
specific and unanticipated types of change in the genetic diversity of wild
types and land races, as well as broader shifts in the ecological relationship
between agriculture and critical ecological functions. In addition, studies
began to consider the way that GMOs would alter land use and the deployment of other technologies, especially chemicals, indirectly causing impact
through changes in practices not specific to GMOs themselves. Although
the reports noted a few case studies where existing or idealized standards
had not been met, the general drift of these reports is that the regulatory

framework was working reasonably well. In effect, they concluded that no pollution from GMOs has in fact occurred.[31]

The implications of the Douglas and Elliott views of pollution for genetic constructs can be further illustrated by considering three cases from the early era of GMOs: Monarch butterflies, the StarLink fiasco, and the dispute over transgenic maize in Mexico. The first case concerns the publication of a brief note indicating that pollen from Bt corn applied to milkweed was harmful to the larvae of *Danaus plexippus*, the charismatic butterfly known for its bright orange color and its perplexing migrations between the United States and Mexico.[32] As reviewed by May Berenbaum, the reaction in the scientific community differed dramatically from that of the broader public. Scientists were critical of the study's methods and followed-up with more detailed studies which indicated that, though Bt pollen is (unsurprisingly) toxic to Monarch larvae, the probability of significant exposure to such pollen among natural populations of Monarchs is very small. Berenbaum cites a number of incidents to document her claim that the public reacted to press coverage of the *Nature* article by presuming harm to butterflies had already happened.[33] If true, Bt pollen would have unambiguously qualified as an environmental pollutant. Although studies refuting alleged risks to Monarch butterflies were widely reported in the early morning editions of American newspapers on September 11, 2001, other events of the day ensured that these reports had little resonance in the public psyche.

In the StarLink case, a version of the Bt protein that had been approved for limited use in animal feeds was discovered in a large number of food products in 2000. The discovery led to a mandatory recall of corn and corn products containing the Cry9C version of the protein. Scientific analysis emphasized the likelihood that Bt proteins could be allergenic when consumed by humans,[34] as well as revisiting risk categories already discussed above.[35] However, the vast majority of the literature generated in the wake of the StarLink controversy emphasized the economic losses both to Aventis and to the global farm economy. The latter were estimated by some sources to exceed $1 billion.[36] Significantly, the category of economic loss was entirely absent from the NRC studies discussed above. My own recollection of the incident is that it was the first time I began to hear the phrase "genetic pollution" being used with any frequency by critics of GMOs and large-scale agriculture. The StarLink case was, for some at least, not only indisputable proof that genetic pollution was possible, but also evidence that it had already occurred.

The case of Bt maize in Mexico is exceedingly complex and the actual facts of the case remain in dispute. Like the Monarch butterfly episode, it began with the publication of a short article in *Nature*, an important scientific journal. This time the article alleged that genetic constructs from Bt maize had introgressed into land races being grown by Mexican farmers.[37] The results reported in the article were contested on the ground that the analysis was flawed by inappropriate methods. Subsequent studies found no transgenes in Mexican land races.[38] Nevertheless, the potential for mixture of artificially introduced nucleotide sequences into land races and wild types was painted vividly. However, there was and remains little agreement on the *harm* associated with such an occurrence. Some authors take it for granted that introgression into land races constitutes a harmful event and go on to speculate on possible modes of remediation.[39] Others note that the hazard is at least contingent on both the likelihood that introgression will occur and on the effect that the resulting phenotype will have on the agronomic performance of land races or the ecological impact on wild relatives.[40]

In the Monarch butterfly case, the effects described by the Cornell University group clearly would qualify Bt pollen as a pollutant on Elliott's criteria but for the fact that, once exposure mechanisms were studied, the scientific community concluded that environmental release of Bt pollen would have little impact on Monarchs. The StarLink case is similar in that allergic responses clearly would qualify the Cry9C varieties of corn as a pollutant, if in fact the evidence to support a causal link between exposure and allergy were forthcoming. Introgression of Bt transgenes into Mexican land race maize is more interesting from a philosophical perspective because, by some criteria, no actual harm ensues even when the land races hybridize with Bt varieties. However, both StarLink and the Mexican case raise the specter of non-biological harms. The economic losses were the main documented impact in the StarLink episode, while Mexican farmers feared that, owing to the illegality of growing genetically engineered crops in Mexico, the discovery of transgenes would be used as a pretext for confiscation of their crops or even land titles. Significantly, however, the hazard of economic loss does not jibe easily with Elliott's analysis of pollution. Although there can be little dispute that economic losses are a form of harm and, as such, can be readily included under the umbrella of risk analysis, Elliott's examples of harm all involve chemical and biological causality. Would people who see the StarLink and Mexican maize cases as instances of genetic pollution have a leg to stand on?

Genetic Pollution as a Cultural Construct

Donald Bruce discusses the problems associated with contamination due to the spread of genes from genetically engineered plants in a 2003 paper. Citing the Mexican case as an example, Bruce analyzes the problem as a conflict between the rights of conventional farmers, who may be growing GMOs, and organic farmers. Organic certification rules banning the use of GMOs determine organic farmers' opportunities for profit. Bruce also notes that the term *genetic pollution* may "beg the question" (his phrase) with respect to the safety of GMOs.[41] Bruce is saying that using the word *pollution* to describe contamination of organic crops assumes precisely what needs to be proved. However, the sheer implicitness of the presumption links it to Douglas's notion of pollution. Douglas's model of cognition and social learning suggests that classification systems emerge in the habitual practice of groups, including but not limited to linguistic practice. Some aspects of social intercourse move to the forefront of consciousness and become the at-issue subject matter of negotiation and debate; others lie conveniently in the background, relying largely on repetitive and unspoken reinforcement in one social context after another. Eventually, the experience of *not* being called upon to justify or defend the cognitive commitments implied by these patterns of interactions becomes reflected in the formation of what philosopher Wilfrid Sellars (1912–1989) calls "we-intentions." I will not discuss the philosophical literature on we-intentions here, offering instead a summary of what I like about Sellars's approach.

For Sellars, we-intentions are patterns of thought or linguistic practice, and, in Sellars's philosophy, there is little difference between the two. They are evident in patterns of conversation where the pronoun "we" becomes the subject of sentences formulated in the optative mood. The optative mood expresses a wish or hope. Sellars's example is "Would that Jones were here!" The person who makes such a statement expresses the wish that Jones (whoever that is) were present, but Sellars was interested in a subclass of sentences in the optative mood where something more than the expression of a personal intent or hope is involved.[42] Statements like "Long live the king!" or "Live long and prosper" (the Vulcan greeting from the Star Trek franchise) are optative, but they are also performative: they function to form a discursive community. If I sigh and utter, "Long live the King!" in a context where others nod in agreement, shared expectations energize the normative aspirations of the statement. Those who call for further explanation set themselves apart. Perhaps they do not understand a critical function of such statements, which has more to do with solidarity than with expressing an individual's wish or hope. However, the "we hope (or wish) that . . ." in these examples is repressed; it is wholly implicit. As an unstated implication, the collective and performative dimension of the intention assumes a power that continues to mystify the rationalistically minded among us.

Sellars explains this aspect of collective intentionality with the example of the Whooping Crane Society. Whooping cranes are one of the most iconic endangered species, with the total population having dropped to fewer than twenty individuals at one point. Sellars's Whooping Crane Society is a fictional group where people are inclined to sigh and say "Would that whooping cranes be saved!" Importantly, to challenge this aspiration is to mark oneself as outside the group, the discursive community in which such sentences are spoken. Claims that challenge the implicit set of beliefs and cognitive commitments operating in the background are, above all else, signaling that a person does not regard themselves as part of the "we" that is implied when said commitments are accepted without explanation. Indeed, as standardly accepted, these commitments are *not* brought into the forefront of consciousness. To ask, "What's so great about whooping cranes?" might be reasonable in some settings, but within the Whooping Crane Society, it merely smudges one's social identity.[43] To situate oneself outside the "we," outside the cultural or linguistic community, can be a risky practice in and of itself. Ever since the pioneering work of George Herbert Mead (1863–1931) it has been recognized that the sheer need for belonging creates incentives for conforming to such group practices, especially when nothing fundamental to a given individual's interests or identity is a stake in doing so.[44] Although I will not belabor the point, I hope that readers will see the connection between this discussion of we-intentions and the earlier reference to discourses of social control.

To reiterate a theme from Douglas's work on pollution, then, the association of biological risks with the word "pollution" and the dissociation of economic losses from biological harms needs no stronger justification than the fact that linguistic or cultural communities follow such patterns habitually. It need not, in other words, be a rationally justifiable practice, and indeed some common set of implicit meanings must typically be in place in order to *apply* criteria of rationality. Importantly, these implicit meanings must be playing such a fundamental role that they are beyond challenge. To ask *why* economic harms do not count as a basis for pollution sets you outside the community that follows this practice. The question "Why?" might be *intended* as substantive, as initiating an inquiry or asking for reasons. Nevertheless, simply asking the question puts one outside the borders of environmental science as it is currently practiced. It is likely to be perceived as a challenge to the authority of science.

Douglas's early work on pollution claims that modern science inoculates certain groups against reactive defense measures taken in support of arbitrary classifications. Galileo Galilei (1564–1642) was sanctioned by Pope Urban VIII (1568–1644) because his scientific findings appeared to challenge the authority of the Roman Catholic Church. Douglas initially thought that liberal democracies had developed cultural formations that place science in a protected sphere, protecting scientists from political, religious, and other "non-scientific" reprisals. Science, on this view, is an institutionalized practice of criticism in which categorical distinctions can be subjected to deliberative review and selectively discarded. By the time she published her influential article "Environments at Risk," in 1975, Douglas had abandoned this thought. She observed the fact of disagreement among scientists and concluded that wider society is thrown back on the same patterns of implicit meaning and cultural group identity that she had observed in primitive religion.[45]

One could argue for an even stronger version of this view: patterns of cognitive commitment operate within the sciences themselves. Thus, one would not be surprised to find that environmental scientists who study pollution develop a linguistic practice in which economic outcomes are excluded from the universe of discourse. This might simply be because economic outcomes never come up in their discourse on pollution and environmental risk (and such outcomes *would not* come up given the training, domain of expertise, and problem set with which environmental scientists are normally occupied). Furthermore, hiring and publication practices are an implicit feature of environmental scientists' social epistemology. They institutionalize these patterns in academic and research organizations. Discipline-based biases are also integrated into laws and regulations through policies that populate government and civil society organizations with people bearing specific academic credentials. When spheres of technical expertise order a discrete normative stance toward a specific class of outcomes (e.g., biological but not economic harms), an implicit practice of characterizing pollution as distinctly biological becomes habitual. Those who would challenge this practice simply identify themselves as outsiders, as people who are not really in the know. Such patterns of reinforcement would be particularly influential in the sciences, where "being in the know" is a front-of-mind criterion for social status. By social status, I mean eligibility for employment on college faculties or publication of one's work. In short, the pattern of usage that implicitly excludes economic harms from pollution beliefs is as much a cultural construct *within* environmental science as alternative beliefs are outside of it.

Now I hasten to add that, as a practicing pragmatist, I do not view this result as plunging science into a pernicious form of relativism. It is always possible to make an implicit practice the focus of an explicit critical discussion and wind up concluding that continuing the practice is warranted; that is what is implied by fallibilism. What makes one a pragmatist as distinct from a dogmatist is that one must critically examine and debate the implicit practice before arriving at such a conclusion. However, the ability to collectively examine and debate also implies some shared linguistic and cognitive commitments. This is why philosophers such as John Dewey and Charles Sanders Peirce rejected the Cartesian attempt to doubt everything and then rebuild science on secure foundations. One can question any given belief, explicit or implicit, but one cannot question everything all at once. The pertinent point in the present context is that critical discourse and debate will be effective within the cultural community implied by the linguistic and cognitive commitments shared by pragmatists (whether they label themselves as such or not). Nevertheless, this same critical discourse will be interpreted as an attack on the collective intentions crucial for group solidarity among those who do not share the pragmatists' commitment to fallibility.

So Tell Me, Are Genes Pollutants?

A series of philosophical points follow with respect to genetic pollution. First, the history recounted at the beginning of the chapter matters. DDT, the Love Canal, and other episodes of chemical contamination are episodes that reinforce the way we understand pollution today. One might say that people just got in the habit of thinking that unseen substances can move through the environment in mysterious ways. These substances cause both familiar forms of havoc (death and disease) and hitherto unimagined calamities (loss of songbirds and biodiversity or climate change). However, when I talk about the way *we* understand pollution, I mean to be signaling the way that this history has functioned to establish discursive communities around specific normative commitments. In line with what I have already said, these commitments are closely aligned with each community's basic system of conceptual categories. They are so closely aligned that even asking questions about them marks the inquirer as an outsider. Outsiders may or may not be perceived as a threat, but the very act of questioning indicates that they do not really speak the community language. At the same time, this history supports an idea of pollution that allows people who understand it in terms of contamination and purity to have at least limited ability to converse with another community of people who understand it in terms of exposures that are probabilistically correlated with biologically classifiable forms of harm. When the habits of these two communities are extended to gene technology, the conversation breaks down.

The next point bears on whether we should continue the implicit practice of excluding economic and possibly other outcomes from the way that we think about risks and pollution from GMOs. Notice that now my use of the word "we" implicitly places me inside the community of environmental scientists and their institutional allies. One normally persuasive justification we in the environmental science community have for continuing our practice is that it has served us well enough in the past. We had no trouble communicating with economists who analyzed the StarLink case. However, to the extent that this practice divides us from those who raise questions about genetic pollution, to continue with our pattern abandons any hope of actually engaging our critics in debate. We rely solely on the status and power accorded to our community in virtue of the way that *our* practices are respected and determinative of legal and regulatory codes and theirs are not. In stronger words, we are content to *force* other people to modify their behavior in order to preserve our linguistic conventions. I have argued at length in other contexts against this kind of reliance on force and power, and I have claimed that it is contrary to norms that characterize science itself.[46] If we scientists wish to expand our community and engage others, we would be wise to soften a cognitive commitment whose warrant resides primarily in the fact that it makes sense to us.

The final and most difficult point concerns the extension of this cognitive model to groups who readily interpret events such as the StarLink and Mexican episodes (and possibly also Monarch butterflies) in terms of genetic pollution. Douglas originally quoted Lord Chesterfield's[47] phrase "matter out of place" in her account of pollution. This is what I would call the "beer can in the woods" view of pollution. I take this image to crystallize what many

Americans associate with the idea of environmental pollution. While non-Americans may be less inclined to carry canned beer into the woods in the first place, the basic point can be extrapolated globally. Quite a few beer cans can accumulate in the woods before they constitute a true biological hazard, yet the wilderness tradition in America combines with an aesthetic of tidiness to reinforce a common belief that they do not belong there. The same traditions support an implicit belief that agriculture is "outside" the environment, or at least outside the environment that needs protection. The ability to track nucleotide sequences brings the blurry biological boundary between nature and agriculture into view. Agricultural crops and wild relatives have always engaged in forms of promiscuity, but it is only with the technological ability to sequence DNA that this becomes something that people can detect. What is more, gene movement is most clearly and unambiguously tractable for transgenes whose sequence has been catalogued and registered for the purpose of protecting intellectual property. Molecular biology makes the migration of genes as visible as a beer can in the woods. Tying this visibility to sequences of human origin, the biotech industry effectively created the category of genetic pollution.

Of course, it is doubtful that the idea of genetic pollution has enough resonance to become an important cognitive category on this basis alone. The salience of genetic pollution arguably follows from many sources. Rachel Carson's exposure of *chemical* pollution in agriculture linked food safety with impact on wildlife, establishing pollution as a cognitive construct that can be plausibly extended to genes. Indeed, biotechnology companies have been mindful of such risks from the start.[48] The way that GMOs have been able to unite a number of hitherto unrelated interests and social causes builds on this platform. Two groups with shared we-intentions may be especially important. First, there are the environmentalists. The possibility of environmental harm has some support within the scientific community itself. Second, the cadre of farmers and food industry firms who have something to gain by keeping non-GM crops isolated form another discursive community. I want to be clear: this is not just (or even primarily) industrial farmers.

The creation of the organic standard in the United States and the demand for non-GM crops and food products in Europe, Japan, and elsewhere are potential markets for a number of American farmers and grain companies. Their economic opportunity depends on a sometimes difficult to implement system for separating GMO from non-GMO. The non-GMO stream is placed at risk of contamination by the presence of GMOs anywhere in the vicinity or equipment used to transport crops. One might add economic and legal risks associated with prosecution of farmers, seed cleaners, and others who are alleged to have violated the intellectual property rights of the biotech companies.[49] The claim that intellectual property rights could be used to intentionally bankrupt farmers in order to prosecute land grabs continues to surface in debates over GMOs.[50] In short, we have one discursive community that has coalesced around environmental risk and another discursive community that coalesced around segregation of GMOs, primarily for economic reasons.

People like my Aunt Orva, who tend to think that human-introduced nucleotide sequences are simply forms of graffiti or dirt, don't fit into either of these groups. However, both of these groups have reasons to find common ground with Orva. The potential for allying economic interests to others' distaste opens the door for a discourse of social control. The ante is raised even further when biological hazards relating to biodiversity, extinction of characteristic megafauna, or allergenicity are added to the mix, and it hardly matters that these hazards are characterized as uncertain and tenuously linked to transgenes. Such contexts create the climate for full-blown pollution ideas to flourish. What is more, intimations that these associations are mere contingencies (intimations such as I am making now) threaten patterns of practice that bind this loose community of activists into a "we." Such intimations demonstrate that one is not part of the community more than they serve to question the underlying warrant for the pollution beliefs. It is also important to note that these observations on the discourse of genetic pollution have brought us (and now I mean my readers and me) back to the discussion of inquiry, persuasion, and social control mentioned way back in the Introduction.

Now, at this juncture, I could write that it would be possible to examine the implicit cognitive commitments that support such beliefs and wind up concluding that continuing the practice is warranted. Those of us (e.g., my readers and me) who choose to pursue that inquiry could conclude that this way of talking binds us into an important political community that has not only served us well so far, but that has the prospect of securing important environmental and social justice goals in the future. However, in doing that, I might cease to be identifying with environmental scientists and *their* allies. I would be partnering with a community that currently sees itself as excluded from the discourse patterns of the socially empowered environmental science community. Although environmental scientists may not think of themselves as all that powerful, they have successfully united the authority of science and the power of administrative law, at least in certain domains.

There is a flipside. Within the community of activists, any hint that the substantive risks might *not* turn out to be validated is disloyalty. Examining the meaning of pollution as I have done in this chapter might *itself* be viewed as disloyalty. It is not at all clear to me that I can have it both ways, however much I quite sincerely might wish to do so. It is this kind of observation that led Douglas into the cultural theory of risk that characterized her later work. One finds oneself situated in one community or another, and while as an analyst one can comment on the way that cultural commitments around pollution beliefs put groups at odds, when the politics actually get rolling it is very hard to occupy a neutral position.[51]

As a philosopher, I say that however much pro- and anti-GM communities stand in opposition to one another with respect to their political goals, the cognitive commitments that lead to and warrant one set of pollution ideas are not, in fact, logically incompatible with the cognitive commitments that lead to (and warrant) competing conceptualizations of risk. There are paths not taken that could reconcile these positions. It is politically difficult to acknowledge this because doing so involves putting oneself in the uncomfortable position of challenging implicit meanings among both communities. Back in the Chapter 1 to this book, Carl Schmidt said that in politics "the friend of my enemy is my enemy." If he is right, the potential for democratic engagement on pollution issues becomes quite limited. Where this political principle is in force, the pragmatist has few friends. My personal observation (unsupported by any data beyond my life experience) is that opposition to gene technology does function as a we-intention among food movement activists. Raising any sort of question about the validity of such opposition marks one as an outsider, an enemy to the food movement.

Pollution, Power, and Philosophy:
A Concluding Soliloquy

Once again, we end by observing that there is more to say but too little time and space to say it. There is much to be gained politically and ethically by maintaining a broadly scientific approach to pollution, which is to say, Elliott's approach rather than Douglas's. Yet, even saying this calls on implicit conventions of speech with normative implications. Economists and anthropologists are every bit as scientific as ecologists, toxicologists, or other environmental scientists, so why are we justified in identifying the latter group's we-intentions with the "broadly scientific approach"? The short answer to this question is that this just how "we" talk. The long answer has to probe the formation of a "we" that talks this way. Yet I have already crossed that hazy line I drew between an overly technical conversation among specialists and the public discourse where philosophical ethics can have some impact.

It *is* important to have some sense of how "we" come to talk in one way rather than another because that is the best way to raise ethical questions about whether this is who "we" want to be. I keep putting the word "we" in quotes to highlight the way that patterns of speaking are the basis of discursive communities. As a member of the community, talking about what we think or do comes pretty naturally. Yet surely everyone has had the experience of talking with someone and then being brought up short when your conversation partner says something that just doesn't jibe with the taken-for-granted background of daily life. Those are the moments when the boundaries of our own discursive community become visible. Usually, we pass over these moments in awkward silence, but philosophy involves unpacking community-forming we-intentions. It can require a seemingly endless series of meta moves—talking about the conversation, then talking about talking about the conversation, and so on. The philosophical series may end in enlightenment, but it may not.

The long answer is worth pursuing. The wistful tone of the preceding paragraph is not meant to indicate the futility of further inquiry. Elliot's approach to pollution has enabled both governmental and non-governmental activities that have improved public health as well as protected habitats for endangered flora and fauna. A conceptualization of pollution emphasizing hazards to health is also important for environmental justice. Definitions of environmental injustice emphasize how groups defined by race and ethnicity experience higher rates of exposure to toxic substances and negative health outcomes.[52] At the same time, a narrowed understanding of pollution may reinforce the tendency to ignore racial exclusion and economic inequality as factors that skew the distribution of negative health outcomes.[53] The pragmatists hope that a more extended examination of these practical implications could inform our judgment about the wisdom of the implicit commitments that underlie Elliott's approach. Douglas's analysis is helpful in its ability to make us more cognizant of these commitments.

Finally, this philosophical approach to pollution may not be consistent with a social movement's emphasis on action in the short term. Protecting the solidarity that gives a social movement its punch may be much more important. This thought takes us from social control back to Socrates' conversation with friends down at the Piraeus. It may be necessary to carve out a discursive space specifically designed to permit challenges to the collective intentions that undergird solidarity in the political sphere. That is, of course, what my conception of food ethics is intended to promote.

7

Sustainable Food Systems

According to a popular understanding, a sustainable food system is one that "meets the needs of the present without compromising future generation's ability to meet their needs." This formula adapts the language of the World Commission on Environment and Development (WCED) chaired by Gro Harlem Brundtland (henceforth the Brundtland report). There is much wisdom in this little nostrum, but there are also hidden meanings that compromise the model of sustainability in important ways. Since philosophy is dedicated to exposing hidden meanings there is thus work to do.

Bryan Norton is philosophy's leading theorist of sustainability. I challenge his approach in this chapter. At the same time, I accept aspects of Norton's view without discussion: Norton is a pluralist with respect to values. Sustainability is a social goal that must accommodate diverse understandings of the right and the good. Norton outlines three ways to do this. Most generally, he argues for adaptive management: policy should require decision-makers to monitor the outcomes of their choices, and it should allow them to make continuous adjustments. This extends even to the goals that policy is implemented to achieve. Understood as adaptive management, sustainability is something that we learn about through experience. Second, Norton argues for democracy: sustainability should be pursued through governance and decision-making processes that are open to all and that are responsive to all perspectives. The guidance for reconciling differences comes from the history of democratic political philosophy. Finally, language is our environment. We must be attentive to the way that talking with one another shapes our understanding of the human condition.[1]

I do not disagree with any of these tenets from Norton's work, though I see them as ancillary to a philosophical analysis of sustainability as such. Neither do I contest a host of additional doctrines espoused by environmental philosophers since 1970. For example, a reader of this chapter might call me an anthropocentrist, or someone who thinks that human beings are the sole source of ethical value. I am neither an anthropocentrist nor do I understand this chapter as engaging this debate in environmental ethics. I do

From Silo to Spoon. Paul B. Thompson, Oxford University Press. © Oxford University Press 2024.
DOI: 10.1093/oso/9780197744727.003.0008

not want to be read as prejudging any of these philosophical debates in virtue of what follows here. My starting point is this: sustainability becomes meaningful as it is applied to many activities as well as to domains that have little to do with the protection of wilderness, ecological processes, or endangered species. They include sustainable cities, sustainable energy, and sustainable business. There would be much more to say about the sustainability of any such practice, and the chapter cannot even fully cover the territory implied by sustainable food systems. Neither the Brundtland nostrum nor Norton's more expansive development is adequate to this diversity.

Sustainable Food Systems: The Origin of Debate

Conversations on sustainable agriculture predated the Brundtland report by at least a century, though the word "sustainability" did not necessarily figure prominently in the discussion at the outset. Working backward in time from the 1987 WCED, "sustainable agriculture" was the term of choice for critics of industrial farming technology throughout the 1970s. Even earlier Liberty Hyde Bailey (1858–1954) promoted the idea of permanent agriculture, by which he meant farming practices that would support household farms while preserving soil and water resources. Contrary to trends observed on American farms when he retired from Cornell University in 1913, Bailey imagined how an alternative kind of farming could continue indefinitely. Hiram King (1848–1911) completed the studies for his book, *Farmers of Forty Centuries, or Permanent Agriculture in China, Korea and Japan* at about the same time. King documented conservation practices such as composting and terracing that allowed continuous intensive cultivation, supporting not only household farmers, but also large populations. Bailey's and King's *permanent agriculture* is one model for a sustainable food system.[2]

Even as early as the 1700s, American agricultural societies decried "skimmers": farmers who denuded unfarmed land, depleted the soils over a just a few years, and then moved on to repeat the process on previously uncultivated prairies, meadows, and forests. Skimming left the land in an unfarmable condition. It was a very temporary form of cultivation, far from permanent in Bailey's and King's sense. Yet the complaints about skimming raised in the farm journals of the time also highlighted the social impact of eroded lands: skimmers lack any commitment to the prosperity of the towns and villages in which they lived. A transient population could not sustain rural communities.[3] The concern for maintaining community capacities joins environmental impact from skimming to anticipate contemporary threats to the sustainability of a food system. A food system might be unsustainable because it destroys its biological base or because it undercuts the social institutions that citizens need.

A somewhat different set of sustainability concerns emerged with Thomas Malthus (1766–1834). Malthus created a mathematical model of the relationship between agriculture and human population growth. His 1798 *Essay on the Principle of Population* suggested that while unchecked populations would grow at an exponential rate, biological constraints on food production would limit the rate of growth of the food supply. Malthus speculated that even under the most optimistic scenarios, the food supply for later generations would grow at a fixed rate of increase. So while a doubled population might double again and again, total food production would be doing well to grow at a rate of a few percent over the lifetime of any individual.[4] A careful reading of his *Essay* shows that Malthus did *not* think food shortages are what actually limits population growth; social conventions and public policy are more influential. Nevertheless, his model marks an important broadening beyond what's happening in farmers' fields. Malthus's model underpins a view of sustainable food systems that stresses the ratio of population (the number of people needing to eat) and the global food supply.[5]

A decade before the Brundtland report, farmers and agricultural experts alike were dividing into camps. Some followed the thinking of Bailey and King, focusing on the regeneration of renewable resources like soil and water. Malthusians focused on meeting the food needs of future generations. They argued that successive waves of chemical, mechanical, genetic, and information technology would be needed to feed a growing global population. Still others were observing the loss of businesses, schools, and other institutions in rural communities as farms consolidated. The clash among these production-focused groups never gained much traction within the food movement, where the tendency is to presume that the injustice that permeates the production, processing, and distribution of food is unsustainable by definition. Attending to injustice broadens the scope of social concerns of earlier critics who attacked skimmers. Practices that exploit labor, cause hunger (*and* obesity), or that oppress people based on class or ethnicity can hardly be called sustainable, given this outlook. Food justice advocates will say that our current food system is unsustainable because of the numerous ways in which we can see how it fails in the fundamental task of meeting basic needs.

There are, then, at least three and possibly four schools of thought on sustainable food systems, but we should be cautious in applying the famous "three pillars" or intersecting circles that represent economic, environmental, and social sustainability. For one thing, no one here is arguing that some form of profit or economic sustainability is critical (though certainly everyone worries about sustaining his or her income).[6] We might say that the soil and water crowd seems focused on environment, but it is important to recognize that the environment they are focused on lies within the confines of a farmers' field. To some extent, the activists focused on present-day injustice match up with social sustainability, but the people who worry about future generations' ability to feed themselves have no complement in the "three circles" view of sustainability. Models emphasizing people, planet, and profit simply do not capture what is at stake in the debates over sustainable food systems.

Sustainable Development and the Brundtland Approach

The wisdom in the Brundtland approach lies in asking people of today to exercise caution in activities that constrain future generations' capacity to fulfill their requirements. The full statement from the Brundtland report goes as follows: "Sustainable development is development that meets the needs of the present generation without compromising future generations' ability to meet their needs."[7] Let's think like logicians for a moment and look closely at the structure of this claim. The Brundtland report is making a distinction between *sustainable* development and other forms of development. It is not proposing to give a definition of sustainability as such. This is important. Bryan Norton overlooks this point when he writes, "Today, the most often-cited definition of sustainability is that of the Brundtland Commission's report, *Our Common Future*," and then follows with the above quoted statement from page 43.[8] Conflating sustainability with sustainable development is the source of many conceptual and normative errors.

As many authors including Norton have said, the series of multilateral efforts leading up to the Brundtland report begins with the 1972 United Nations Conference on the Human Environment in Stockholm. The conference revealed a rift between countries in Europe and North America and what was then called the developing world, including China. Less industrialized economies were reluctant to ratify all of the environmental priorities being floated by representatives from Europe and the industrialized world. Nevertheless, the meeting produced a consensus statement consisting of twenty-six principles known as the Stockholm Declaration. The first seven principles endorse various conservation goals, as well as the priority of human rights. Principle 8 states "Development is needed to improve the environment." The Declaration then continues with fifteen principles either referencing development explicitly or noting that science and education (marks of a developed economy) are prerequisites for environmental protection. The declaration concludes with a statement calling for the elimination of weapons of mass destruction.[9]

Less than a decade later, Willy Brandt (1913–1992), former Chancellor of Germany and recipient of the 1971 Nobel Peace Prize, chaired an international commission on disparities between the developed North and the less developed South. Many of the independent nations of the global South were less than a quarter of a century old at that time, having emerged from colonial domination only after the end of World War II. In contrast to the Stockholm Conference emphasis on environment, the Brandt Commission concentrated on economic inequality and quality of life. The 1980 Brandt report framed these problems in terms of the South's less advanced state of economic development. The poverty and absence of social services in the South were a consequence of exploitation by the North but could be remedied through economic growth. The Brandt Commission concluded that wealthy countries had a both a self-interest and a moral obligation to promote development in the Global South. Just a few years later, the WCED was charged with reconciling the environmental imperatives identified by the Stockholm Declaration with the ethically based obligation to address disparities highlighted in the Brandt report.

Making sense of the Brundtland report's approach requires some prior understanding of what its authors mean by development. A detailed discussion would take the reader deep into MEGO territory ("my eyes glaze over"), so I will simplify. For nearly a hundred years, development has been measured by growth in a country's gross domestic product (GDP). When talking heads on the evening news discuss economic growth or recession, they are talking about whether this number has increased and, if so, by how much. However, GDP has many recognized deficiencies as an indicator of human *welfare*. For example, if the population of a country increases spending on healthcare, that will show up as an increase in GDP. It might mean that more and more people are sick. Healthcare spending soared in the COVID-19 pandemic, buoying GDP at a time when most sectors were contracting.[10] Despite the obvious detriment to general welfare, such increases in healthcare spending still factor into GDP as a positive indicator of economic health. If we think that development should have something to do with improving human welfare, GDP is a non-starter. Alternative approaches to measuring development identify elements of a modern, industrialized economy that contribute to quality of life better than GDP.[11] Two of these alternative approaches are important for understanding the sustainable development debate. One is the *basic needs approach*, associated with the work of economist Paul Streeten (1917–2019). The other is *natural capital*, a concept developed by Herman Daly (1938–2022).[12]

In outline, the basic needs approach identifies both minimal physiological requirements for survival, such as food, water, and shelter, and capacities that individuals would need to survive and protect themselves in a given social setting. This might include literacy and police protection, for example, though one can imagine settings in which neither would be requisite for mere survival. Streeten argued that efforts to improve the quality of life in countries that had suffered from colonial exploitation should give priority to meeting these basic needs before attempting to deliver luxury consumption goods and, in some cases, even basic political liberties. Even if there are historical correlations between growth in GDP and a country's satisfaction of basic needs, there is nothing in GDP that assures this connection. Streeten and his supporters argued that the policies intended to promote development should emphasize needs rather than year-to-year growth in GDP.[13] Crucially, the language of the Brundtland report is endorsing Streeten's emphasis on needs rather than the capital accumulation implied by growth in GDP.

In contrast, Daly's work has been the focus of many philosophers, including Norton. The assumptions about development that motivate Daly's approach do not take up Streeten's challenge to the dominance of capital. Instead, the question of whether development is actually happening is framed in terms of a debate between two ways to measure capital accumulation: weak and strong sustainability. *Weak sustainability* is associated with Robert Solow, a theorist of economic development who argued that capital in the form of knowledge, skill, and the capacities we associate with science, technology, engineering, and mathematics (STEM) can expand indefinitely. These are called *human capital*. In his lecture "An Almost Practical Step

Toward Sustainability," Solow argued that human capital could substitute for declines in the natural resource base (e.g., natural capital).[14] Hence, sustainable development would be development in which increases in human capital offset declines in the productive capabilities of natural resources. Daly, by contrast, provides many reasons why growth in scientific and technological capacities cannot fully compensate for declines in natural capital. Significantly, Daly does think that *some* forms of human or social capital *do* compensate for declines in resources of ecosystem services, but his point is that we cannot expect this intersubstitutivity of capitals to continue indefinitely. Hence, sustainable development for Daly is development that meets the natural capital requirements of future generations.[15]

In short, the weak versus strong sustainability debate turns on whether one thinks that there are limits to humanity's ability to replace natural capital with science and technology. I do not mean to suggest that this question is unimportant, and I will return to it in the balance of this chapter. However, it is vital to begin the inquiry into sustainability by recognizing how longstanding debates over development get imported into the definition of sustainable development. Some economists continue to think that, contrary to Streeten's view, accumulating capital *is* the best way to improve quality of life, even among the poorest of the poor.[16] A fair evaluation of the differences between the Brundtland definition and the approaches of Solow and Daly would delve deeply into these other debates in the theory of economic development and poverty alleviation. That would be a very rude way to treat readers who thought they were going to learn something about sustainable food systems, so I will cut it short. The key point to note is that *all* of this is about *development*,[17] hence we should begin by asking whether any of it carries over to a discussion of sustainability as such, or to the idea of a sustainable food system.

Defining Sustainability

The root problem occurs when we interpret the Brundtland report's criteria for sustainable development as a definition of sustainability itself. Here is a case where analytic philosophy's use of formal logic is helpful. We might render the definition as follows:

(1)   Sustainability$_{def}$ = $\forall x\ S(x) \leftrightarrow x$ meets the needs of the present and x allows future generations to meet their needs.

Then, for development, d,

> S(d) ↔ development that meets the needs of the present and also allows future generations to meet their needs.

Stated very broadly (1) says that any activity, process, or other entity that fails to meet needs both now and in the future is unsustainable. This logical analysis does allow us to see the Brundtland Commission's remarks on sustainable development as an instance of a general form. (Readers who don't find the use of symbols helpful can flip to the endnotes at the back of the book and read a more detailed [albeit much longer] discussion in English.)[18] If this logical analysis is the correct way to understand sustainability as such, it should be possible to use a similar approach to evaluate other activities, such as business or agriculture:

> For business activity β, S(β) ↔ β meets the needs of the present and also allows future generations to meet their needs.
> For agriculture α, S(α) ↔ α meets the needs of the present and also allows future generations to meet their needs.

Several points emerge, some of which are just technical points in logical grammar. There is some ambiguity on whether every business or every farm has to satisfy the requirements of this definition. On one view, it is the composite whole represented by *all* businesses or *all* agricultural practices that must meet the needs of the present while allowing future generations to meet their needs. This grammatical oddity does not arise in the case of sustainable development because development is already defined as a property of the economy as a whole rather than a feature of firms, governments, or households. In the cases of business activity or agriculture, it is the *system* of practices that is relevant rather than the practice of every individual firm or farm. Yet we do want to evaluate the sustainability of specific farming practices, such as large-scale monocultures or relying on synthetic fertilizer. When we try to instantiate the definition given in (1) to individual farms, it becomes torturous. Consider a large-scale monoculture (LSM) such as a 1,000-acre farm growing corn and soybeans or cotton and peanuts.

> S (LSM) [e.g., LSM is sustainable] ↔ LSM meets the needs of the present generation and also allows future generations to meet their needs.

No single farm, no matter how large, can feed the present generation. It is the overall food system in which LSMs operate that does or does not meet needs rather than the activity of any specific farm. The agricultural end of the food system comprises an enormous diversity of different farming practices, and this definitional adaptation of the Brundtland language does not tell us much about how to evaluate any given farming practice. In short, the approach generates silliness rather than insight.

Now, I am not saying that the language of meeting needs is *irrelevant* to the evaluation of large-scale monoculture. I repeat that there is wisdom in the Brundtland approach. However, someone would have to fill in the definition with a lot of information about the cumulative social and environmental impacts of large-scale monocultures to make an evaluation of their sustainability. This is the reason that I have argued for a different approach to understanding sustainability.

(2) S_{def} = $\forall$x such that x is a process, practice or system of practice, S(x) $\rightarrow$ $\exists$(y) y measures or evaluates whether or to what extent x can continue.

In this approach, sustainability is determined by one or more measures of the process's ability to continue. "Ability to continue" can be a strictly *temporal* criterion (e.g., α is more sustainable than β because it will last longer), or it could be in virtue of its *vulnerability* to disruption (e.g., α is more sustainable than β because it is less likely to collapse as a response to its internal organization or an external threat). Operationalizing (2) requires criteria for deciding whether a practice is sustainable or unsustainable or using the measure to rank one process as more sustainable than another.[19] Under my approach, there is quite a bit more to say about sustainability on a case-by-case basis. The balance of the chapter says some of it as we think of sustainable food systems.

Although specifying the meaning of continuance for sustainability can become convoluted, the criteria are often clear in context. When a television news reporter asks a pundit whether the rise in real estate prices is sustainable, they mean over the next six months to a year. When Bailey and King raised the question of agricultural sustainability through the lens of permanent agriculture, they were thinking in terms of generations (perhaps a dozen or more). That would approach 400 years. Four centuries is a long time, but still not infinity—the agricultural systems they were describing would not survive the death of the Sun, for example. To the extent that this time-scale thinking applies to the Brundtland Commission's interest in the process of development, it was a matter of decades or one century, at most.

My approach can be applied comprehensively (to development or to the food system) as well as to a specific practice (such as LSM) or even to the practice of a single individual farmer. Importantly, it also points us toward the hierarchical relationships that obtain among the various levels of system organization. These relationships are not additive. On the one hand, large-scale monoculture might not be able to continue as a general practice even if there are specific farms that have done it (and still could do it) over many generations. On the other hand, it is implausible to think a food system entirely dependent on LSM farms could continue to function if the practice exhausts the resources required for agriculture. That was Bailey's and King's concern.[20] In addition, one does not need to be a specialist in some arcane area of expertise (like economic development theory) to understand what sustainability means. Expertise will still be needed, of course. It is not obvious *why* LSM might not be sustainable, but explaining this will be much more straightforward if the focus is on what threatens to bring large-scale monocultures to a halt.

The Ethics of Sustainability

When we say that a practice or system is unsustainable, we seem to be making a claim that is open to empirical evidence. If a pundit says that the increase in housing costs is unsustainable, this means he thinks it will stop, perhaps within the year, perhaps sooner. If housing prices do continue to rise over that time period, we look back and say he was wrong: the rate of increase was sustainable. This is the *system-describing* sense of sustainability. It may not be easy to determine whether a statement about the sustainability of a system is true or false, particularly when it involves a prediction about the future. It is a truth-apt claim, nonetheless. However, many claims about sustainable food systems do not hang on matters of fact, or at least not unambiguously. If someone says that the treatment of agricultural field workers is unsustainable, they might mean that it is a gross injustice. This might not be something that one could evaluate empirically, but it is clearly saying that the practice *should* not continue.

The distinction between system-describing and *goal-prescribing* senses of sustainability is not necessarily a problem, but it can lead to confusion about what is meant when a particular aspect of the food system is evaluated. Although they did not use the word "sustainability," Bailey, King, and critics of the skimmers were speaking in a system-describing sense. They saw that depletion of soils and water would prevent farmers in the future from continuing to use their current methods or that rural communities would disappear when farms are abandoned. To be sure, they saw these events as bad. They were not shying away from an ethical judgment. However, the evils that motivated their judgment derived from their understanding of how food systems ought to serve human needs, as opposed to the thought that soil depletion or transiency were intrinsically wrong. They were not simply *defining* the sustainability of the food system according to whether or not it conforms to a moral standard.

My approach to sustainability (a measure of whether or to what extent a process or system of activity can continue) privileges the system-describing line on sustainability. This approach does not presume a quantitative or technically complex understanding of measures. Sometimes our judgment of a system's ability to continue is nothing more than a seat-of-the-pants intuition, a highly subjective guess. Other times, the measure does indeed incorporate data collection, system modeling, and the identification of indicators for sustainability that rest on complex scientific procedures. Although there will be circumstances in which the complex scientific approach is superior to someone's subjective guess, my view does not mean guessers are failing in every respect. People who doubt climate science are, in effect, adopting a measure of the sustainability for our current way of life that contradicts the measures that have been developed by the Intergovernmental Panel on Climate Change (IPCC). According to a system-describing approach to sustainability, at least one of them is wrong. (I'm placing my own bets on who is right with the IPCC.) I take it as one virtue of my approach that we can frame this as a disagreement about which measures we should adopt when making queries into the sustainability of our current way of life.

Nevertheless, the system-describing approach to sustainability is not "value free" (whatever that might mean). The emphasis on description and prediction does not mean that there is no ethics of sustainability. The act of focusing one's attention on a process or system is replete with value judgments. Certain features of the world are judged to be relevant. What makes them relevant? They help us single out the practice, process, or system whose continuity is to be estimated and exclude other features that might have been included given a different perspective or evaluative stance. Most crucially, conceptualizing anything as a system implies boundary judgments. We must have some understanding of how a system is bounded to evaluate whether or how long it can continue. Even when the sustainability of a process (the spinning of a toy top, for example) is a matter of mere curiosity, conceptualizing what the process is (e.g., what distinguishes the top from the table on which it spins; what distinguishes its motion from the rotation of the Earth) can take different paths. These judgments bound the process under review as distinct from a larger system of processes.

We have already seen that concern about the sustainability of soils was an early focus for Liberty Hyde Bailey and F. H. King. A deeper dive into the systems view of soil illustrates the role of ethics in estimating whether a given farming practice can continue. When Bailey and King attempted to identify the criteria for permanent agriculture, they were thinking about things that farmers might do to compensate for the constant outflow of nutrients that accompanies farming. Some of the organic matter in a crop flows out of the soil system in the form of food eaten by people and animals, who may deposit their organic wastes far from the site where their food is grown. When the soil system is viewed from the standpoint of ecological integrity, it is sustainable only if the inflows and outflows remain in balance. (In fact, this system has many more variables than described here.[21] We have not even begun to think about the roles of wind and water, for example.) Further discussion would almost certainly invoke a MEGO reaction from many readers. Just fix upon the way that soil sustainability has to be conceptualized (e.g., measured) through a description of interacting stocks and flows, and we can get back to ethics.

Notice that Bailey and King give farmers a role to play in the interaction of organic matter, soil metabolizing organisms, and plant nutrients: they can compost crop residue, apply manure, or rotate crops, for example. This reflects a value-laden standpoint that would have been rejected by many of Bailey's or King's contemporaries who called themselves ecologists. Early ecology disclaimed interest in systems that incorporated human activity as an element in the interaction of biophysical stocks like organic matter or energy (i.e., nutrients). In contrast, Bailey and King were interested in *agriculture*, a system that inherently incorporates human activity. A value-laden standpoint separates Bailey and King from the ecologists of their generation, though contemporary ecology has no difficulty in seeing humans as crucial components of an ecosystem.

These value judgments are reflected in the way analysts bound the system of interest. Bailey and King included farmers in their understanding of soil metabolism, but they did not think of farmers themselves as stocks that were affected by inflows and outflows. In retrospect, we can see why they should have been interested enough in the "stock" of farmers to include it in within the system. As the number of farmers has declined since 1900, that has surely affected soil metabolism. Today's agroecologists sometimes argue that when their farms get too big, the number of farmers declines. The remaining farmers are unable to deploy the management practices needed to sustain the metabolic interactions among organic matter, soil organisms, and plant nutrients. At larger scales, farmers become addicted to synthetic fertilizer.

This observation points us toward new boundary judgments. The farmer who manages for ecological integrity exists in an economic system in which the price they will receive for their crop depends on supply and demand. If farmers using synthetic fertilizer are able to sell profitably at a lower price, farmers who maintain soil with King's methods may not be profitable. Their higher production costs will not be recouped in the sale of their crops, and they will eventually exhaust their savings (or credit). They will go broke. Here we have introduced a whole new set of stocks and flows: savings, credit (forms of capital), farm commodities (whose inflow is production, outflow is sales), and, of course, prices. Do these stocks and flows belong in the system we use to evaluate the sustainability of a farming system? That is a question that one cannot answer without adopting a particular valuational stance. Which standpoint is the right one? The pragmatist answer to that ethical question is that it depends on the situation that has led you to launch an inquiry into sustainability. A geologist or soil physicist might be quite interested in the eons-long processes that form a soil's mineral composition, but Bailey and King were interested in the balance of soil components as it changes over a few generations or less.

Getting System Boundaries Right

"It depends," usually *is* the ethically appropriate answer because different perspectives lead people toward different conceptions of the relevant system. But can't we say more about which valuational stance we ought to adopt?

Shouldn't ethics have something to say about *that*? Many situations issue from a standpoint so obvious there is no serious possibility of doubt or dispute. One example comes from Roger Pielke, Jr.'s discussion of Tornado Politics, or decisions about what matters in emergencies. When a tornado is rapidly approaching and visible out the window, everyone in the room can agree that the situation demands action. The imminent threat leaves no room for debate about what the problem is.[22] The sheer obviousness of what matters in a life-or-death situation obscures the fact that value judgments are active in conceptualizing the problem one is attempting to understand and resolve. One does not need a philosopher to help with the ethical imperatives that arise in response to local food systems compromised by hurricanes, earthquakes, or tornados. Nevertheless, the fact that there is nothing controversial about the valuational standpoint of Tornado Politics does not imply that value judgments have not been made.

Even beyond emergencies, a widely shared and non-controversial valuational standpoint may not be problematic. The we-intentions discussed in Chapter 6 are crucial for the coordination of action and social epistemology. Arguably, scientific disciplines are able to function because individual scientists accept an implicit agreement on what constitutes the appropriate subject matter for research. Many (but perhaps not all) disciplines will be able to formulate measures that speak to the sustainability of processes and systems that fall within the scope of the discipline. Implicit norms will also determine the methods or datasets that can be called on to develop those measures. As unspoken, these norms may be so obvious as to seem fact-based or objective to practitioners. A soil ecologist asked to evaluate the sustainability of a farming system will gravitate toward the systematic interaction of organic matter, metabolic processes, and energy. An agricultural economist will focus on whether farmers who deploy that system are likely to survive the vicissitudes of the commodity markets. *Within* the disciplinary contexts in which both scientists work, shared understanding of *what* depends on what makes them a discursive community, a "we." Yet there are larger questions about which of these threats to sustainability—bankruptcy or soil exhaustion—should be viewed as the problem that makes a measure of sustainability important. Both standpoints have a partial grasp of a larger set of systematic interactions.[23]

Expanding the scope of the relevant system would have salutary effects, but it would not resolve the problem of system boundaries. We might, for example, note that technological innovation is itself a system with stocks and flows. Stephen Stoll's history of soil conservation suggests that the development of the Haber-Bosch process for capturing atmospheric nitrogen relieved threats to the sustainability of soil metabolism in the 19th century.[24] Yet diving into the innovation system reveals still more layers of complexity. Nitrogen's role in the explosives needed for the weapons of World War I drove growth in the industrial capacity for producing ammonia (a compound of nitrogen and hydrogen) through the Haber-Bosch process. After the war, this capacity was available for the production of synthetic fertilizer. It is an open question as to whether the demand for nitrogen within agriculture would have been enough to incentivize the creation of this industrial base.[25] Very few specialists in agriculture include military technology within the innovation system of the food system.[26]

There is no final answer here, but ethics does provide a direction for inquiry. Becoming more aware of how one is oneself embedded within systems is a start. Then one can use systems thinking to ask how one's own perspective is a function of system affordances. Standpoints derived from the disciplinary divisions in science need to be augmented with reflection on way that problems in the food system intersect. At the same time, this requires much more understanding of food system ecology than the average philosophy professor is going to have. In summation, the question of bounding systems is inherently ethical, but it is not *only* ethical.

Resource Sufficiency and Functional Integrity

The systems just described emphasize notions of balance. Stocks that range from soil microorganisms to financial capital grow or shrink in virtue of inflows and outflows. Other events or processes are described as drivers that affect the rate of flows, much like adjusting the flow of water into your bathtub by turning the faucet. The water level in the tub (the stock) is stable when the amount coming in through the faucet is exactly equal to the amount going out through the drain. The balance between inflows and outflows underlies our intuition of sustainability in systems like this. Boundaries are determined by deciding which stocks and flows to include. In the bathtub model just described, I did not include outflow from evaporation, for example. However, someone else might be interested in the sustainability of this system over a much longer timeframe. Evaporation might matter.

This bathtub thinking is especially relevant to food systems because eating anything is an outflow to the total stock of food, while the farm sector's production of edible commodities is the primary inflow. As we have just seen, this inflow is affected by a complex set of factors, but as long as they remain in balance, the food system can continue to function indefinitely. "Continuing to function indefinitely" is what Bailey and King had in mind when they wrote about permanent agriculture. This is *functional integrity*. As long as the basic structure of the system is maintained, it can be expected to chug along without any of us having to think too much about sustainability. Systems that resist threats to their sustainability are *robust*, while systems that are able to recover from short-term disruptions are *resilient*.[27] Most importantly, the food system has often proved to be *adaptive* over time. It has experienced change in its stocks and flows as well as in key system elements, but it has maintained the integrity of its basic functions, at least in so far as they are understood as providing food for people. Or, at least, that is the way we understand sustainability of food systems. Local food systems have experienced short-term perturbations (the Irish Potato Famine is a case in point) that have led to death and social disruption. Global and national food systems have also developed structural issues that produce recurring deficits in food security for subpopulations. These and other looming challenges to food system sustainability point us toward further adaptive changes that still need to be made.

This general theme of balancing stocks and flows is central in many but not all discussions of sustainability. Ulrich Grober's history of sustainability traces the concept to Hans Carl von Carlowitz (1645–1714), who balanced the German mining industry's use of trees as timber supports in mineshafts (the outflow) against their rate of growth in German forests (the inflow). Mining could continue (it was sustainable) as long as this balance was respected. When the pace of cutting to reinforce mineshafts exhausted the trees, mining was forced into costly periods of stoppage as the forests recovered.[28] Here, too, the functional integrity of the system is at issue. However, if you get in your car and start driving, the major constraint on your ability to continue that process is the amount of gasoline in your tank. The engine's consumption of gas is an outflow, though you can affect the rate of this flow by adjusting your speed. This notion of adjusting the rate at which we consume a finite resource underpins a *resource sufficiency* view of sustainability.

There is little doubt in my mind that many people think of sustainability more along the model of exhausting resources than keeping stocks and flows balanced. The food system has some features that *are* amenable to this way of thinking. Industrial farming consumes a lot of fossil fuel, and fossil fuel is a finite resource like that amount of gas in your tank. Unlike your tank, there is no obvious way to refill our fossil fuel reserves. When the global supply of fossil fuels are gone, the farming practices that depend on them will have to stop. One can introduce a measure of how long these practices can continue by measuring consumption and estimating the total supply. That would, indeed, be a logically coherent way to understand the sustainability of industrial farming. It is not, in my view, the most perspicacious way to think about sustainability in a system that depends on balancing the inflows and outflows of potentially renewable resources.

An aphorism attributed to architect William McDonough captures the point. If you are trying to get to Canada but you find yourself driving 120 miles per hour in the direction of Mexico, slowing down to 20 does not help.[29] Thinking about sustainability as conserving limited or finite resources obscures the sense in which our activities are embedded in systems that have the potential to reproduce the stocks we need to continue our way of life, a process McDonough calls "cradle to cradle." The resource sufficiency perspective has arguably limited many people's ability to think of sustainability in the way that it really needs to be understood in the context of food systems. Yet resource sufficiency and functional integrity can also be thought of as alternative philosophies of sustainability. Unfortunately, I do not see the leading philosophical theorists of sustainability attending to this distinction.[30]

Describing Systems, Seeking Justice

Additional philosophical problems trouble the interpretation of the Brundtland aphorism as a definition for sustainable food systems. These problems relate to the sense in which sustainability is thought to express an ethical commitment to future generations. This becomes more obvious when we try to apply (1) to activities or processes other than development. Consider this minor twist on a sustainable agriculture:

For a food system f, $S(f) \leftrightarrow f$ meets the needs of the present and also allows future generations to meet their needs.

In order to meet the criteria specified in this definition, f has to satisfy both conjuncts. It has to meet needs in the present *and* in the future. Now, this is fine as a heuristic device, but, from a logical standpoint, it undercuts the ethical claim that many advocates of sustainable food systems want to make. A Bailey or King, for example, might recognize failings in the food systems that used regenerative and soil-conserving practices. A permanent agriculture might *not* fully meet the needs of the present. Yet Bailey and King still want to argue against short-term fixes that undercut future generations' ability to meet their needs. Indeed, this is arguably the position of the WCED. Authors of the report could not have thought that the state of world in 1987 fully met needs of the then current generation.

If we switch to (2), we get:

If a food system (e.g., a system of practices) f, is sustainable [e.g., S(f)], →

$\exists(y)$ y measures or evaluates whether or to what extent x can continue.

In Bailey and King's case, y is a measure of soil quality and water availability. The ethical argument to justify this measure depends on an assumption that is seldom made clear by Bailey or King, but it becomes explicit in the language of the Brundtland Commission. The food system is not just for today; it should serve the needs of future generations. To say that a food system should be sustainable is to recognize the moral standing of future generations and to balance their interests against those of people living in the present generation.

Notice the fact–value tension here. On one hand, the point of asking whether any process or practice is sustainable is to assess whether it is likely to continue and to identify what circumstances might threaten its operation. That is the system-describing sense of sustainability. On the other hand, we sometimes say that something is unsustainable when what we mean is that it *should* not come to a stop, whether it is likely to or not (the goal-prescribing sense). In the first usage, a reporter on the evening news asks an economist whether the rate of growth in GDP is sustainable. In the second usage, a frustrated teacher stands in front of the class, bangs the desk, and says "This disrespectful behavior is unsustainable!" Meanwhile, the smart-alecks in the back of the room are whispering to each other, "Why not? We can keep it up indefinitely." The tension endures because there is an ambiguity between system-describing and goal-prescribing meanings of the word "sustainability."[31]

I have emphasized the system-describing sense of sustainability. Yet in some contexts claiming that a process or practice is unsustainable is a way to make a moral claim, and it does so in a very straightforward manner. When people say that hunger or exploitation of labor is unsustainable, they are making a moral claim. What should we make of this from the standpoint of philosophical ethics? I must admit that my first reaction was to see this as trivializing the very idea of sustainability.[32] It is not as if we were without any ability to make an ethical assessment of failings in the contemporary food system apart from saying that it is unsustainable. We already have the philosophical tools we need to criticize injustice to poor or racially marginalized people in the food system. Allowing some to go hungry while others revel in excess drew moral condemnation in the earliest ages of the historical record. It cuts across virtually all cultural groups. We have fully adequate language and concepts to denounce both failings of the food system (to workers and to the hungry). We have the words to decry these failings as moral evils and as forms of injustice. To put the point differently, the word "sustainability" does not come up in Chapter 3 of this book.

But there is more. When we limit our scope to the industrial era of food systems—roughly the 20th century and beyond—we see a situation in which the well-fed may be ignorant of deficiencies in the food system. Social criticism is needed to raise awareness, and the word "sustainability" is often used in this context. Again, my first impulse is to point out how the well-fed whose consciousness is being raised already have the moral concepts that allow them to grasp the ethical significance of these deficiencies once they become aware of them. I would stress making them aware of the *facts* rather than chastening them on moral grounds. Using the word "sustainability" to point out moral failings of the current food system seems redundant at best. It does not add anything new to our understanding of food systems. What is more, logical analysis shows how using the word sustainability to decry injustice in a given situation obscures the things the language of sustainability was intended to highlight. If one half of the present-*and*-future generations conjunction fails, the other half is irrelevant. The truth criteria have already been satisfied.

Although I support raising the average person's awareness of injustice in the current food system, the commitment to justice in the present can obscure environmental ethics' commitment to consider future consequences. When saying our food system is unsustainable simply calls out present-day injustice, the sense that we have obligations to future generations ceases to have much bearing. Unsustainability has already been proved by the injustice in the present. When justice for future generations ceases to function in evaluating sustainability, the conservation concerns noted by Bailey and King also become marginalized. In fact, we may lose the sense that sustainability has any connection to the environmental impact of agriculture entirely. Taken as a goal-prescribing concept, meeting the needs of the present generation becomes a condition that must be satisfied before giving any consideration to the needs of future generations or to the ecological integrity of farming practices.

All of the above weighs against "meeting needs of the present" as the guiding ethical norm for sustainable food systems. However, I have become more sensitive to the importance of the philosophical debate between those who apply system-describing approaches to the food system and those who understand sustainability as purely normative concept. Patricia Allen is a leading advocate of the view that sustainable food systems must incorporate a foundational commitment to social justice. She develops a detailed argument for this view in a series of publications over the past forty years. The account I provide here cannot do full justice to her position, but it is important to see how my own analytic argument (summarized above) fails to grapple with Allen's primary thrust. Much of her work on sustainable food systems consists in precisely the sort of sociological scholarship that I see as exposing moral deficiencies in the current food system. Our differences of opinion do not arise in connection with the judgment that there *are* moral deficiencies with respect to social justice or with the ethical commitment toward actions that address them. Food ethics certainly encompasses the issues Allen has documented. However, Allen advocates for such action under the banner of sustainability, while, for reasons just discussed, I have seen this as philosophically problematic.

The case for Allen's view rests on an institutional analysis of sustainability discourse rather than the logical analysis I have emphasized. Here, we need to focus on discourses of social control rather than inquiry. Sustainability functions symbolically as a rallying point for coordinating social action. Rather than resorting to the type of logical scrutiny given earlier in this chapter, the social theorist interprets the word's significance as a function of the cooperative endeavors that it serves to mobilize. Allen observed the synchronization of food system activists around the idea of sustainability beginning in the 1970s and 1980s. As characterized in an important essay by Gordon Douglass (1927–2017), they had the same three different orientations discussed earlier in the chapter. Some understood agricultural sustainability in terms of the total productivity of the global food system, especially in light of projected population growth. That is, the food system is sustainable if it produces enough food to feed everyone. Others followed Bailey and King in emphasizing the ecological integrity of mainstream farming practices. Finally, Douglass noted that still others focused on the economic failure of small and mid-sized farms and the correlative decline in rural schools, commercial enterprises, and social services, a view that recapitulated late 18th-century critiques of skimming.[33]

According to Douglass the idea of sustainability was functioning to co-ordinate social action around these three objectives. While Douglass was largely just *mapping* this coordination, Allen took an explicitly normative position. She noted that none of these three groups included a commitment to relieving the oppression of food system workers or addressing the actually experienced hunger of people living in industrialized societies. Even the concern with "feeding the world" was interpreted strictly as a function of productive capacity, with no attention to whether food actually reaches hungry people. Emphasizing the way that sustainability was bringing people together around goals for food system change, Allen saw the omission of these dimensions as a serious flaw. For Allen, any symbol or banner serving as the rallying point for people engaged in efforts to steer the production, distribution, and consumption of food in new directions should incorporate a commitment to social justice. Since sustainability was, in her view, the emergent symbolic form oriented to this task, it must, on pain of moral inadequacy, include a commitment to social justice.[34]

In short, Allen saw that a food movement was emerging in the 1980s and that sustainability was a symbolic pivot for coordinating social change. There were many overlapping reasons to incorporate goals of social justice into this new social movement. It would forge an alliance between activists emphasizing ecological integrity and older movements focused on food security and rights for farmworkers, especially in California, where Allen did her early research. Working together strengthens the bargaining position of each partner in such an alliance. Normatively, it addresses the lacuna in Douglass's analysis of sustainability, the omission of social justice concerns that were both obvious and well established within the political landscape of food system activism. Given Allen's social interactionist approach to sustainability, we can see why incorporating a commitment to social justice might be philosophically justifiable.

Sustainability and Social Justice Redux

Patricia Allen's influential work on sustainable food systems provides a counterpoint to the emphasis that I have laid on systems thinking throughout this chapter. If one starts with the view that sustainability has an inherently critical dimension, it makes sense to approach sustainability in terms of its ability to mobilize social change within food systems. Given that starting point, Allen has been extremely effective in exposing the deficiencies in forms of advocacy that neglect classic ethical problems. Combating the oppression and abuse of workers within the food system then becomes a criterion for sustainability. Similarly, structural features that limit both access and control over food systems among the poor, as well as those whose autonomy is compromised by cultural oppression based on race or gender, come to be viewed as markers of an unsustainable (because unjust) food system.

Can my approach be reconciled with Allen's? Although there are things we lose with the institutional, social movement approach to sustainability, there are also ways in which emphasizing functional integrity complements Allen's efforts. First, trying to fathom the functional integrity of food systems is wholly consistent with Allen's ethical or political commitments even if the interpretation of sustainability continues to emphasize the potential for a system collapse. We can and do articulate ethical commitments through more traditional philosophical ideas: equity, fairness, equality, autonomy, or justice in recognition and distribution of social goods. These ideas inform the ethics of labor relations in the food system, and they have long been present in efforts to improve food security or secure the universal human right to food. Recent analyses of food sovereignty add further dimensions to the food justice literature without necessarily defining sustainability through criteria for meeting the needs of the present generation. As such, the functional integrity of food systems can become part of a more comprehensive inquiry into food justice. There is, in short, no reason for understanding an event-predicting approach to sustainability as a challenge to the pursuit of social justice in food systems.

Second, reform-minded political theorists have long asked whether oppressive and unjust regimes are sustainable, even if they have not used that particular word. The question presupposes something like a functional integrity approach. Here is how that thinking might go: a class conflict or a specific form of oppression (like slavery or racism) creates tension within society. Oppressed peoples become more and more angry, and their resentment against the regime (or the current institutional structure) grows. Eventually there is a tipping point, after which violence escalates, creating a legitimate threat to the continuation of a regime and its attendant social forms. The dialectical materialism of Karl Marx and Friedrich Engels (1820–1895) provides a prominent example, but conservative theorists like David Hume (whom we met way back in the Chapter 1) make a similar argument to warn ruling elites of the need to monitor such tensions. It is as if resentment and resistance are stocks that build to boiling point, eventually increasing destruction of property and revolutionary violence. In the absence of some pressure-relieving outflow, the entire system goes into collapse. This is one way to understand how oppression and poverty are unsustainable in a system-describing sense. One would need to say more to reconcile this pattern of thinking in political theory with Allen's goal-describing notion of sustainability. Nevertheless, this is a second opening to conversation with those who have been attracted to sustainability as a type of social movement.

More fundamentally, Allen's approach may reflect a more sophisticated systems analysis of social control—the discursive domain that disciplines behavior and creates the social capacity for every kind of ethical discourse. Although philosophers like to stand apart from the discourse of social control, they should be mindful of its machinations and the current state of play. Although I have said that ideas such as equity, fairness, equality, autonomy, or justice in recognition and distribution of social goods articulate the moral telos of Allen's position, it is not at all clear that appealing to these ideas is persuasive in the current milieu. From the standpoint of social control, each of these words has been co-opted by the antagonistic, winner-take-all politics of the current era. They function more as markers signaling fealty toward a particular alignment of socioeconomic interests (or gender, racial, and ethnic identities) than as philosophically contested concepts. As a result, appeals to equity, fairness, equality, autonomy, or justice in recognition and distribution of social goods simply reinforce already existing political alliances. These words function to indicate loyalty to an established outlook—a we-intention—but, as such, using them only reproduces the current structure of we/they political alliances.

Given this diagnosis of the sociopolitical environment in which one must function, broadening a social movement or forming new alliances may be more readily achieved through innovation in our moral concepts. In this respect, the ambiguous nature of sustainability can be an advantage. Allen hopes the goal-prescribing sense can be exploited to build new alliances. At the same time, it is one thing to *hope* that oppression and poverty are unsustainable and something else to ask whether this is true. Gender oppression and structural racism have thus far shown themselves to withstand reform efforts, resurfacing in a new guise. Even as progress is made in key directions, processes of oppression and racial discrimination persist. Wealth disparities reproduce inequality in educational access, employment opportunities, and rates of incarceration. In food systems, institutionalized forms of inequality have led to declines in locally owned food businesses and the availability of healthy foods. National chains have displaced black-owned businesses, only to abandon neighborhoods when chain managers have recalculated their profit margins.[35] I am inclined to say that racism is all too sustainable. It must be one of the most resilient institutions of American culture, if not globally. Indeed, Allen herself recognizes that when sustainability is viewed strictly as a symbolic form for coordinating action, institutionalizations that further oppression are also possible.[36] But I hasten to add that, in saying this, I do *not* mean to weaken or undercut the sense in which discourses on sustainability might serve as a conduit to changing these circumstances.

Perhaps systems thinking could help us understand how to dismantle the connected stocks and flows that maintain patterns of discrimination and oppression. We could draw upon our knowledge of what makes systems we want to sustain more robust, resilient, and adaptive to target the linkages in systems we want to break. To paraphrase F. Scott Fitzgerald (1896–1940), advocates for sustainability must learn to "hold two opposed ideas in the mind at the same time, and still retain the ability to function."[37] When we *equate* sustainability with justice, we hamper our ability to think about why *in*justice is so persistent, so resilient, and seemingly so adaptably responsive to attempts at change. Yet when we insist upon a system-describing perspective simply for the sake of logical consistency, we may undercut sustainability's power to motivate social change.

8

Agrarian Pragmatism

Earlier chapters criticize mainstream ethical theory and applied ethics. This chapter sketches a more positive approach to food ethics. Agrarianism stresses the role of farming, fishing, and other components of the food system in structuring a society's political institutions. Many contemporary writers associate agrarian philosophy with Thomas Jefferson (1743–1826), yet agrarian thinking dates back to the ancient Greek founders of the Western philosophical tradition. Here, I explore a contemporary version of this standpoint, outlining a form of virtue ethics derived from Jefferson, 19th-century American transcendentalists, and early 20th-century thinkers who were contemporaries of John Dewey. "Agrarian pragmatism," is the term that I use to characterize this environmental philosophy. Unlike previous chapters that deal with specific problems in food ethics, this chapter offers a succinct (and hence incomplete) overview of the philosophical commitments that guide my thought.

Perhaps the most straightforward way to lead readers into the themes of this chapter is to explain how I came to these ideas myself. As a new assistant professor at Texas A&M University in 1981, I was charged with teaching a course on agricultural ethics. I saw this as fully compatible with my interest in philosophical dimensions of environmentalism.[1] However, I eventually came to the conclusion that the most influential philosophical theories in environmental ethics were incapable of addressing the moral quandaries of farming and food systems. As I learned more about agriculture, I gradually developed my approach to the history of philosophical thought. Up through the 17th century, some form of food provisioning would have been the dominant activity of any society. Even if philosophers did not write about food systems during these times, it would have been the water they were swimming in. Everyone would have had a knowledge of food systems that has become quite rare in the present age. I began to read classic philosophical texts with an eye toward the way subsistence activities like farming, hunting, herding, or fishing would have been part of the presumptive background knowledge—what everyone knows. As utterly *obvious*, it might have seemed

From Silo to Spoon. Paul B. Thompson, Oxford University Press. © Oxford University Press 2024.
DOI: 10.1093/oso/9780197744727.003.0009

pointless to say very much about it. The fact that the philosophical canon includes few overt discussions of food and farming should not be taken to imply that philosophers thought it was irrelevant.

On the one hand, I was coming to the view that farmers (here understood to include pastoralists, fishers, and gatherers harvesting from uncultivated sources) exhibit a characteristic standpoint incompatible with the logic of 20th-century moral theory, including work by environmental ethicists. They have a distinct moral outlook on their activity, to which I will return. On the other hand, I was discerning the influence of mechanical industrialization on theorists' understanding of the material basis for social life. Over the course of the 19th century, agriculture begins to be evaluated in the same terms as factory work, transportation, energy production, and other sectors of an industrial economy. By the 20th century, agriculture is viewed as an industry like any other. Philosophers and other moralists working from this point of view were adopting an *industrial philosophy of agriculture*. This view of agriculture does not jibe easily with the notion that farming and food production tend toward a distinctive understanding of moral agency, especially as it concerns the wider environment. This tension generates important problems in food ethics. What should we call the alternative to an industrial philosophy? Why not *agrarian philosophy of agriculture*?

From a personal standpoint, agrarian pragmatism is simply the result of conjoining my reflections on these problems with my training in philosophical pragmatism. As I discuss in this chapter, I see aspects of pragmatist ontology and epistemology as especially congenial to a philosophically robust account of environmental ethics as an agrarian might see it. Pragmatists stress the role of environment in forming the moral personality of an era, but they also understand the environment to include the technological infrastructure in addition to social and cultural forms. Twentieth-century moral theory can be seen as an adaptive response to changes wrought by the industrial milieu, but now our environing world has changed again. Some forms of agrarianism challenge dominant habits of thinking in contemporary environmental philosophy, but I withhold unqualified endorsement of either industrialist or agrarian outlooks. It is the tension between these accounts that opens the space for inquiry in food ethics.

The chapter begins with some initial orientation to agrarian thought. Many references to agrarians or agrarianism do not imply any sort of philosophical perspective, while some philosophies that are authentically agrarian are also morally problematic. After this throat-clearing, I make an abrupt switch to problems with mainstream environmental ethics. This sets up a more positive and thorough account of an agrarian moral philosophy that makes deep connections to the pragmatist tradition. The chapter concludes by emphasizing the fecundity of the agrarian hypothesis, even if we might not want to endorse an unqualified version of agrarian thinking as a contemporary environmental ethic.

Agrarianism: A Preliminary Account

Agrarianism is not a foreign term in contemporary speech, but it cannot have a particularly robust meaning for very many people.[2] Thomas Jefferson is the most frequently noted exponent of agrarianism, while Wendell Berry is the contemporary prophet and spokesperson for agrarian themes. Both authors are often disqualified on grounds of their alleged patriarchy, their insensitivity to racial hierarchies, and their neglect of power. Jefferson will be discussed at intervals throughout the rest of this book, with attention to his unsavory qualities emphasized in Chapter 9. My characterization of agrarian philosophy in this book will not involve deep engagement with Berry's thought or substantive discussion of his claims. Nevertheless, having some awareness of Berry's writing is important in the cultural milieu of the 21st century.

Wendell Berry is primarily a literary figure associated with a group of environmentally oriented American writers who studied under the tutelage of Wallace Stegner (1909–1993). Edward Abbey (1927–1989) and Gary Snyder are also emblematic figures in this literary genre. Berry's novels, poetry, and essays give prominence to the decline of family-style farms and the rural communities associated with them in the years since World War II. His 1977 book *The Unsettling of America* is probably the most systematic statement of his ideas as they pertain to a philosophical outlook or their relevance to policy. The book contains a number of diatribes against the agricultural policies favored by Earl Butz (1909–2008), who was Secretary of Agriculture to Richard M. Nixon (1913–1994). Butz was the most vocal advocate of industrial agriculture in his generation. Berry is especially vociferous in attacking the influence of efficiency, as a normative criterion, and specialization, as the social form in which a modernist outlook has been institutionalized. He is a persistent critic of capitalism, but he is no socialist. Berry's positive program commends things like farming with horses instead of tractors, something he has done himself on his Kentucky farm near the Ohio River.[3] In sum, Berry is associated with a leftward-leaning environmentalism closer to anarchism than Marxism. If Berry is criticized as having insufficient views on matters of race and gender (and he is),[4] readers should at least be aware that he is quite far from the prototypical type of white supremacist that caricatures a white male from the American South.

In certain respects, Berry's advocacy for farming is a misleading indicator of his agrarianism. For some, the term is primarily associated with land reform movements aimed at breaking up large parcels assembled under colonialism. Indeed, the online version of the Merriam Webster dictionary defines agrarianism as "a social or political movement designed to bring about land reforms or to improve the economic status of the farmer."[5] However, advocates of land reform appeal to many different philosophical principles, only a few of which are agrarian in a manner consistent with the view I will defend. For example, many development-oriented authors understand land reform as a way to increase agriculture's contribution to gross domestic product (GDP)—discussed in Chapter 7. Here, one might compare how redistribution of land holdings compares with increased mechanization or chemical use to evaluate proposals for change in land tenure arrangements. In either case, the criterion is the farm sector's contribution to economic growth.[6] Growth in the agricultural sector's contribution to the overall economy probably does improve the prospects of some farmers, but it may also weaken the standing of the farmer as a political actor of any special significance.

The "agrarian myth" creates a second barrier to understanding agrarianism in philosophical terms. All philosophical schools of thought—all isms—function as archetypes open to different interpretations and more detailed specification. To treat these schools or their specific variants philosophically is to query how they get things right or wrong, the specific sense of right or wrong itself to be specified through philosophical inquiry. Myths, in contrast, are more like free-floating literary or ideational forms. They may have so little conceptual content as to make serious examination of their veracity bootless. Myths may have functional implications in a given setting, but only in so far as they serve to organize and coordinate social and ideological factors that subsist and gain influence independent from what a myth literally says. Nobody really needs to believe or advocate a myth to make it effective as a mechanism of social control. This makes myths especially receptive to articulation and revision that realign their significance to people for

whom they have salience.[7] Nonetheless, questioning whether a given alignment of a mythic structure—the Garden of Eden and the Fall, Persephone's
annual visit with Demeter—is more or less adequate can only be done against
the background of the truth-apt commitments that philosophy provides.

My interest in agrarianism lies in treating it as a philosophical school of
thought, one open to multiple interpretations. This approach treats alternative ways to specify the archetypal structure of the agrarian tradition as
competing interpretations. (This is, in fact, the way that philosophers understand all isms.) M. Thomas Inge (1936–2021) wrote an introductory essay for
a collection of literary examples that sketches the contours of agrarianism as
follows:

- Cultivation of the soil provides direct contact with nature; through the
  contact with nature the agrarian is blessed with a closer relationship to
  God. Farming has within it a positive spiritual good; the farmer acquires
  the virtues of "honor, manliness, self-reliance, courage, moral integrity,
  and hospitality" and follows the example of God when creating order
  out of chaos.
- The farmer "has a sense of identity, a sense of historical and religious
  tradition, a feeling of belonging to a concrete family, place, and region,
  which are psychologically and culturally beneficial." The harmony of
  this life checks the encroachments of a fragmented, alienated modern
  society which has grown to inhuman scale.
- In contrast, farming offers total independence and self-sufficiency. It
  has a solid, stable position in the world order. But urban life, capitalism,
  and technology destroy our independence and dignity while fostering
  vice and weakness within us. The agricultural community can provide
  checks and balances against the imbalances of modern society by its fel-
  lowship of labor and cooperation with other agrarians while obeying
  the rhythms of nature. The agrarian community is the model society for
  mankind.[8]

James A. Montmarquet (1947–2018) situated these themes within a philosophical tradition beginning with Hesiod's *Works and Days* and culminating
in the 20th century in the writings of Berry. Montmarquet's analysis stresses
the claim that it is only through practical work activity that higher virtues
(such as justice or piety) become accessible to individuals. Citing Benedict
of Nursia (480–548), Monmarquet notes how "agricultural work avoids the

secular attractions and temptations of sometimes more engaging commercial activities," and how it is done "under an aspect of necessity rather than mere human preference or caprice"[9] gives the virtues associated with agricultural work a particularly compelling justification. Montmarquet regards agrarian uprisings as having less to do with egalitarian redistribution of wealth than with the displacement of the dignity associated with agricultural work by the emergence of capitalist acquisition.[10]

Agrarian philosophies thus propose a relational interpretation of human experience as a praxis with respect to the natural world. They are, in that sense, environmental philosophies. However, agrarian views are distinguished from other environmental philosophies by their emphasis on material practice in the formation of norms, values, and social institutions—what we might call *morals*. Oddly, neither Inge nor Montmarquet notes how the most relevant material practices involve sourcing food. Meeting food needs is a prerequisite for biological reproduction in any species, though humans are one of several species for which satisfaction of this prerequisite can be characterized as a group accomplishment. Features of the biophysical environment partially determine whether group behavior in conformity with social norms is successful in meeting basic biological needs. In this sense, the natural environment "selects" for culture—a theme that is commonplace in certain domains of anthropology and archeology.[11] The history of philosophical geography includes many figures that interpret norms and sociocultural institutions as both originating from and (in some sense) being justified by the way that they facilitate material practices vital to a social groups' survival.[12]

Although there are many variations in agrarian thought, most approaches presume that soil, climate, and other geographical features lead to different material practices. These, in turn, tend to produce corresponding differences in the norms, values, and social institutions of human populations. Each of the three key elements in this triad of nature, practice, and normative institutions is dynamic. The natural environment is both intentionally modified by human beings and undergoes gradual change processes of both anthropogenic and non-anthropogenic origin. Agronomic practices (such as soil tillage, slash and burn, fertilization, irrigation, or seed saving) change from year to year in response to both natural variations as well as the social environment in which they are embedded. Normative institutions (such as harvest rituals, property rights, work rules [including slavery], and credit practices) may change more slowly than agronomic practices but also evolve over time. Because of this dynamism, prescriptive agrarian philosophy is often expressed by alleging progressive or degenerative tendencies in the character of individuals or a social group rather than applying strict criteria of right and wrong to their actions or the outcome of those actions. As such, agrarian views often talk about corruption or strength of character and apply this criterion to individuals as well as to social groups.

In fact, agrarian thinking of this ilk was virtually ubiquitous in both science and political philosophy prior to the second half of the 18th century. Charles-Louis de Secondat, Baron de Montesquieu (1689–1755) is a particularly apt and influential example. He pioneered a set of fundamental concepts for political economy, such as the distinction between administrative, legislative, and judicial functions of the state, and argued that the specific form and functionality of any political entity would result from the way a form of government (monarchy, republic, despotism) combines with natural forces derived from soil and climate in a given region. Montesquieu held that the agriculture made possible by the soil and climate in a given region plays a strong role in the evolution of political institutions. If the environmental conditions are too harsh, no polity is possible. However, when nature is too generous, there is no need for the political institutions that ultimately give rise to culture and economic growth.[13] Montesquieu's views are a precursor of contemporary ecology, directly influencing the writing of Georges-Louis Leclerc, Count de Buffon (1707–1788). Buffon's *Histoire naturelle* was the immediate stimulus for works cataloging and analyzing the natural endowments of various world regions with an eye toward their ability to support European-style civilization. *Notes on the State of Virginia* (1785) by Thomas Jefferson is such a work.[14]

This type of agrarian thinking lingers well into the 19th century. G. W. F. Hegel produced a philosophy of history that was, perhaps, the culmination of Montesquieu's climate theory. Hegel believed that history is a developmental process culminating in the ultimate realization of freedom. Following Montesquieu's logic directly, Hegel assumes that the ready availability of food in tropical climes vitiates any impulse for political consciousness. Hegel traces the emergence of spirit in its early stages through Asiatic and Middle Eastern civilizations, where centrally administered irrigated agriculture demands social coordination, eventually giving rise to the idea of a "people." The notions of polity, citizenship, and freedom emerge in ancient Greece because the soil and climate of the Peloponnesus peninsula facilitated a food system composed of small, diversified farms (the *hoi mesoi*). These, in turn, led to the family structure described in Aristotle's *Politics*, which, in turn, give rise to the distinctive Greek political institutions. The subjective standpoint of a free people is the work of the historical process, but it is only after the creation of the Christian church that it is formed through cultural, as opposed to material, forces. Once viewed as the preferred entrée into Hegel's thought, the lectures on the philosophy of history are not widely read today. While the determinism and explicit Eurocentrism in Hegel's narrative will strike many contemporary readers as problematic, it nevertheless takes environment very seriously and as such deserves more comment from contemporary environmental philosophers than it has thus far received.

These elements in modern philosophy need to be examined for implicit racism. Buffon's interest in whether other regions could support European civilization was doubly racist. On the one hand, he presumed that *only* the characteristic landscape and climate of Europe would support the development of a civilized mentality. Other peoples would be deficient, even subhuman. On the other hand, his work functioned as an instruction manual for colonization. Buffon's classification system helped colonizers scope out new regions where crops of value to Europe might be grown, as well as providing guidance on what would have to be taken in hand in order to do so successfully.[15] Jefferson's own entanglement with racism will be taken up shortly. Oddly, it is in attending to the legacies of racism that agrarianism may have its best chance of becoming intelligible to contemporary readers.

By the late 20th century, the term "agrarian" was more likely to be associated with literature and paintings involving rural or pastoral themes than the above-described tradition in philosophy. Inge sketched five themes:

1. *Religion.* Farming reminds humanity of its finitude and dependence on God.
2. *Romance.* Technology corrupts; nature redeems.
3. *Moral ontology.* Farming produces a sense of harmony and integration, while modern society is alienating and fragmenting.
4. *Politics.* Rural autochthony provides the backbone for democracy.
5. *Society.* Rural interdependencies and reciprocities provide a model for healthy community.[16]

A reformulation of these tenets is clearly in order if we are to move toward a philosophically defensible agrarianism.[17] In the balance of this chapter, I focus on the moral ontology tenet.

Thomas Jefferson and Agrarianism

Other than Berry, Thomas Jefferson himself is today seen as the preeminent spokesperson for agrarianism as a system of thought. Jefferson's *Notes on the State of Virginia* announces "Those who labour in the earth are the chosen people of God," while an oft-quoted letter to John Jay (1745–1829) declares, "Cultivators of the earth are the most valuable citizens."[18] These quotations are cited as elements of the agrarian myth when they are interpreted as the bald assertion of a farming people's moral superiority, especially in comparison to the corruption and vice of city life.[19] One can see how these words might support such a sentiment, and there is ample evidence that similar praise of farming's virtues was sounded frequently to support Western settlement of the North American continent throughout the 19th century.[20] This is not the only way to read Jefferson, however. His letters and farm notes show that he was not naïve about the virtue of farmers. His praise in the two quoted passages was directed specifically to the way in which landowners could not easily disentangle themselves from their nation's solvency and defense. They are valuable *as citizens* in a way that traders and manufacturers were not simply because their assets cannot be easily moved to a new polity when times get tough.[21]

If Buffon's natural history and Jefferson's tribute to the farmer functioned as a prolegomenon to colonization and the assertion of European white supremacy, we should be suspicious of this praise. Jefferson is now considered to be a deeply problematic figure in American history, especially in light of his failures with regard to race. Historian Garry Wills takes some pains to demonstrate how Jeffersonian agrarianism was anything but original, concluding that Jefferson lifted his agrarianism from *An Essay on Public Happiness* by François Jean marquis de Chastellux (1734–1788).[22] Wills also points out the connection between contemporary racism and Europe's ambition to displace indigenous peoples and exploit the labor of enslaved Africans. He describes Jefferson as the figure who insinuates white supremacy into the very foundations of the American freedom ideal.[23] This places Jefferson squarely in the tradition of political thought that Charles Mills (1951–1921) has called the Racial Contract—a nexus of philosophical conceits that conspire to deny the full measure of humanity to non-European, non-white peoples. On Mills's reading, the social contract that was coming to be viewed as the basis for social ethics in Jefferson's time excluded non-whites just as it excluded women. The flexibly interpretable construction of race that became explicit in Kant denied black, brown, yellow, and red races (and, at junctures, the Irish and the Jews) the mutual protection and opportunity being accorded to whites.[24]

Other Jefferson scholars portray his philosophy in strikingly different terms. Willard Sterne Randall makes repeated reference to Jefferson's *opposition* to slavery, leaving out much discussion of Jefferson's slaveholding practice. He describes Jefferson as a gradualist in his approach to ending slavery, pointing out that the young Jefferson argued for ending the importation of slaves in the Virginia legislature. Jefferson's draft of a model constitution also called for a ban on the introduction of persons not already enslaved and stated that anyone born after 1800 would be declared free. Randall moderates the outrage a present-day reader might feel when learning of Jefferson's efforts to capture a runaway slave in 1769 by pointing out how, in stealing Jefferson's horse, the runaway had committed a felony and repudiated favors that had previously been bestowed on him. At the same time, Randall disapprovingly quotes a passage from *Notes on the State of Virginia* where Jefferson speculates that blacks are "inferior to whites in the endowments of both mind and body."[25] For my part, it is important to notice that Jefferson maintained a commitment to white supremacy even while condemning enslavement as a social practice. My argument appears in Chapter 9.

Attention to Jefferson's understanding of the environmental conditions that support a virtue of citizenship helps to moderate the tension between these two views of his legacy. Adrienne Koch (1913–1971) argues that Jefferson's remarks on race are actually an attempt to rebut the materialistic determinism he saw in Buffon's thought. In Koch's reading, Buffon was contributing to the strand of enlightenment philosophy promulgated by Claude Adrien Helvétius (1715–1777) and Paul-Henri Thiry, Baron d'Holbach (1723–1789). Helvétius and d'Holbach each authored explicit defenses of the view that conscious perception, emotion, and other features of the mind are reducible to the movement of matter. They denied the existence of supernatural or spiritual entities (including God) as well as the view that mind can be understood as a distinct substance or form of being apart from matter. In Koch's view, this materialism undergirds Buffon's view of the manner in which soil and climate are determinative for the phenotype and behavior of living organisms, including human beings. Although Jefferson admired these French thinkers' appeal to empirical evidence in constructing their philosophies, he viewed human nature as a composite of material and sociocultural formations.

Jefferson's farmers (they are planters, not fishers or foragers) have long-term interests in maintaining their soils. If they plant trees or vines, it takes years or even decades to realize the full benefit. Furthermore, these assets are not portable; they are firmly affixed to the territory of the polity in which the farmer resides. This gives farmers an inclination to participate in the polity's governance and defense, and Jefferson is claiming that a factory operator or a factory worker will not be so strongly inclined. While Jefferson's agrarian argument does indeed accord a prominent role to property holdings, it is important to see that it does not apply to every kind of property that we might think of in a contemporary sense. Ownership of portable or easily exchangeable types of property would not support Jefferson's argument, and financial forms of capital undermine it. The political virtue of citizenship arises from the close identification between the farmer's economic interests and a plot of land that is irrevocably fixed in a specific geographical place. Koch stresses how this element in Jefferson's though differs from a view that sees rational capacity and moral virtue as fixed by a hereditary material like blood, or what today we might call genes. Whether Helvétius and d'Holbach would have thought this explicitly, the notion that moral character is wholly determined by heritable properties becomes a fixture of Eurocentric doctrines of racial identity. In Koch's interpretation of Jefferson's philosophy, his insistency on the influence of environmental conditions led him to reject the deterministic racial classifications that Buffon applied to Africans and Native Americans.[26]

The racial nexus of Jefferson's thinking is taken up in more detail in the succeeding chapter. For now, it is the difference between Jefferson's philosophy (as interpreted by Koch) and the classic forms of materialistic naturalism that provides entry into agrarian philosophy. Koch refers to an exchange of letters between Jefferson and John Adams (1735–1826) in which Jefferson explains away the atheism of French *philosophes*, claiming that it is a product of the way that the Catholic Church dominates their social milieu.[27] The intolerance built into the social fabric of their environing conditions demanded a posture of strict resistance, while the American social climate favored creeds that accommodate a plurality of theisms, including his own deistic religious beliefs. Similarly, traits of indigenous people (Jefferson referred to them as aboriginals) reflect forms of socialization peculiar their collective solution to the imperatives of surviving on the North American continent (in other words, their culture). This was nurture rather than nature. However, Jefferson did not see nurture as a product of an individual's education or upbringing so much as a longer-term process of social accommodation that might take a number of generations to work out. He made remarks suggesting that a planter's ownership of slaves was adversely determinative for the evolution of "the most valuable citizens," but he did not hold out much hope that this could be reversed simply by ending slavery or giving black Americans the opportunity to farm.[28]

Mainstream Environmental Ethics and Its Discontents

As noted earlier, my particular interest in agrarianism arose from my disenchantment with mainstream philosophical approaches to environmental ethics. These views do not provide much ethical guidance for the stewardship of agricultural land. Environmental ethicists debated alternative ways to understand the value of nature, natural entities (such as forests, watersheds, the Grand Canyon, or the Ogallala Aquifer) and ecosystem processes (the hydrogen cycle or the global climate system). Most economists and some philosophers argue that value is derived either from human use of nature, natural entities, and the impact of ecosystem processes, or from preferences. Values derived from use are, in a philosophical sense, instrumental: the value of the natural entity derives from its capacity to achieve some further end. Preferences are evaluative attitudes or dispositions. They may be observed in the economizing behavior of humans or through other measurement strategies, such as surveys. People may want to preserve natural entities and ecosystem processes because they deliver goods that humans need (such as clean air and water). Alternatively, someone may just prefer that these things exist and continue to thrive. In either case, the human beings doing the valuation need not look beyond themselves to discover a source of value.

Contrarily, many environmental activists and environmental philosophers believe that value is an intrinsic feature of sentient creatures, living organisms, or even autopoetic, self-reproducing systems such as species, ecosystems, or the Earth itself. On this view, human beings should not think of themselves as assigning value to natural entities and ecosystem processes. Rather, humans *discover* a value that exists independently of humanity's encounter with the natural world. On this view, the self-interested uses that humans make of natural entities are utterly distinct from their intrinsic value. Eugene Hargrove, the founding editor of *Environmental Ethics*, regards establishment of an approach to valuation without regard to human preferences as a foundational question for environmental philosophy.[29] Disagreements over the source and scope of valuation were the very stuff of mainstream environmental philosophy between 1970 and 2010. A plethora of philosophical positions were introduced to account for environmental values. My treatment of mainstream environmental ethics will not attempt to catalog all of them.

Applying the instrumentalist/preference-based approach to agricultural land is straightforward. Farmland is clearly being used, and one can even assess its value through consulting the market price. However this approach to valuation cannot stand up to Liberty Hyde Bailey's or F. H. King's goal of permanent agriculture (discussed in Chapter 7). In particular, there would be no reason to engage in conservation practices that did not repay themselves over a relatively short period of time. Mainstream environmental ethics leaves us with two alternatives. Perhaps there is some obscure sense in which Bailey and King are thinking of farms as intrinsically valuable ecosystems, even if the value of farmland itself derives from its use. Alternatively, some version of duties to future generations might generate a morally persuasive reason to make a food system sustainable and regenerative in Bailey's and King's sense. Although the future generations argument has some plausibility, it also implies that farms and ranches are simply resources. They are not actually part of the environment that environmental ethics is sworn to preserve and protect.

Put differently, the duties-to-future-generations view makes no commitment to farmers (now again including the fishers, pastoralists, and foragers) or to the land and aquatic ecosystems in which these subsistence activities take place. Humans could get their food in other ways. Back in the 1980s, two U.S. Department of Agriculture (USDA) scientists speculated on future food systems: slime pits filled with genetically engineered microorganisms would capture solar energy, which would be piped to machines where other advanced technologies transform the sludge into familiar-looking foods.[30] Like the George and Jane Jetson family, future generations would meet their food needs by pressing buttons that deliver meals without the bother of farmers or farmland. The food system would then be fully industrialized, though the standard questions of the industrial philosophy remain: Does this system make an optimal use of resources? Are costs fairly distributed? Does it violate anyone's rights? In the 21st century, synthetic meats and other industrially processed animal products are taking steps to realize this vision. While there are certainly ethical arguments favoring this transformation, we should at least be curious about what it was in the agrarian valorization of the farmer's role that might be lost in the fully industrialized Jetson family food system.

A 2005 article by philosopher Ben Minteer and conservation biolo-
gist James Collins helps to appreciate a related concern situated squarely
in the tradition of environmental philosophy's engagement with conservation biology and the protection of endangered species and ecosystems.
They claimed that the first generation of environmental philosophers—
Australasian philosophers such as John Passmore (1914–2004) and
Richard Sylvan (1935–1996) or Americans such as Holmes Rolston or
Baird Callicott—had not developed an approach that could challenge the
dominance of natural resource economics in influencing actual conservation practice. Minteer and Collins see the passive appreciator of natural
beauty or ecological integrity as a key part of the problem. The primary
force of the claim that something has an intrinsic value in environmental
ethics is to assert that it should not be sacrificed to achieve any amount of
value obtained (or protected) in less fundamental terms. While this claim
might be understood to block or override the tradeoff calculations of resource economics, it fails to situate human beings within their ecological
context. The standpoint of the ethical evaluator is outside the system of
biotic and abiotic forces or predator and prey relationships. In the disen-
gaged spectator view that lays the groundwork for decision-making, the
ecological significance of human activity is, at best, occluded, and potentially obscured altogether.[31]

Minteer and Collins's observation connects with the discussion of
decisionism from Chapter 4. Although environmental philosophers disagree over the source and character of environmental values, most share the
assumption that values of some sort form the basis for preserving natural
goods and protecting them from consumptive or destructive use. It is important to notice how most of these approaches to valuation derive their
moral ontology from a model of rational choice that emerged in the late 18th
century and that continues to be very influential in environmental policy
today. Here, values become prescriptive through a linear model of rational
action: the decision-maker estimates how each option for taking action
achieves a quantum of environmental value, however it is conceived, then
applies decision criteria to select the favored option. There are strengths to
this model. It is flexible. The decision-maker can be an individual or an organization. It can even be an idealized subject, such as society as a whole. The
values applied can be instrumental or intrinsic. The decision rule might involve a scheme for adding and subtracting commensurate values and might
even include procedures for reconciling incommensurables. Alternatively, a

decision rule can regard one class of values as overriding. Such values drive decision-making; they trump other values.

Instrumental use and preference values can be subjected to comparative, cost-benefit style optimization, while intrinsic values may take the form of constraints on use and mandated actions to protect or preserve intrinsic values. But however one comes down with respect to these philosophical approaches to assigning value, the model of choice looks rather much like an ordinary business decision, where alternative courses of activity are arrayed before the manager.[32] Furthermore, it is decision-making that an ethics is assumed to be addressing in in this model. As such, decisionism has been the default assumption, especially in public policy settings. As Minteer and Collins note, there is nothing particularly ecological about this approach in ethics. Ecologists have struggled to conform to this model for environmental ethics by proposing a number of ways in which ecology might be used to help predict the outcome associated with a given policy option, but the weak predictive value of ecological models has limited ecology's role.[33]

Of course, Minteer and Collins are not the only ones to be frustrated. Other philosophers reject elements of this mainstream model. One school emphasizes environmental virtue ethics, which extends widespread discontent about choice-oriented ethical theories to environmental questions. Feminists have argued that the main problem in environmental ethics is not anthropocentrisim (centering valuation on human interests) versus bio- or ecocentrism (attributing intrinsic value to nonhuman entities), but centrism itself. Environmental philosophers should take a more relational approach. Environmental pragmatism is yet another alternative. Each of these perspectives shares elements with the agrarianism I will develop at some length in the balance of this chapter. A detailed discussion of these alternatives and overlaps would risk that my eyes glaze over (MEGO) reaction, so I will be brief.

It is not immediately obvious how either virtue ethics or environmental pragmatism offers the more ecological approach sought by Minteer and Collins. It is not even clear that they offer an alternative to decisionism. Indeed, the environmental pragmatism developed by Andrew Light and Bryan Norton is intended to be compatible with styles of policymaking that have been profoundly shaped by economists and public choice theorists. Although Alasdair MacIntyre does offer an important critique of decisionist tendencies in contemporary ethics,[34] environmental virtue theorists describe virtues as dispositions that align with environmental preservation and

sustainability goals.[35] This emphasis on dispositions brings virtue ethics per-
ilously close to natural resource economists' understanding of preferences.
Arguably, environmental virtue ethics and a utilitarianism sensitive to environmental values are isomorphic: they both pick out an identical set of decision options as ethically justified.

In contrast, I have a great deal of sympathy with the path charted by
feminists such as Val Plumwood (1939–2008). It might be possible to develop an environmental philosophy out of critical feminist and race theorist materials that would not be recognizably agrarian in its outlook. Yet
some of the relational themes argued by feminists have historical precedents
in agrarian accounts of the household economy, though the implicit patriarchy in these accounts points toward yet another way in which classical
agrarian philosophies must be reconstructed. I believe agrarian pragmatism complements the work of many feminists and race theorists, but too
often the feminists and critical race theorists I admire overlook humanity's
deep dependence on food systems. There are snares and pitfalls that must
be avoided in reconciling these philosophies, and I would not claim that the
account I am developing here has avoided all of them. Agrarian pragmatism
must not fall prey to the nostalgia of the agrarian myth, and it must develop
an ecological understanding of the moral agent that avoids typecasting the
farmer in white supremacist terms. I agree that my philosophy could profit
from a deeper engagement with feminist and critical race schools of thought.

Agrarian Thought and Cultural Formation

As discussed at more length later, consideration of habits and institutions
became the focus of John Dewey's pragmatism. In order to see how this
theme in 20th-century philosophical pragmatism descends from philosophical predecessors who focused on material practices associated with subsistence provisioning, it is instructive to consider Scottish Enlightenment
philosophers for whom social norms and institutions were presumed to
reflect a specific type of subsistence production. On this model, hunter-
gatherer societies develop moralities around group needs for sharing of
provisions and protection. With pastoral societies, it becomes necessary to
develop institutions of chattel property and trade for exchange of livestock.
With settled agriculture, these institutions become associated with land
holdings and crops, but there are also reciprocities that become established

among well-defined social roles (butcher, miller, and baker). In each case, moral codes emerge for social groups in an ecological fashion: particular social norms reflect the way that habits and patterns of action allow a given group to cope effectively with the challenge if provisioning themselves, given their environment. Individuals are expected to conform to norms characteristic of their given station, but reciprocities continue to exist between specific individuals who will know and interact with one another not only throughout their lifetimes, but also over generations.[36]

This is *not* an "evolutionary ethics" that sees morality coded in the genes. An evolution of sorts is occurring, but it is a cultural rather than a genetic selection. It is nonetheless appropriate to call this "evolution" because the "selecting" is not a process of conscious choice. Rather, norms that survive to be passed from one season or generation to the next do so in virtue of their contribution to keeping people fed, among other biophysical needs. Material subsistence practices in these agrarian societies channel moral sentiments in a unique way, producing characteristic moral norms and expectations functional for the societies in question. These mores and customs are functional in the sense that they regulate human conduct and allow the societies to persist over generations. Adam Smith's *Wealth of Nations* is known for theoretical innovations that blossomed into contemporary notions of the market, economic equilibrium, and capitalism. However, the book was also intended to investigate how the emerging commercial and industrial environment might work on moral sentiments to produce habits and institutions quite unlike those of the agrarian societies that had been the primary focus of Smith's earlier moral theory. Smith was aware that norms functional for agrarian societies might not be functional in the newly emergent capitalistic world. He believed, however, that formal social institutions (e.g., laws and public policies) that channel self-interested behavior into mutually beneficial forms of practice eventually form habits and norms, making industrial trading states as functional as (and considerably more prosperous than) the agrarian societies they replaced.

From Smith to Dewey, the centrality of farming becomes increasingly less critical to the analysis, and, as such, it may not be appropriate to characterize these clearly adaptive (and in that sense "ecological") theories as agrarian. Furthermore, as societies become more complex, it becomes less plausible to view norms critical for successful farming as making a decisive contribution to the overall stability and permanence of society. Nevertheless, the traditional linkage between agriculture and cultural transmission directs us toward an ethical philosophy grounded in the adaptive nature of personal virtues and social institutions. Emphasis on agriculture also makes clear the sense in which nature, land, and environment are active both in the adaptive mechanism (a people that starves does not reproduce) and within the focal area of the farmer's (or society's) consciousness. The farmer is not necessarily thinking about an adaptive response, but he or she most certainly *is* thinking about what we today call "the environment." This suggests that discussions of "good farming" (as developed by Wendell Berry) are ethically fecund in virtue of the way that they make fairly complex ideas about adaptation, selection, and even ecology more understandable.

In these philosophies, human beings are part of a larger system that has a formative role in their activities and practices and, subsequently, in what is valuable or important for them. Here, one might understand ethics as addressing the relationships, the fit, or the harmony that obtains between a human being and the larger whole in which they live their lives. Such approaches to ethics are not novel or new. Aristotle's *Politics*, for example, describes how human beings function within a nested hierarchy of systems that extend from the family up to the polis, the functional community that provides the basis for society and subsistence for a given population of human beings. Aristotle believed that human beings possessed an innate purpose or *telos*, which was to express to the fullest extent possible a rational life, but he believed that the specific shape and content of rationality would be configured by the society in which a person lives. Rationality was, for Aristotle, a virtue that must be realized through practice rather than a criterion of decision-making or optimal choice. Agrarian pragmatist ethics proceeds by arguing that it is necessary to expand the circles of systematic embedding that frame Aristotle's ethics beyond the state or polis to be inclusive of the broader environment. An ethics seeking to harmonize the natural and social worlds in which we find ourselves would then be alternative to mainstream environmental ethics because it would see human experience as determined by and reflective of interactions with the broader ecosystem.

Virtue theorists then argue that inquiry into what counts as human excellence or rationality must proceed in light of a rich understanding of how the broader environment shapes (and then is shaped by) the character traits that human beings develop in their interactions with the environment. Philip Cafaro argues that Henry David Thoreau (1817–1862) should be read as a virtue theorist who, like MacIntyre, aims to recover a commitment to comprehensive moral excellence that has been lost in contemporary life. He writes, "Thoreau recognizes that besides recovering the concept of virtue, we must recover an ethical space for virtue's pursuit."[37] Cafaro goes on to document Thoreau's extensive use of virtue terminology before likening the pursuit of virtue to the artist's pursuit of perfection. "The artist or striver after virtue must choose his own path, guided partly by tradition, but primarily by his own inner light."[38] However, Cafaro's claim that Thoreau seeks to *recover* an understanding of virtue lost to the modern world is anachronistic. Cafaro is explicitly endorsing a virtue ethic in *contrast* to the rights theories or utilitarian approaches, and he takes pains to document the way that Thoreau navigates between an Aristotelian notion of virtue and deontological formulations of duty or moral law. There is, however, little evidence to support the idea that Thoreau formulated his ideas in conformity with the tripartite consequences-rights-virtues distinction characteristic of late 20th-century Anglo-American academic philosophy. Nor does it seem likely that *Walden* is written in reaction to the work of English utilitarians such as Jeremy Bentham or John Stuart Mill. It is, in fact, only in the 20th century that philosophers made sharp distinctions between approaches that utilize a vocabulary of rights and those that stress the utility of consequences. Virtually all 18th- and 19th-century writers in ethics (including Kant and Mill) would have utilized vocabularies that draw equally on rights, virtues, and use-values.

What distinguishes Thoreau from Kant or Mill, who were laying the stones for the 20th-century's fascination with subjectivity, is that he was drawing consciously on an agrarian approach. Like his friend and one-time mentor Ralph Waldo Emerson (1802–1882), Thoreau believed that practical experiences such as planting beans, building a home, gathering huckleberries, or fathoming the depth of a pond are formative for human personality and character. Emerson and Thoreau both believed that nature was the most reliable guide to character and a balanced, self-reliant personality. However, what Emerson and Thoreau mean by *nature* is not wilderness or endangered species but simply their gardens and backyards—a world not totally given over to urban rhythms and the built environment.[39] If we follow Thoreau, it is agrarian philosophy, as opposed to recent forms of virtue ethics, that will provide the most useful connections to ecological ethics.

In contrast to anthropocentric and ecocentric schools in environmental philosophy, agrarian views have tended to focus attention on elements of human conduct that are less well adapted to a rational choice model but arguably more congenial to people who think in ecological terms. Like virtue ethics, agrarian views tend to state moral claims through a discussion of character traits. Unlike Cafaro's account, agrarian views saw norms and character traits as products of the interaction between an organism (a person) and its environment. Also unlike late 20th-century virtue ethics, agrarians view societies or social groups as having a distinct character in virtue of their having evolved norms and cultures in response to the natural environments in which they developed. Thus, personal virtues are responses that individuals acquire as a result of the way that their natural and social environment selects or reinforces certain attitudes, predispositions, and behavioral repertoires rather than others. Societies or cultures consist of socially reproduced norms (or tendencies to reinforce personal conduct) that are themselves the result of selection pressure exerted over time.

Finally, contrary to the late 20th-century presumption that cultivating virtue requires a moral agent to categorically reject any appeal to rights and duties, on the one hand, or consequentialist reasoning, on the other, a *pragmatist* ethic views these archetypical depictions of morality as logically independent capacities that have themselves been shaped by the evolutionary forces governing cultural formation. It may be wholly appropriate to think like a utilitarian, a neo-Kantian rights theorist, or even a contractualist when the situation in which an individual or group finds themselves matches the depiction of moral agency implied by each of these orientations. In many (arguably most) cases, the three perspectives cohere, and there will also be situations in which only one appears to provide any basis for guidance. However, the independence of these capacities also implies that cognitive capacities for questioning pat answers are always at hand. When each factor points in a different direction (or when none appears to be relevant) a person or group is thrown back on general procedures for innovative resolution of problematic circumstances. The situation calls for inquiry.

Norms, Habits, and Evolutionary Process

A simple model for the evolution of norms can be grasped by considering how an ecosystem might select for decision rules about animal stocking rates for pastoral systems. William Grant and I developed a quantitative ecological model for this type of "norm selection" by ecosystem processes. A community of pastoralists using a decision rule of maximizing output are compared to a community of pastoralists using a simple decision rule of "do what your neighbor did last time." Even if maximizing pastoralists have perfect information about ecosystem functioning, under plausible biological assumptions they drive themselves to extinction by depleting resources needed for animal production. As such, it is easy to see how a social norm of conformity might displace norms directing individuals to optimize outcomes. Given some plausible assumptions about ecosystem organization, a social group practicing conformity survives indefinitely, while a rationally maximizing social group is "selected against" by the natural environment.[40] Our goal was to show both that a "rational choice" model of norm-formation does not necessarily lead to the adoption of ecologically stable norms and that it is entirely possible for ecologically stable norms to evolve without calculative, outcome-anticipating rational choice.[41]

Within pragmatist philosophy, the most commonly used term for such acquired norms and dispositions is "habit." William James (1842–1910) used this term to refer to personal or individual modes of non-reflective response behavior, and Dewey adapted the term to socially institutionalized behavioral patterns. Although it is possible to describe and analyze habitual behavior as "choices," habits seldom involve (and are often quite resistant to) deliberate weighing of alternatives and conscious selection of decision rules for choosing the final course of action. Habits tend to evolve as relatively unreflective responses to situations that are encountered frequently. They are adaptive in the sense that they reproduce behavior (often a fairly complex repertoire of behavior) that a person or group deploys while coping with routine challenges. Behaviors that are not adaptive in this sense, or that result in the need for explicit, deliberative decision-making, generally do not become habitual. This is as true for "social habits" (more typically referred to as "institutions") as it is for an individual's habituated conduct.[42]

More recently, work in the pragmatist tradition has focused on the framing of choice itself. George Lakoff brought *framing* into the policy lexicon, and ethicists should take note. In public policy, framing is the way governmental or social activity is presumed to turn upon a certain specific set of issues, or present a specific set of live options. Even in individual behavior, however, decision-makers never give consideration to the full range of possible options available. There is always a limited set of "ends-in-view" and a similarly limited set of plausible means that are given consideration.[43] Indeed, failing to approach both individual and public choice without such limitations would impose intolerable costs on decision-making. Here, Lakoff is adapting one of Dewey's key insights: conduct always reflects a *poise*, an anticipatory orientation that facilitates an ability to behave in response to some elements in an organism's environment rather than others. For Dewey, an ethic must explore ways in which organisms, including individual human beings as well as social groups, are attuned toward features that function as a stimulus for some habituated response.

As such, understanding how individual and public choice are limited and shaped by framing is of intrinsic philosophical interest. In work with pragmatist philosopher Mark Johnson, Lakoff has argued that thinking with frames and metaphors is ecologically appropriate for embodied human beings with limited time and presence of mind.[44] Our ability to use language and carry on successful conversations becomes possible in virtue of the way that a limited set of possible framings come to the fore and shape our universe of possibilities in common life. Lakoff's framing work is "ecological" in that frames are "selected" from the limitless number of possible ways to orient and interpret a linguistic act not by conscious choice but by an adaptive process that is reflected in our very ability to use language itself. One might see this selection process as a competition among diverse symbolic forms (or "memes" in the terminology of Richard Dawkins). Some of these symbolic forms are reproduced in that they are remembered, communicated, and passed along in the symbolic practices of human beings. They are "selected" in at least two senses. First, processes of memory, communication, and education exert selection pressure: symbolic forms that are too complicated or obscure die out. Second, they either help people negotiate their environments or they do not, and groups of people who adopt less successful symbolic forms themselves die out.

Framings also have an enormous influence on our ability to conceptualize any given situation as ethically significant. Indeed, framings orient ethical thinking toward a distinct set of possibilities, on the one hand, but also toward what philosophers might call a particular conceptualization of normativity. That is, people will frame an issue or situation as "ethical" in a certain way and may be relatively insensitive to alternative framings. For example, Lakoff's political work indicates that messages framed in terms of burden sharing or fairness resonate more fully as having ethical significance than messages framed in the language of tradeoffs or redistribution.[45] As such, framing (and the way that a given population becomes adapted to one framing rather than another) is a subject of importance to ecological ethics. Unfortunately, its importance far exceeds the limited space that can be given to it in the present context. One might succinctly restate much of what has been said above as follows: framings commonplace among environmental philosophers have failed to engage framings commonplace among ecologists (or the general public). Abetted by Lakoff and Johnson's work, the pragmatist approach allows us to see *why* this is the case, but this does not necessarily imply that talking like a pragmatist is likely to get you very far, either.

Habits and framing are elements of human conduct that emerge from repetitive encounters with things, people, and entrenched ideas or practices in a given environment. Such environments have social, natural, and cultural elements in contemporary society. A full development of pragmatist ecological ethics would demand more robust accounts of habit and framing, accounts that would be anchored not only in the work of recent figures such as Norton, Minteer, or Lakoff and Johnson, but also in the thinking of classical pragmatists such as John Dewey or Charles Sanders Peirce. One weakness in such an account is that the analysis of habits, institutions, and framing is grounded in a 20th-century philosophical tradition that stressed *social* reinforcers as distinct from the way that habits or framing might evolve through interactions with the *natural* environment. It has thus not been obvious that there is anything of relevance to environmental philosophy in classical pragmatism. Here a return to the more explicitly agrarian orientations of an Emerson or Thoreau might be an improvement.

The Moral Ontology of Evolutionary Norms

It is time to confront a problem that has probably already occurred to many readers. There is no reason to think that the habits we form are good ones, nor is there any reason to think that adaptive cultures are morally superior to those that are consigned to the dustbin of social evolution. What is worse, some of the philosophies that have celebrated evolution promoted racist ideals that were used to rationalize some of the most oppressive social practices of the 19th and 20th centuries. Herbert Spencer (1820–1903) described evolution as "survival of the fittest." The idea was conjoined with older ideals of social progress in which human associations move from savagery and barbarism toward civilized society. It is easy to see how these themes can be used to place European culture at the pinnacle, justifying the exploitation of putatively inferior races. Some of these topics are explored in Chapter 9. Inspecting the evolutionary elements in the pragmatism of Peirce,

James, and Dewey for hidden elements of white supremacy is a vital and compelling philosophical task.

Contrary to the way that the word *pragmatic* is sometimes used in ordinary language, no philosophical pragmatist has ever claimed that the sheer functionality of norms proves their ethical justifiability. Pragmatists do claim that an ability to be functionally sustained, whether by memory, habituated cognition, or social institutions is relevant to a norm's viability, but I am not sure that even this amounts to a logically necessary condition. Stated as succinctly as I can manage, the pragmatist view is that humanity's entire tradition of philosophical thought, including Aristotle, Kant, and the utilitarians, equips us for normative inquiry. The best we can do is subject ethical questions to a sustained inquiry that draws on all of these traditions (and more) in order to inform the judgment that occurs at the natural termination of reflective questioning. No person, no social group can be certain that they have gotten it right, but the process of inquiry must be guided by "getting it right" as a regulative principle.

No one writing from the perspective of a white male in the first quarter of the 21st century can be entirely confident that he has purged his philosophy of elements that contribute to the resilience of white supremacist ideology. Nevertheless, the point of agrarian pragmatism is to develop an alternative to the decisionistic moral ontology that undergirds both utilitarian and rights-based thinking. Here, it will be helpful to draw on a metatheory Michel Foucault (1926–1984) discussed in conversation with Paul Rabinow (1944–2021) and Hubert Dreyfus (1929–2017). Foucault explains how we can gain insight into the comparative logic of ethical systems by examining four elements. First, there is the ethical substance or *substance éthique*. This is "the material that's going to be worked over by ethics."[46] Foucault is calling attention to the sense in which ethics is understood to be a practice or activity aiming to condition, modify or control something. The something that is to be conditioned, modified, or controlled is commonly thought to be some aspect of the self or soul. Perhaps it is the will: a component of the self comprising our intentions or desires. Perhaps it is the executive function of the mind: the governor of choice. In Foucault's last writings, he was exploring how Greek and early Christian ethics posited a very different *substance éthique*. It was an aspect of ourselves that experiences pleasure, gratification, or consummation.

We start to appreciate a fuller range of potential for ethics when we realize that it is possible to experience an ethic quite unlike the 20th century's focus

on choice. At the same time, the ethics of the 20th century began to incorporate conceptions of the *substance éthique* that transcended the individual
self. Even society as a whole can occupy the role of "the decision-maker"
who contemplates and evaluates alternative futures. Nevertheless, the comparative strength of Foucault's model comes into greater focus when we
consider the other three elements. There is the mode of subjectivation, or
mode d'assujettissement. This is the manner in which the *substance éthique*
is invited to engage in ethical activity. Although 20th-century rights theory
and utilitarianism or other versions of consequentialism have very similar
understandings of the *substance éthique*, they differ dramatically with respect to their *mode d'assujettissement*. In both cases, it is some version of
the executive that ethics is supposed to guide or discipline, but utilitarians
invite this decision-maker to consider the outcomes that his, her, its, or
their actions will produce. Rights theorists invite the decider to consider
how the range of permissible options is constrained, perhaps by the social
contract or by some master rule, such as "Do unto others as you would have
them do unto you."[47]

The third element is the *practique du soi*, which I interpret as a form
of *techne*: an art, craft, or science that specifies what the ethical subject
will do in response to the invitation or demand expressed in the *mode
d'assujettissement*. Foucault also calls this *l'ascétisme*, an ascesis or form of
self-discipline.[48] This is, of course, a key to much of Foucault's more celebrated work. Power exerted from the outside, possibly in the form of threats
or violence, can condition our activity and dictate our choices, but we do not
think of this kind of power as having much to do with ethics. However, power
also circulates when the cultural milieu specifies asceses of self-discipline.
Many adopt and practice these asceses unreflectively. Here, freedom emerges
as form of self-understanding that counters ascesis-as-power (at least in part)
when someone recognizes how their own forms of self-discipline function as
impositions on the *practique du soi* of others.

This characterization of freedom expresses a *téléologie*, an expression of
the ideal type, or the kind of person that an ethical agent hopes to be. In the
example just cited, which Foucault associates with Immanuel Kant, persons
engage in ethical reflection (itself a form of *techne*) in order to free themselves from mindless participation in the replication of moral platitudes. One
does this by considering how one's morality simultaneously takes the form of
oppressing others while constraining the fullest expression of the moral will
(e.g., Kant's *substance éthique*). Becoming truly self-governed is the *téléologie*

in Kant's ethics. It requires a *practique du soi* in which persons become the kind of decision-maker that freely constrains their own activity in light of its effect on others. It is important to see that this is not teleology in the normal sense of the word. Teleological morality typically portrays the end state as a *mode d'assujettissement* in Foucault's sense. In consequentialism we are invited to consider the state of affairs we want to bring about, while in many forms of virtue ethics, we are encouraged to emulate persons we take to have strong moral character.

Two points of qualification should be noted. First, with respect to Foucault's reading of Kant, we should question whether the idealized self-governing subject, the *téléologie* in Kant's ethics, embodies and perpetuates elements of white supremacy and male patriarchy. At a minimum, the form of subjectivity developed in Kant's second critique seems to sketch a domain in which the reader is invited to consider himself as equipped with all the power needed to execute the asceses prescribed in the categorical imperative. The 21st century demands more humility. Other authors have drawn on Kant's racial ideas to make an even more damning assessment of his achievements.[49] Second, I would not suggest that Foucault's four-part structure for characterizing the ontological commitments of an ethos or moral theory represents a well-worked out or internally consistent account that can be applied to any and every cultural system of moral practice. I do, however, think that it is helpful for the discussion at hand.

And how *does* all this relate to the evolutionary account of norms and habits sketched above? Foremost, I take Peirce, James, and Dewey to be articulating a radically different understanding of the *substance éthique*. Human beings are products of their environment, but not in the sense that a psyche is somehow shaped by forces wholly outside of it. Dewey writes that organisms are in the environment not as marbles are in a box but as events are in history.[50] The organism–environment unity is an ontological whole that may be specified into distinct moments given the overarching goals and purposes embedded within a nexus of events occurring at a particular place and time. Once these specifications have been made, truth-apt assertions about them are possible for Dewey: we can talk meaningfully (and either truthfully or falsely) about spotted owls in Oregon forests or farmers working in their fields. In these contexts, organisms and environments are separate things. But when we wish to talk about that thing that is the target of ethical reflection or ethically motivated modification, we must treat the organism–environment as a unified whole.

As such, we must reject invitations to ethical reflection that encourage us to think of human beings (or human societies) in terms of a psyche, soul, or even an embodied mind. An evolutionary, habit-oriented pragmatism does not seek asceses directed solely toward some element that is abstracted from the organism–environment totality. It matters little whether that element is conceived as some psychological capacity like rational evaluation, or some social functionality like policymaking or governance. In either case, what we do (singularly or plurally) is a situated response affected within an environment that also and immediately reconfigures the organism–environment totality. Or, to put it a bit too simply, we are always natural, we are always in nature, and our conduct redounds throughout nature.

How does this shift to a different understanding of the *substance éthique* play out with respect to agrarian pragmatists' *mode d'assujettissement*, their *practique du soi* and their *téléologie*? That is a large question that I cannot even attempt to answer here. It is an agenda for future work in agrarian pragmatism. Dewey emphasizes a method of inquiry. Whether they understand themselves as individuals or as members of a public, people are presumed to be situated; that is, they are environed both geographically and historically. They can exercise their ability to respond more effectively by working systematically through different approaches to learning: divergent, assimilative, convergent, and accommodative learning styles.[51] As for *practique du soi*, ethical inquiry will be most effective when it recognizes how each of the major divisions in philosophical ethics, utilitarian/consequentialist, deontological, and virtue ethics, develops a logically independent factor that has, at one time or another, helped human beings act responsibly given the situations in which they found themselves. Morality is thus a complex component of humanity's historical environment that prepares people with response-ability, even as it is adaptively reshaped by the response that people adopt in the present moment.[52] For Dewey, we do not lack resources or the ability to question the moral validity of any trajectory that evolution and habit set us on. But we are moving deep into MEGO territory, and it is past time to drop back.

Agrarian Pragmatist Ecological Ethics?

In this chapter, I have argued that, unlike contemporary policy models in agriculture, which descend from utilitarian conceptions of optimizing outcomes, older agrarian thinking saw agricultural production as a form of three-way co-production. The farmer produces crops and livestock, to be sure, but in doing so adapts to soil and climate in producing the farm. The farm (and the life of farming) in turn produce the farmer, meaning that the goodness of the farmer's work is more evident in the character of the farm family and the farm community than in the quantity of farm commodities.[53] Here, it is fallacious to resolve questions of value into either subjective use-values or intrinsic values associated with features or traits of entities (such as farms or ecosystems). It is instead the complex functional integrity of reinforcement and co-production seen in farmer-community-nature interactions that creates the context for moral evaluation.

In fact, underappreciated aspects of Jefferson's thought process suggest an even stronger connection to pragmatist philosophy. Echoing a theme emphasized by Peirce, Adrienne Koch writes "Philosophical problems were recognized only if they were genuine problems confronting Jefferson, bearing in some fashion on his political, agricultural, moral, scientific or religious affairs."[54] Koch does not include either pragmatism or agrarianism in her repertoire of philosophical orientations, but she describes Jefferson as a thinker whose pluralistic approach prevented him from identifying too closely with a doctrinaire version of the positivist, empiricist, materialist, and utilitarian ideas from which he drew. At the same time, Jefferson was able to resolve tensions and potential contradictions arising from these various schools of thought by retaining a focus on the circumstances that created a disturbance, evaluating theory in terms of its ability to generate action that would relieve the problematic aspects of a particular situation. Koch writes that some observers cite this tendency to argue that Jefferson was unphilosophical in his thinking, but she prefers to think of him as made uncomfortable by the certainty with which some of the *philosophes* he met in Paris could assert their positions.[55] She might have described this as an early form of pragmatist fallibilism.

Future attempts to utilize agrarian pragmatism in practical decision-making or in a broader environmental policy context will need to be attentive to Jefferson's unsavory ties to racism and settler colonialism. Ironically, the first steps toward decolonizing agrarian thought may involve a deeper appreciation of the way that white supremacist themes are tied not only to the forms of agriculture being practiced during the era of colonization, but also to the way that agricultural practices penetrate the metaphysics and epistemology of the modern era. I offer some thoughts to that end in the final chapter of this book.

9

Food Ethics and the Philosophy of Race

Every epoch calls for its own approach to philosophy. My work is part of my generation's response to the environmental crisis. Coinciding roughly with the first Earth Day in 1970, the growing awareness of humanity's impact on regional and global ecosystems sparked philosophical reflection on the values embedded within or attributable to non-humans and, in some cases, non-sentient entities such as eco-systems or *Gaia*, the superorganism of the entire planet. Environmental philosophy explores the dilemmas of collective responsibility and joins the sciences in seeking remedies to resource depletion, declines in biodiversity, and the transformative effects of climate change. Food ethics is a central part of the challenge. Writing on food system reform, legal scholar John Head appeals to the ancient Greek notion of *kleos apthatan*—the task whose completion wins enduring fame and admiration to a person or the people of an age. He writes, "Surely our *kleos* revolves around addressing the issues of ecological degradation."[1]

Yet, there is another great challenge to philosophy in our time. In 1903, W. E. B. Du Bois (1868--1963) saw the problem of the 20th century as the "color line." The color line is Du Bois's metaphor for a complex web of racial classifications, implicit norms, and systems of oppression that constitute white supremacy. Attempts to understand race and gender and promulgate progressive social change have stimulated thought on the nature of social identity, the experience and epistemology of oppression, and the sources of racial and gender stereotyping in the philosophical systems that gave rise to modern science. Throughout the world and especially in the United States, humanities scholars have unquestionably given significant attention to Du Bois's diagnosis of the central problem, the *kleos apthatan*, of the current age. Although black intellectuals have been calling attention to issues of race since the time of Ottobah Cugoano (1757–1791) or David Walker (1785–1830), the academic discipline of philosophy came to its senses about race rather late: important work began to be recognized in white- dominated philosophy departments only during the last decades of the 20th century.[2] Many

From Silo to Spoon. Paul B. Thompson, Oxford University Press. © Oxford University Press 2024.
DOI: 10.1093/oso/9780197744727.003.0010

philosophers would join other scholars in the humanities and social sciences in saying that Du Bois's agenda takes priority over environmental crisis.

The Problem

The fact that we can even speak of two separate crises shows that these trends have had too little intercourse. It is not entirely clear why that is. On the environmental side, the philosophical work that followed the first Earth Day emphasized the health risks of industrial technology and the protection of "untrammeled wilderness." A 1989 paper by Ramachandra Guha challenged the American tendency to overlook questions of justice in the distribution of recreational benefits and environmental harms,[3] but Guha's paper was read as an appeal to consider environmental issues in what he called the Third World. New philosophical work on race and gender may have had an implicitly urban focus following the example set by Alain LeRoy Locke (1885–1954) in his writing on the Harlem Renaissance or Jane Addams's (1860–1935) work in the ethnic neighborhoods of Chicago. Although this chapter will emphasize the themes of race, the feminist, queer, and transgender philosophies have also made important contributions to the discipline's turn toward novel issues. In all of these domains, the city is subliminally presumed to be the milieu in which these identities are performed.[4]

Environmental justice is a bridge between these conversations, but, even here, the emphasis has been on an urban population's exposure to industrial pollution. In food studies, scholars and social activists have recognized the disproportional harm experienced by women, ethnic minorities, people of color, and non-conforming gender identities. These harms run the full length of the food chain, from dispossession of farmland to lack of access to healthy food in urban favelas, projects, and racially segregated neighborhoods.[5]

Food sovereignty was originally coined to convey smallholding peasant farmers' interest in fending off the power of industrial agriculture and globally organized food processors and retailers. It has expanded to resist incursion on food systems that are of both cultural and nutritional significance to marginalized groups. Advocates for environmental justice have pressed for an understanding that encompasses the need for recognition and restorative measures as well as fair distribution for goods such as food or farmland.[6] But, these efforts notwithstanding, the connections between food ethics and the philosophy of race remain underdeveloped, at best. John Head does not even mention racial justice in his account of the task that will win lasting credit to our generation, should we choose to face it.

Chapter 8 introduced a heuristic dichotomy for philosophical inquiry into food systems. The industrial philosophy sees ethical issues in the production, processing, distribution, and consumption of food as similar to those in the industrial organization of transportation, manufactured goods, housing, healthcare, or entertainment. Agrarian philosophies stand in contrast to this view. Agrarian views are united by starting with the lived experience and material organization of a food system and deriving a philosophical understanding of food and agriculture from history and practice. How do these contrasting approaches influence work on environmental justice? Traditional applied ethics simply fills in the abstract statements of utilitarianism or rights theory with facts about practice within each sector of the economy. This generates ethical evaluations of the options facing a decision-maker, generating a straightforwardly industrial, as opposed to agrarian, approach.

In contrast, feminist philosophy and the philosophy of race are contributing new diagnoses of the moral problem with industrially organized society. Often it goes like this: economic development was not achieved without slavery and other forms of oppression. The political underpinnings of modern, democratic welfare-states were assembled on the back of Europe's prior refusal to regard non-white peoples as fully human, as possessing the requisites for true citizenship. The concerns of racial and gender justice can be made sensitive to many of food's distinctive characteristics, including its necessity for health and survival. Much of the writing on environmental justice takes this approach. However, most writers who make the critique never question the presumption that food and agriculture constitute but one sector within a complex industrial economy. Although much of this recent philosophical work can be read as a rejection of applied philosophy's decisionist biases, it seldom if ever attempts to take the food system as a starting point in its genealogy of power relations.

As discussed in Chapter 8, many agrarian philosophies put the sociopolitical efficacy, normative importance, and historical significance of food and agriculture in a central place. Other sectors of the economy such as manufacturing, healthcare, defense, and the arts derive their ethical significance in relationship to the agrarian core. If race and gender are critical social forms, an agrarian view of the food system would hold that ideas and practices governing the food chain should have decisive influence over the construction and reproduction of the arrangements and cultural ideals that constitute them. I can by no means claim to have a comprehensive knowledge of contributions to feminist philosophy or the philosophy of race over the past fifty years, so I offer the analysis of this chapter as a contribution to a conversation that may not even exist.

This concluding chapter speculates on what an agrarian philosophy might contribute if it were to address the philosophy of race and racism in a forthright manner. Given the scope and complexity of recent work on race, it cannot hope but be inadequate. I begin with a tentative framing on race and racism and then identify two logically distinct forms of racism in contemporary food systems: the exploitation of racialized groups within the food system and European displacement of food systems through colonialism. I apply this distinction in discussing racial slavery's link to plantation agriculture and white settler's dispossession of indigenous land. Finally, I return to Thomas Jefferson, and provide a counterweight to themes introduced in Chapter 8 with a frank assessment of his implication in racist ideology and practice. I offer these thoughts in the spirit of allyship, rather than as ideas that should substitute for the philosophical work born of struggle.

Philosophical Frames

Recent work in philosophy and political theory presents many options for understanding race and racism. White readers always need to be reminded of the egregious violence with which the victims of racism have been persecuted. Some narratives recount well-known incidents such as the killing of Emmett Till (1941–1955), the murder of three civil rights workers in Mississippi in 1964, or the assassinations of black leaders including Medgar Evers (1925–1963) and Martin Luther King, Jr. (1925–1968). Annette Gordon-Reed begins by recounting the fate of Joe Winters (≈1903–1922) who was burned at the stake after being accused of rape by a white teenager. She goes on to discuss Bob White (≈1920–1943), who was beaten by Texas Rangers to extract a confession for the rape of a white woman. Although White's confession was thrown out by the U.S. Supreme Court, he was eventually forced to stand trial in Conroe, Texas. The woman's husband shot White in the head in the open courtroom, but the killer was acquitted by a white jury that took less than two minutes to reach its verdict.[7] Leonard Harris describes a well-documented episode in which a white mob in Mississippi tied a black couple, the Holberts, to a tree and forced them hold out their hands so that their fingers could be cut off, one by one. The mob drove a large corkscrew into both of them at several places, "in the arms, legs and body, and then pulled out, the spirals tearing out big pieces of raw, quivering flesh every time it was withdrawn."[8] Harris defines racism as "a polymorphous agent of death, premature births, shortened lives, debilitating theft, abusive larceny, degrading insults and insulting stereotypes forcibly imposed."[9]

Almost all the terminology in philosophy of race is controversial owing to the way that patterns of speaking and writing play into specific manifestations of racism and white supremacy. Some philosophers writing on racism stress a distinction between overt and attitudinal forms of racism manifest in conscious motives and emotions and other forms of racism that are structural. These structural racisms reproduce racially distributed forms of harm through laws and conventional practices that reflect a legacy of earlier times. Structural racism may or may not be accompanied by racial animus or implicit bias on the part of individuals in order to remain effective.[10] Both types of racism find support in the work of philosophers, and I suppose I am a "both/and" philosopher, rather than an "either/or." The arguments that I develop speak to the sense in which an interlocking set of institutions and discursive practices reinforce patterns of conduct that favor people raced as white over all others, no matter how they are racially classified. This does not imply that there are no gradations or differences in the way that non-white groups are affected, and there are also intersections with feminist and queer thought. The chapter is already long, and I hope readers will forgive me for not delving deeply into the lively discussion on these themes.

As discussed in Chapter 8, philosophers of the ancient world developed theories of the relationship between soil and climate, on one hand, and personality traits thought characteristic of a regional population, on the other. The Roman philosopher Marcus Terentius Varro (116–27 BCE) developed a complex system of climate and soil classification reflecting this kind of practical farming wisdom. For Varro, the character of a people was also shaped by the climate-soil-farming complex of the region in which they lived.[11] Varro's style of soil and climate determinism continues to figure in the perpetuation of racial stereotypes that view putatively inferior racial groups as a threat to civilization. Simon Donner summarizes the view as one that argues for the superiority of Mediterranean peoples (e.g., the ancient Greeks and Romans) in light of the stifling impact that hotter or colder climes have on human development. On this view, non-whites are lazy and less intelligent.[12] Neil Altman and Johanna Tiemann describe neo-Nazi William Pierce

(1933–2002) as promoting the superiority of the white race based on the pseudo-evolutionary claim that having evolved in temperate zones, whites were endowed with the ability to delay gratification, leading to stronger planning and problem-solving skills. The ideology holds that "races that developed in warmer, more consistent climes were not required to develop higher mental functions or the capacity for self-restraint."[13] Also in Chapter 8, Hegel saw no trace of civilization in Africa because life is too easy: the food grows on trees.

By the 17th century, natural philosophers were cataloging climate–soil relationships with an eye toward European colonization of distant regions. Buffon's thirty-six-volume *Histoire Naturelle* was simultaneously a masterpiece of curiosity-driven science and an instruction manual for colonizers who hoped to convert the globe into a plantation supplying Europe with industrial inputs and cheap food commodities for the proletariat. This classificatory taxonomy was fully of a piece with writings by celebrated philosophers classifying *Homo sapiens* into racial groups. Recent work in the philosophy of race has emphasized how John Locke, David Hume, Jean-Jacques Rousseau, and Immanuel Kant participated in the construction of a racial hierarchy.[14] The development of a philosophical rationale for racial classification occurred along with the rise of social contract theory and was effected by the same men we see as crucial figures in that tradition of political thought. The sense in which their ideas rationalized an expansion of Europe's foodshed (the geographical basin from which a population draws agriculturally produced goods) is less frequently recognized.

Charles Mills tells us that a reading of Enlightenment philosophers should start from the fact that whatever the philosophers *thought* they were doing, Europeans had already agreed to cooperate in the subjection of non-Europeans. The practice of white supremacy preceded racism. Mills does not mean that there was an agreement in the literal sense. He means the social contract tradition in philosophy—as well as the notions of subjectivity and consent that it mobilized—were embroiled in projects to put white Europeans in power right from the start.[15] Social contract theories were designed to combat the rationales for maintaining the political dominance of titled aristocracy. As such, they tied the legitimacy of the state to a putatively universalizable conception of personhood, but Mills notes that, as a matter of practice, these white male property owners were deeply engaged in the oppression of women and non-whites. They needed a theory to explain why the oppressed others were not fully deserving of personhood, and, from that, the modern classification of races was born.[16] Mills argues that structural forms of racism may be more philosophically significant because white supremacy—the systematic advantaging of those raced as white—can and does persist even among individuals who harbor no conscious racial animus and who are largely unaware of the advantages that their racial position affords.[17]

Yet I do not think that Mills would disagree with the observation that much of the oppression and violence in the American food system derives from overtly racist attitudes. For example, in 1960, four black students from North Carolina A&T staged a sit-in at the Greensboro Woolworth's all-white lunch counter. The protest was a signal event in the early years of the U.S. civil rights movement, and it was connected to food in several ways. Most obviously, it was a lunch counter—a public eatery. Practices of food consumption are frequent sites of ritual practice in all cultures, and the Jim Crow South was no exception. White Southerners' maintained and even cultivated distaste for eating with Blacks, and everybody knew it. Whites, Blacks, and even anti-racist whites understood this segregationist practice as a form of attitudinal racism. Upton Sinclair (1878–1968) said that his muckraking 1906 exposé of meatpacking missed its intended target of America's heart, but hit its stomach. The A&T students went for the stomach, right from the start.

The lunch counter protests also reflect elements of structural racism in the food system that would not be obvious to many readers. North Carolina A&T is both a public (e.g., state-supported) and a historically black university. It was established in 1890, to allow Southern land-grant universities—the publicly supported institutions that maintain programs tied to the U.S. Department of Agriculture (USDA) to remain segregated. The maintenance of this separate but putatively equal system of secondary education reflected the implicit Racial Contract. Funding for the 1890 schools has never come close to that of the original 1860 land-grant colleges. Although the segregation maintained by the creation of 1890 land-grants was *intentional*, Mills also discusses how the presumptive racial hierarchy supporting lower funding for black universities became enshrined in law. Mills quotes Chief Justice Roger Taney (1777–1864) with reference to the U.S. Constitution's language on the rights of citizens.

[Blacks are] . . . of an inferior order, and altogether unfit to associate with the white race. . . . This opinion was at that time [when the framers wrote the Constitution] fixed and universal in the civilized portion of the white race. It was regarded as an axiom in morals as well as politics, which no one thought of disputing or supposed to be open to dispute.[18]

Given the presumed intellectual inferiority of Blacks, the white power structure inferred that their educability was limited. As farmers, they could not be expected to adopt the scientific methods being developed at white colleges of agriculture.

I see the general framework that I have developed in the book as compatible with Mills approach and supportive of his prescriptive agenda. Mills would not, I think, have characterized himself as a pragmatist, but my emphasis on social control suggests how Taney's view could be reproduced through discourses dominated by whites, even as slavery is abolished and Jim Crow dismantled after the civil rights protests of the 1960s. Racial hierarchy would be the implicit background or, as Jason Stanley suggests, the "not-at-issue" context that survived "at-issue" discourses to end chattel slavery. If "everybody already knows" that Blacks are not fully men in the self-evident sense Jefferson proclaimed in the opening words of *The Declaration of Independence* (as Taney claimed), the Racial Contract survives as a resilient background element even in progressive discourses that make important, if also limited, reforms.[19]

Now let me be clear: it was certainly not the case that everyone thought Blacks to be less than fully human even in Taney's day, much less during the 1960s, when many elements of Jim Crow were overturned. I am drawing on Stanley's approach to suggest a weaker but more sinister epistemological claim with powerful ethical implications. When I write "everybody already knows," I am calling attention to the pragmatic background of persuasive discourse. There might be quite a bit of difference and disagreement about what is true and false among participants in a discourse, but while these differences remain in the background of the expressed or "at issue" points being contested, they continue to be reproduced in the discourse of social control. Decisionist applied ethics will be an inadequate response because no one, neither utilitarians nor deontologists, needs to be reflecting any ill will toward Blacks in their framing of decision options that will be subjected to an explicit moral evaluation (e.g., the "at issue" subject matter of philosophical persuasion). Because persuasive moral discourse aims at adjustments in its audience's belief system, it can miss ways in which the imaginable courses of action are shaped by the institutional environment. As I understand the Racial Contract, it is an unspoken element of this background, what "everybody already knows" even when there are many people who would reject it were it to be expressed explicitly.

The balance of this chapter is an inquiry into the food system's contribution to the Racial Contract. I want to distinguish two forms: racism *within* food systems and racist *dispossession* that occurs when one racially identified group undermines the food system of another group. In the United States, Blacks and Hispanics are the primary victims of racism within the food system, though Chinese, Japanese, and Filipino immigrants have also suffered. In contrast, Native Americans have seen their food systems disposed of and destroyed. In this, I am following Mills's practice of including the repression of all these groups under the Racial Contract. Although I have not developed a precise definition of a food system, the idea implies a coordinated interaction of various elements, including firms, government bodies, and institutionalized practices. I would include cultural forms within these elements as well. The distinction emphasizes the difference between racisms that oppress through the operation of an existing food system and those that subjugate or obliterate the functional food system of a racially oppressed group. Calling attention to this difference promotes a more complete understanding of the way that food systems have contributed to the institutionalization of white supremacism in global food systems.

Racism in Contemporary Food Systems

How do racist elements survive in the background of food system discourse? As occurring *within* food systems, racism is incorporated into production, processing, distribution, and consumption in all the ways that racism *can* appear. In some cases, people are motivated by racial animus or bias or see the cultural instantiation of racist practice as an opportunity to further their interests at the expense of racially oppressed people. In other cases, racism is wholly implicit. In the United States, racism within the food system is structural in the racial distribution of primary farm operators. Out of just over two million farmers in the 2012 Census of Agriculture, only 33,371 or 1.65 percent are black, while 12.2 percent of the total U.S. population are black.[20] Although non-racial characteristics might account for some aspects in this skewed distribution, racial minorities' disproportionate absence among farm operators reflects the legacy of explicitly racist efforts to exclude them from farm proprietorship. Even if no one is consciously targeting black farmers today, the numbers reveal an ongoing form of structural racism.

In addition, the evidence for explicitly racist efforts to oppress Blacks, Hispanics, and Asians within North American farms and food systems is overwhelming. The economic drivers for this oppression are access to land and availability of labor. The list of actions to limit black farmers' access to land is lengthy. Immediately after the American Civil War, plans to redistribute lands to formerly enslaved Blacks were cancelled.[21] Subsequently, the USDA denied black farmers in the American South access to information about the existence of government programs to improve profitability. White-controlled agricultural extension services refused black farmers' application for benefits without explanation. Officers of white-run banks turned down loan applications from black farmers, and white landowners refused offers for purchase or rental from black operators.[22] White farmers' access to these benefits and services created an overwhelming competitive advantage, which black smallholders resisted through the formation of cooperatives and the development of farming methods that minimized the need for purchased inputs. A U.S. Federal Court recognized this history in the 1999 *Pigford et al. v. Glickman*, which awarded substantial damages based on racial discrimination in the administration of USDA programs.[23]

In the Western United States, cooperation among white farmers and government officials prevented waves of Chinese, Japanese, and Filipino immigrants from establishing successful farms. Like Africans brought to North America in the slave trade, these Asian immigrants were experienced farmers. While they were an important source of labor for the California fruit and vegetable industry, their proficiency posed a competitive threat to white landowners whenever they were able to gain control over their own land. White landowners took advantage of government policies (such as the Chinese Exclusion Act of 1882 and the internment of Japanese Americans in World War II) to force land sales. Local communities harassed and bullied both workers and Asian farmers. The white community developed a system for playing different ethnic groups— Chinese, Japanese, Filipino, and Hispanic—against one another to keep wages low and deprive them of the opportunity to become agricultural proprietors. In this respect, efforts to prevent Asian farmers from entering food system proprietorship connected with large growers' effort to resist the unionization of farmworkers during the 1960s.[24]

The United Farm Workers of America (UFWA) strikes of the 1960s and 1970s intersect with the racist underpinnings of immigration debates. Fruit and vegetable growers have long depended on a short-term expansion of the work force during harvest. The people who do this work move from farm to farm and, in many locales (not just the United States), cross international borders in doing so. Although most industrial democracies have developed policies intended to protect these workers (and hence support the economic interests of the growers who depend upon them), abuses continue.[25] Horrendously abusive practice extends into non-farm components of the food chain, as restaurants and food retailers are among the firms who exploit undocumented workers. As I have written in *From Field to Fork*, these are among the most obvious ethical issues in the food system, and it is not clear that we need philosophers to endorse their condemnation.[26] More subtly, immigration policy is also a race matter. Growers in Florida and neighboring states have followed the Californian strategy of pitting the distinct racial identities of undocumented field workers from Haiti and Central America against one another to create conditions in which their uncertain immigration status makes them especially vulnerable to exploitation.[27] Any attempt at food ethics that fails to acknowledge the racial dimension of these issues is failing a key moral responsibility.

Sharecropping also exhibits racism within the food system. It was dominant in the southern states well into the 1960s, and it combined with Jim Crow to function as the overriding enforcement mechanism for anti-black racism in the American South prior to World War II. As most readers will know, sharecropping is a form of contract where one party supplies inputs, another supplies labor, and both take a share of the proceeds when the crop is sold. Various models of a sharecropping system are available, and the system is widely practiced on a global basis, today. Sharecropping is not intrinsically unjust, but as inequality comes to pervade the context for these arrangements, opportunities for exploitation grow. After President Andrew Johnson (1808–1875) vetoed the Civil Rights Act of 1866, freed black fieldworkers had only their manual labor to contribute in the years following emancipation, while whites contributed land, machinery, and annually purchased inputs such as seed and guano. What is more, white landowners extended food, housing, and other essentials to their workforce in the form of a loan (or furnish) that was to be repaid when workers received their share. Even when whites did not cheat their workers by "cooking the books"—as they often did—workers could finish each season more deeply in debt to their patron. As such, they were not really free to refuse a renewal of the agreement in the following season.[28]

From one perspective (e.g., *my* perspective), the oppressive aspects of contemporary food systems are obvious. Indeed, they are so obvious that I have tended to omit even cursory mention of them in my earlier writings.[29] It is nonetheless important to notice how racism patterns their impact. From the perspective of someone whose engagement with food systems is limited to buying and eating, racisms in the distributive and consumptive end of the food system will be less obvious. It is therefore important for readers less attuned to agricultural practice than I am to see how these difficult to perceive patterns continue. Racial difference structures poverty in many industrial societies, where food consumption depends on the ability to pay for food. Profit-driven food retailers (e.g., food markets and restaurants) abandon areas where margins are low. Efforts to improve food security (soup kitchens, food pantries, government entitlements) become instruments for reinforcing racist stereotypes.[30] With the production practices just noted, this configuration of the food system illustrates how racisms (sometimes overt, sometimes structural) exist *within* the food system.

Settler Colonialism and the Displacement of Food Systems

A different set of social justice issues emerge from colonial *displacement* of indigenous food systems. Unlike the racist distribution of injustice within food systems, these forms of injustice are more difficult to capture in the utilitarian and rights-based ethical systems of the industrial mindset. As noted already, European colonialism took shape as the imposition of plantation-style agricultural production systems intended to supply the homeland with inputs to their nascent industrial economies. These farms required a large, violently disciplined labor force as well as control over a significant portion of arable lands in colonized territory. While one can condemn the takings, as well as the cruelty and rights-violations of plantation agriculture from the perspective of utilitarian or rights-based ethics, the twin requirements for control over labor and land point toward a different set of food justice issues. The first and most obvious point to notice is that plantations for cotton, tobacco, and sugar cane required large tracts. Colonists had to remove indigenous people from these lands, imposing a European style of property rights in place of local institutions for allocating access and use of fields, forests, and sources of water. Then they had to obtain a workforce able to manage a monoculture of these commodity crops. That intensified the geographical dislocation of indigenous groups, substituting a new population composed either of European immigrants or (more frequently) enslaved Africans. These are the material underpinnings of settler colonialism. An alternative colonialism might have extracted tribute from conquered peoples without also disrupting the internal organization of their society. *Settler* colonialism, in contrast, is characterized as the systematic attempt to replace an indigenous population, a sometimes literal but necessarily cultural genocide that reconfigures the norms, expectations, and practices at a given locale.[31] Settler colonialism is overtly racist in its condemnation and eradication of the indigenous people's own norms and practices. It is structurally racist in its institutionalization of alternative patterns that reproduce the behavior and mindset of settlers.

Analyses of settler colonialism that ignore the role of agriculture overlook not only the material basis for this pattern of oppression, but they also fail to appreciate some of its most ethically problematic consequences. Kyle Whyte's work on settler colonialism emphasizes activity that disrupts how environment functions in indigenous people's worldview and practice. Although Whyte does not reference John Dewey, Dewey understands organisms (including humans) as always-already-environed entities. An organism (a person) acts from a poise or standpoint comprising species, group, and individual histories. Whyte lays stress on the role of provisioning and food consumption in patterning the interactions among members of Native American peoples and bands. Collective capacities (e.g., culture) emerge and are reproduced by food systems. Just as plantations required control over land and labor, so do the complex and intricately articulated systems of practice that constitute indigenous food systems, generally evolved over centuries. Incompatibility is to be expected. What is more, settler colonialists brought invasive plant, animal, and microbial species along with them, further upsetting the poise—the collective capacities oriented to the environment— of indigenous food systems.[32]

How are we to characterize the forms of injustice that Whyte sees in the wholesale displacement of indigenous food systems? It is first of all important to see that the utilitarian and neo-Kantian rights theories that support an industrial orientation to food systems are poorly suited to this philosophical task.[33] Mills calls our attention to the way that these classic forms of ethical reasoning revert back to Europe's participation in the African slave trade and the colonization of Africa, the Americas, and parts of Asia. Perhaps to avoid becoming embroiled in philosophical debate over the Racial Contract,

Whyte resorts to the concept of food sovereignty, an idea coined to assert the interests of smallholding farmers and the rural communities in which they reside against disruption by industrial food systems. In that context, loss of food sovereignty counters those who defend industrial food systems in virtue of their alleged capacity to improve food security. In other contexts, food sovereignty has been expanded to assert any individual's right to consume anything, without regard to a public interest in food safety or environmental integrity.[34] This pattern in the discourse of social control is typical of a food movement aimed squarely at expanding its base, but, from a philosophical perspective, the increase in political efficacy comes at the cost of capitulating to an industrial philosophy of food systems. It is pragmatic not in the sense of philosophical pragmatism, but that of expediency. My interest here is not one of rejecting Whyte's or other food activists' political objectives, but rather in being clear-eyed about the price we pay. Occlusion of the role that race plays in the history of sovereignty arguments is part of that price.

There is little risk that Whyte's readers will overlook the role of white privilege in his treatment of settler colonialism. Nevertheless, his attempt to mount an argument familiar to an audience steeped in the philosophical commitments of industrial society also obscures the agrarian orientation of the indigenous knowledge systems whose loss he laments. The worldview of colonized peoples in both North and South America as well as Australasia and much of the Middle East was agrarian in the sense that their food systems anchored their entire system of cultural practice, *and* they were aware of this fact.[35] In contrast, the plantation agricultures developed to serve the manufacturing economies of Europe were encouraging a philosophical transition to thinking of agriculture as just one sector of the economic system. 18th- and 19th-century elites were willing to make exceptions for agriculture, but the view that it would ideally conform to the dictates of efficient production while internalizing social costs was well on the way. I would count the erasure of agrarian thinking as a component of the racial injustice issuing from the displacement of indigenous food systems.

Now, some readers will object to my characterization of indigenous food systems in agrarian terms. The objection is well-founded to the extent that my suggestion is viewed as a Western or European reinterpretation of an indigenous world view. As the balance of this chapter demonstrates, European-derived agrarian philosophies incorporated many objectionable elements. If agrarianism implies a neo-liberal productionist standpoint, this may reinforce a vision of human beings disembedded from their environing conditions, acting upon plants and animals that serve as food as if they were mere resources. Alternatively, obtaining food may be a form of mutualism, or even a gift in which living nature plays the active part. My own positionality means that I cannot speak *for* those who see their nourishment in such strongly relational terms. I must respect those who reject the terminology of agrarianism because they see it as too deeply implicated in the Eurocentric projects they are resisting. Nevertheless, I hope to open a philosophical space in which subsistence provisioning can be understood as a nodal nexus for human praxis.

In summary, Whyte is calling our attention to epistemic oppression. Indigenous agro- ecological knowledge systems secure a people's ability to sustain themselves in a given biome, but the biotic elements of their environment are disrupted when plantation agriculture enters the region. This voids the traditional ecological knowledge (TEK) of the indigenous population. However, it is possible to see this as but one element in a broad spectrum of epistemic oppressions that cut across every aspect of socioeconomic life. There would not be anything important about the fact that the epistemic injustice involves knowledge of food systems, on that view. That would be to take what I call an industrial view of epistemic oppression. I am arguing that a deeper epistemic injustice consists in obliterating the possibility of understanding the problem in agrarian terms. On the one hand, the epistemic injustice consists not simply in undercutting the effectiveness of TEK, but also in blocking an entire way of thinking about the human condition. On the other hand, this form of epistemic injustice rebounds to affect the worldview of the oppressors, the settler colonialists, who are cut off from the possibility of understanding their own philosophical heritage. Even European forms of agrarian thinking disappear from the universe of philosophical possibilities.

Agriculture, Oppression, and the Agrifood System from 1600

As noted already, the expression *food system* emphasizes the systematic organization of actors. It also puts food in the forefront as distinct from other goods produced by agriculture. Foregrounding food might arouse the imagination of people who eat but take no particular interest in farming, ranching, fishing, forestry, and other forms of renewable natural resource curation.

However, the producers themselves take a rather different view. Even small-holder subsistence households will see provisioning of food, energy, and fiber for clothing and other uses as all of a piece. Traditionally, the term "agriculture" connotes this ensemble of practices, which may include hunting and foraging as well as animal husbandry undertaken for draft animals or household security rather than food consumption. As the focal point of our study drifts back to the agriculture and food systems of the 17th, 18th, and 19th centuries, this perspective becomes important. Appreciating the full meaning of racism in the food system requires this broadened perspective.

An overly narrow focus on food is misleading because large-scale global trade in non- food agricultural commodities (cotton, tobacco, hides, and pelts) has a long history, including trade in quasi foods like sugar and spice.[36] When we include these non-food products in our understanding of an *agri*food system, colonization comes into focus as an agricultural project. European consumption of luxury goods like tobacco and furs extended a trade pattern built on the Silk Road network, which was first established during the Han Dynasty of China during the 2nd century BCE. By the 13th century, the demand for such luxury goods precipitated the growth of a sea-going shipping industry. The opening to North and South America during the 16th century created lucrative opportunities for trading new types of luxury good, including tobacco and cocoa (as well as precious minerals). Settlements intended for agricultural production of these goods grew throughout the 17th century.

When we view this history from an agricultural perspective, we see how this period of trade in luxury commodities created the infrastructure for racism in the 18th century: the rise of cotton, tobacco, and sugar plantations. Textile mills throughout Europe (especially in the English Midlands) created an enormous demand for raw cotton, a crop never grown at scale in any European country. This demand in turn triggered a phenomenon that historian Sven Beckert has called "war capitalism": deploying military power to secure the supply chain for a homeland textile industry. Sidney Mintz (1922–2015) argues that the creation of the industrial workforce also stimulated the demand for another plantation crop grown under tropical conditions. Imported sugar was an inexpensive way to supply calories to factory workers, even if the jams and sweetened teas they consumed were lacking in nutritional quality.[37] In comparison to the earlier era, both cotton and sugar were amenable to large-scale plantation-style plant production. These highly profitable crops incentivized control over relatively large tracts of land. They also required attention from field labor on an almost daily basis, with the need for an increased workforce during a lengthy harvest season. In short, they put the settler in settler colonialism.

Unlike cereal crops, cotton, sugar, and tobacco require almost constant attention. Sugar cane and tobacco plants must be trimmed frequently. Cane is grown in soils that do not retain water, but also flood, so water management is a day-by-day process of adjustment. Tobacco is harvested selectively (e.g., leaf by leaf) to assure top quality. Cotton is naturally a perennial crop that flowers and produces bolls continuously through the later period of the growing season.

This means that workers must be in the field to pick ripe bolls, leaving others to develop for later harvest. When grown at plantation scale, cotton develops susceptibility to pests and must be plowed under after the last harvest and replanted in the spring. These three plantation crops thus required a full-time field labor force skilled enough to exercise appropriate agronomic practices, at least through the eight to ten months of the year from planting to harvest. Rice, a fourth plantation crop grown in the southern United States and parts of Latin America, also required forms of highly specialized labor.[38]

What does any of this have to do with agrarianism? An agrarian philosophical outlook can take many forms, but the one that emerged between 1700 and 1900 saw these features of plantation production systems as providing a justification for social institutions that were resisted by the people they oppressed and opposed on moral grounds in urban centers. In one sense, emergent ideas of white racial superiority simply jibed well with a society that envisioned a cruelly disciplined agricultural workforce as an unavoidable ill. Aristotle's statement that some people are naturally destined to be slaves reinforced this pattern of thinking. Aristotle was almost certainly thinking of Greek agriculture when he made this comment.[39] One can trace an agrarian argument for slavery that stresses first the inherent risks and vulnerabilities of plantation agriculture and then emphasizes how the landowner's absolute control over every aspect of his worker's lives secures the continued reproduction of what its defenders regarded as an absolutely essential social form. Given these imperatives, it is particularly convenient to have race-oriented philosophical rationales at hand for characterizing a class of human beings as fit for enslavement.

Yet why would anyone think that plantation agriculture is an essential form? I think we can track two lines of thought, only one of which I find even remotely convincing. Economic thinkers (such as the physiocrats) who argued that agriculture was the only legitimate source of social wealth followed the less convincing path. They claimed that other forms of production, such as manufacturing, only rearrange existing materials. Only agriculture can actually expand wealth by producing goods of value where literally nothing existed before. Adam Smith put the kibosh to this doctrine, but it was influential during the 18th century and might have been cited to encourage the growth of farming systems capable of supplying Europe's growing demand for cotton, sugar, and other commodity crops. The (slightly) more plausible way of reasoning starts with the idea that we do, indeed, need farm commodities. We have to eat, after all, and we need clothes on our back. If the benefits of plantation production outweigh the social costs, one can generate a utilitarian argument for accepting the inevitable. This is the thought that eventually takes shape in the industrial philosophy of agriculture. I am not convinced by this argument, but I do think that philosophers have to take it seriously.

In sum, the above noted imperatives of agricultural production are more widely applicable to the emergence of racial theories than the silence of most ˙ philosophers writing on race would imply. Nevertheless, there is no reason why we should view the plantation system of commodity production as an unavoidable, much less ethically justifiable, way to organize an agri-food system. There are two points to stress. First, plantations were not inevitable. In 19th-century America, plantation systems existed side by side with smallholder household farming, where labor was supplied by household members with occasional help from volunteer neighbors and hired hands. Southern smallholders were poor, but they did grow cotton and cane (and some owned slaves). On a global scale, cotton farming in Egypt and India—two of the American South's key competitors—was primarily managed by smallholders. Second, the view that agriculture must of necessity supply sugar, cotton, or tobacco for European markets was already a significant step toward viewing agriculture merely as one sector in an industrial economy. Native American food systems deployed a complex mix of swidden agriculture, foraging, hunting, and harvesting from closely monitored populations of wild fish and game. While indigenous people's approach excelled at sustainability, it might have had trouble supplying the cotton mills in Manchester and Birmingham.

It is, then, quite misleading when defenses of the plantation system are taken to be emblematic of an agrarian philosophical outlook.

White Supremacist Agrarian Philosophy

Although I hope to open the space for a more congenial form of agrarianism, the appropriation of Varro or Hegel for neo-Nazi versions of evolutionary norms is a good reason to approach agrarian philosophy with healthy skepticism. When one looks deeply into the rationales advanced under the agrarian banner, more reasons can be added. As noted in Chapter 8, many view Thomas Jefferson as the authoritative source on agrarian philosophy. Although Jefferson was far more nuanced than some of his contemporaries, the complexities in Jefferson's vision serve to make him an apt paradigm for a white supremacist form of agrarian philosophy. My own book, *The Agrarian Vision*, emphasized Jefferson's understanding of the connection between farming and democracy as an entry point for thinking about sustainability. While I do not back down from what I wrote there, I might have offered readers a more rounded picture of Jefferson the man.

Jefferson's insulting and ill-informed remarks on Blacks in his *Notes on the State of Virginia* are a staple of recent scholarship in the philosophy of race. Explaining differences between Whites and Blacks that are "fixed in nature," he begins with skin color and goes on to note "a very strong and disagreeable odor," "a want of forethought," and a "disposition to sleep when abstracted from their diversions, and unemployed in labor." Jefferson continues, "They are more ardent after their female, but love seems with them to more an eager desire, than a tender delicate mixture of sentiment and sensation." Though he admits their musical abilities compare favorably to Whites, he goes on to describe Blacks as "in reason much inferior." Jefferson closes this section in the *Notes* with disparaging remarks about the literary accomplishments of Phyllis Whately (1753–1784) and Ignatius Sanchez (c. 1729–1780). The literary accomplishments of these two black writers belied Jefferson's stereotyping judgments, but Jefferson is unmoved. Of Whately, he writes, "Among the blacks is misery enough, God knows, but no poetry," and on Sanchez, "his imagination is wild and extravagant, escapes incessantly from every restraint of reason and taste, and, in the course of its vagaries, leaves a tract of thought as incoherent and eccentric, as is the course of a meteor through the sky."[40]

Quotations from the *Notes* can suggest an oversimplified version of Jefferson's views. For example, Tamas Pataki makes a passing reference to Jefferson in an introductory overview of philosophical approaches to the theorization of race. He writes,

> Thomas Jefferson (1782), reflecting on the supposed inferiority of his black slaves concluded: "It is not their condition, then, but nature, which has produced the distinction."[41]

A close reading of the *Notes* qualifies the picture we would form of Jefferson's views given Pataki's rendering of the quotation. The passage appears in a section where Jefferson is comparing the racial slavery of his own Virginia to that of the ancient Greeks. Jefferson overlooks important differences in the "condition" of slaves in these two contexts. Nevertheless, his point in comparing Virginia to Ancient Greece is to document how *others* have presumed the heritability of uncomplimentary characteristics among blacks. Jefferson does not necessarily disagree, but his very next sentence describes this inference as a conjecture.[42] As Charles Mills himself notes, these passages in the *Notes* are brought to a conclusion by a remark in which Jefferson characterizes them as a "suspicion only."[43]

Jefferson might not have been as racist as many of his contemporaries, but his attitude is ethically and philosophically problematic in ways that call for special recognition. First, Jefferson articulated philosophical principles that he did not uphold in either his political career or personal life. He made numerous legislative proposals for ending the institution of slavery, and, as President, he signed the law ending the importation of slaves. Yet Jefferson did not free his slaves, as George Washington (1732–1799) did. In fact, the connections between Jefferson's agrarianism and his views on slavery and race helps illuminate the possibilities of agrarian philosophy. Although Jefferson's agrarianism contextualizes his view of race, his statements on blacks and native peoples do not yield a smooth or internally consistent understanding. What is more, Jefferson's actual conduct appears to be flatly contrary to his expressed views in crucial respects. I am willing to examine his contributions to political thought apart from his private life or conduct of office, though I respect others who take a different view.

Jeffersonian Agrarianism

First, it is important to be clear about the agrarian views that Jefferson held. Mark Tauger summarizes agrarian views in his history of global agriculture. They "idealized the peasant or farmer as the true and fundamental representative of the nation. Adherents of this view considered peasants and farmers better than urban people because they worked on the land, producing crops and livestock that satisfied civilization's basic needs, uncorrupted by towns, capitalism and foreigners."[44] Again following up on a theme from the previous chapter, a quick glance at Jefferson could link him to this form of agrarian populism, but my reading is different. Jefferson is drawing on a much older political argument for tying the political rights we now associate with citizenship to land ownership. In contrast to shop owners and manufacturers, farmers' key productive assets (what we today call capital) are arable lands.[45] Improvements (fencing, irrigation, and improving soils) can increase farm productivity, but they are not very portable. In contrast, Jefferson had watched traders and manufacturers pick up their assets and leave the thirteen colonies that eventually rebelled against England's King George III (1738–1820). Landowners were more responsible *as citizens* because their personal interests were more closely aligned with the physical territory of the state. Elsewhere this reasoning might have supported vesting power in the nobility, but Jefferson envisioned an America in which the vast majority of citizens would be landholding farmers. Agrarianism was a plan for navigating between what Jefferson saw as the aristocratic threat to individual liberties and the populist threat to good government.[46]

Execution of this plan required economic development emphasizing smallholding owner-operators holding down the American land mass. These were not plantations, such as Jefferson's own, but household farms. In fact, the need for a large plantation workforce cut against Jefferson's vision. Agricultural workers with no ownership stake in farms would lack the tie that binds their interest to that of the nation. Given the onerous nature of farm work, they would have every incentive to cut corners and shirk responsibility. This kind of reasoning also lies at the core of Jefferson's opposition to slavery. The field work done by slaves was no more conducive to the virtue of citizenship than working in a factory. What might have been just as bad from Jefferson's perspective, reliance of slave labor encouraged habits of cruelty and indolence among slave owners.[47] Jefferson perceived a pernicious system of feedbacks in which the institution of slavery induces vices among the slaveholders, whose conduct quite justifiably creates resentment and anger among the enslaved. This in turn causes fear among slaveholders who become more adamant in their commitment to slavery as a defense against retribution from their slaves. Jefferson believed that, sooner or later, something had to give; the slave system was not politically viable over the long run.

In sum, it is logically possible to articulate a variety of Jeffersonian agrarianism that is actually contrary to the simplistic version derived from the passages in *Notes on the State of Virginia*. This is what I had in mind in *The Agrarian Vision*. However, Jefferson's farming and his political career were both conducted within a historical context characterized by the mentality Charles Mills calls the Racial Contract. Both farmers and politicians have to think in the short run in order to get *to* the long run, and Jefferson's short-term thinking reflects an implicit acceptance of white supremacy. The Southern planters (of which he was one) could not see their way out of slavery, and Jefferson's natural political alliances were thus with people who opposed his philosophical position on slavery.[48]

Jefferson on Race

Jefferson's *Notes on the State of Virginia* is not the only source we have for inferring key elements in his view of race. A paragraph that was omitted from Jefferson's original draft of the *Declaration of Independence* is an important document. Voiced as a complaint against King George III, it offers Jefferson's most straightforward condemnation of slavery as violating the rights of "persons of a distant people who have never offended him, captivating and carrying them into slavery in another hemisphere, or to incur miserable death in their transportation thither."[49] The passage goes on to refer to enslaved Africans as MEN (all caps in the original), directly countering Justice Taney's doctrine. The author of the *Declaration* did think that black slaves were men; Taney was just wrong on that point. The same passage shows how Jefferson also understood that slaves would resent their status as well as their treatment. This would make them a threat to landowning citizens. Blacks were, for Jefferson, fully capable of political agency.

Notice, however, that even in the deleted passage from the *Declaration* Jefferson does not oppose slavery on grounds of racial equality. Although the deleted sentences state that non-whites are men, the insulting words in his *Notes* explicitly express a belief in a racial hierarchy. The contradictory nature of these texts is relaxed a bit when we remember that Jefferson probably did not understand this hierarchy in genetic terms. Darwin was seventeen when Jefferson died in 1826, and Mendel was a child of four. Jefferson's reading of philosophical race theories was not as deterministic as that of the French materialists he encountered in Paris. Adrienne Koch quotes a letter from Jefferson to Nicholas de Condorcet (1743–1794) that offsets the insults to Whately and Sanchez with praise of Benjamin Banneker (1731–1806). Here Jefferson expresses his hope that "the want of talents observed in them [e.g., Blacks] is merely the effect of their degraded condition, and not proceeding from any difference in the structure of the parts on which intellect depends."[50] That is, Jefferson took Banneker's accomplishments to be evidence against the hypothesis of inevitable or hereditary racial inferiority that he had ventured in the *Notes*.

Nevertheless, the Condorcet letter should not be interpreted to mean that he denied any role to biology at all. Comparing Jefferson's remarks on blacks to his remarks on Native Americans is instructive in this respect. In contrast to his remarks on blacks, Jefferson devoted extensive passages in his *Notes on the State of Virginia* to extolling the intelligence, nobility, and capability of Native Americans. He argued that their putatively savage nature was, in fact, an entirely rational accommodation to the conditions in which they lived. They would adapt quickly to the habits of a civilized people given the education, inducements, and opportunities available to Europeans at the time.[51] Although characterizing indigenous peoples of North America as a distinct racial group can certainly be challenged, Jefferson (along with Mills) accepts this approach. The fact that he does not appear to hold a biologically racist view toward the indigenous people of North America supports the thesis that he was *not* simply a man of his time with respect to his conceptualization of race and anti-black racism.

I have suggested that the categorization of races in Jefferson's time was also a legacy of climate determinism, which is itself an agricultural inheritance. This philosophical heritage descends from Varro, as mentioned above, and is apparent in Buffon's system of natural history. I am arguing that Jefferson's view does in fact differ from white supremacists who extended Varro, Buffon, or Hegel's reasoning to all non-whites. In contrast, Jefferson sees cultural adaptations as explaining dangerous or unsavory traits settler colonists observed in the character of indigenous peoples. Of course, he is less generous with respect to blacks, and that is a source of consternation for those of us who take logical consistency seriously. When we note his views on indigenous peoples and the qualifying remarks on the heritability of putatively disreputable traits among blacks, Jefferson does not regard mentality or character traits as biologically determined features of race, at least as we understand biological determination in the 21st century.

Jefferson might have had a more Lamarckian view. He might have thought that traits learned or acquired during an individual's lifetime were somehow—perhaps weakly—passed from parent to progeny,[52] but I would be speculating to assert that. In any case, Jefferson does not qualify as a pure instance of the type that Charles Mills characterized as a racial realist.[53] However, Jefferson's more flexible views on race and heredity only make his anti-black racism ethically problematic in a different sense. They are even inexplicable save, perhaps, as yet another instance of the resilience of Mills's Racial Contract. The naturalistic philosophical grounds offered for racial groupings by men like Hume and Kant provided a logically consistent rationale that applied to all races, including Whites. While Jefferson thought that indigenous people were culturally adapted (rather than hereditarily disposed) to a wilderness environment, Blacks seem to have lived in a state of exception for Jefferson. Their racial constitution would prevent them from escaping it, at least for many generations.[54]

Taking stock of the argument thus far, Jefferson's agrarianism is a view that stresses the connection between a person's subsistence activity and the development of political virtues. A person who works for wages will not have the same orientation to his or her polity as a person who farms and neither will someone whose wealth is based on moveable assets. The cultural evolution–environmental selection aspect of the human condition that is at work in this argument does carry over into Jefferson's view on what differentiates colonial whites from Native Americans, but he sees enslaved Africans as less capable of any short-term adaptive change. They are in some manner limited by heredity in a way that Whites and Native Americans are not. So Jefferson *did* believe in racial difference, at least at the time he was writing the *Notes*. We cannot exclude the possibility that this belief accounts for the way he treated his slaves. However, Jefferson does not always behave in a manner that is consistent with his expressed beliefs. With that, we turn to his actions.

What Jefferson Did

I have earlier noted that Jefferson's attempts at legislatively restricting and even ending the institution of slavery did not prevent him from engaging in a political alliance with some of the most vociferous defenders of slavery. In fact, Jefferson's hypocrisy on the continuance of slavery runs deeper still. Henry Wiencek's analysis of the account books at Monticello have convinced him that Jefferson made a lot more money selling slaves than by selling crops. The domestic slave trade was the only thing on Jefferson's Virginia plantation that was keeping the operation afloat. Wiencek believes that Jefferson knew that, and that made it unlikely he would take any personal measures based on his philosophical beliefs.[55] Jefferson's treatment of slaves exemplifies what I have called an internal form of racist oppression with respect to agriculture. He was running a plantation and he was willing to do things to his enslaved black workforce to make it financially viable. Though he may not have been among the cruelest Virginia slaveholders, he approved the use of violence in their discipline and employed overseers known for their brutality. His ill treatment of enslaved Blacks included not only his fieldworkers, but also his household staff. Jefferson's sexual exploitation of Sally Hemmings (1773–1835) is now widely accepted. We could end by saying that whatever he professed, he was simply of his time with respect to his treatment of black Americans.[56]

It is worse than that, however. His more positive attitude toward Native Americans notwithstanding, Jefferson damaged indigenous peoples sorely in his practice as a political leader. If he was not beholden to prejudices that relegated native peoples to reduced racial status, neither was he above doing things that caused them irreparable harm. As the third President of the United States, Jefferson supported violence against indigenous tribes, bands, and confederacies. He laid out a plan of subterfuge that would make Native American claims over tracts of land vulnerable to dispossession based on indebtedness. He did this while exposing the evils of debt in his philosophical writings, even calling for policies that would relieve people from debt peonage.[57] Jefferson was thus a central figure in the subversion of indigenous food systems and their replacement by the European model of household management. Aside from Andrew Jackson, no American president was more disastrous for indigenous people.

Jefferson's actions are consistent with his agrarian vision. With respect to the Africans enslaved at Monticello, the simple imperatives of doing whatever it takes to keep a farm going are indicative of this view, but Jefferson's political activities with respect to the indigenous peoples of North America are even more telling. He saw the removal of Native Americans as a key to the realization of his vision for an agrarian democracy. Jefferson was quite open about this. His second inaugural address to Congress praises the "aboriginal inhabitants of these countries" but notes that they have been "overwhelmed by the current, or driven before it" and are now (in 1805) "reduced within limits too narrow for the hunter's state." Jefferson hopes to draw them into farming, a lifestyle that will "prepare them for that state of society, which to bodily comforts adds the improvement of the mind and morals."[58] An 1802 message to Handsome Lake (1735–1815) of the Iroquois extols the benefits of settled agriculture as "advantageous to a society, as it is to an individual, who has more land than he can improve."[59] Jefferson is suggesting that Native Americans hold more territory than they need for farming. If they can be induced into abandoning the complex food systems that have sustained them for generations and turning to European-style crop production, they can afford to sell their excess land to white settlers.

An 1803 letter to William Henry Harrison (1773–1841) repeats this thought, but Jefferson goes on to suggest something beyond a discourse of philosophical persuasion for gaining control of aboriginal land holdings.

> When they withdraw themselves to the culture of a small piece of land, they will perceive how useless to them are their extensive forests, and will be willing to pare them off from time to time in exchange for necessaries for their farms & families. To promote this disposition to exchange lands which they have to spare and we want for necessaries, which have to spare and they want, we shall push our trading houses, and be glad to see the good and influential individuals among them run in debt, because we observe that when these debts get beyond what the individuals can pay, they become willing to lop them off by a cession of lands.[60]

The same letter notes that when indigenous groups become "extinct" or are "driven off" their lands, the United States is justified in claiming them by the doctrine of sovereignty.[61] Given *these* passages, we are justified in characterizing Jeffersonian agrarianism as white supremacist in its overarching implications.

Alternatives?

Beyond noticing two modes of racial oppression—*within* food systems and *displacement* of food systems—this chapter catalogs ways in which European agriculture has supported white supremacist visions of race and ethnicity. This observation can be conjoined with Mills's theory of the Racial Contract, as well as with other work in the philosophy of race tracing the deep connections between idealistic egalitarian conceptions of respect for persons and the reality of racial subjection. The oppression of factory laborers in the Industrial Revolution moved European philosophers to develop a moral critique asserting the equality of workers in their standing as persons. Yet philosophers' interest in the conditions of the working class simultaneously concealed how the textile mills of the Industrial Revolution were coming from an agricultural production system that had to deny the humanity of *its* workforce in order to secure a constant stream of raw materials (e.g., cotton) supplying the manufacturing process. Even as the factory system expanded beyond textiles, the workforce had to be fed with cheap commodities (e.g., sugar), also produced under conditions that required dehumanizing procedures for disciplining field labor. There is thus an important sense in which the Racial Contract is written in the agricultural underpinnings of the Industrial Revolution. What would the alternative to this tradition be?

One answer is more technology. The development of power machinery for farming obviates the need for oppressive forms of field labor. However, the actual history of machine harvestable crops reveals ambiguities. Mechanization of field crop farming required genetic modifications making it feasible for all the plants to be harvested on the same day. This was difficult for some plantation crops, and especially cotton because workers needed to be in the field periodically to select mature bolls, leaving others for a later day. Cotton was one of the last commodity crops to be mechanically harvested, and the timing of this transition is suspect. Mechanically harvestable cotton varieties became available in the 1930s. Mechanization allowed Southern landowners to resist the Depression Era USDA's efforts to enforce rules that would have helped black sharecroppers get a fair share of subsidy payments.[62] Rather than reforming the institution of sharecropping, Southern planters adopted this new technology and terminated agreements (many of which included housing) with their predominantly black workforce. Some scholars have argued that this racially skewed collapse in the rural economy was a proximate cause of the Great Migration of Blacks to Northern cities.[63]

What is more, plants that have been bred for uniformity are more vulnerable to devastating losses. Fungi, insects, and plant diseases spread rapidly in a monoculture of genetically identical specimens. Although there are managerial responses to this problem, the actual history of 20th-century agriculture is once again telling. Farmers have attacked pests with a succession of chemical and biotechnological agents. Toxins accumulate in the environment, damaging beneficial species, such as Rachel Carson's songbirds. What is more, pests rapidly acquire resistance to toxins, putting farmers on a "pesticide treadmill" requiring constant development of new chemical formulations.[64] In practice, the technological response must bear significant responsibility for the environmental problems of food systems. Although I would not dismiss the role of new technology in alleviating both social and environmental problems, the notion of a technological fix for agricultural elements of the Racial Contract is naïve. That is one reason why we need the more active conversation outlined at the beginning of this chapter.

Alternatively, we can look for other versions of agrarian thinking. In fact, I think they are not too hard to find. The *Pachamama* (or Mother Earth) ethic of respect for nature is grounded in the daily planting and harvesting practices of Latin America's Aymara peoples.[65] This is arguably an indigenous form of agrarianism that could function as a competitor to Jefferson's. However, there are structural and epistemological reasons why old white men should be cautious about translating the work of non-whites into the philosophical language they happen to prefer. As Kristie Dotson has argued, reinterpreting the words of people who have suffered intersectional oppressions is inherently disrespectful and liable to be distorting in ways that further the oppression of the people being translated.[66] Concepts derived from Aymara vocabularies have been reinterpreted for exploitative practices. At the same time, some scholars who expose distortions in the way that indigenous worldviews are being appropriated prefer to interpret them as committed to an "intrinsic value" view of nature.[67] If my analysis is correct, this runs counter to the thought that the Aymara worldview is an expression of agrarian philosophy. It would be more reflective of work by Holmes Rolston III, Arne Naess, and the advocates of Deep Ecology. I remind readers of my pragmatist fallibilism. I could be wrong about this, and wrong in a moral sense.

If many of the Native American food systems displaced by colonial settler states can be understood as resting on agrarian foundations, suggestive sources can also be found among African American authors. *Freedom Farmers: Agricultural Resistance and the Black Freedom Movement* by Monica

White begins by noting that the tension between African-American leaders Booker T. Washington (1856–1915) and W .E. B. Du Bois (1868–1963) was in part animated by Washington's focus on rural blacks as opposed to Du Bois's emphasis on advancement in urban contexts. White also notes that Du Bois's praise for black agricultural cooperatives is underemphasized in recent scholarship. White situates George Washington Carver (1864–1953) between Washington and Du Bois. Carver achieved renown as a scientist while conducting research specifically intended to be useful to resource-limited household farmers (what today we might call sustainable agriculture). This sketch of the range in opinion among black leaders circa 1900 sets up White's primary topic, which is a detailed discussion of four farming initiatives. Each of them operated on the basis of a strongly placed-based organizing principles and conceived the ability to produce food for the community as a source of solidarity and a way to resist oppression by the surrounding white community.[68]

The Detroit Black Community Food Security Network (DBCFSN)[69] is one of White's case studies. It is a collaborative project that mobilizes various urban agriculture projects in the City of Detroit intended to fulfill simultaneously neighborhood revitalization, youth employment, and improved access to fresh produce grown without pesticides and synthetic chemicals. A large (by urban standards) community farm on city-owned land is a centerpiece of the project, overseen by Malik Yakini, who has been a mainstay of the DBCFSN. Yakini stresses the cooperative element of the DBCFSN as a form of resistance to the alienating impact of capitalist social relations. However, his anti-capitalism is less oriented to socialism than to the ideal of displacing market relations with localized, place-centered collaboration.[70] Yakini's focus on urban food systems recalls agrarian syndicalist movements that link more strongly to the agrarian anarchism of Charles Fourier (1772–1837) or Peter Kropotkin (1842–1921) than to Karl Marx.[71] When I visited Yakini at the Detroit farm in 2015, he told me that the collective memory of slavery and sharecropping in the black community presents an obstacle to organizing in connection with the food production end of urban food systems.

Coming from the other end of the food chain, Ashanté Reese offers a detailed study of the role that retail food shops played in establishing a sense of identity and community solidarity in a Washington, DC, area neighborhood in the 1950s. These relationships began to suffer as increased mobility gave residents the opportunity to seek lower food prices at major grocery chain stores and big-box outlets. Although Reese's study does not put producers in the foreground, it does a nice job of explaining how aspects of food sovereignty contribute to the quality of life for people who experience racism in its multiplicity of forms. She articulates a longing for the sense of community associated with agrarian ideals and suggests that people in this neighborhood may not have fully appreciated how it helped them resist the force of white supremacy until the system teetered into an advanced state of decline. She suggests that alternative food system strategies (co-ops, farmers markets) need to be evaluated in terms of their ability to revive what I would call agrarian ideals.[72]

Still others interpret anti-racist action in terms of resisting the way that modernist ideology encouraged the institutionalization of white supremacist ideals through the influence of the agricultural and food sciences. Contributors to A. Breeze Harper's *Sistah Vegan* combine ideas from local food and organics threads in the food movement with reflections on the movement's exclusion of black women, on the one hand, and the racist eugenic science that has engendered mistrust of science in the black community.[73] Harper's contributors document a wide variety of reasons why they have chosen vegan lifestyles, with some reflecting agrarian-like principles and archetypes. However neither Reese's nor Harper's contributors make reference to agrarianism or agrarian ideals, and White's treatment is noticeably sparing in this respect. It is thus crucial to recognize that connecting these intersectional works to agrarianism is fraught with the potential for epistemic oppression.

This potential may be most potent in the context of the food movement, if such a thing can be said to exist. The Detroit People's Food Co-op opened in the spring of 2022. This long-term project of the DBNFSN is intended to address the kind of issues that Reese documents in a more systematic and far-reaching form. In discussing the project, Yakini said that they faced something of a conundrum with respect to the participation of white allies. Clearly, they want the support of allies, and they understand it as well intentioned. It is an expression of the activist food ethics discussed in Chapter 2 of this book. At the same time, Yakini noted how white activists needed to be reminded that they are not in a leadership role. He also expressed ambivalence about a member-owned cooperative that could potentially have a large portion of its membership coming from whites who want to show their support for its aspirations.[74]

And Finally . . .

I hope that anti-racists can be at least a bit open-minded about agrarian traditions of thinking, though the exploration of agrarian ideas will be easier for racially oppressed groups that are not burdened with the collective memory of enslaved field labor and sharecropping. As I have tried to show in this chapter, settler colonialist destruction of indigenous food systems is an injustice in part *because* these were agrarian systems. The practices of food procurement and distribution in these Native American food systems were central to a metaphysics in which the human condition is understood as a function of relations with and integration into the world of plants and animals. The food system was hardly just one sector or function of the indigenous worldview. It was in crucial respects its totality and certainly the central node in determining the habitus and ethos of native cultures. One component of settler colonialist displacement was to disintegrate indigenous practice from its immediate environment and recast it as a form of religious mythology.

Such observations could continue by exploring how immigrant communities work to reproduce elements of their food system through gardening projects, how Chinese, Japanese, and Filipino diasporas grew from a connection to farming, or how the kibbutz became a central feature in late 20-century Jewish identity politics. Perhaps when the agrarian orientation of these philosophical systems begins to be appreciated we can begin to understand how fundamental their interpenetration with racial justice actually is. A totalizing refusal of agrarian philosophy because some racists were agrarians (as they certainly were) only serves the reproduction of white supremacy. It conceals settler colonialism's repression of the land-food-people nexus. If philosophers of race are correct in tying the Enlightenment conception of the human condition to racist ideals and practices (and surely they are), then opposing the industrial vision of what matters about food systems should follow. Perhaps then a recovery of the agrarian vision will be possible, and perhaps it will prove to be a bridge between two most compelling philosophical conversations of our time.

Notes

Introduction

1. Yang Jisheng, *Tombstone: The Great Chinese Famine, 1958–1962.* S. Moser and J. Guo, Tr., E. Friedman, S. Moser and J. Guo, eds. (New York: 2008, Farrar, Straus and Giroux).
2. Warren J. Belasco, *Appetite for Change: How the Counterculture Took On the Food Industry,* 2nd ed. (Ithaca, NY: 2014, Cornell University Press).
3. Paul B. Thompson, *From Field to Fork: Food Ethics for Everyone* (New York: 2015, Oxford University Press).
4. Peter Singer, "Famine, affluence and morality, *Philosophy and Public Affairs* 1(1972): 229–243.
5. Vibha Kapuria-Foreman and Mark Perlman, "An economic historian's economist: Remembering Simon Kuznets," *The Economic Journal* 105(1995): 1524–1547. Clearly, more could be said about this. Thomas Piketty traces a historical transition in the meaning of national accounts that ends with the merger of British, French and American approaches (the last associated with Kuznets) to produce the conception that undergirds contemporary theories of economic development. Thomas Piketty, *Capital in the Twenty-First Century* (Cambridge, MA: 2014, Harvard University Press).
6. Laura-Anne Minkoff Zern, *The New American Farmer: Immigration, Race, and the Struggle for Sustainability* (Cambridge, MA: 2018, The MIT Press), 8.
7. Ibid. p. 162.
8. Teju Cole, "The white-savior industrial complex," *The Atlantic* March 21, 2012, accessed October 10, 2021, at https://www.theatlantic.com/international/archive/2012/03/the-white-savior-industrial-complex/254843/
9. Reinterpreting the words of racially marginalized speakers can be an oppressive form of epistemic disrespect. See Kristie Dotson, "Conceptualizing epistemic oppression," *Social Epistemology* 28(2018): 115–138.
10. For those readers who have some familiarity with what philosophers have been saying about non-human animals, I would say that my view is more similar to that of Peter Singer than Tom Regan, save for the fact that I do not think any form of utilitarianism suffices as an adequate moral theory. I am probably more receptive to the idea that preserving species-typical behaviors is morally significant than Singer because I think they are significant even in the absence of any evidence that constraining these behaviors is a source of pain or stress. Singer is right to note that agricultural animals suffer under the conditions in which they are currently raised, and I would agree that their interests must be reflected in any ethical evaluation of livestock production or consumption of meat, milk, or eggs. Singer's work has brought these issues to a wide audience, while mine has been focused on making reforms in contemporary animal agriculture.

With other colleagues, I have worked to reduce suffering in present-day production systems. *From Field to Fork* outlined some of the reasons why that is more difficult than many people seem to think. The fact that welfare is multidimensional is one philosophical problem. Not only are we unsure how to trade one aspect of welfare off against another, there are problems in understanding how species-typical behavior is related to welfare. (For more on this, see Paul B. Thompson, "The opposite of human enhancement: Nanotechnology and the blind chicken problem," *NanoEthics* 2(2008): 305–316.) Singer has remarkably little to say about how livestock should be treated. He focused on convincing readers not to eat them. Aspects in which my view differs from that of Singer are discussed in Paul B. Thompson, "Getting pragmatic about farm animal welfare," in *Animal Pragmatism: Rethinking Human-Nonhuman Relationship*s. E. McKenna and A. Light, eds. (Bloomington: 2004, Indiana University Press), 140–159 and Paul B. Thompson, "Analytic and pragmatist food ethics: Method and approach," *Pragmatism Today* 8, 2(2017): 10–23, Available at http://www.prag matismtoday.eu/winter2017/Analytic-vs-Pragmatist-Food-Ethics-Method-and-Approach-Paul-B-Thompson.pdf. I also think that many philosophers are badly informed about the condition of animals in industrial production settings. See Paul B. Thompson, "Philosophical ethics and the improvement of farmed animal lives," *Animal Frontiers* 10(2020): 21–28. They have taken a highly superficial approach to the study of animal ethics: Paul B. Thompson, "The vanishing ethics of husbandry," in *The Animals in Our Midst: The Challenges of Co-Existing with Animals in the Anthropocene*, B. Bovenkerk and J. Keulartz, eds. (Cham: 2021, Springer), 203–221. Collectively, the papers cited in this note add up to over 100 pages on animal agriculture, much of which is Open Access or available from most libraries.

11. IPPC (Intergovernmental Panel on Climate Change). *Climate Change 2014: Impacts, Adaptation and Vulnerability*, accessed May 23, 2018, at https://www.ipcc.ch/pdf/ass essment-report/ar5/wg2/ar5_wgII_spm_en.pdf

12. I have addressed a portion of these issues in Paul B. Thompson, "Emerging (food) technology as an environmental and philosophical issue in the era of climate change," in *Food, Environment and Climate Change: Justice at the Intersections*, E. Gilson and S. Kenehan, eds. (Lanham, MD: 2019, Rowman and Littlefield), 195–212.

13. Tina L. Saitone, K. Aleks Schaefer, and Daniel P. Scheitrum, "COVID-19 morbidity and mortality in U.S. meatpacking counties," *Food Policy* 101(2021): https://doi.org/10.1016/j.foodpol.2021.102072

14. Zeina Nakat and Christelle Bou-Mitri, "COVID 19 and the food industry: Readiness assessment," *Food Control* 121(2021): https://doi.org/10.1016/j.foodcont.2020.107661

Chapter 1

1. Peter Singer, *Practical Ethics*, 2nd ed. (New York: 1993, Cambridge University Press).

2. Jason Carmichael, "Social control," *Oxford Bibliographies*, 2012, accessed October 12, 2021, at https://www.oxfordbibliographies.com/view/document/obo-9780199756 384/obo-9780199756384-0048.xml

3. Jason Stanley has written enlightening philosophical essays on the use of language to effect social control. See Jason Stanley, *How Fascism Works: The Politics of Us and Them* (New York: 2018, Random House). I include the techniques that Stanley describes in my conception of social control, but I also include more innocent habituation that occurs in the day-to-day process of living.

4. I do admit that there are occasions when highly abstruse points from academic ethical theory or metaethics have impact. There is such a thing as expertise in ethics. It consists less in knowing how to act than in having an arsenal (or is it a shopping bag?) of concepts, tropes, and thought experiments at one's disposal *and* in having cultivated the art of deploying these tools in ways that help non-specialists further their personal quests for moral clarity. Academic discourses that seem to be unconnected to common morality may have an indirect impact in building ethical expertise. There is also the possibility that there is some intrinsic value in these conversations, at least for the people who participate in them, and universities might be the place where such conversations are encouraged.

5. According to *Encyclopedia Britannica*, group-think derives from the work of social psychologist Irving Janis (1918–1990). It applies when two or more individuals are gripped by the illusion of infallibility and an inability to question the accepted morality of the group. Those who hold contrary views are stereotyped as opponents or enemies, leading to deficits in the ability to consider alternatives and a cognitive bias to favor evidence that supports the dominant point of view. Janis focused on the phenomenon of group-think to explain catastrophic errors in foreign policy. Anna Schmidt, "Groupthink, psychology," *Encyclopedia Britannica*, n.d., accessed October 4, 2021, at https://www.britannica.com/science/groupthink

6. Moynihan is the figure most frequently cited for the aphorism, "Everyone is entitled to his own opinion, but not to their own facts." Quote Investigator suggests that Bernard Baruch produced the earliest version and that former U.S. Secretary of Defense James Schlesinger coined the wording used here. See https://quoteinvestigator.com/2020/03/17/own-facts/, accessed October 5, 2021.

Chapter 2

1. John Ryder argues for a distinction between *inquiry*, which he understands as a research activity structured by a preconceived account of what could count as an adequate answer, and *query*, which is more open-ended and receptive to findings or events that would substantially change the focus and direction of thought. Ryder derives the distinction from the writings of our mutual teacher, Justus Buchler. There is also *enquiry*, which may have an accusative connotation: We don't conduct an enquiry unless we suspect some form of wrongdoing. I do not follow Ryder's usage, and will mostly just use the word "inquiry" without regard to the difference Ryder points out. However, I will occasionally use *query* in place of *inquiry* when the connotation of the alternative wording suits my goal of calling attention to more open-ended investigative activity. See John Ryder, *The Things in Heaven and Earth: An Essay in Pragmatic Naturalism* (New York: 2013, Fordham University Press).

2. Erland Mårald says this in his contribution to Per Sandin, Erland Mårald, Aiden Davison, David E. Nye, and Paul B. Thompson, "Book symposium on *The Agrarian Vision: Sustainability and Environmental Ethics* by Paul B. Thompson," *Philosophy & Technology* 26(2013): 301–320.

3. The argument for this claim is made in *From Field to Fork*, pp. 24–30 and pp. 80–89. This is not meant to imply that earlier generations failed to recognize social and ethical questions associated with farming and the distribution of food. Nor do I deny that diets were subject to duties of religious piety. Nevertheless, by 1800, specifically moral dimensions of eating that might have occupied ancient or medieval philosophers had been displaced by the view that one's personal interest in healthy diets is a matter of prudent decision-making rather than moral responsibility. Paul B. Thompson, *From Field to Fork: Food Ethics for Everyone* (New York: 2015, Oxford University Press).

4. Helen Zoe Veit, *Modern Food, Moral Food: Self-Control, Science and the Rise of Modern Eating in the Early Twentieth Century* (Chapel Hill: 2013, University of North Carolina Press). Other historians document this sentiment among U.S. farmers nearly a century earlier. See Kristen Hoganson, *The Heartland: An American History* (New York: 2019, Penguin Books).

5. Ann Vileisis, *Kitchen Literacy: How We Lost the Knowledge of Where Our Food Comes From, and Why We Need to Get It Back* (Washington DC: 2008, Island Press).

6. Ron Sandler, *Food Ethics: The Basics* (New York: 2012, Routledge).

7. Jack Lewis, "The birth of EPA," *EPA Journal* 11(1985): 6–11.

8. Indeed, consumer concerns about chemical additives used in processed food date back to the first decade of the 20th century, when Harvey Wiley's laboratory in the U.S. Department of Agriculture's Bureau of Chemistry began to undertake studies on adulterated foods. This led to the passage of the Pure Food and Drug Act of 1906, and the creation of the U.S. Food and Drug Administration. See Vileisis, *Kitchen Literacy*.

9. Someone might say it goes back to Shay's Rebellion in 1786, if not to the activism of Gerrard Winstanley (1609–1676) in England. I do not think that the activists who mounted campaigns on behalf of small farmers in the 1980s and 1990s were much motivated by Winstanley, but I do think that they were conscious of populist movements from a century previous. I do not think that much depends on whether these social issues are viewed as descending from the 19th century or an earlier era, but neither would I object to different tellings of the food ethics story.

10. Douglas Hurt, *American Agriculture: A Brief History*, rev. ed. (Lafayette, IN: 2002, Purdue University Press).

11. Warren Belasco, *Appetite for Change: How the Counterculture Took On the Food Industry*, 2nd ed. (Ithaca, NY: 2014, Cornell University Press).

12. Paul B. Thompson, "Agricultural ethics: Then and now," *Agriculture and Human Values* 32(2015): 77–85.

13. A few of them: Orville Schell, *Modern Meat* (New York: 1984, Random House); Michael Fox, *Agricide: The Hidden Crisis that Affects Us All* (New York: 1986, Schocken Books); John Robbins, *Diet for a New America* (Wallpole, NH: 1987, Stillpoint); Brewster Kneen, *From Land to Mouth* (Toronto: 1989, NC Press).

14. Schlosser and Pollan are journalists who had been publishing on food, agriculture, and the environment for some time. See Eric Schlosser, "In the strawberry fields," *Atlantic Monthly* November 1995, accessed February 10, 2022, at https://www.thea tlantic.com/magazine/archive/1995/11/in-the-strawberry-fields/305754/;   Michael Pollan, "Playing God in the garden," *New York Times Magazine* October 25, 1998, p. 44, accessed January 4, 2021, at https://www.nytimes.com/1998/10/25/magazine/ playing-god-in-the-garden.html; Michael Pollan, "How we live now: 10-23-03: The (agri)cultural contradictions of obesity," *New York Times Magazine* October 23, 2003, accessed January 4, 2021, at https://www.nytimes.com/2003/10/12/magazine/the- way-we-live-now-10-12-03-the-agri-cultural-contradictions-of-obesity.html

15. Gabriel Axel, *Babette's Feast* (Copenhagen: 1987, Nordisk Film); Kathy Schiffer, *Babette's Feast* is Pope Francis' favorite film (and mine), *National Catholic Register*, November 27, 2016, accessed March 31, 2021, at https://www.ncregister.com/blog/ babettes-feast-is-pope-francis-favorite-film-and-mine

16. Vittoria Ferrandino and Valentia Sgro, Italian migration and entrepreneurship's origins in the United States of America: A business history analysis from the post Second World War period to the present day, *Book of Proceedings: 25th International Conference on Multidisciplinary Studies* (Los Angeles: 2021, European Center for Science Education and Research), 343–359.

17. I. Cheney (Dir), *The Search for General Tso* (Wicked Delicate Films, 2014).

18. Lisa Heldke, *Exotic Appetites: Ruminations of a Food Adventurer* (New York: 2003, Routledge).

19. Carlo Petrini, *The Slow Food Revolution: Why Our Food Should Be Good, Clean and Fair* (New York: 2013, Rizzoli).

20. A. Breeze Harper, "Vegans of color, racialized embodiment, and problematics of the "exotic," in *Cultivating Food Justice: Race, Class and Sustainability*, A. H. Alkon and J. Agyeman, eds. (Cambridge, MA: 2011, MIT Press), 221–238.

21. According to *The Republic*, Socrates and Glaucon did not go the Piraeus in order to philosophize about justice. They went to observe a religious rite. Nevertheless, they have the liberty to philosophize without fear that their speculations will be viewed as seditious once they are outside the political sphere of Athens.

22. Peter Singer, "Famine, affluence and morality," *Philosophy and Public Affairs* 1(1972): 229–243.

23. Peter Singer, *The Life You Can Save: Acting Now to End World Poverty* (New York: 2009, Random House).

24. Peter Singer, "Animal liberation," *New York Review of Books*, April 5, 1973, accessed January 4, 2021, at https://www.nybooks.com/articles/1973/04/05/animal-liberat ion/; *Animal Liberation: A New Ethic for Our Treatment of Animals* (New York: 1975, New York Review Press).

25. Peter Singer and Jim Mason, *The Ethics of What We Eat: Why Our Food Choices Matter* (Emmaus, PA: 2006, Rodale Press).

26. Michael Pollan, *The Ominovore's Dilemma: A Natural History of Four Meals* (New York: 2006, Penguin Books).

27. The idea that we can regard society as a whole as a choice-making agent is controversial, and some theorists reject it altogether. It can be distinguished from the claim that we can talk meaningfully about social welfare or a general quality of life that prevails across any given group of people. It is also possible to adopt the perspective of social choice (i.e., evaluating both public policy and the organization of economic institutions and cultural mores *as if* they were choices made by society as a whole) without also committing to the utilitarian's principle of optimizing social welfare; see Amartya Sen, *The Idea of Justice* (Cambridge, MA: 2009, Harvard University Press). My discussion of Singer is not intended to challenge the social choice perspective. With Sen, I would argue that it implies neither optimizing welfare nor a metaphysically literalist interpretation of society as a choice-making agent.

28. Utilitarian consequentialism also assumes that the welfare impacts from all affected parties are included in the assessment and that the additive result of summing welfare impacts produces a ranking. See Amartya Sen, *On Ethics and Economics* (Oxford: 1987, Basil Blackwell).

29. Peter Singer, *Practical Ethics*, 2nd ed. (Cambridge: 1993, Cambridge University Press).

30. Jeremy Bentham (1748–1832) implied this in the title of his book *An Introduction to The Principles of Morals and Legislation* (Oxford: 1789, Clarendon Press).

31. In both "Famine, Affluence and Morality" and *Animal Liberation*, Singer says that everyone will agree that when someone can do a significant amount of good at little cost to themselves, they should do it, and he takes some pains to explain why deontologists should accept this principle.

32. Thrasymachus shows up shortly after Cephalus's departure in Plato's *Republic* and is bested by Socrates in one of the most famous philosophical exchanges in Western literature.

33. I am not aware of any place in Singer's writings where he has adopted a premise solely in order to persuade his audience. I read Singer as someone whose professional ethos precludes overt sophism. Rationalizing insincerity when it produces a good outcome seems inconsistent with what he takes philosophy to require.

34. As a side point, the actual impact of this law on the welfare of laying hens is a point of some dispute. There are variations both in the interpretation of the law and in enforcement of standards. Mara Miele, A., C. Lomellini-Dereclenne, L. Mounier, and I. Veissier, "Implementation of the European legislation to protect farm animals: A case-study on French inspections to find solutions to improve compliance," *Animal Welfare Journal* 26, 3(2017): 311–321; C. S. Vogeler, "Why do farm animal welfare regulations vary between EU member states? A comparative analysis of societal and party political determinants in France, Germany, Italy, Spain and the UK," *JCMS: Journal of Common Market Studies*, 57, 2(2019): 317–335.

Chapter 3

1. The argument is developed in considerably more detail in Paul B. Thompson, *From Field to Fork: Food Ethics for Everyone* (New York: Oxford University Press, 2015), 106–129.

2. Peter Singer, "Famine, Affluence, and Morality," *Philosophy and Public Affairs* 1(1972): 229–243; Garret Hardin, "Lifeboat Ethics: The Case Against Helping the Poor," *Psychology Today Magazine* 8 (September 1974): 38–43, 123–126.

3. Thomas Pogge and Keith Horton, *Global Ethics: Seminal Essays* (New York: Paragon House, 2008).

4. Singer, "Famine, Affluence, and Morality."

5. This focus continues on the human ability to muster enough willpower to meet the standards implied by Singer's analysis. Hugh Lafollette provides a succinct and inclusive overview of the twentieth-century philosophical literature on hunger and famine relief that followed publication of Singer's article. It is striking how the displacement of Singer's emphasis on hunger has continued well into the twenty-first century. Richard Miller reviews and endorses arguments for seeing human capacity for moral concern as limited by cognitive considerations. Kit Wellman and Andrew Cohen renew the debate over famine relief in terms of whether it is legitimate to favor those near to us when discharging duties of charity. Constanze Binder and Conrad Heilmann offer a refinement of the problem by focusing attention on the significance of geographical distance. Keith Burgess-Jackson provides an assessment of whether Singer himself has been able to meet these burdens. Artúrs Logins and Travis Timmerman have conducted a debate over how much sacrifice Singer's principle actually requires. The points under dispute in this literature could apply to virtually any form of charitable aid, including vaccines, clothing, or building supplies.

See Hugh LaFollette, "World Hunger," in *A Companion to Applied Ethics,* R. Frey and C. Wellman, eds. (Oxford: Blackwell, 2003), 238–253; Richard W. Miller, "Beneficence, Duty and Distance," *Philosophy and Public Affairs* 32(2004): 357–383; Christopher Heath Wellman, "Famine Relief: The Duties We Have to Others," in *Contemporary Debates in Applied Ethics.* A. I. Cohen and C. H. Wellman, eds. (New York: Blackwell, 2005), 313–325; Andrew I. Cohen, "Famine Relief and Human Virtue," in *Contemporary Debates in Applied Ethics*, A. I. Cohen and C. H. Wellman, eds. (New York: Blackwell, 2005), 26–342; Constanze Binder and Conrad Heilmann, "Duty and Distance," *Journal of Value Inquiry* 51(2017): 547–561; Keith Burgess-Jackson, "Famine, Affluence, and Hypocrisy," *Philosophy* 10(2020): 397–413; Artúrs Logins, "Save the Children!" *Analysis* 76(2016), 418–422; Travis Timmerman, "Save (Some of) the Children," *Philosophia* 46(2018): 465–472.

6. Garrett Hardin, "The Tragedy of the Commons," *Science* 162(1968): 1243–1248.

7. Hardin, "Lifeboat Ethics."

8. Peter J. Taylor, *Unruly Complexity: Ecology, Interpretation and Engagement* (Chicago: University of Chicago Press, 2005). See also LaFollette, "World Hunger."

9. See, Jessica Leann Urban, "Interrogating Privilege/Challenging the 'Greening of Hate,'" *International Feminist Journal of Politics* 9, 2(2007): 251–264; Paul M. Pulé, Martin Hultman, and Angelica Wågström, "Discussions at the Table," in *Men, Masculinities, and Earth*, P. M. Pulé and M. Hultman, eds. (London: Palgrave, 2021), 17–101.

10. At least one reader of *From Field to Fork* took me to be endorsing Hardin's argument against food aid, but, as I hope to have made clear in this chapter, my approach to

this issue has nothing to do with Hardin's racially suspect deployment of population ecology. Issues of race are addressed directly in Chapter 9.

11. Peter Singer, *Practical Ethics,* 2nd ed. (New York: Cambridge University Press, 1993), 246; and *The Life You Can Save: Acting Now to End World Poverty* (New York: Random House, 2009).

12. David A. Crocker, *Ethics of Global Development: Agency, Capability, and Deliberative Democracy* (Cambridge: Cambridge University Press, 2008), 6–7.

13. Amartya Sen, *Poverty and Famines: An Essay on Entitlement and Deprivation* (Oxford: Oxford University Press, 1981). See also Thompson, *From Field to Fork,* pp. 110–112.

14. Crocker, *Ethics of Global Development.*

15. LaFollette, "World Hunger."

16. David A. Crocker, "Development Ethics," in *Routledge Encyclopedia of Philosophy,* E. Craig, ed. (Milton Park, UK: Taylor and Francis, 1998), doi:10.4324/9780415249126-L016-1. https://www.rep.routledge.com/articles/thematic/development-ethics/v-1

17. Henry Shue, *Basic Rights: Subsistence, Affluence and U.S. Foreign Policy* (Princeton: Princeton University Press, 1980).

18. Jean Drèze and Amartya Sen, *Hunger and Political Action* (Oxford: Oxford University Press, 1989). See also Sen, *Poverty and Famines.*

19. Amartya Sen, *Development as Freedom* (New York: Alfred A. Knopf, 1999).

20. Rawls argued for a "duty to assist other people" as a component of his "law of peoples." The duty is conceptualized specifically within the context of international relations and justified as a necessary means for strengthening civil institutions in other societies. Within a domestic political context, food security is one among other primary goods that contribute to the realization of any plan of life. In consequence, ensuring food security becomes a component of any well-ordered society, and all duties to offer foreign assistance, including food aid, are covered under the more comprehensive goal of promoting development. See John Rawls, "The Law of Peoples," *Critical Inquiry* 20(1993): 36–68.

Thomas Pogge bundles food and water among basic needs that also include shelter, clothing, and basic medical care. He shows that people in extreme poverty lack secure access to all these needs, then develops his substantive development ethic by attempting to show that extreme poverty is itself the product of unjust and coercive actions that, in fact, violate even the negative rights that Shue had argued were insufficient. Intuitions and statistics about the compelling nature of food needs are recruited in service to Pogge's account of poverty, but all of Pogge's energies are dedicated toward elucidating the moral significance of poverty and arguing for duties to redress existing injustices while avoiding future ones. Thomas Pogge, *World Poverty and Human Rights: Cosmopolitan Responsibilities and Reforms* (Cambridge: Polity Press, 2002).

21. Elizabeth Ashford, "The Duties Imposed by the Human Right to Basic Necessities," in *Freedom From Poverty as a Human Right: Who Owes What to the Very Poor?,* T. Pogge, ed. (New York: Oxford University Press, 2007), 190.

22. Sylvia Berryman, "Is Global Poverty a Philosophical Problem?" *Metaphilosophy* 50(2019): 405–420.

23. Helen Veit, *Modern Food, Moral Food: Self-Control, Science and the Rise of Modern American Eating in the Early Twentieth Century* (Chapel Hill: University of North Carolina Press, 2013).

24. Christopher B. Barrett and Daniel G. Maxwell, *Food Aid After Fifty Years: Recasting its Role* (Abingdon, UK: Routledge, 2005).

25. Theodore W. Schultz, "Value of US Farm Surpluses to Underdeveloped Countries," *Journal of Farm Economics*, 42(1960): 1019–1030.

26. C. Peter Timmer, *Getting Prices Right: The Scope and Limits of Agricultural Price Policy* (Ithaca: Cornell University Press, 1986).

27. Luis Camacho, "Agriculture Intensification from the Perspective of Development Ethics," in *The Ethics of Intensification: Agricultural Development and Cultural Change*, P. B. Thompson, ed. (New York: Springer, 2008), 97–110.

28. Vernon W. Ruttan, "The Politics of US Food Aid Policy: A Historical Review," in *Why Food Aid?*, V. W. Ruttan, ed. (Baltimore: Johns Hopkins University Press, 1993), 2–36.

29. Vernon W. Ruttan, "Does Food Aid Have a Future?" in *Why Food Aid?*, V. W. Ruttan, ed. (Baltimore: Johns Hopkins University Press, 1993), 216–228.

30. Raymond F. Hopkins, "Reforming Food Aid for the 1990s," in *Why Food Aid?*, V. W. Ruttan, ed. (Baltimore: Johns Hopkins University Press, 1993), 200–215.

31. M. A. Keyser and L. van Wesenbeeck, "Food Aid and Governance," in *Development Economics Between Markets and Institutions: Incentives for Growth, Food Security and Sustainable Use of the Environment*, E. Bulte and R. Ruben, eds. (Wageningen, NL: Wageningen URI, 2007), 183–208.

32. Edward Clay, "Food Aid, Development and Food Security," in *Agriculture and the State: Growth, Employment and Poverty in Developing Countries*, C. P. Timmer, ed. (Ithaca: Cornell University Press, 1991), 232.

33. U.S. Agency for International Development, Food assistance frequently asked questions, accessed April 1, 2021 at https://www.usaid.gov/food-assistance/faq

34. Hugh Lafollette and Larry May, "Suffer the Little Children," in *World Hunger and Morality*, W. Aiken and H. LaFollette, eds. (Upper Saddle River: Prentice-Hall, 1996), 70–84.

35. While a doctor's visit and nursing services have low exclusion costs, medical treatment has knock-on benefits to public health that have high exclusion cost.

36. E. P. Thompson, "The Moral Economy of the English Crowd in the 18th Century," *Past and Present* 50(1971): 76–136.

37. People may, of course, be reluctant and even unable to make effective use of particular foods that are totally unfamiliar. This does not contradict my basic point.

38. Noah Zerbe, "Feeding the Famine? American Food Aid and the GMO Debate in Southern Africa," *Food Policy* 29(2004): 593–608.

39. Alan P. Fiske, "The Four Elementary Forms of Sociality: Framework for a Unified Theory of Social Relations," *Psychological Review* 99(1992): 689–723.

40. Barrett and Maxwell, *Food Aid After Fifty Years*.

41. Paul B. Thompson, *The Ethics of Aid and Trade: U.S. Food Policy, Foreign Competition and the Social Contract* (New York: Cambridge University Press, 1992).

42. Barrett and Maxwell, *Food Aid After Fifty Years*, pp. 47–48.

43. Thompson, *The Ethics of Aid and Trade*, pp. 37–40.

44. In Thompson, *The Ethics of Aid and Trade*. I argued that, like security assistance, a contractualist, enlightened self-interest rationale provides the justification for development assistance. I am less enamored with contractualist arguments today, and I fully support capability theorists' challenge to the conception of development that guided assistance programs prior to the creation of the Millennium Development Goals.

45. Thompson, *From Field to Fork*, pp. 114–121.

46. Jack Holmes, "Here's What Life Is Like in Puerto Rico 3 Months after Hurricane Maria," *Esquire* December 17, 2017, accessed April 2, 2021 at https://www.esquire.com/news-politics/a14474788/puerto-rico-3-months-after-hurricane/; José Andrés with Richard Wolfe, *We Fed an Island: The True Story of Rebuilding Puerto Rico One Meal at a Time* (New York: HarperCollins, 2018).

47. Integrated Food Security Phase Classification (IPC), Yemen brief, 2020, accessed April 2, 2021 at http://www.ipcinfo.org/fileadmin/user_upload/ipcinfo/docs/IPC_Yemen_AcuteFoodInsecurity_2020FebDec_Report_English.pdf

48. Cormac Ó Gráda, *Famine: A Short History* (Princeton: Princeton University Press, 2009).

49. Singer, "Famine, Affluence, and Morality," p. 229.

50. See "The Concert for Bangladesh," accessed April 2, 2021 at https://en.wikipedia.org/wiki/The_Concert_for_Bangladesh

51. Sen, *Poverty and Famines*.

52. Peter Bowbrick, "The Causes of Famine: A Refutation of Professor Sen's Theory," *Food Policy* 11(1986): 105–124.

53. Phillip Spencer, *Genocide Since 1945* (New York: Routledge, 2012), 62–65.

54. Martha Nussbaum does this in her capabilities list, for example. See Martha C. Nussbaum, *Women and Human Development: The Capabilities Approach* (New York: Cambridge University Press, 2001).

55. This is the argument in Thompson, *From Field to Fork*, pp. 106–129.

56. The debate between Logins and Timmerman, turns upon how burdensome the organizational obligations become. I believe that the distinction between emergency and development assistance speaks to this point. Although I read *The Life You Can Save* as applying Singer's principle to issues that must be classified as development rather than emergency assistance, addressing emergency needs on a global basis is well within the capabilities of "the richer countries," to use Singer's phrase. See Logins, "Save the Children!" and Timmerman, "Save (Some of) the Children."

Chapter 4

1. See Paul B. Thompson, *From Field to Fork: Food Ethics for Everyone* (New York: 2015, Oxford University Press), 187–188.

2. Samantha Noll, "Local food as social change: Food sovereignty as a radical new ontology," *Argumenta* 5(2020): 215–230, at 215.

3. Jules Pretty, Andrew S. Ball, Tim Lang, and James I. L. Morison, "Farm costs and food miles: An assessment of the full cost of the UK weekly food basket," *Food Policy* 30(2005): 1–19.

4. Tim Lang, David Barling, and Martin Caraher, *Food Policy: Integrating Health, Environment and Society* (Oxford: 2009, Oxford University Press).

5. Thompson, *From Field to Fork*, 188.

6. Bill McKibben, "A grand experiment," in *Food, Ethics and Society: An Introductory Text with Readings*, A. Barnhill, M. Budolfson, and T. Doggett, eds. (New York: 2016, Oxford University Press), 490–495; Alisa Smith and J. MacKinnen, *Plenty: Eating Locally on the 100 Mile Diet* (New York: 2007, Random House); Barbara Kingsolver, *Animal, Vegetable, Miracle: Our Year of Seasonal Eating* (London: 2010, Faber & Faber).

7. Noll, Local food as social change.

8. Helen De Bres, "Local food: The moral case," in *Food, Ethics, and Society: An Introductory Text with Readings*, A. Barnhill, M. Budolfson, and T. Doggett, eds. (New York: 2016, Oxford University Press), 495–509.

9. Carson Young, "Should you buy local?," *Journal of Business Ethics* (2022): https://doi.org/10.1007/s10551-020-04701-3

10. James E. McWilliams, *Just Food: Where Locavores Get It Wrong and How We Can Truly Eat Responsibly* (New York: 2009, Little Brown); Pierre Desrochers and Hiroku Shimizu, *The Locavore's Dilemma: In Praise of the 10,000 Mile Diet* (New York: 2012, PublicAffairs).

11. This is, of course, the argument of John Stuart Mill, discussed at more length in Chapter 5.

12. Young, "Should you buy local?"

13. McWilliams, *Just Food*; Desrochers and Shimizu, *The Locavore's Dilemma*.

14. Mark C. Navin, "Local food and international ethics," *Journal of Agricultural and Environmental Ethics* 27, 3(2014): 349–368, emphasizes how the locavore ethic is implicitly directed toward better-off consumers in industrial societies. Anne Barnhill, "Does locavorism keep it too simple?," in *Philosophy Comes to Dinner*, Andrew Chignell, Terence Cuneo, and Matthew C. Halteman, eds. (New York: 2015, Routledge), 242–263), emphasizes the incompleteness of the locavore ethic. Benjamin Ferguson and Christopher Thompson, "Why buy local?," *Journal of Applied Philosophy* 38(2021): 104–120, note that purchasing carbon offsets and similar measures may be a more effective way to achieve environmental objectives.

15. Liz Goodnick, "Limits on locavorism," in *Just Food: Philosophy, Justice and Food*, J. M. Dieterle, ed. (New York: 2015, Rowman & Littlefield), 195–211.

16. Christopher L. Weber and H. Scott Matthews, "Food-miles and the relative climate impact of food choices in the United States," *Environmental Science and Toxicology* 42(2008): 3508–3513.

17. De Bres, "Local food: The moral case"; Desrochers and Shimizu, *The Locavore's Dilemma*, do discuss the potential contribution to social capital, which is certainly one plausible way to interpret De Bres's claims about support for relationship building

within one's local community. However, De Bres's first interpretation makes a less technically complex claim about what it would mean to support one's local community, namely, that local purchases provide income to neighbors and nearby fellow citizens.

18. For this argument, see Anthony Flaccavento, *Building a Healthy Economy from the Bottom Up: Harnessing Real-World Experience for Transformative Change* (Lexington: 2016, University Press of Kentucky).

19. Peter Singer and Jim Mason, *The Ethics of What We Eat* (Emmaus, PA: 2007, Rodale Press).

20. De Bres, "Local food: The moral case."

21. See Richard Marosi, "Desperate workers on a Mexican mega-farm: 'They treated us like slaves,'" *Los Angeles Times*, December 14, 2014, accessed September 25, 2016, at http://graphics.latimes.com/product-of-mexico-labor/

22. See Sarah Lyon, "Fair trade's impact on smallholders," in *Handbook on the Human Impact of Agriculture*, H. S. James, Jr., ed. (Northampton, MA: 2021, Edward Elgar), 194–217.

23. Andrew Chignell, "Can we really vote with our forks? Opportunism and the threshold chicken," in *Philosophy Comes to Dinner: Arguments About the Ethics of Eating*, Andrew Chignell, Terence Cuneo, and Matthew C. Halteman, eds. (New York: 2015, Routledge). 182–202; Mark Bryant Budolfson. "Is it wrong to eat meat from factory farms? If so, why?," in *The Moral Complexities of Eating Meat*, Bob Fischer and Ben Bramble, eds. (New York: 2015, Oxford University Press), 80–98; Eliot Michaelson, "Act consequentialism and inefficacy," in *Food, Ethics, and Society: An Introductory Text with Readings*, A. Barnhill, M. Budolfson, and T. Doggett, eds. (New York: 2016, Oxford University Press), 215–219. For a view that critiques the inefficacy argument from the perspective of economic theory, see Steven McMullen and Mathew C. Halteman, "Against inefficacy objections: The real economic impact of individual consumer choices on animal agriculture," *Food Ethics* 2(2019): 93–110. https://doi.org/10.1007/s41055-018-00030-4

24. Michael J. Driscoll and Ashok K. Lahiri, "Income-velocity of money in agricultural developing economies," *Review of Economics and Statistics* 65(1983): 393–401.

25. Unfortunately, life in the food movement is never this easy. One group promoting local food systems does so under the banner of "slow money." See https://slowmoney.org, accessed October 12, 2021.

26. This observation is not intended as a rebuke to Singer. There is no evidence that he ever thought of his work as illuminating such problems.

27. We could pursue these points further by considering tweaks to consequentialist ethical theory such as "two-level" utilitarianism. I will not do that because I may have already pushed even interested readers well beyond their patience for technical issues. That is, we are approaching MEGO territory, if we haven't already been there for the last five paragraphs. Locating the boundary between philosophy that is enlightening and useful and philosophy that has become so abstruse that its discourses cannot be brought back into the public sphere is a matter of judgment. I judge that it is time to move on to other topics.

28. De Bres, "Local food: The moral case," 503.

29. De Bres's two and half pages on agrarian views presents the most extended discussion of such viewpoints in the entirety of the 664-page reader on food ethics in which her contribution appears, an omission that would lead one to think that these arguments have little bearing on food ethics generally.

30. De Bres, "Local food: The moral case," 504.

31. I have made a study of Berry's thought in *The Spirit of the Soil* and will resist the temptation to engage in a lengthier discussion of how his thought differs from that of Wirzba. See Paul B. Thompson, *The Spirit of the Soil: Agriculture and Environmental Ethics*, 2nd ed. (New York: 2017, Routledge).

32. See Wendell Berry, *What Are People For?* (Berkeley, CA: 1990, Counterpoint Press); Norman Wirzba, *Food and Faith: A Theology of Eating*, 2nd ed. (New York: 2019, Cambridge University Press).

33. I am aware of the irony in translating these anti-decisionist views into the decisionist language of payoffs. Unfortunately, an exploration of irony's role in morality would take us into MEGO territory, but see Kierkegaard on this.

34. Hubert L. Dreyfus and Stuart E. Dreyfus, "Peripheral vision: Expertise in real world contexts," *Organization Studies* 26(2005): 779–792.

35. One of the pre-publication readers of the book balks at this juncture, reading me as claiming that virtue ethics does not involve rules. Certainly some versions of virtue ethics afford a major place for rules and rule-following, but my inquiry reaches a different inflection point: What is a rule? Are heuristics and ethos rule-like in important respects? Delving into this tangent would take me into the work of Ludwig Wittgenstein (1889–1951), one personal influence that I have found ways to avoid mentioning in the main text. Here is what I can say briefly: the rules that interest consequentialists and many deontologists (I'm not sure about virtue theorists) must be decisively determinative for selecting which of several discrete options for future action are morally required, permissible, or optimal (the possible criteria here become a source of theoretical dispute). In contrast, a heuristic or ethos may help guide us "how to go on" without necessarily specifying any set of decision options, at all.

36. Kingsolver, *Animal, Vegetable, Miracle*.

37. I will not drag readers too deeply into the details of political theory, but those who have familiarity with the work of Nancy Fraser or Ernesto Laclau (1935–2014) and Chantal Mouffe may recognize the tune. See Nancy Fraser, "Rethinking the public sphere: A contribution to the critique of actually existing democracy," *Social Text* 25, 26(1990): 56–80; Ernesto Laclau and Chantal Mouffe, *Hegemony and Socialist Strategy: Towards a Radical Democratic Politics* (New York: 2001, Verso).

38. Jürgen Habermas, "New social movements," *Telos* 49(1981): 33–37.

39. Michiel Korthals, "Taking consumers seriously: Two concepts of consumer sovereignty," *Journal of Agricultural and Environmental Ethics* 14(2001): 201–215; Mark Sagoff, "Values and preferences," *Ethics* 96(1986): 301–316.

40. I am making a superficial allusion to Jacques Derrida (1930–2004). The relevant work is *Rogues: Two Essays on Reason*, Pascale-Anne Brault and Michael Naas, tr. (Palo Alto, CA: 2005, Stanford University Press).

Chapter 5

1. The phrase "whole foods" distinguishes a food item such as beans, peas, tomatoes, or apples from foods that are prepared from ingredients, such as baked goods, processed meats, and prepared foods such as canned or frozen soups or dinners. It is a distinction with many levels of qualification and refinement. My reference to Aunt Orva's preference for whole foods is intended to convey that she seldom buys prepared foods, such as canned or frozen chow mien or Tater Tots. She would be preparing meals "from scratch," that is, starting with whole ingredients that she would cut, chop, and cook. Orva exists only in my imagination, but this description shouldn't conjure up fanatical behavior.

2. IGA stands for Independent Grocers Association. It was a co-op of locally owned grocery stores formed to achieve economies of scale in their supply chain. A&P and Piggly-Wiggly were similar co-ops of independent grocers. At this writing, a few of these stores remain in the United States. Large corporations own most grocery stores in North America and Europe.

3. Howard Markel, *The Kelloggs: The Battling Brothers of Battle Creek* (New York: 2017, Pantheon Books).

4. Ann Vileisis, *Kitchen Literacy: How We Lost the Knowledge of Where Food Comes From, and Why We Need to Get It Back* (Washington, DC: 2007, Island Press).

5. See Harvard T. H. Chan School of Public Health (n.d.), "Shining the spotlight on trans fats," accessed April 29, 2021, at https://www.hsph.harvard.edu/nutritionsou rce/what-sh ould-you-eat/ fat s-and-ch oleste rol/ types-of—fat/transfats/

6. Warren Belasco, *Appetite for Change: How the Counterculture Took on the Food Industry*, 2nd ed. (Ithaca, NY: 2014, Cornell University Press). My glib summary of this history could be disputed. As Belasco knows well, advocacy for health food goes back at least to the Rodale Press's first issue of *Organic Farming and Gardening* in 1942, if not to John Harvey Kellogg or the 19th-century views of Sylvester Graham (1794–1851). Nevertheless, I do not mean to dispute the counterculture's role in starting a food movement.

7. Julie Guthman, *Agrarian Dreams: The Paradox of Organic Farming in California*, 2nd ed. (Berkeley: 2007, University of California Press).

8. Dan Flynn, "Enforcement stepped up in past year to protect USDA's organic label," *Food Safety News*, accessed March 16, 2022, at http://www.foodsafetynews.com/ 2021/05/enforcement-stepped-up-in-past-year-to-protect-usdas-organic-label/

9. Vileisis, *Kitchen Literacy*.

10. Debates over the labeling of genetically engineered food provided the original context for my invention of the fictional Aunt Orva in Paul B. Thompson, "Why food biotechnology needs an opt out," in *Engineering the Farm: Ethical and Social Aspects of Food Biotechnology*, B. Bailey and M. Lappe, eds. (Washington, DC: 2002, Island Press), 27–43. In this chapter, I adopt the convention of describing these foods as "GM foods" (for genetically modified) or "GMOs" (for genetically modified organisms). This terminology is itself controversial, and the controversy is discussed at some length in Paul B. Thompson, *Food and Agricultural Biotechnology in Ethical Perspective*, 3rd ed.

(New York: 2020, Springer). In a nutshell, one could argue that everything we eat is genetically modified, but conventions of speech involve lots of shortcuts that do not stand up to literal analysis.

11. John Stuart Mill, *On Liberty* (London: 1859, John W. Parker & Son).

12. The FDA does mandate speech in its regulation of drugs. Manufacturers are required to disclose known risks. When it comes to foods, the policy has been to take a *de minimus* approach to risk. Although it is scientifically (indeed epistemologically) impossible to ensure that foods have zero risk, the *de minimus* approach means that probability of injury is so remote that the risk is too small to raise concern. Unless there is some compelling offsetting benefit, a food safety agency will usually ban a product that exceeds the *de minimus* standard. Artificial sweeteners, for example, are judged to provide benefits to obese and diabetic people that offset their small but non-negligible risks. In a few other cases, such as warnings on tobacco and alcohol products, regulatory agencies have chosen to compel speech.

13. See, for example, Barbara A. Almanza, Douglas Nelson, and Stella Chai, "Obstacles to nutrition labeling in restaurants," *Journal of the American Dietetic Association* 97, 2(1997): 157–161.

14. Carmen Bain and Tamera Dandachi. "Governing GMOs: The (counter) movement for mandatory and voluntary non-GMO labels," *Sustainability* 6, 12(2014): 9456–9476.

15. T. Havinga, "Regulating kosher and halal foods: Differing arrangements between state, industry and religious actors," *Erasmus Law Review* 3, 4(2010): 241–255.

16. Alexandra Pliakas, *Thinking Through Food: A Philosophical Introduction* (Peterborough, ON: 2018, Broadview Press).

17. Ibid.

18. The United States entered an agreement with the European Union in 2006 that limits American companies' use of terms like "champagne," "chablis," or "chianti," though products bearing these labels that were on the market prior to the agreement have been allowed to continue. To my knowledge, use of the term "prosciutto" is not regulated in the United States.

19. This line of reasoning is followed in the concluding chapter of Paul B. Thompson, *From Field to Fork: Food Ethics for Everyone* (New York: 2015, Oxford University Press), 227–255.

20. The organic standard in place at this writing permits a few chemicals derived from natural sources as well as natural fertilizers such as mulch or composted manure. In addition, the standard emphasizes farming practice so chemicals that are in the environment (perhaps resulting from spraying by a neighbor) do not keep a crop from qualifying as organic. The details of the organic standard are enough to make the eyes glaze over, and they change over time. At this writing, there is a debate over whether hydroponic crops qualify as organic, for example.

21. Debra M. Strauss, "Genetically modified organisms in food: Ethical tensions and the labeling initiative," in *Ethical Tensions from New Technology: The Case of Agricultural Biotechnology*, H. S. James, Jr., ed. (Wallingford, UK: 2018, CABI International), 83–96.

22. The USDA system establishes criteria for *process labels*—that is, marketing labels that refer to some process by which a food is grown or processed but which cannot be

determined by inspection or scientific tests performed on the final product. In addition to non-GMO, Fair Trade is a process label.

23. This utilitarian perspective was taken in a putatively neutral report by the U.S. Congressional Research Service:

D. U. Vogt and M. Parrish, *Food Biotechnology in the United States: Science, Regulation and Issues* (Washington, DC: 1999, Government Printing Office).

24. Herbert G. McCann, "McDonald's settles over beef fries," *CBS News*. 2002, accessed October 13, 2021, at https://www.cbsnews.com/news/mcdonalds-sett les-beef-over-fries/

25. A. O. Hirschmann, *Exit, Voice, and Loyalty: Responses to Decline in Firms, Organizations, and States* (Cambridge, MA: 1970, Harvard University Press).

26. Ibid.

27. Nancy Fraser, "Rethinking the public sphere: A contribution to the critique of actually existing democracy," *Social Text* 25, 26(1990): 56–80; Ernesto Laclau and Chantal Mouffe, *Hegemony and Socialist Strategy: Towards a Radical Democratic Politics* (New York: 2001, Verso).

28. One could argue that process claims and food labels do not provide exit for people who cannot afford the foods that carry these labels. I agree in principle, but there are more nuanced points to debate. What does it take to "afford" these options? I would argue that people who economize on food choices simply so that they exercise discretion with respect to other areas of their household budget probably do not have commitments that rise to the level of a religious or spiritual belief. I concede that it would be difficult to devise a test for this, however. I also accept that some individuals in 21st-century industrial democracies do not enjoy exit because of their economic straits. The same goes for impoverished nations where almost everyone's food choices are constrained. Food labels are not going to fix these problems, which involve much more basic issues in social justice. The considerations discussed in this chapter do not speak to these more fundamental issues, but if a critic claims that the continuing existence of fundamental injustice vitiates the need to configure exchange-mediated food systems according to principles of religious freedom and liberty of conscience, I would want to inspect the argument for that.

29. Flashing back to the 1990s one more time, the USDA's initial proposal for its organic certification program would have permitted the use of gene technology in organically grown crops. It was not, in the view of USDA, a chemical technology in the sense stipulated by the gurus of organic farming, J. I. Rodale (1898–1971) and Sir Albert Howard (1873–1947). An enraged public shouted down the proposal, and, when the USDA organic label went live in 1998, GM foods were not eligible. One might say that even before non-GMO marketing labels became available, these measures accommodated the liberty of conscience issues exemplified by Aunt Orva and discussed throughout this chapter. In Europe and Japan, her exit was protected by her ability to look for the GM label. The United States protected her through the ability to choose organic. The U.S. labeling law of 2016 left labeling advocates dissatisfied. As I write, we appear poised for a new round of debate as advocates of gene technology are arguing that a specific class of gene-edited foods should be exempt from

the regulatory and labeling requirements established for GMOs. See Thompson, *Food and Agricultural Biotechnology in Ethical Perspective.*

30. See, for example, Stelin Welin, "Introducing the new meat: Problems and prospects," *Etikk i praksis-Nordic Journal of Applied Ethics* 1(2013): 24–37.

31. Cor van der Weele, "How to save cultured meat from eco-modernism? Selective attention and the art of dealing with ambivalence," in *Animals in Our Midst: The Challenges of Co existing with Animals in the Anthropocene*, B. Bovenkerk and J. Keulartz, eds. (New York: 2021, Springer). 545–557.

32. I would be remiss if I failed to bring several important exceptions to readers' attention. Robert Streiffer and Alan Rubel, "Democratic principles and mandatory labeling of genetically engineered food," *Public Affairs Quarterly* 18(2004): 223–248; Alan Rubel and Robert Streiffer, "Respecting the autonomy of European and American consumers: Defending positive labels on GM foods," *Journal of Agricultural and Environmental Ethics* 18(2005): 75–84; Paul Weirich, ed., *Labeling Genetically Modified Food: The Philosophical and Legal Debate* (New York: 2007, Oxford University Press). In this chapter, my goal of dissociating the philosophical issues from the food biotechnology debate has prevented me from engaging with the philosophical claims in this literature more directly.

Chapter 6

1. For further reading on bioaccumulation, see the following website from The Open University: https://www.open.edu/openlearn/science-maths-technology/biology/water-and-human-health/content-section-4.1.1, accessed October 15, 2021.

2. Courtney Lindwall, "Industrial agricultural pollution 101." *NRDC.org* July 31, 2019, accessed December 28, 2021, at https://www.nrdc.org/stories/industrial-agricultural-pollution-101#whatis

3. See Carolyn Raffensperger's comments in Carolyn Raffensperger, Moira Campbell, and Paul B. Thompson, "Considering *The Spirit of the Soil* by Paul B. Thompson," *Agriculture and Human Values* 15(1998): 161–176. https://doi.org/10.1023/A:100747 3217074

4. See, for example, Joseph R. Des Jardins, *Environmental Ethics* (Detroit: 2012, Cengage Learning).

5. Elizabeth D. Blum, *Love Canal Revisited: Race, Class, and Gender in Environmental Activism* (Lawrence: 2008, University Press of Kansas).

6. This is a broad gloss on the way economists define externalities, but I'm going to stick with it in this chapter.

7. A cost-benefit analysis might also view the pollution costs of dioxin in comparison to the benefits of manufacturing products of which it is a byproduct. The moral difference consists in the way that restricting the use of agricultural pesticides affects moral agents (e.g., farmers) who have reasons to use a substance that others view as a pollutant.

8. David Pimentel and Hugh Lehman, eds., *The Pesticide Question: Environment, Economics and Ethics* (New York: 1993, Chapman and Hall).

9. My book, *The Spirit of the Soil*, first published in 1995, includes a more detailed discussion of pesticide use as an assurance problem. Paul B. Thompson, *The Spirit of the Soil: Agriculture and Environmental Ethics*, 2nd ed. (New York: 2017, Routledge).

10. Mary Douglas, *Purity and Danger: An Analysis of Concept of Pollution and Taboo* (London: 1966, Routledge and Keegan Paul), 245.

11. Shaker communities emphasized the adoption of orphans and welcomed converts as a way to repopulate their churches. My citation of the obvious impact of cultural mores on sexual reproduction does not imply that Shaker communities had means of continuance that did not depend upon sexual reproduction.

12. Alison Eldridge, "Jonestown," *Britannica* n.d., accessed March 18, 2022, at https://www.britannica.com/event/Jonestown

13. Jared Diamond, *Collapse: How Societies Choose to Fail or Succeed*, rev. ed.) New York: 2011, Penguin Books).

14. Ibid.

15. Hyam Maccoby, *Ritual and Morality: The Ritual Purity System and Its Place in Judaism* (New York: 1999, Cambridge University Press), vii.

16. Douglas, *Purity and Danger*, 54

17. Ibid., 58.

18. Roy F. Ellen, *Environment, Subsistence, and System: The Ecology of Small-Scale Social Formations* (Cambridge: 1982, Cambridge University Press). A fully developed system of culture will also stipulate categorical classifications relating to sexual and kinship practices, status hierarchies and a host of material and symbolic practices

19. Susan McHugh, *Dog* (London: 2004, Reaktion Books).

20. Ingvar Svanberg and Åsa Berggren, "Insects as past and future food in entomophobic Europe," *Food, Culture and Society* 24(2021): 624–638, https://doi.org/10.1080/15528014.2021.1882170 There is a moral debate here reflecting critiques of Western culture's categorization of animal minds. See Bob Fischer, "Bugging the strict vegan," *Journal of Agricultural and Environmental Ethics* 29(2016): 255–263; Jeff Sebo and Jason Schukraft, "Don't farm bugs," *Aeon* July 27, 2021, accessed June 13, 2022, at https://aeon.co/essays/on-the-torment-of-insect-minds-and-our-moral-duty-not-to-farm-them?fbclid=IwAR1uppTQcx1u8xqhNZD2dnkch7m96X8vjNDJCJe4ebMoPP4Eeje95Y3rGsU

21. Kevin C. Elliott, "Pollution," in *Encyclopedia of Environmental Ethics and Philosophy*, J. Baird Callicott and Robert Frodeman, eds., vol. 2 (New York: 2009, Macmillan Reference USA), 158–162.

22. Kevin C. Elliott, *Is a Little Pollution Good for You? Incorporating Social Values in Environmental Research* (New York: 2011, Oxford University Press).

23. Though not a scientific document, the World Wildlife Fund's web article on pollution introduces the subject with, "Pollution may muddy landscapes, poison soils and waterways, or kill plants and animals" WWF (World Wildlife Fund) n.d. Pollution, accessed May 3, 2021, at https://www.worldwildlife.org/threats/pollution

24. When I say "now" I mean circa the third decade of the 21st century. GMO—short for genetically modified organism—does have a legal meaning in some regulatory contexts, where it is derived from the living modified organism (LMO) of the Cartagena Protocol.

25. A sampling of authors making this claim over the past quarter of a century: Brian P. Bloomfield and Theo Vurdubakis, "Disrupted boundaries: New reproductive technologies and the language of anxiety and expectation," *Social Studies of Science* 25(1995): 533–551; Mark Sagoff, "Genetic engineering and the concept of the natural," in *Genetically Modified Food and the Consumer*, Allan Eaglesham, Steven G. Pueppke, and Ralph W. F. Hardy, eds. (Ithaca, NY: 2001, National Agricultural Biotechnology Council), 127–140; Jason Scott Robert and Françoise Baylis, "Crossing species boundaries," *American Journal of Bioethics* 3, 3(2003): 1–13; Melissa L. Finucane and Joan L. Holup, "Psychosocial and cultural factors affecting the perceived risk of genetically modified food: An overview of the literature," *Social Science & Medicine* 60(2005): 1603–1612; Jakub Kwieciński, "Genetically modified abominations?," *EMBO Reports* 10(2009): 1187–1190; Abby Kinchy, *Seeds, Science, and Struggle: The Global Politics of Transgenic Crops* (Cambridge, MA: 2011, MIT Press); Myles Carroll, "Narrating technonatures: Discourses of biotechnology in a neoliberal era," *Journal of Political Ecology*, 25(2018): 186–204; Henk ten Have and Maria do Céu Patrão Neves, "Genetic modification (GMOs), general," in *Dictionary of Global Bioethics* (New York: 2021, Springer), 559–560.

26. The related notions of boundary-crossing, boundary work, and boundary objects became important in science studies at about the same time that the GMO debate was heating up in the 1990s. Examining these connections would burden the already complex discussion in this chapter with even more MEGO. See Susan Leigh Star and James Griesemer, "Institutional ecology, 'translations,' and boundary objects: Amateurs and professionals on Berkeley's museum of vertebrate zoology," *Social Studies of Science* 19(1989): 387–420. Some of the authors cited in Note 25 had this notion of boundaries in mind.

27. See Martin W. Bauer, "Distinguishing red and green biotechnology: Cultivation effects of the elite press," *International Journal of Public Opinion Research* 17(2005): 63–89.

28. Sheila Jansanoff, "Ordering knowledge, ordering society," in *States of Knowledge: The Co-Production of Science and Social Order*, Sheila Jasanoff, ed. (New York: 2004, Routledge), 13–45.

29. This was Sheila Jasanoff's point, made in several contexts. While I take the point, I think Jasanoff's analysis underplays the significance of a literal—or perhaps it would be better to say *physicalist*—sense of pollution. See Jasanoff, Ibid.

30. This is the primary sense in which organisms with antibiotic-resistance genes were considered as pollutants, but antibiotic resistance is itself a complex phenomenon and other impacts are possible.

31. Although these reports use a conceptual approach that conforms to the philosophical analysis of pollution offered by Kevin Elliott, "pollution" is not a term of analysis in any of them. It would thus be misleading to suggest that these reports are intended to

be read as a scientific analysis of genetic pollution. In describing these NRC reports as conforming to a theory of pollution, I am taking an interpretive liberty, but I believe it can be justified by one of several extrapolations from the text of these reports. They apply a framework for environmental risk assessment that theoretically *could have* resulted in classifying nucleotide sequences as pollutants but in fact did not. On this view, genetic constructs in GMOs were evaluated as potential forms of pollution, but the reports concluded that no plausible mechanism for realizing a speculative hazard could be identified. An alternative way to interpret the reports takes the position that pollution risks were small and did not warrant change in regulatory practice in the NRC committees' opinion. On this view the nucleotide sequences are minor pollutants. A positivistic reading of the reports might hold that since the reports don't discuss pollution in connection with GMOs, extrapolative interpretations such as the ones I am offering here are unwarranted. The NRC committees may have considered using the terminology of pollution and deliberately rejected it, or it simply might not have occurred to them. In any case, the analytic approach taken in all the reports is consistent with a definition that stresses the potential for hazards transported physically through the biophysical environment. In Elliott's terminology: pollution.

32. John E. Losey, Linda S. Rayor, and Marianne E. Carter, "Transgenic pollen harms monarch larvae," *Nature* 399(1999): 214.

33. May Berenbaum, "Interpreting the scientific literature: Differences in the scientific and lay communities," *Plant Physiology* 125(2001): 509–512.

34. Steve L. Taylor and Susan L. Hefle, "Will genetically modified foods be allergenic?," *Journal of Allergy and Clinical Immunology* 107(2001): 765–771.

35. Mike Mendelsohn, John Kough, Zigfridais Vaituzis, and Keith Matthews, "Are Bt crops safe?," *Nature Biotechnology* 21(2003): 1003–1009; Rebecca M. Bratspies, "Myths of voluntary compliance: Lessons from the StarLink Corn fiasco," *William & Mary Environmental Law & Policy Review* 27(2003): 593–648.

36. Colin MacIlwain, "US launches probe into sales of unapproved transgenic corn," *Nature* 434(2005): 423.

37. David Quist and Ignacio H. Chapela, "Transgenic DNA introgressed into traditional maize landraces in Oaxaca, Mexico," *Nature* 414(2001): 541–543.

38. S. Ortiz-García., E. Ezcurra, B. Schoel, F. Acevedo, J. Soberón, and A. A. Snow, "Absence of detectable transgenes in local landraces of maize in Oaxaca, Mexico (2003–2004)," *PNAS* 102(2005): 12338–12343.

39. Kristin L. Mercer and Joel D. Wainwright, "Gene flow from transgenic maize to landraces in Mexico: An analysis," *Agriculture, Ecosystems & Environment* 123(2008): 109–115.

40. Stewart C. Neal, Jr., Matthew D. Halfhill, and Suzanne I. Warwick, "Transgene introgression from genetically modified crops to their wild relatives," *Nature Reviews: Genetics* 4(2003): 806–817. I was personally involved in the Mexican case, and I hope that even the brief discussion in this chapter demonstrates that I do not endorse an interpretation that defines the risks of gene technology in narrowly agronomic or ecological terms.

41. Donald Bruce, "Contamination, crop trials and compatibility," *Journal of Agricultural and Environmental Ethics* 16(2003): 595–604.

42. Sellars's key paper is W. Sellars, "On reasoning about values," *American Philosophical Quarterly* 17(1980): 81–101. People wonder who Jones was. My guess is the character played by Gary Cooper in the 1945 film *Along Came Jones.*

43. Ibid.

44. Mead's book is *Mind, Self, and Society,* C. W. Morris, ed. (Chicago: 1967 [1934], University of Chicago Press). These connections are indicative of my philosophical pragmatism, which will not be exposited here, but see Chapter 8.

45. The paper is reprinted in Mary Douglas, *Implicit Meanings: Selected Essays in Anthropology,* 2nd ed. (New York: Routledge, 1999), 224–237.

46. This was the point of one of my favorite but least frequently read papers: Paul B. Thompson, "Science policy and moral purity: The case of animal biotechnology," *Agriculture and Human Values* 14(1997): 11–27;

47. Philip Stanhope, 4th Earl of Chesterfield (1694–1773).

48. In 1996, the *New York Times* reported work by Steve Taylor and Julie Nordless on the inadvertent transfer of allergens from Brazil nuts into a GMO soybean. It is yet another episode in the GMO saga that can be seen two ways. While opponents of GMOs used it to highlight dangers, my view is that this work, and the fact that the Pioneer Hi-bred International seed company immediately suspended work on this particular modification, demonstrates the seriousness with which the industry takes food safety risks. See Warren A. Leary, "Genetic engineering of crops can spread allergies, study shows," *New York Times,* March 14, 1996, accessed January 27, 2022, at https://www.nytimes.com/1996/03/14/us/genetic-engineering-of-crops-can-spread-allergies-study-shows.html

49. A series of lawsuits and legal actions revolved around corporate claims that farmers who saved seed or even inadvertently planted seed containing patented genes had violated the company's intellectual property rights. I am not aware of any cases where corporate plaintiffs who were successful in establishing facts to that effect were denied victory in the courts. The case of Monsanto's prosecution of Canadian farmer Percy Schmeiser (1931–2020) is most frequently cited. For further discussion, see Bruce Ziff, "Travels with my plant: *Monstanto vs. Schmeiser* revisited," *University of Ottawa Law and Technology Journal* 2(2005): 493–510. This does not mean that observers of these cases endorsed the biotechnology industry's view of their property rights on moral rather than legal grounds.

50. Mohamed Behnassi and Sanni Yaya, "Land resource governance from a sustainability and rural development perspective," in *Sustainable Agricultural Development: Recent Approaches in Resources Management and Environmentally Balanced Production Enhancement,* Mohamed Behnassi, Shabbir A. Shahid, and Joyce D'Silva, eds. (Dordrecht: 2011, Springer), 3–23.

51. Mary Douglas and Aaron Wildavsky, *Risk and Culture: An Essay on the Selection of Technical and Environmental Dangers* (Berkeley: 1982, University of California Press).

52. See Bunyon Bryant and Paul Mohai, eds., *Race and the Incidence of Environmental Hazards: A Time for Discourse* (Boulder, CO: 1992, Westview Press).

53. On the exclusion of social determinants of health, see Sean Valles, *Philosophy of Population Health: Philosophy for a New Public Health Era* (New York: 2018, Routledge). Valles does not use the concept of pollution in his framing of the analysis.

Chapter 7

1. Bryan G. Norton, *Sustainability: A Philosophy of Adaptive Ecosystem Management* (Chicago: 2005, University of Chicago Press).

2. On Bailey and King, see Paul B. Thompson, *The Agrarian Vision: Sustainability and Environmental Ethics* (Lexington: 2010, University Press of Kentucky).

3. On skimmers, see Stephen Stoll, *Larding the Lean Earth: Soil and Society in Nineteenth Century America* (New York: 2002, Hill and Wang).

4. The distinction between growth rates is often described as the difference between exponential and geometric or arithmetic functions. As I was struggling to explain this in common English, I found an interesting discussion on the web that led me to drop that language altogether. See "Is it more accurate to use the term geometric growth or exponential growth?" *StackExchange*, accessed January 27, 2022, at https://math.stackexchange.com/questions/1611050/is-it-more-accurate-to-use-the-term-geometric-growth-or-exponential-growth

5. On my reading of the *Essay*, Malthus does not predict that population will outrun the food supply. Rather, he produces this famous model of the underlying stocks and flows in agriculture and population ecology in order to motivate an analysis of what checks population growth in a manner that *prevents* the famines predicted by his model from occurring. In this connection, Malthus (implausibly on my view) cites social institutions linked to poverty and vice as preventing the doubling that would, according to his model, allow population growth to outrun food production. See Thomas Robert Malthus, *An Essay on the Principle of Population*, Donald Winch and Patricia James, eds. (Cambridge: 1992, Cambridge University Press). Nonetheless, the more common understanding of Malthus's models does presume that growth in population and agricultural production exists in a competition that threatens the sustainability of the global food system. Authors writing in this tradition point out that growth in agricultural yields has in fact kept pace with global population growth since Malthus wrote, and they cite this observation to support new research on yield-increasing technology. See Anthony Trewavas, "Malthus foiled again and again," *Nature*, 418(2002): 668–670.

6. Miguel Altieri, *Agroecology: The Science of Sustainable Agriculture*, 2nd ed. (Boca Raton, FL: 2018, CRC Press) included an early rendering of the three-circle diagram in its first edition, published in 1987. Altieri was, on the one hand, responding to the work of Gordon Douglass (see Note 33) and linking to business management literature on socially responsible investment and the triple bottom line. The business literature implicitly took the economics circle to include traditional accounting practices

oriented to a firm's balance sheet, extending that idea to environment and impacts on community stakeholders. Altieri's approach is true to this model in taking economics to indicate farm profitability. But this is a significant departure from Douglass's model, and it is on that basis that I have avoided a lengthy tangent in the main text.

7. World Commission on Environment and Development, *Our Common Future* (New York: 1987, Oxford University Press), 43.

8. Bryan G. Norton, *Searching for Sustainability: Interdisciplinary Essays in the Philosophy of Conservation Biology* (New York: 2003, Cambridge University Press), 169. The statement was originally made in a 1992 article published in *Environmental Values*.

9. See Simon Dresner, *The Principles of Sustainability*, 2nd ed. (New York: 2002, Earthscan Press). Norton mentions this U.N. conference in Norton, *Sustainability*. I am quoting from the representation of the Stockholm Declaration that appears in the Wikipedia article on the conference, accessed July 2, 2021, at https://en.wikipedia. org/wiki/United_Nations_Conference_on_the_Human_Environment#cite_note-9

10. Micah Hartman, Anne B. Martin, Benjamin Washington, and Aaron Catlin, "National health care spending in 2020: Growth driven by federal spending in response to the COVID-19 pandemic," *Health Affairs* 41, 1(2022): 13–25.

11. V. Kapuria-Foreman and M. Perlman, "An economic historian's economist: Remembering Simon Kuznets," *Economic Journal* 105(1995): 1524–1547.

12. The capabilities approach (discussed in Chapter 3) would be a third approach, and one that might be more familiar to philosophers than the two I discuss here. A capabilities approach would examine how environmental integrity influences a person's ability to choose which goods to pursue. The contrast between Streeten and Daly provides a more straightforward illustration of the tensions that animated the work of the WCED.

13. See Paul Streeten, Shahid Javed Burki, Mahbub Ul-Haq, Norman Hicks, and Frances Stewart, *First Things First: Meeting Basic Human Needs in the Developing Countries* (New York: 1981, Oxford University Press). I

14. In other writings on sustainability I criticize this equation of natural capital with "the natural resource base." In this context, I'm working hard to minimize the MEGO effect. See, for example, Paul B. Thompson, "Norton and sustainability as such," in *A Sustainable Philosophy: The Work of Bryan Norton*, S. Sarkar and B. A. Minteer, eds. (New York: 2018, Springer), 7–26; or Paul B. Thompson and Patricia A. Norris, *Sustainability: What Everyone Needs to Know* (New York: 2021, Oxford University Press). For Solow's approach, see Robert M. Solow, *An Almost Practical Step Toward Sustainability* (Washington DC: 1992, Resources for the Future).

15. Herman E. Daly, "Sustainable development-definitions, principles, policies," in *The Future of Sustainability*, M. Keiner, ed. (Dordrecht: 2005, Springer), 39–53; Herman E. Daly and John B. Cobb Jr., *For the Common Good: Redirecting the Economy Toward Community, the Environment, and a Sustainable Future* (Boston: 1989, Beacon Press).

16. This is the view of Jeffery Sachs, *The End of Poverty* (New York: 2005, Penguin).

17. This point is made definitively and at greater length by Aiden Davison, *Technology and the Contested Meanings of Sustainability* (Albany: 2002, SUNY Press).

18. The general goal here is to apply a specific method of formal logic to achieve clear definitions of key terms. On this approach, a good definition should preserve the meaning of a sentence whenever the definition is substituted for the term being defined. The discussion in the text emphasizes logical quantifiers. Quantifiers allow us to represent the logical implications of relationships or predicates that hold in every possible case (universal quantification: "for all x," symbolized as $\forall$x) or in at least one case (existential quantification: "there is at least one X," symbolized $\exists$x). The symbolic expression $S(x)$ just means "x is sustainable" in ordinary English. So when we translate

(1) $\forall x\, S(x) \leftrightarrow x$ meets the needs of the present and x allows future generations to meet their needs}

into English we can break the symbolic notation down as follows: the first part of the sentence— $\forall x\, S(x)$—is saying "for anything (any word or concept we substitute for the variable x) of which we would say "x is sustainable. . . ." The part after the two-headed arrow goes on to stipulate the defining conditions. In this case, there are two conditions that must be true of x whenever one can truly assert $S(x)$ (e.g., say that x is sustainable). First, x must meet the needs of the present and, second, x must allow future generations to meet their needs. The fact that the arrow points in both directions (e.g., $\leftrightarrow$) tells us that if $S(x)$ is false (e.g., x is *not* sustainable), then one of the conditions stated in the second half must also be false. Either x doesn't meet the needs of present generations, or it doesn't allow future generations to meet their needs. We can then test the definition by instantiating x (e.g., trying out different concepts, processes, or practices where x appears in the definition). If the definition is a good one, the truth of both conditions will hold in every case where we want to say that x is sustainable, and, in every case where we want to say that x is *not* sustainable, one or the other of these conditions must be false. This is what the analytic approach *means* by a definition.

If we skip down to (2), the universal quantifier $\forall$x is still referring to anything (any instantiation of the variable x) that we might want to call sustainable or unsustainable. But the definition is doing a different job. Now it is restricting the scope of sustainability (e.g., $S(x)$) to practices, processes, and systems of practice. It says that when we say a practice, process, or system of practice is sustainable, then there must be some metric or measure y (e.g., $\exists(y)$) that tells us whether or how long x can or will continue. Here, there is no biconditional ($\leftrightarrow$). We have an arrow pointing in one direction: $\rightarrow$. This means *if* we say "some practice, process or system of processes is sustainable," then we are committing ourselves to finding some metric for determining whether or how long it continue. It also says that it would be false to predicate sustainability of anything that lacks such a metric. It neither tells us anything about what the metric is nor whether the existence of such a metric implies that the given practice, process, or system of processes is sustainable. In other words, there will be more to say, more things to predicate, about those things we want to call sustainable. There is thus an important sense in which this is *not* a definition in the classic sense of analytic philosophy: it does not tell us the necessary and sufficient conditions for attributing sustainability.

I'm willing to let further details slide in the present context. I do think that the analytic philosopher's practice of testing definitions by substituting different ways to instantiate variables is a useful way to gain clarity about the difference between sustainable development and sustainability as such, and that is the point I want to get across. Notice that I am just now reaching the end of a 600-word footnote intended help readers who have no familiarity with symbolic logic navigate the basic procedure for instantiating variables under universal and existential quantification. The virtue of symbolic logic lies in the efficiency of expression; the vice in its obtuseness for the uninitiated.

19. In the spirit of analytic philosophy (and consistent with the concluding comments in the preceding footnote), I concede that additional factors should be incorporated into my definition. However, I'm also trying to be at least minimally accessible here, so, while I welcome amendments to my criterion, I hope the logic choppers will cut me some slack when they offer them.

20. Ian Werkheiser and Zachary Piso, "People work to sustain systems: A framework for understanding sustainability," *Journal of Water Resources Planning and Management* 141(2015): A4015002.

21. Agricultural soils are not inert bodies of dirt or dust that serve only to anchor plant root systems or transport water and fertilizer. A soil is a system of interacting processes that includes the slow breakdown of rock and minerals as well as the decay of organic matter, generally abetted by insects, worms, and microorganisms. The geophysical processes that contribute to mineral content are so slow that soil specialists regard mineral content as a fixed stock, but organic matter flows into the soil system from fallen leaves, broken stems, and animal manure. The insects, worms, and microorganisms that convert organic matter into nutrients that will support the growth of future plants are also a variable stock. They enter the soil system based on their reproductive rate and predator–prey relationships within soils, and they exit the system when they die. However, farmers can affect inflows and outflows of organic matter, soil-metabolizing organisms (like worms or microorganisms), and plant nutrients (like nitrogen, phosphorus, and potassium [e.g., NPK]). Adding composted manure provides an inflow of organic matter that is preloaded with soil-metabolizing organisms. Adding synthetic fertilizer is a direct inflow of plant nutrients, but synthetic fertilizers also kill off microorganisms, thus increasing the outflow (e.g., death rate) of soil-metabolizing organisms. Legumes fix atmospheric nitrogen in soils, making it available as a nutrient for future crops. This feature undergirds the sustainability of "three sisters" cropping systems practiced by Native Americans.

22. Pielke draws a contrast with abortion politics, where it is equally obvious that radically different value orientations make decision-making difficult. Robert Pielke, Jr., *The Honest Broker: Making Sense of Science in Policy and Politics* (New York: 2007, Cambridge University Press), especially 43–50.

23. Zachary Piso, Ian Werkheiser, Samantha Noll, and Christina Leshko, "Sustainability of what? Recognising the diverse values that sustainable agriculture works to sustain," *Environmental Values* 25(2016): 195–214.

24. Stoll, *Larding the Lean Earth*.

25. This is a point that I have returned to repeatedly in my career of writing on ethics and agriculture. Each time, I am struck by the lack of coherence in the literature on this point, and I have cited at least a half-dozen sources on the links between military research and industrial agriculture in my other publications. For readers needing an orientation to soil ecology more generally, the best source is probably Vaclav Smil, *Enriching the Earth: Fritz Haber, Carl Bosch, and the Transformation of World Food Production* (Cambridge, MA: 2001, MIT Press).

26. Vernon Ruttan and Yujiro Hayami developed an influential theory of agricultural innovation which held that drivers are endogenous to the farm economy. Vernon Ruttan and Yujiro Hayami, "Toward a theory of induced institutional innovation," *Journal of Development Studies* 20, 4(1984): 203–223.

27. For this and succeeding points, see Thompson, *The Agrarian Vision*.

28. Ulrich Grober, *Sustainability: A Cultural History*, Ray Cunningham, tr. (Totnes, UK: 2012, Green Books).

29. See Matt Tynauer, "Industrial revolution, take two," *Vanity Fair*, 2008, accessed August 13, 2021, at https://www.vanityfair.com/culture/2008/05/mcdonough200805

30. See Thompson, 2018, "Norton and sustainability as such."

31. My book, *The Spirit of the Soil: Agriculture and Environmental Ethics*, 2nd ed. (New York: 2017, Routledge), was published in its first edition in 1995. In the second edition, the discussion of sustainability occurs at pages 172–180.

32. Some of the considerations discussed here were included in my discussion of sustainable agriculture from the first edition of *The Spirit of the Soil* (Ibid.). Others were mentioned in "Agricultural sustainability: What it is and what it is not," *International Journal of Agricultural Sustainability* 5(2007): 5–16.

33. Gordon K. Douglass, "The meanings of agricultural sustainability," in *Agricultural Sustainability in a Changing World Order*, G. K. Douglass, ed. (Boulder, CO: 1984, Westview Press), 3–29. See also Werkheiser and Piso, "People work to sustain systems."

34. Allen's early work on this theme includes Patricia Allen and Carolyn Sachs, "The poverty of sustainability: An analysis of current discourse," *Agriculture and Human Values* 9, 4(1992): 30–37, and especially her edited book *Food for the Future: Conditions and Contradictions of Sustainability* (New York: 1993, Wiley), as well as many other highly cited papers. In this phase of her work, Allen emphasized the symbolic role of sustainability in mobilizing a social movement around food system reform, and other papers noted how this movement would be opposed by dominant interests in capitalist society (see Patricia Allen, "Sustainable agriculture at the crossroads," *Capitalism Nature Socialism* 2(1991): 20–28). Her focus on "the food movement" should be read against my view that an overriding focus on mobilizing social actions undercuts the philosopher's commitment to open-ended inquiry (see Chapter 2).

35. Ashanté M. Reese, *Black Food Geographies: Race, Self-Reliance, and Food Access in Washington, DC* (Chapel Hill: 2019, University of North Carolina Press).

36. See Patricia Allen and Julie Guthman, "From 'old school' to 'farm-to-school': Neoliberalization from the ground up, *Agriculture and Human Values* 23(2006): 401–415.

37. F. Scott Fitzgerald, *The Crack Up* (New York: 1945, New Directions), 1.

Chapter 8

1. Paul B. Thompson, "Agricultural ethics—then and now," *Agriculture and Human Values* 32(2015): 77–85.
2. Book-length treatments by James Montmarquet, Kimberly Smith, and Eric Freyfogle have been important for me. James A. Montmarquet, *The Idea of Agrarianism: From Hunter-Gatherer to Agrarian Radical in Western Culture* (Moscow: 1989, University of Idaho Press); Kimberly K. Smith, *Wendell Berry and the Agrarian Tradition: A Common Grace* (Lawrence: 2003, University of Kansas Press); Eric T. Freyfogle, *Agrarianism and the Good Society: Land, Culture, Conflict, and Hope* (Lexington: 2007, University Press of Kentucky).
3. Wendell Berry, *The Unsettling of America: Culture and Agriculture* (San Francisco: 1977, Sierra Club Books).
4. Kimberly Smith has reviewed and rebutted the allegations of patriarchy and racism in Berry's work from a feminist perspective. See Kimberly Smith, "Wendell Berry's feminist agrarianism," *Women's Studies* 30(2001): 623–646. My treatment of Berry can be found in Paul B. Thompson, *The Spirit of the Soil: Agriculture and Environmental Ethics*, 2nd ed. (New York: 2017, Routledge), 93–112, 198–201.
5. Anonymous, n.d. Agrarianism, *Merriam-Webster Dictionary*, accessed September 12, 2021, at https://www.merriam-webster.com/dictionary/agrarianism
6. See Zvi Lerman, "Land reform, farm structure and agricultural performance in CIS countries," *China Economic Review* 20(2009): 316–326. Lerman's is a fairly standard approach to understanding agriculture's contributions to development, and his question is whether land reforms succeed in advancing welfare as reflected by GDP. I do not intend to be critical of this approach here. My point is only to illustrate how many people who study or advocate for land reform do not have a philosophically agrarian orientation in the sense that I am attempting to develop in this chapter.
7. Three communication scholars have produced a very useful examination of agrarian themes from the standpoint of mythos. Their study examines the historical roots of agrarian themes in the United States through detailed examination of several distinct episodes and goes on to discuss the reproduction, transformation, and exploitation of these mythic structures in popular culture. Ross Singer, Stephanie Houston Grey, and Jeff Motter, *Rooted Resistance: Agrarian Myth in Modern America* (Fayetteville: 2020, University of Arkansas Press).
8. This summary of Inge's essay was originally prepared by my coauthor in Thomas C. Hilde and Paul B. Thompson, "Agrarianism and pragmatism," in *The Agrarian Roots of Pragmatism*, P. B. Thompson and T. C. Hilde, eds. (Nashville, TN: 2000, Vanderbilt University Press), 1–21.
9. Montmarquet, *The Idea of Agrarianism*, 107.
10. Ibid., 146–148.
11. Roy A. Rappaport, *Pigs for the Ancestors: Ritual in the Ecology of a New Guinea People* (New Haven, CT: 1967, Yale University Press); Marvin Harris, *Cannibals and Kings: The Origins of Culture* (New York; 1977, Random House); Roy F. Ellen, *Environment, Subsistence, and System: The Ecology of Small-Scale Social Formations* (New York: 1982, Cambridge University Press).

12. Clarence J. Glacken, *Traces on the Rhodian Shore: Nature and Culture in Western Thought from Ancient Times to the End of the Eighteenth Century* (Berkeley: 1976, University of California Press).

13. Charles Montesquieu, *The Spirit of the Laws*, A. M. Cohler, B. C. Miller, and H. S. Stone, tr. and eds. (Cambridge: 1989, Cambridge University Press).

14. Jack Greene, "The intellectual reconstruction of Virginia in the age of Jefferson," in *Jeffersonian Legacies*, P. S. Onuf, ed. (Charlottesville: 1993, University of Virginia Press), 225–253.

15. I do not mean to imply that agricultural expansion was the immediate goal of colonizers.

16. M. Thomas Inge, *Agrarianism in American Literature* (New York: 1969, Odyssey Press).

17. Readers whose interest is piqued by such a prospect are referred to Paul B. Thompson, *The Agrarian Vision: Sustainability and Environmental Ethics* (Lexington: 2010, University Press of Kentucky).

18. Thomas Jefferson, *Writings*, M. D. Peterson, ed. (New York: 1984, Literary Classics of the United States), 290, 818.

19. See David B. Danbom, "Romantic agrarianism in twentieth-century America," *Agricultural History* 65, 4(1991): 1–12; Laura Sayre, "The politics of organic farming: Populists, evangelicals, and the agriculture of the middle," *Gastronomica* 11, 2(2011): 38–47.

20. Henry Nash Smith, *Virgin Land: The American West in Symbol and Myth* (New York: 1950, Vintage Books). Smith's history of Western settlement is contested, but there is little doubt that the dozens of journalists and other writers he quotes in this classic study were promoting an agrarian ideal in which the natural virtue of the farming life was a central tenet.

21. Thompson, *The Agrarian Vision*, 45–50.

22. Garry Wills, *Inventing America: Jefferson's Declaration of Independence* (New York: 1979, Vintage Books), 160.

23. Garry Wills, "American Adam," *New York Review of Books*, March 6, 1997, accessed September 9, 2021, at https://www.nybooks.com/articles/1997/03/06/american-adam/. Wills does not use the phrase "white supremacy" in his article.

24. Charles Mills, *The Racial Contract* (Ithaca, NY: 1997, Cornell University Press).

25. Willard Sterne Randall, *Thomas Jefferson: A Life* (New York: 1993, Henry Holt & Co.). For the runaway episode, see 143–144; for the quotation, at 302.

26. Adrienne Koch, *The Philosophy of Thomas Jefferson* (New York: 1943, Columbia University Press), 89–104.

27. Ibid., 96.

28. See Paul B. Thompson, "Thomas Jefferson and agrarian philosophy," in *The Agrarian Roots of Pragmatism*, P. B. Thompson and T. C. Hilde, eds. (Nashville, TN: 2000, Vanderbilt University Press), 118–139.

29. Eugene Hargrove, *Foundations of Environmental Ethics* (Englewood Cliffs, NJ: 1989, Prentice-Hall).

30. Martin H. Rogoff and Stephen l. Rawlins, "Food security: A technological alternative," *BioScience* 37(1987): 800–807.

31. Ben A. Minteer and James P. Collins, "Ecological ethics: Building a new tool kit for ecologists and biodiversity managers," *Conservation Biology* 19(2005): 1803–1812.

32. There may be some call here for a more extensive discussion of the distinction between "consequentialist" and "deontological" approaches in environmental philosophy—a typology that is enormously popular among philosophers. Consequentialist ethical theories associate ethical value with the outcomes or "end states" that result from any decision or action, while deontological theories associate ethical value or "normativity" with the choice itself or with the intentions of the decision-maker. Common interpretations of the deontological school connect it with views that place special emphasis on rights, on obtaining consent from affected parties, or on proscribing a domain of actions as wholly prohibited, without regard to the consequences they produce. Indeed, such theories are often characterized as "rights views." Thus, in environmental philosophy, many environmental economists would qualify as consequentialists, along with well-known figures such as Peter Singer and Robin Attfield. Other influential figures in environmental ethics almost certainly think of themselves as deontologists, including Paul Taylor (1923–2015) and Holmes Rolston. Consequentialist views tend to encourage "tradeoffs" among good and bad outcomes, while deontological views try to block certain outcomes altogether. What is more significant than this distinction so prized by philosophers is the way that both of these schools of thought frame ethical questions through the lens of decision-making. It is either the outcome of decisions (for consequentialists) or constraints on decisions (for rights theorists) that matter ethically. It is in this respect that both of these approaches can be seen as alternatives within the decisionist, rational choice model. See Peter Singer, *One World: The Ethics of Globalization* (New Haven, CT: 2002, Yale University Press); Robin Attfield, *Environmental Ethics: An Overview for the Twenty-First Century* (Cambridge: 2003, Cambridge University Press); Paul W. Taylor, *Respect for Nature: A Theory of Environmental Ethics* (Princeton, NJ: 1986, Princeton University Press); and Holmes Rolston III, *Environmental Ethics: Duties to and Values in the Natural World* (Philadelphia: 1988, Temple University Press).

33. Minteer and Collins, "Ecological ethics."

34. Alasdair MacIntyre, *After Virtue: A Study in Moral Theory*, 2nd ed. (Notre Dame, IN: 1984, University of Notre Dame Press).

35. Ronald L. Sandler, *Character and Environment: A Virtue-Oriented Approach to Environmental Ethics* (New York: 2007, Columbia University Press).

36. Aaron Garrett, "Anthropology: The 'original' of human nature," in *Cambridge Companion to the Scottish Enlightenment*, A. Broadie, ed. (Cambridge: 2003, Cambridge University Press), 79–93.

37. Phillip Cafaro, *Thoreau's Living Ethics: Walden and the Pursuit of Virtue* (Athens: 2004, University of Georgia Press), 51.

38. Ibid., 75.

39. Robert S. Corrington, "Emerson and the agricultural midworld," *Agriculture and Human Values* 7(1990): 20–26; Douglas R. Anderson, "Wild farming: Thoreau and agrarian life," in *The Agrarian Roots of Pragmatism*, P. B. Thompson and T. C. Hilde, eds. (Nashville, TN: 2000, Vanderbilt University Press), 153–163.

40. William E. Grant and Paul B. Thompson, "Integrated ecological models: Simulation of socio-cultural constraints on ecological dynamics," *Ecological Modeling* 100(1997): 43–59.

41. This approach to the evolution of norms has a more extensive development in game theoretic models that simulate the evolution of cooperative strategies. I do not reject that approach, but it is not what I am talking about here. What Grant and I did was to connect an ecological model to a simple problem in game theory, showing how it could simulate the games being studied in behavioral and evolutionary economics. This implies a more robust understanding of biological selection (e.g., cultures die out because people starve) than is seen in this literature. See, for example, Bryan Skyrms, *The Stag Hunt and the Evolution of Social Structure* (New York: 2003, Cambridge University Press).

42. For a more detailed exposition, see Hugh LaFollette, "Pragmatic ethics," in *Blackwell Guide to Ethical Theory*, H. LaFollette, ed. (Oxford: 2003, Blackwell Publishers), 400–419.

43. George Lakoff, *Don't Think of an Elephant: Know Your Values and Frame the Debate: The Essential Guide for Progressives* (White River Junction, VT: 2004, Chelsea Green Publishers).

44. George Lakoff and Mark Johnson, *Philosophy in the Flesh: The Embodied Mind and Its Challenge to Western Thought* (New York: 1999, Basic Books).

45. Lakoff, *Don't Think of an Elephant*.

46. See Michel Foucault, "On the genealogy of ethics: An overview of work in progress," in *Ethics, Subjectivity and Truth: The Essential Works of Foucault*, vol. 1., Paul Rabinow, ed., Robert Hurley, tr. (New York: 1997, New Press), 253–280. Quotation on 263. This chapter is derived from "working sessions" conducted in English that Rabinow and Dreyfus held with Foucault in 1983. The text includes both French and English renderings of the four elements I discuss here. I prefer to quote the French because it helps dissociate Foucault's ideas from potentially misleading ways in which an English translation might be interpreted.

47. Foucault himself explains the *mode d'assujettissement* by drawing a contrast between the Stoics' attentiveness to their own life and Isocrates's focus on relations with others. Ibid., 264.

48. Ibid., 265.

49. Robert Bernasconi, "Will the real Kant please stand up," *Radical Philosophy* 117(2003): 13–22.

50. John Dewey, "Experience and nature," in *The Later Writings of John Dewey*, vol. 1, Jo Ann Boydston, ed. (Carbondale: 2008, Southern Illinois University Press), 224.

51. Paul B. Thompson, *From Field to Fork: Food Ethics for Everyone* (New York: 2015, Oxford University Press), 16–21.

52. Gregory Pappas, "Dewey's moral theory: Experience as method," *Transactions of the Charles S. Peirce Society* 33(1997): 520–556.

53. This argument can be developed in light of the way that Albert Borgmann and David Strong link philosophy of technology to environmental ethics. See Paul B. Thompson,

"Farming as focal practice," in *Technology and the Good Life?*, E. Higgs, A. Light, and D. Strong, eds. (Chicago: 1999, University of Chicago Press), 166–181.

54. Koch, *The Philosophy of Thomas Jefferson*, 90.

55. Ibid., 97.

Chapter 9

1. John W. Head, *Deep Agroecology and the Homeric Epics: Global Cultural Reforms for a Natural-systems Agriculture* (New York: 2021, Routledge), 44.

2. As university philosophy departments have quickened the pace in considering race or gender during the 21st century, the work of many earlier thinkers has resurfaced and been reincorporated into the catalog of writings considered to be philosophical. Prior to recent times, philosophy teachers regarded figures such as Du Bois as sociologists or social activists, rather than as philosophers. See Erin McKenna and Scott L. Pratt, *American Philosophy: From Wounded Knee to the Present* (New York: 2015, Bloomsbury Academic).

3. Ramachandra Guha, "Radical American environmentalism and wilderness preservation: A third world critique," *Environmental Ethics* 11(1989): 71–83.

4. Food ethics takes cognizance of race in studies of food and identity, especially with respect to cooking and social rituals associated with eating. Lee McBride draws on the philosophy of Alain Locke to argue that many foods and food traditions are cultural products arising conjointly with the struggle against oppression. Failing to acknowledge this history constitutes an injustice in recognition. However, McBride also concludes that such histories do not establish collective ownership of foodways by racially defined groups and that consumption and adaptation of foods can have morally salutary consequences. See Lee McBride III, "Racial imperialism and food traditions," in *The Oxford Handbook of Food Ethics*, A. Barnhill, M. Budolfson, and T. Doggett, eds. (New York: 2018, Oxford University Press), 333–344.

5. On dispossession, see Shakara S. Tyler and Eddie A. Moore, "Plight of black farmers in the context of USDA farm loan programs: A research agenda for the future," *Professional Agricultural Workers Journal* 1, 1(2013): 6, accessed August 24, 2021, at https://tuspubs.tuskegee.edu/pawj/vol1/iss1/6 On food access see Ashanté Reese, *Black Food Geographies: Race, Self-Reliance and Food Access in Washington D.C.* (Chapel Hill: 2019, University of North Carolina Press).

6. For example, Mark Navin, "Food sovereignty and gender justice: The case of La Via Campesina," in *Just Food: Philosophy, Justice and Food*, J. Dieterle, ed. (London: 2015, Rowman and Littlefield), 87–100; Samantha Noll, "Food sovereignty in the city: Challenging historical barriers to food justice," in *Food Justice in U.S. and Global Contexts*, I Werkheiser and Z. Piso, eds. (New York: 2017, Springer), 95–111; Kyle Powys Whyte, "Food sovereignty, justice, and indigenous peoples: An essay on settler colonialism and collective continuance," in *The Oxford Handbook of*

Food Ethics, A. Barnhill, M. Budolfson, and T. Doggett, eds. (New York: 2018, Oxford University Press), 345–366.

7. Annette Gordon-Reed, *On Juneteenth* (New York: 2021, W. W. Norton).

8. Trudier Harris, *Exorcising Blackness: Historical and Literary Lynching and Burning Rituals* (Bloomington: 1984, Indiana University Press), 2, quoted in *A Philosophy of Struggle: The Leonard Harris Reader*, L. McBride, ed. (London: 2020, Bloomsbury Academic), at 56.

9. Ibid., 55.

10. Luc Faucher, "Racism," in *The Routledge Companion to the Philosophy of Race*, P. C. Taylor, L. M. Alcoff, and L. Anderson, eds. (New York: 2018, Routledge), 406–422.

11. See Clarence J. Glacken, *Traces on the Rhodian Shore: Nature and Culture in Western Thought from Ancient Times to the End of the Eighteenth Century* (Berkeley: 1976, University of California Press).

12. Simon Donner, "The ugly history of climate determinism is still evident today," *Scientific American* June 24, 2020, accessed January 13, 2023, at https://www.scientificamerican.com/article/the-ugly-history-of-climate-determinism-is-still-evident-today/

13. Neil Altman and Johanna Tiemann, "Racism as a manic defense," in *Racism in Mind*, M. R. Levine and T. Pataki, eds. (Ithaca, NY: 2004, Cornell University Press), 127–141. The quoted passage is on page 136.

14. Robert Bernasconi, "Critical philosophy of race and philosophical historiography," in *The Routledge Companion to Philosophy of Race*, P. C. Taylor, L. M. Alcoff, and L. Anderson, eds. (New York: 2018, Routledge), 3–13; Frank M. Kirkland, "Kant on race and transition," in *The Routledge Companion to Philosophy of Race*, P. C. Taylor, L. M. Alcoff, and L. Anderson, eds. (New York: 2018, Routledge), 28–42.

15. Charles Mills, *The Racial Contract* (Ithaca, NY: 1997, Cornell University Press). Mills would have been one of those who thinks that anyone who attempts something like an environmental philosophy without confronting the reality of racism cannot fail to promote racist ideology.

16. Charles Mills, *Blackness Visible: Essays on Philosophy and Race* (Ithaca, NY: 1998, Cornell University Press), 151–166. See also Leonard Harris, "The concept of racism: An essentially contested concept," "What, then is racism?" and "Necro-being: An actuarial account of racism," in L. Harris, *A Philosophy of Struggle*, 43–96.

17. Mills, *The Racial Contract*

18. Taney is quoted in Mills, *The Racial Contract*, 184.

19. Stanley develops this view in Jason Stanley, *How Propaganda Works* (Princeton, NJ: 2015, Princeton University Press).

20. U.S. Department of Agriculture, "Farm Demographics," May 2014, accessed March 27, 2023, at https://www.nass.usda.gov/Publications/Highlights/2014/Farm_Demographics/Highlights_Farm_Demographics.pdf

21. Rick Beard, "A promise betrayed: Reconstruction policies prevented freedmen from realizing the American dream," HistoryNet, 2017, accessed September 15, 2021, at https://www.historynet.com/a-promise-betrayed.htm

22. Pete Daniel, *The Shadow of Slavery: Peonage in the South, 1901–1969* (New York: 1972, Oxford University Press).

23. Bruce J. Reynolds, *Black Farmers in America, 1865–2000: The Pursuit of Independent Farming and the Role of Cooperatives*, Rural Business Cooperative Report 194. Washington: DC: 2002, USDA, accessed August 29, 2021, at https://www.rd.usda.gov/files/RR194.pdf. Monica White also discusses this period of racial repression while highlighting the success of resistance efforts that emphasized cooperative farming. Monica M. White, *Freedom Farmers: Agricultural Resistance and the Black Freedom Movement* (Chapel Hill: 2019, University of North Carolina Press).

24. Cecilia M. Tsu, *Garden of the World: Asian Immigrants and the Making of Agriculture in California's Santa Clara Valley* (New York: 2013, Oxford University Press).

25. Susan Ferris and Ricardo Sandoval, *The Fight in the Fields: Cesar Chavez and the Farmworkers Movement* (New York: 1997, Harcourt and Brace).

26. Paul B. Thompson, *From Field to Fork: Food Ethics for Everyone* (New York: 2015, Oxford University Press), 54–79.

27. Barry Esterbrook, *Tomatoland: How Modern Industrial Agriculture Destroyed Our Most Alluring Fruit* (Kansas City, MO: 2012, Andrews McMeel Publishing).

28. Daniel, *The Shadow of Slavery*; Joseph D. Reid, "Sharecropping in history and theory," *Agricultural History* 49(1975): 426–450, provides an alternative analysis that explains how arrangements can be economically rational for all parties. Reid's paper stresses that in the postwar South, sharecropping existed along with hired labor.

29. In *From Field to Fork*, I argued that virtually any normative approach to social justice would find these forms of oppression problematic. My treatment of food justice there does not adequately reflect the significance of racism in producing and reproducing these problems. See Thompson, *From Field to Fork*, 58–62.

30. Janet Poppendieck, *Sweet Charity?: Emergency Food and the End of Entitlement* (New York: 1998, Penguin Books).

31. Lorenzo Veracini, *Settler Colonialism: A Theoretical Overview* (London: 2010, Palgrave Macmillan).

32. Kyle P. Whyte, "Indigenous food sovereignty, renewal and U.S. settler colonialism," in *The Routledge Handbook of Food Ethics*, M. Rawlinson and C. Ward, eds. (New York: 2016, Routledge), 354–365. See also Whyte, "Food sovereignty, justice, and indigenous peoples"; and Ian Werkheiser, "Community epistemic capacity," *Social Epistemology* 30(2015): 25–44.

33. This is not to say that they are entirely lacking in their resources for moral condemnation. Utilitarians can stress the adverse impact on the welfare of indigenous peoples and might go further, acknowledging the utility of indigenous knowledge systems in valuing ecosystem services. Rights theorists will have no difficulty with short-term impacts on immediately affected individuals, but efforts to expand the discourse of rights to collective capacities have spawned a large and contentious literature that it is best to acknowledge without further comment. See Will Kymlicka, *Liberalism, Community and Culture* (New York: 1989, Oxford University Press); and, for the reaction, Michael Freeman, "Are there collective human rights?" *Political Theory* 43(1995): 25–40.

34. Thompson, *From Field to Fork*, 72–76.

35. It is less clear to me that the same thing can be said about Africa, though the history of black slavery could have had a deleterious impact on cultural forms that valorize

farming and food systems. My comment here reflects the almost unilateral opinion of Africanists I know. While throughout Asia and the Americas farmers are venerated, even while being neglected and oppressed, they say that this is not the case in Africa.

36. See Marcel Mazoyer and Lawrence Roudart, *A History of World Agriculture from the Neolithic Age to the Current Crisis*, J. H. Membrez, tr. (New York: 2006, Monthly Review Press). See also David Goodman and Michael Watts, "Agrarian questions: Global appetite, local metabolism: Nature, culture and industry in *fin-de-siècle* agro-food systems," in *Globalizing Food: Agrarian Questions and Global Restructuring*, D. Goodman and M. Watts, eds. (London: 1997, Routledge), 1–32. The title of Goodman and Watts's book notwithstanding, they include fiber production as a component of "agro-food systems."

37. Sven Beckert, *Empire of Cotton: A Global History* (New York; 2014, Vintage); Sidney Mintz, *Sweetness and Power: The Place of Sugar in Modern History* (New York: 1985, Penguin).

38. It is significant that Africans already had experience with many of these crops. Plantations in the Americas might not have been successful if not for the prior agricultural knowledge of enslaved Africans. James F. Hancock, *Plantation Crops, Plunder and Power: Evolution and Exploitation* (New York: 2017, Routledge).

39. Well, "almost certainly" is a bit of an overstatement. Aristotle's observation appears in Book 1 of the *Politics*, and a prolific literature has emerged among scholars trying to understand what he meant by it. Later in the *Politics*, Aristotle extolls the *hoi mesoi* or middle-class farming households of the Greek world, most of whom would have relied on a rather small slave workforce for executing farming tasks. The institutions of the *hoi mesoi* are not so much good for the slaves themselves (though their life conditions were generally better than those of enslaved blacks), but because they enabled the Greek way of life.

40. Thomas Jefferson, *Writings*, M. D. Peterson, ed. (New York: 1984, Library of America), 264–267.

41. Tamas Pataki, "Introduction," in *Racism in Mind*, M. P. Levine and T. Pataki, eds. (Ithaca, NY: 2004, Cornell University Press), 1–23. The quoted passage appears on page 6. Pataki is himself quoting from Michael Banton, *Racial Theories*, 3rd ed. (Cambridge: 1998, Cambridge University Press).

42. Jefferson, *Writings*, 268.

43. "I advance it therefore as a suspicion only, that the blacks, whether originally a distinct race, or made distinct by time and circumstances, are inferior to the whites in the endowments both of body and of mind." Jefferson, *Writings*, 270. See also Mills, *The Racial Contract*, 191.

44. Mark Tauger, *Agriculture in World History*, 2nd ed. (New York: 2021, Routledge), 88. Tauger is rehearsing a view argued at more length by David B. Danbom, "Romantic agrarianism in twentieth-century America," *Agricultural History* 65, 4(1991): 1–12. It had been argued even earlier by Henry Nash Smith, *Virgin Land: The American West as Symbol and Myth* (New York: 1950, Vintage Books). Smith reproduces many quotations from 19th-century sources who make bald statements on the superior morality of American farmers.

45. Well into the 20th century (and, in some quarters, still today) land was distinguished from capital in part because of its intrinsic non-portability.

46. Paul B. Thompson, *The Agrarian Vision: Sustainability and Environmental Ethics* (Lexington: 2010, University Press of Kentucky), 62–86.

47. Ibid.

48. See the discussion of Jefferson's alliance with John Taylor of Caroline (1753–1824) in Kimberly Smith, *Wendell Berry and the Agrarian Tradition: A Common Grace* (Lawrence: 2003, University of Kansas Press).

49. Quoted in Willard Sterne Randall, *Thomas Jefferson: A Life* (New York: 1992 [2014], Harper Perennials), 276–277.

50. Quoted in Adrienne Koch, *The Philosophy of Thomas Jefferson* (New York: 1943, Columbia University Press), 118–119.

51. Jefferson, *Writings*, 183–190.

52. Jean-Baptiste Lamarck (1744–1829) was a French botanist who argued for the heritability of phenotypically acquired characteristics, a view that was rejected after Darwin. It seems likely that Jefferson would have crossed paths with him during his years in France, but I have not seen discussions of such a meeting in any of the secondary sources on Jefferson that I have consulted, nor am I aware that Jefferson discussed Lamarck's theories in his correspondence.

53. Mills, *The Racial Contract*, 44–50.

54. I argued for this view in Paul B. Thompson, "Thomas Jefferson and agrarian philosophy," in *The Agrarian Roots of Pragmatism*, P. B. Thompson and T. C. Hilde, eds. (Nashville, TN: 2000, Vanderbilt University Press), 118–139.

55. Henry Wiencek, *Master of the Mountain: Thomas Jefferson and His Slaves* (New York: 2012, Farrar, Straus and Giroux).

56. Paul Finkelman, "Thomas Jefferson and antislavery: The myth goes on," *Virginia Magazine of History and Biography* 102(1984): 193–228; and "Jefferson and slavery," in *Jeffersonian Legacies*, P. F. Onuf, ed. (Charlottesville: 1993, University of Virginia Press), 181–221. I think Finkelman runs together Jefferson's views on slavery with his views on race in these articles.

57. Paul B. Thompson, "Thomas Jefferson's land ethics," in *Thomas Jefferson and Philosophy: Essays on the Philosophical Cast of Jefferson's Writings*, M. A. Holowchak, ed. (Lanham, MD: 2014, Lexington Books), 61–77.

58. Jefferson, *Writings*, 520.

59. Ibid., 556.

60. Ibid., 1118.

61. Ibid., 1119.

62. Bill Winders, *The Politics of Food Supply: U.S. Agricultural Policy in the World Economy* (New Haven, CT: 2009, Yale University Press).

63. Harry C. Dillingham and David F. Sly, "The mechanical cotton-picker, Negro migration, and the integration movement," *Human Organization* 25 (1966): 344–351.

64. See Paul B. Thompson, *The Spirit of the Soil: Agriculture and Environmental Ethics*, 2nd ed. (New York: 2017, Routledge), 53–57.

65. Vincenta Mamani-Bernabé, "Spirituality and the *Pachamama* in the Andean Aymara worldview," in *Earth Stewardship. Ecology and Ethics*, vol 2., R. Rozzi, F. S. Chapin III, J. B. Callicott, S. T. A. Pickett, M. E. Power, J. J. Armesto and R. H. May Jr., eds. (New York: 2015, Springer), 65–76.

66. Kristie Dotson, "Conceptualizing epistemic oppression," *Social Epistemology* 28(2014): 115–138.

67. Johannes M. Waldmueller and Laura Rodriguez, "*Buen vivir* and the rights of nature: Alternative visions of development," in *Routledge Handbook of Development Ethics*, J. Drydyk and L. Keleher, eds. (New York: 2019, Routledge), 234–247.

68. White, *Freedom Farmers*.

69. In 2021, the DBNFSN announced that henceforth the S in their name would stand for sovereignty, rather than security. However, this change is not reflected on their website as of late 2022.

70. Malik Yakini, "Visions of a new economy from Detroit: A conversation with Malik Yakini," *Non Profits Quarterly* July 11, 2018, accessed February 3, 2022, at https://non profitquarterly.org/visions-of-a-new-economy-from-detroit-a-conversation-with-malik-yakini/

71. For an exploration of these links, see Antonio Roman-Alcalá, "Agrarian anarchism and authoritarian populism: towards a more (state-)critical 'critical agrarian studies.'" *Journal of Peasant Studies* 48(2021): 298–328.

72. Reese, *Black Food Geographies*.

73. A. Breeze Harper, *Sistah Vegan: Black Women Speak on Food, Identity, Health and Society* (Brooklyn, NY: 2020 [2010], Lantern Publishing).

74. Malik Yakini, "Building black food sovereignty: An update," Zoom lecture delivered March 15, 2022; accessed May 5, 2022, at https://www.youtube.com/watch?v=Daez RQDgHDg

Bibliography

Allen, Patricia. 1991. "Sustainable agriculture at the crossroads." *Capitalism Nature Socialism* 2: 20–28.

Allen, Patricia, ed. 1993. *Food for the Future: Conditions and Contradictions of Sustainability.* New York: John Wiley and Sons.

Allen, Patricia, and Carolyn Sachs. 1992. "The poverty of sustainability: An analysis of current discourse." *Agriculture and Human Values* 9(4): 30–37.

Allen, Patricia, and Julie Guthman. 2006. "From 'old school' to 'farm-to-school': Neoliberalization from the ground up." *Agriculture and Human Values* 23: 401–415.

Almanza, Barbara A., Douglas Nelson, and Stella Chai. 1997. "Obstacles to nutrition labeling in restaurants." *Journal of the American Dietetic Association* 97: 157–161.

Altieri. Miguel. 2018. *Agroecology: The Science of Sustainable Agriculture,* 2nd ed. Boca Raton, FL: CRC Press.

Altman, Neil, and Johanna Tiemann. 2004. "Racism as a manic defense." In *Racism in Mind,* M. R. Levine and T. Pataki, eds. Ithaca, NY: Cornell University Press, 127–141.

Anderson, Douglas R. 2000. "Wild farming: Thoreau and agrarian life." In *The Agrarian Roots of Pragmatism,* P. B. Thompson and T. C. Hilde, eds. Nashville, TN: Vanderbilt University Press, 153–163.

Andrés, José, with Richard Wolfe. 2018. *We Fed an Island: The True Story of Rebuilding Puerto Rico One Meal at a Time.* New York: HarperCollins.

Ashford, Elizabeth. 2007. "The duties imposed by the human right to basic necessities." In *Freedom From Poverty as a Human Right: Who Owes What to the Very Poor?* T. Pogge, ed. New York: Oxford University Press, 183–218.

Attfield, Robin. 2003. *Environmental Ethics: An Overview for the Twenty-First Century.* Cambridge: Cambridge University Press.

Axel, Gabriel. 1987. *Babette's Feast.* Copenhagen: Nordisk Film.

Bain, Carmen, and Tamera Dandachi. 2014. "Governing GMOs: The (counter) movement for mandatory and voluntary non-GMO labels." *Sustainability* 6: 9456–9476.

Banton, Michael. 1998. *Racial Theories,* 3rd ed. Cambridge: Cambridge University Press.

Barnhill, Anne. 2015. "Does locavorism keep it too simple?" In *Philosophy Comes to Dinner,* A. Chignell, T. Cuneo, and M. C. Halteman, eds. New York: Routledge, 242–263.

Barrett, Christopher B., and Daniel G. Maxwell. 2005. *Food Aid After Fifty Years: Recasting Its Role.* Abingdon, UK: Routledge.

Bauer, Martin W. 2005. "Distinguishing red and green biotechnology: Cultivation effects of the elite press." *International Journal of Public Opinion Research* 17: 63–89.

Beckert, Sven.2014. *Empire of Cotton: A Global History.* New York: Vintage.

Behnassi, Mohamed, and Sanni Yaya. 2011. "Land resource governance from a sustainability and rural development perspective." In *Sustainable Agricultural*

Development: Recent Approaches in Resources Management and Environmentally-Balanced Production Enhancement, M. Behnassi, S. A. Shahid, and J. D'Silva, eds. Dordrecht: Springer, 3–23.

Belasco. Warren J. 2014. *Appetite for Change: How the Counterculture Took on the Food Industry*, 2nd ed. Ithaca, NY: Cornell University Press.

Bentham, Jeremy. 1789. *An Introduction to The Principles of Morals and Legislation.* Oxford: Clarendon Press.

Berenbaum, May. 2001. "Interpreting the scientific literature: Differences in the scientific and lay communities." *Plant Physiology* 125: 509–512.

Bernasconi, Robert. 2003. "Will the real Kant please stand up." *Radical Philosophy* 117: 13–22.

Bernasconi, Robert. 2018. "Critical philosophy of race and philosophical historiography." In *The Routledge Companion to Philosophy of Race,* P. C. Taylor, L. M. Alcoff, and L. Anderson, eds. New York: Routledge, 3–13.

Berry, Wendell. 1977. *The Unsettling of America: Culture and Agriculture.* San Francisco: Sierra Club Books.

Berry, Wendell. 1990. *What Are People For?* Berkeley, CA: Counterpoint Press.

Berryman, Sylvia. 2019. "Is global poverty a philosophical problem?" *Metaphilosophy* 50: 405–420.

Binder, Constanze, and Conrad Heilmann. 2017. "Duty and distance." *Journal of Value Inquiry* 5: 547–561.

Bloomfield, Brian P., and Theo Vurdubakis. 1995. "Disrupted boundaries: New reproductive technologies and the language of anxiety and expectation." *Social Studies of Science* 25: 533–551.

Blum, Elizabeth D. 2008. *Love Canal Revisited: Race, Class, and Gender in Environmental Activism.* Lawrence: University Press of Kansas.

Bowbrick, Peter. 1986. "The causes of famine: A refutation of Professor Sen's theory." *Food Policy* 11: 105–124.

Bratspies, Rebecca M. 2003. "Myths of voluntary compliance: Lessons from the StarLink Corn fiasco." *William and Mary Environmental Law and Policy Review* 27: 593–648.

Bruce, Donald. 2003. "Contamination, crop trials and compatibility." *Journal of Agricultural and Environmental Ethics* 16: 595–604.

Bruce J. Reynolds, "Black farmers in America, 1865–2000: The pursuit of independent farming and the role of cooperatives," Rural Business Cooperative Report 194. Washington, DC: USDA, 2002. Accessed August 29, 2021, at https://www.rd.usda.gov/files/RR194.pdf.

Bryant, Bunyon, and Paul Mohai, eds. 1992. *Race and the Incidence of Environmental Hazards: A Time for Discourse.* Boulder, CO: Westview Press.

Budolfson, Mark Bryant. 2015. "Is it wrong to eat meat from factory farms? If so, why?" In *The Moral Complexities of Eating Meat,* B. Fischer and B. Bramble, eds. New York: Oxford University Press, 80–98.

Burgess-Jackson, Keith. 2020. "Famine, affluence, and hypocrisy." *Philosophy* 10: 397–413.

Cafaro, Phillip. 2004. *Thoreau's Living Ethics: Walden and the Pursuit of Virtue.* Athens: University of Georgia Press.

Camacho, Luis. 2008. "Agriculture intensification from the perspective of development ethics." In *The Ethics of Intensification: Agricultural Development and Cultural Change,* P. B. Thompson, ed. New York: Springer, 97–110.

Carmichael, Jason. 2012. "Social control." *Oxford Bibliographies*. Accessed October 12, 2021, at https://www.oxfordbibliographies.com/view/document/obo-9780199756 384/obo-9780199756384-0048.xml

Carroll, Myles. 2018. "Narrating technonatures: Discourses of biotechnology in a neoliberal era." *Journal of Political Ecology* 25: 186–204.

Cheney, Ian. 2014. *The Search for General Tso*. Wicked Delicate Films. https://www. wickedelicate.com/about

Chignell. Andrew. 2015. "Can we really vote with our forks? Opportunism and the threshold chicken." In *Philosophy Comes to Dinner: Arguments About the Ethics of Eating*, A. Chignell, T. Cuneo, and M. C. Halteman, eds. New York: Routledge, 182–202.

Clay, Edward. 1991. "Food aid, development and food security." In *Agriculture and the State: Growth, Employment and Poverty in Developing Countries*, C. P. Timmer, ed. Ithaca, NY: Cornell University Press, 202–236.

Cole, Teju. 2012, March 21. "The white-savior industrial complex. *The Atlantic*. Accessed October 10, 2021, at https://www.theatlantic.com/international/archive/2012/03/the-white-savior-industrial-complex/254843/

Corrington, Robert S. 1990. "Emerson and the agricultural midworld." *Agriculture and Human Values* 7: 20–26.

Crocker, David A. 1998. "Development ethics." In *Routledge Encyclopedia of Philosophy*, E. Craig, ed. Milton Park, UK: Taylor and Francis, doi:10.4324/9780415249126-L016-1.

Crocker, David A. 2008. *Ethics of Global Development: Agency, Capability, and Deliberative Democracy*. Cambridge: Cambridge University Press.

Daly, Herman E. 2005. "Sustainable development: Definitions, principles, policies." In *The Future of Sustainability*, M. Keiner, ed. Dordrecht: Springer, 39–53.

Daly, Herman E., and John B. Cobb Jr. 1989. *For the Common Good: Redirecting the Economy Toward Community, the Environment, and a Sustainable Future*. Boston: Beacon Press.

Danbom, David B. 1991. "Romantic agrarianism in twentieth-century America." *Agricultural History* 65(4): 1–12.

Daniel, Pete. 1972. *The Shadow of Slavery: Peonage in the South, 1901–1969*. New York: Oxford University Press.

Davison, Aiden. 2001. *Technology and the Contested Meanings of Sustainability*. Albany, NY: SUNY Press.

De Bres, Helen. 2016. "Local food: The moral case." In *Food, Ethics, and Society: An Introductory Text with Readings*, A. Barnhill, M. Budolfson, and T. Doggett, eds. New York: Oxford University Press, 495–509.

Derrida, Jacques. 2005. *Rogues: Two Essays on Reason*. Pascale-Anne Brault and Michael Naas, Tr. Palo Alto, CA: Stanford University Press.

Des Jardins, Joseph R. 2012. *Environmental Ethics*. Detroit: Cengage Learning.

Desrochers, Pierre and Hiroku Shimizu. 2012. *The Locavore's Dilemma: In Praise of the 10,000 Mile Diet*. New York: PublicAffairs.

Dewey, John. 2008 [1925]. *Experience and Nature* republished as *The Later Writings of John Dewey*. vol. 1, Jo Ann Boydston ed. Carbondale: Southern Illinois University Press.

Diamond, Jared. 2011. *Collapse: How Societies Choose to Fail or Succeed*, rev. ed. New York: Penguin Books.

Dillingham, Harry C., and David F. Sly. 1966. "The mechanical cotton-picker, Negro migration, and the integration movement." *Human Organization* 25: 344–351.

Donner, Simon. 2020. "The ugly history of climate determinism is still evident today." *Scientific American*. Accessed June 24, 2020, at https://www.scientificamerican.com/article/the-ugly-history-of-climate-determinism-is-still-evident-today/

Dotson, Kristie. 2018. "Conceptualizing epistemic oppression." *Social Epistemology* 28: 115–138.

Douglas, Mary. 1966. *Purity and Danger: An Analysis of Concept of Pollution and Taboo*. London: Routledge and Keegan Paul.

Douglas, Mary. 1999. *Implicit Meanings: Selected Essays in Anthropology*, 2nd ed. New York: Routledge.

Douglas, Mary, and Aaron Wildavsky. 1982. *Risk and Culture: An Essay on the Selection of Technical and Environmental Dangers*. Berkeley: University of California Press.

Douglass, Gordon K. 1984. "The meanings of agricultural sustainability." In *Agricultural Sustainability in a Changing World Order*, G. K. Douglass, ed. Boulder, CO: Westview Press, 3–29.

Dresner, Simon. 2002. *The Principles of Sustainability*, 2nd ed. New York: Earthscan Press.

Dreyfus, Hubert L., and Stuart E. Dreyfus. 2005. "Peripheral vision: Expertise in real world contexts." *Organization Studies* 26: 779–792.

Drèze, Jean, and Amartya Sen. 1989. *Hunger and Political Action*. Oxford: Oxford University Press.

Driscoll, Michael J., and Ashok K. Lahiri. 1983. "Income-velocity of money in agricultural developing economies." *Review of Economics and Statistics* 65: 393–401.

Eldridge, Alison. n.d. "Jonestown." *Britannica*. https://www.britannica.com/event/Jonestown

Ellen, Roy F. 1982. *Environment, Subsistence, and System: The Ecology of Small-Scale Social Formations*. Cambridge: Cambridge University Press.

Elliott, Kevin C. 2009. "Pollution." In *Encyclopedia of Environmental Ethics and Philosophy*, J. B. Callicott and R. Frodeman, eds. Farmington Hills, MI: Macmillan Reference USA, 158–162.

Elliott, Kevin C. 2011. *Is a Little Pollution Good for You? Incorporating Social Values in Environmental Research*. New York: Oxford University Press.

Esterbrook, Barry. 2012. *Tomatoland: How Modern Industrial Agriculture Destroyed Our Most Alluring Fruit*. Kansas City, MO: Andrews McMeel Publishing.

Faucher, Luc. "Racism." In *The Routledge Companion to the Philosophy of Race*, P. C. Taylor, L. M. Alcoff, and L. Anderson, eds. New York: Routledge, 406–422.

Ferguson, Benjamin, and Christopher Thompson. 2021. "Why buy local?" *Journal of Applied Philosophy* 38: 104–120.

Ferrandino, Vittoria, and Valentia Sgro. 2021. "Italian and Entrepreneurship's Origins in the United States of America: A history analysis from the Post Second World War period to the present day." In *Book of Proceedings: 25th International Conference on Multidisciplinary Studies*, A. Singh, B. Barrett, G. Gui, E. Vieira, and V. Chkoniya, eds. Los Angeles: European Center for Science Education and Research, 343–359.

Ferris, Susan, and Ricardo Sandoval. 1997. *The Fight in the Fields: Cesar Chavez and the Farmworkers Movement*. New York: Harcourt and Brace.

Finkelman, Paul. 1984. "Thomas Jefferson and antislavery: The myth goes on." *Virginia Magazine of History and Biography* 102: 193–228.

Finkelman, Paul. 1993. "Jefferson and slavery." In *Jeffersonian Legacies*, P. F. Onuf, ed. Charlottesville: University of Virginia Press, 181–221.

Finucane, Melissa L., and Joan L. Holup. 2005. "Psychosocial and cultural factors affecting the perceived risk of genetically modified food: An overview of the literature." *Social Science and Medicine* 60: 1603–1612.

Fischer, Bob. 2016. "Bugging the strict vegan." *Journal of Agricultural and Environmental Ethics* 29: 255–263.

Fiske, Alan P. 1992. "The four elementary forms of sociality: Framework for a unified theory of social relations." *Psychological Review* 99: 689–723.

Fitzgerald, F. Scott. 1945. *The Crack Up.* New York: New Directions.

Flaccavento, Anthony. 2016. *Building a Healthy Economy from the Bottom Up: Harnessing Real-World Experience for Transformative Change.* Lexington: University Press of Kentucky.

Flynn, Dan. 2021. "Enforcement stepped up in past year to protect USDA's organic label." *Food Safety News.* Accessed March 15, 2022, at https://www.foodsafetynews.com/2021/05/enforcement-stepped-up-in-past-year-to-protect-usdas-organic-label/

Foucault, Michel. 1997. "On the genealogy of ethics: An overview of work in progress." In *Ethics, Subjectivity and Truth: The Essential Works of Foucault,* vol. 1, Paul Rabinow, ed., Robert Hurley, Tr. New York: New Press, 253–280.

Fox, Michael. 1986. *Agricide: The Hidden Crisis that Affects Us All.* New York: Schocken Books.

Fraser, Nancy. 1990. "Rethinking the public sphere: A contribution to the critique of actually existing democracy." *Social Text* 25/26: 56–80.

Freeman, Michael. 1995. "Are there collective human rights?" *Political Theory* 43: 25–40.

Freyfogle, Eric T. 2007. *Agrarianism and the Good Society: Land, Culture, Conflict, and Hope.* Lexington: University Press of Kentucky.

Garrett, Aaron. 2003. "Anthropology: The 'original' of human nature." In *Cambridge Companion to the Scottish Enlightenment,* A. Broadie, ed. Cambridge: Cambridge University Press, 79–93.

Glacken, Clarence J. 1976. *Traces on the Rhodian Shore: Nature and Culture in Western Thought from Ancient Times to the End of the Eighteenth Century.* Berkeley: University of California Press.

Goodman, David, and Michael Watts. 1997. "Agrarian questions: Global appetite, local metabolism: Nature, culture and industry in fin-de-siècle agro-food systems." In *Globalizing Food: Agrarian Questions and Global Restructuring,* D. Goodman and M. Watts, eds. London: Routledge, 1–32.

Goodnick, Liz. 2015. "Limits on locavorism." In *Just Food: Philosophy, Justice, and Food,* J. M. Dieterle, ed. New York: Rowman and Littlefield, 195–211.

Gordon-Reed, Annette. 2021. *On Juneteenth.* New York: W. W. Norton.

Grant, William E., and Paul B. Thompson. 1997. "Integrated ecological models: Simulation of socio-cultural constraints on ecological dynamics." *Ecological Modeling* 100: 43–59.

Greene, Jack. 1993. "The intellectual reconstruction of Virginia in the age of Jefferson." In *Jeffersonian Legacies,* P. S. Onuf, ed. Charlottesville: University of Virginia Press, 225–253.

Grober, Ulrich. 2012. *Sustainability: A Cultural History,* Ray Cunningham, Tr. Totnes, UK: Green Books.

Guha, Ramachandra. 1989. "Radical American environmentalism and wilderness preservation: A third world critique." *Environmental Ethics* 11: 71–83.

Guthman, Julie. 2007. *Agrarian Dreams: The Paradox of Organic Farming in California,* 2nd ed. Berkeley: University of California Press.

Habermas, Jürgen. 1981. "New social movements." *Telos* 1981(49): 33–37.

Hancock, James F. 2017. *Plantation Crops, Plunder, and Power: Evolution and Exploitation.* New York: Routledge.

Hardin, Garrett. 1968. "The tragedy of the commons." *Science* 162: 1243–1248.

Hardin, Garret. 1974. "Lifeboat ethics: The case against helping the poor." *Psychology Today Magazine* 8 (September 1974): 38–43, 123–126.

Hargrove, Eugene. 1989. *Foundations of Environmental Ethics.* Englewood Cliffs, NJ: Prentice-Hall.

Harper, A. Breeze. 2010. *Sistah Vegan: Black Women Speak on Food, Identity, Health, and Society.* Brooklyn, NY: Lantern Publishing.

Harper, A. Breeze. 2011. "Vegans of color, racialized embodiment, and problematics of the 'exotic.'" In *Cultivating Food Justice: Race, Class and Sustainability*, A. H. Alkon and J. Agyeman, eds. Cambridge, MA: MIT Press, 221–238.

Harris, Leonard. 2020. *A Philosophy of Struggle: The Leonard Harris Reader*, L. McBride, ed. London: Bloomsbury Academic.

Harris, Marvin. 1977. *Cannibals and Kings: The Origins of Culture.* New York: Random House.

Hartman, Micah, Anne B. Martin, Benjamin Washington, and Aaron Catlin. 2022. "National health care spending in 2020: Growth driven by federal spending in response to the COVID-19 pandemic." *Health Affairs* 41: 13–25.

Havinga, T. 2010. "Regulating kosher and halal foods: Differing arrangements between state, industry, and religious actors." *Erasmus Law Review* 3(4): 241–255.

Head, John W. 2021. *Deep Agroecology and the Homeric Epics: Global Cultural Reforms for a Natural-Systems Agriculture.* New York: Routledge.

Heldke, Lisa. 2003. *Exotic Appetites: Ruminations of a Food Adventurer.* New York: Routledge.

Hilde, Thomas C., and Paul B. Thompson. 2000. "Agrarianism and pragmatism." In *The Agrarian Roots of Pragmatism*, P. B. Thompson and T. C. Hilde, eds. Nashville, TN: Vanderbilt University Press, 1–21.

Hirschmann, A. O. 1970. *Exit, Voice, and Loyalty: Responses to Decline in Firms, Organizations, and States.* Cambridge, MA: Harvard University Press.

Hoganson, Kristen. 2019. *The Heartland: An American History.* New York: Penguin Books.

Holmes, Jack. 2017. "Here's what life is like in Puerto Rico 3 months after Hurricane Maria." *Esquire* December 17, 2017 https://www.esquire.com/news-politics/a14474788/puerto-rico-3-months-after-hurricane/

Hopkins, Raymond F. 1993. "Reforming food aid for the 1990's." In *Why Food Aid?* V. W. Ruttan, ed. Baltimore, MD: Johns Hopkins University Press, 200–215.

Hurt, Douglas. 2002. *American Agriculture: A Brief History*, rev. ed. Lafayette, IN: Purdue University Press.

Inge, M. Thomas. 1969. *Agrarianism in American Literature.* New York: Odyssey Press.

IPPC, AR5 WG2. 2014. *Climate Change 2014: Impacts, Adaptation, and Vulnerability.* Part A. Accessed May 23, 2018, at https://www.ipcc.ch/pdf/assessment-report/ar5/wg2/ar5_wgII_spm_en.pdf

Jansanoff, Sheila. 2004. "Ordering Knowledge, Ordering Society." In *States of Knowledge: The Co-Production of Science and Social Order*, Sheila Jasanoff, ed. New York: Routledge, 13–45.

Jefferson, Thomas. 1984. *Writings*. M. D. Peterson, ed. New York: Literary Classics of the United States.

Kapuria-Foreman, Vibha, and Mark Perlman. 1995. "An economic historian's economist: Remembering Simon Kuznets." *Economic Journal* 105: 1524–1547.

Keyser, M. A., and L. van Wesenbeeck. 2007. "Food aid and governance." In *Development Economics Between Markets and Institutions: Incentives for Growth, Food Security, and Sustainable Use of the Environment*, E. Bulte and R. Ruben, eds. Wageningen, NL: Wageningen URI, 183–208.

Kinchy, Abby. 2011. *Seeds, Science, and Struggle: The Global Politics of Transgenic Crops.* Cambridge, MA: MIT Press.

Kingsolver, Barbara. 2010. *Animal, Vegetable, Miracle: Our Year of Seasonal Eating.* London: Faber and Faber.

Kirkland, Frank M. 2018. "Kant on race and transition." In *The Routledge Companion to Philosophy of Race*, P. C. Taylor, L. M. Alcoff, and L. Anderson, eds. New York: Routledge, 28–42.

Kneen, Brewster. 1989. *From Land to Mouth.* Toronto: NC Press.

Koch, Adrienne. 1943. *The Philosophy of Thomas Jefferson.* New York: Columbia University Press.

Korthals, Michiel. 2001. "Taking consumers seriously: Two concepts of consumer sovereignty." *Journal of Agricultural and Environmental Ethics* 14: 201–215.

Kwieciński, Jakub. 2009. "Genetically modified abominations?" *EMBO Reports* 10: 1187–1190.

Kymlicka, Will. 1989. *Liberalism, Community, and Culture.* New York: Oxford University Press.

Laclau, Ernesto, and Chantal Mouffe. 2001. *Hegemony and Socialist Strategy: Towards a Radical Democratic Politics.* New York: Verso.

LaFollette, Hugh. 2003. "Pragmatic ethics." In *Blackwell Guide to Ethical Theory*, H. LaFollette, ed. Oxford: Blackwell Publishers, 400–419.

LaFollette, Hugh. 2003. "World hunger." In *A Companion to Applied Ethics*, R. Frey and C. Wellman, eds. Oxford: Blackwell, 238–253.

LaFollette, Hugh, and Larry May. 1996. "Suffer the little children." In *World Hunger and Morality*, W. Aiken and H. LaFollette, eds. Upper Saddle River, NJ: Prentice-Hall, 70–84.

Lakoff, George. 2004. *Don't Think of an Elephant: Know Your Values and Frame the Debate: The Essential Guide for Progressives.* White River Junction, VT: Chelsea Green Publishing.

Lakoff, George and Mark Johnson. 1999. *Philosophy in the Flesh: The Embodied Mind and Its Challenge to Western Thought.* New York: Basic Books.

Lang, Tim, David Barling, and Martin Caraher. 2009. *Food Policy: Integrating Health, Environment, and Society.* Oxford: Oxford University Press.

Leary, Warren A. 1996. "Genetic engineering of crops can spread allergies, study shows." *New York Times*, March 14, 1996. Accessed July 15, 2023, at https://www.nytimes.com/1996/03/14/us/genetic-engineering-of-crops-can-spread-allergies-study-shows.html

Lerman, Zvi. 2009. "Land reform, farm structure and agricultural performance in CIS countries." *China Economic Review* 20: 316–326.

Lewis, Jack. 1985. "The birth of EPA." *EPA Journal* 11: 6–11.

Lindwall, Courtney. 2019. "Industrial agricultural pollution 101." *NRDC.org* July 31, 2019. Accessed December 28, 2021, at https://www.nrdc.org/stories/industrial-agricultural-pollution-101whatis

Logins, Artūrs. 2016. "Save the children!" *Analysis* 76: 418–422.

Losey, John E., Linda S. Rayor, and Marianne E. Carter. 1999. "Transgenic pollen harms monarch larvae." *Nature* 399: 214.

Lyon, Sarah. 2021. "Fair trade's impact on smallholders." In *Handbook on the Human Impact of Agriculture*, H. S. James, Jr., ed. Northampton, MA: Edward Elgar, 194–217.

Maccoby, Hyam. 1999. *Ritual and Morality: The Ritual Purity System and Its Place in Judaism*. New York: Cambridge University Press.

MacIlwain, Colin. 2005. "U.S. launches probe into sales of unapproved transgenic corn." *Nature* 434: 423.

MacIntyre, Alasdair. 1984. *After Virtue: A Study in Moral Theory*, 2nd ed. Notre Dame, IN: University of Notre Dame Press.

Malthus, Thomas Robert. 1992 [1798]. *An Essay on the Principle of Population*. Donald Winch and Patricia James, eds. Cambridge: Cambridge University Press.

Mamani-Bernabé, Vincenta. 2015. "Spirituality and the Pachamama in the Andean Aymara worldview." In *Earth Stewardship. Ecology and Ethics*, vol. 2. R. Rozzi, F. S. Chapin III, J. B. Callicott, S. T. A. Pickett, M. E. Power, J. J. Armesto, and R. H. May, Jr., eds. Cham: Springer, 65–76. https://doi.org/10.1007/978-3-319-12133-8_6

Markel, Howard. 2017. *The Kelloggs: The Battling Brothers of Battle Creek*. New York: Pantheon Books.

Marosi, Richard. 2014. "Desperate workers on a Mexican mega-farm: 'They treated us like slaves.'" *Los Angeles Times*, December 14, 2014.

Mazoyer, Marcel, and Lawrence Roudart. 2006. *A History of World Agriculture from the Neolithic Age to the Current Crisis*, J. H. Membrez, Tr. New York: Monthly Review Press.

McBride, Lee III. "Racial imperialism and food traditions." In *The Oxford Handbook of Food Ethics*, A. Barnhill, M. Budolfson, and T. Doggett, eds. New York: Oxford University Press, 333–344.

McCann, Herbert G. 2002. "McDonald's settles over beef fries." *CBS News*, June 5, 2002. https://www.cbsnews.com/news/mcdonalds-settles-beef-over-fries/

McHugh, Susan. 2004. *Dog*. London: Reaktion Books.

McKenna, Erin, and Scott L. Pratt. 2015. *American Philosophy: From Wounded Knee to the Present*. New York: Bloomsbury Academic.

McKibben, Bill. 2016. "A grand experiment." In *Food, Ethics, and Society: An Introductory Text with Readings*, A. Barnhill, M. Budolfson, and T. Doggett, eds. New York: Oxford University Press, 490–495.

McMullen, Steven, and Mathew C. Halteman. 2019. "Against inefficacy objections: The real economic impact of individual consumer choices on animal agriculture." *Food Ethics* 2: 93–110.

McWilliams, James E. 2009. *Just Food: Where Locavores Get It Wrong and How We Can Truly Eat Responsibly*. New York: Little Brown.

Mead, George Herbert. 1967 [1934]. *Mind, Self, and Society*, C. W. Morris, ed. Chicago: University of Chicago Press.

Mendelsohn, Mike John Kough, Zigfridais Vaituzis, and Keith Matthews. 2003. "Are Bt crops safe?" *Nature Biotechnology* 21: 1003–1009.

Mercer, Kristin L., and Joel D. Wainwright. 2008. "Gene flow from transgenic maize to landraces in Mexico: An analysis." *Agriculture, Ecosystems, and Environment* 123: 109–115.

Michaelson, Eliot. 2016. "Act consequentialism and inefficacy." In *Food, Ethics, and Society: An Introductory Text with Readings*, A. Barnhill, M. Budolfson, and T. Doggett, eds. New York: Oxford University Press, 215–219.

Miele, Mara, A. C. Lomellini-Dereclenne, L.Mounier, and I. Veissier. 2017. "Implementation of the European legislation to protect farm animals: A case-study on French inspections to find solutions to improve compliance." *Animal Welfare Journal* 26(3): 311–321.

Mill, John Stuart. 1859. *On Liberty*. London: John W. Parker and Son.

Miller, Richard W. 2004. "Beneficence, duty, and distance." *Philosophy and Public Affairs* 32: 357–383.

Mills, Charles. 1997. *The Racial Contract*. Ithaca, NY: Cornell University Press.

Mills, Charles. 1998. *Blackness Visible: Essays on Philosophy and Race*. Ithaca, NY: Cornell University Press.

Minkoff-Zern, Laura-Anne. 2018. *The New American Farmer: Immigration, Race, and the Struggle for Sustainability*. Cambridge, MA: MIT Press.

Minteer, Ben A., and James P. Collins. 2005. "Ecological ethics: Building a new tool kit for ecologists and biodiversity managers." *Conservation Biology* 19: 1803–1812.

Mintz, Sidney. 1985. *Sweetness and Power: The Place of Sugar in Modern History*. New York: Penguin.

Montesquieu, Charles. 1989 [1748]. *Montesquieu: The Spirit of the Laws*. A. M. Cohler, B. C. Miller, and H. S. Stone, trs. and eds. Cambridge: Cambridge University Press.

Montmarquet, James A. 1989. *The Idea of Agrarianism: From Hunter-Gatherer to Agrarian Radical in Western Culture*. Moscow, ID: University of Idaho Press.

Navin, Mark C. 2014. "Local food and international ethics." *Journal of Agricultural and Environmental Ethics* 27: 349–368.

Navin, Mark. 2015. "Food sovereignty and gender justice: The case of La Via Campesina." In *Just Food: Philosophy, Justice and Food*, J. Dieterle, ed. London: Rowman and Littlefield, 87–100.

Neal, Stewart C., Jr., Matthew D. Halfhill, and Suzanne I. Warwick. 2003. "Transgene introgression from genetically modified crops to their wild relatives." *Nature Reviews: Genetics* 4(2003): 806–817.

Noll, Samantha. 2017. "Food sovereignty in the city: Challenging historical barriers to food justice." In *Food Justice in U.S. and Global Contexts*, I Werkheiser and Z. Piso, eds. New York: Springer, 95–111.

Noll, Samantha. 2020. "Local food as social change: Food sovereignty as a radical new ontology." *Argumenta* 5: 215–230.

Norton, Bryan G. 2003. *Searching for Sustainability: Interdisciplinary Essays in the Philosophy of Conservation Biology*. New York: Cambridge University Press.

Norton, Bryan G. 2005. *Sustainability: A Philosophy of Adaptive Ecosystem Management*. Chicago: University of Chicago Press.

Nussbaum, Martha C. 2001. *Women and Human Development: The Capabilities Approach*. New York: Cambridge University Press.

Ó Gráda, Cormac. 2009. *Famine: A Short History*. Princeton, NJ: Princeton University Press.

Ortiz-García, S., E. Ezcurra, B. Schoel, F. Acevedo, J. Soberón, and A. A. Snow. 2005. "Absence of detectable transgenes in local landraces of maize in Oaxaca, Mexico (2003–2004)." *Proceedings of the National Academy of Sciences* 102: 12338–12343.

Pappas, Gregory. 1997. "Dewey's moral theory: Experience as method." *Transactions of the Charles S. Peirce Society* 33: 520–556.

Pataki, Tamas. 2004. "Introduction." In *Racism in Mind*, M. P. Levine and T. Pataki, eds. Ithaca, NY: Cornell University Press, 1–23.

Petrini, Carlo. 2013. *The Slow Food Revolution: Why Our Food Should Be Good, Clean, and Fair*. New York: Rizzoli.

Pielke, Robert, Jr. 2007. *The Honest Broker: Making Sense of Science in Policy and Politics*. New York: Cambridge University Press.

Piketty, Thomas. 2014. *Capital in the Twenty-First Century*. Cambridge, MA: Harvard University Press.

Pimentel, David, and Hugh Lehman, eds. 1993. *The Pesticide Question: Environment, Economics, and Ethics*. New York: Chapman and Hall.

Piso, Zachary, Ian Werkheiser, Samantha Noll, and Christina Leshko. 2016. "Sustainability of what? Recognising the diverse values that sustainable agriculture works to sustain." *Environmental Values* 25: 195–214.

Plato. 1941. *Plato's The Republic*, B. Jowett, Tr. New York: Modern Library.

Pliakas, Alexandra. 2018. *Thinking Through Food: A Philosophical Introduction*. Peterborough, ON: Broadview Press.

Pogge, Thomas. 2002. *World Poverty and Human Rights: Cosmopolitan Responsibilities and Reforms*. Cambridge: Polity Press.

Pogge, Thomas, and Keith Horton. 2008. *Global Ethics: Seminal Essays*. New York: Paragon House.

Pollan, Michael. 1998. "Playing God in the garden." *New York Times Magazine* Oct. 25, 1998, 44.

Pollan, Michael. 2003. "How we live now: 10-23-03: The (agri)cultural contradictions of obesity." *New York Times Magazine*, October 23, 2003. Accessed July 15, 2023, at https://www.nytimes.com/2003/10/12/magazine/the-way-we-live-now-10-12-03-the-agri-cultural-contradictions-of-obesity.html

Pollan, Michael. 2006. *The Ominovore's Dilemma: A Natural History of Four Meals*. New York: Penguin Books.

Poppendieck, Janet. 1998. *Sweet Charity?: Emergency Food and the End of Entitlement*. New York: Penguin Books.

Pretty, Jules, J., Andrew S. Ball, Tim Lang, and James I. L. Morison. 2005. "Farm costs and food miles: An assessment of the full cost of the UK weekly food basket." *Food Policy* 30: 1–19.

Pulé, Paul M., Martin Hultman, and Angelica Wågström. 2021. "Discussions at the table." In *Men, Masculinities, and Earth*, P. M. Pulé and M. Hultman, eds. London: Palgrave, 17–101.

Quist, David, and Ignacio H. Chapela. 2001. "Transgenic DNA introgressed into traditional maize landraces in Oaxaca, Mexico." *Nature* 414: 541–543.

Raffensperger, Carolyn, Moira Campbell, and Paul B. Thompson. 1998. "Considering *The Spirit of the Soil* by Paul B. Thompson." *Agriculture and Human Values* 15: 161–176.

Randall, Willard Sterne. 1993. *Thomas Jefferson: A Life*. New York: Henry Holt and Co.

Rappaport, Roy A. 1967. *Pigs for the Ancestors: Ritual in the Ecology of a New Guinea People*. New Haven, CT: Yale University Press.

Rawls, John. 1993. "The law of peoples." *Critical Inquiry* 20: 36–68.

Reese, Ashanté M. 2019. *Black Food Geographies: Race, Self-Reliance, and Food Access in Washington, DC*. Chapel Hill: University of North Carolina Press.

Reid, Joseph D. 1975. "Sharecropping in history and theory." *Agricultural History* 49: 426–450.

Reynolds, Bruce J. 2002. *Black Farmers in America, 1865–2000: The Pursuit of Independent Farming and the Role of Cooperatives. Rural Business Cooperative Report 194*. Washington, DC: United States Department of Agriculture.

Robbins, John. 1987. *Diet for a New America*. Wallpole, NH: Stillpoint.

Robert, Jason Scott, and Françoise Baylis. 2003. "Crossing species boundaries." *American Journal of Bioethics* 3(3): 1–13.

Rogoff, Martin H., and Stephen L. Rawlins. 1987. "Food security: A technological alternative." *BioScience* 37: 800–807.

Rolston, Holmes, III. 1988. *Environmental Ethics: Duties To and Values In The Natural World*. Philadelphia: Temple University Press.

Roman-Alcalá, Antonio. 2021. "Agrarian anarchism and authoritarian populism: Towards a more (state-critical) critical agrarian studies." *Journal of Peasant Studies* 48: 298–328.

Rubel, Alan, and Robert Streiffer. 2005. "Respecting the autonomy of European and American consumers: Defending positive labels on gm foods." *Journal of Agricultural and Environmental Ethics* 18: 75–84.

Ruttan, Vernon W. 1993. "The politics of U.S. food aid policy: A historical review." In *Why Food Aid?* V. W. Ruttan, ed. Baltimore, MD: Johns Hopkins University Press, 2–36.

Ruttan, Vernon, and Yujiro Hayami. 1984. "Toward a theory of induced institutional innovation." *Journal of Development Studies* 20(4): 203–223.

Ruttan, Vernon W. 1993. "Does food aid have a future?" In *Why Food Aid?* V. W. Ruttan, ed. Baltimore, MD: Johns Hopkins University Press, 216–228.

Ryder, John. 2013. *The Things in Heaven and Earth: An Essay in Pragmatic Naturalism*. New York: Fordham University Press.

Sachs, Jeffery. 2005. *The End of Poverty*. New York: Penguin.

Sagoff, Mark. 1986. "Values and preferences." *Ethics* 96: 301–316.

Sagoff, Mark. 2001. "Genetic engineering and the concept of the natural." In *Genetically Modified Food and the Consumer*, A. Eaglesham, S. G. Pueppke, and R. W. F. Hardy, eds. Ithaca, NY: National Agricultural Biotechnology Council, 127–140.

Saitone, Tina L., K. Aleks Schaefer, and Daniel P. Scheitrum. "COVID-19 morbidity and mortality in U.S. meatpacking counties." *Food Policy* 101(2021): 102072.

Sandin, Per, Erland Mårald, Aiden Davison, David E. Nye, and Paul B. Thompson. 2013. "Book symposium on *The Agrarian Vision: Sustainability and Environmental Ethics* by Paul B. Thompson." *Philosophy and Technology* 26: 301–320.

Sandler, Ronald L. 2007. *Character and Environment: A Virtue-Oriented Approach to Environmental Ethics*. New York: Columbia University Press.

Sandler, Ronald L. 2012. *Food Ethics: The Basics*. New York: Routledge.

Sayre, Laura. 2011. "The politics of organic farming: Populists, evangelicals, and the agriculture of the middle." *Gastronomica* 11(2): 38–47.

Schell, Orville. 1984. *Modern Meat*. New York: Random House.

Schiffer, Kathy. 2016. "*Babette's Feast* is Pope Francis' favorite film (and mine)." *National Catholic Register,* November 27, 2016, Blogs. Accessed July 15, 2023, at https://www.ncregister.com/blog/babettes-feast-is-pope-francis-favorite-film-and-mine

Schlosser, Eric. 1995. "In the strawberry fields." *The Atlantic Monthly.* November 1995. Accessed July 15, 2023, at https://www.theatlantic.com/magazine/archive/1995/11/in-the-strawberry-fields/305754/

Schmidt, Anna. n.d. "Groupthink, psychology." *Encyclopedia Britannica.* Accessed October 4, 2021, at https://www.britannica.com/science/groupthink

Schultz, Theodore W. 1960. "Value of U.S. farm surpluses to underdeveloped countries." *Journal of Farm Economics* 42: 1019–1030.

Sebo, Jeff, and Jason Schukraft. 2021. "Don't farm bugs." *Aeon* July 27, 2021. Accessed July 15, 2023, at https://aeon.co/essays/on-the-torment-of-insect-minds-and-our-moral-duty-not-to-farm-them

Sellars, Wilfrid. 1980. "On reasoning about values." *American Philosophical Quarterly* 17: 81–101.

Sen, Amartya. 1981. *Poverty and Famines: An Essay on Entitlement and Deprivation.* Oxford: Oxford University Press.

Sen, Amartya. 1987. *On Ethics and Economics.* Oxford: Basil Blackwell.

Sen, Amartya. 1999. *Development as Freedom.* New York: Alfred A. Knopf.

Sen, Amartya. 2009. *The Idea of Justice.* Cambridge, MA: Harvard University Press.

Shue, Henry. 1980. *Basic Rights: Subsistence, Affluence, and U.S. Foreign Policy.* Princeton, NJ: Princeton University Press.

Singer, Peter. 1972. "Famine, affluence, and morality." *Philosophy and Public Affairs* 1: 229–243.

Singer, Peter. 1973. "Animal liberation." *New York Review of Books,* April 5, 1973. Accessed January 1, 2021, at https://www.nybooks.com/articles/1973/04/05/animal-liberation/

Singer, Peter. 1975. *Animal Liberation: A New Ethic for Our Treatment of Animals.* New York: Random House.

Singer, Peter. 1993. *Practical Ethics,* 2nd ed. New York: Cambridge University Press.

Singer, Peter. 2002. *One World: The Ethics of Globalization.* New Haven, CT: Yale University Press.

Singer, Peter. 2009. *The Life You Can Save: Acting Now to End World Poverty.* New York: Random House.

Singer, Peter, and Jim Mason. 2006. *The Ethics of What We Eat: Why Our Food Choices Matter.* Emmaus, PA: Rodale Press.

Singer, Ross, Stephanie Houston Grey, and Jeff Motter. 2020. *Rooted Resistance: Agrarian Myth in Modern America.* Fayetteville: University of Arkansas Press.

Skyrms, Bryan. 2003. *The Stag Hunt and the Evolution of Social Structure.* New York: Cambridge University Press.

Smil, Vaclav. 2001. *Enriching the Earth: Fritz Haber, Carl Bosch, and the Transformation of World Food Production.* Cambridge, MA: MIT Press.

Smith, Alisa, and J. MacKinnen. 2007. *Plenty: Eating Locally on the 100 Mile Diet.* New York: Random House.

Smith, Henry Nash. 1950. *Virgin Land: The American West in Symbol and Myth.* New York: Vintage Books.

Smith, Kimberly K. 2001. "Wendell Berry's feminist agrarianism." *Women's Studies* 30: 623–646.

Smith, Kimberly K. 2003. *Wendell Berry and the Agrarian Tradition: A Common Grace.* Lawrence: University of Kansas Press.

Solow, Robert M. 1992. *An Almost Practical Step Toward Sustainability.* Washington D. C.: Resources for the Future.

Spencer, Phillip. 2012. *Genocide since 1945.* New York: Routledge.

Stanley, Jason. 2015. *How Propaganda Works.* Princeton, NJ: Princeton University Press.

Stanley, Jason. 2018. *How Fascism Works: The Politics of Us and Them.* New York: Random House.

Star, S. L., and J. Griesemer. 1989. "Institutional ecology, 'translations,' and boundary objects: Amateurs and professionals on Berkeley's Museum of vertebrate zoology." *Social Studies of Science* 19: 387–420.

Stoll, Stephen. 2002. *Larding the Lean Earth: Soil and Society in Nineteenth-Century America.* New York: Hill and Wang.

Strauss, Debra M. 2018. "Genetically modified organisms in food: Ethical tensions and the labeling initiative." In *Ethical Tensions from New Technology: The Case of Agricultural Biotechnology*, H. S. James, Jr., ed. Wallingford, UK: CABI International, 83–96.

Streeten, Paul, Shahid Javed Burki, Mahbub Ul-Haq, Norman Hicks, and Frances Stewart. 1981. *First Things First: Meeting Basic Human Needs in the Developing Countries.* New York: Oxford University Press.

Streiffer, Robert, and Alan Rubel. 2004. "Democratic principles and mandatory labeling of genetically engineered food." *Public Affairs Quarterly* 18: 223–248.

Svanberg, Ingvar, and Åsa Berggren. 2021. "Insects as past and future food in entomophobic Europe." *Food, Culture and Society* 24: 624–638.

Tauger, Mark. 2021. *Agriculture in World History*, 2nd ed. New York: Routledge.

Taylor, Paul W. 1986. *Respect for Nature: A Theory of Environmental Ethics.* Princeton, NJ: Princeton University Press

Taylor, Peter J. 2005. *Unruly Complexity: Ecology, Interpretation and Engagement.* Chicago: University of Chicago Press.

Taylor Stephen L., and Susan L. Hefle. 2001. "Will genetically modified foods be allergenic?" *Journal of Allergy and Clinical Immunology* 107: 765–771.

ten Have, Henk, and Maria do Céu Patrão Neves. 2021. "Genetic modification (GMOs), general." In *Dictionary of Global Bioethics*. New York: Springer, 559–560.

Thompson, E. P. 1971. "The moral economy of the English crowd in the 18th century." *Past and Present* 50: 76–136.

Thompson, Paul B. 1992. *The Ethics of Aid and Trade: U.S. Food Policy, Foreign Competition and the Social Contract.* New York: Cambridge University Press.

Thompson, Paul B. 1997. "Science policy and moral purity: The case of animal biotechnology." *Agriculture and Human Values* 14: 11–27.

Thompson, Paul B. 1999. "Farming as focal practice." In *Technology and the Good Life?* E. Higgs, A. Light and D. Strong, eds. Chicago: University of Chicago Press, 166–181.

Thompson, Paul B. 2000. "Thomas Jefferson and agrarian philosophy." In *The Agrarian Roots of Pragmatism*, P. B. Thompson and T. C. Hilde, eds. Nashville, TN: Vanderbilt University Press, 118–139.

Thompson, Paul B. 2002. "Why food biotechnology needs an opt out." In *Engineering the Farm: Ethical and Social Aspects of Food Biotechnology*, B. Bailey and M. Lappe, eds. Washington, DC: Island Press, 27–43.

Thompson, Paul B. 2004. "Getting pragmatic about farm animal welfare." In *Animal Pragmatism: Rethinking Human-Nonhuman Relationships*, E. McKenna and A. Light, eds. Bloomington: Indiana University Press, 140–159.

Thompson, Paul B. 2007. "Agricultural sustainability: What it is and what it is not." *International Journal of Agricultural Sustainability* 5: 5–16.

Thompson, Paul B. 2008. "The opposite of human enhancement: Nanotechnology and the blind chicken problem." *NanoEthics* 2: 305–316.

Thompson, Paul B. 2010. *The Agrarian Vision: Sustainability and Environmental Ethics.* Lexington: University Press of Kentucky.

Thompson, Paul B. 2014. "Thomas Jefferson's land ethics." In *Thomas Jefferson and Philosophy: Essays on the Philosophical Cast of Jefferson's Writings*, M. A. Holowchak, ed. Lanham, MA: Lexington Books, 61–77.

Thompson, Paul B. 2015. "Agricultural ethics: Then and now." *Agriculture and Human Values* 32: 77–85.

Thompson, Paul B. 2015. *From Field to Fork: Food Ethics for Everyone*. New York: Oxford University Press.

Thompson, Paul B. 2017. "Analytic and pragmatist food ethics: Method and approach." *Pragmatism Today* 8(2): 10–23.

Thompson, Paul B. 2017. *The Spirit of the Soil: Agriculture and Environmental Ethics*, 2nd ed. New York: Routledge.

Thompson, Paul B. 2018. "Norton and sustainability as such." In *A Sustainable Philosophy—The Work of Bryan Norton*, S. Sarkar and B. A. Minteer, eds. New York: Springer, 7–26.

Thompson, Paul B. 2019. "Emerging (food) technology as an environmental and philosophical issue in the era of climate change." In *Food, Environment, and Climate Change: Justice at the Intersections*, E. Gilson and S. Kenehan, eds. Lanham, MD: Rowman and Littlefield, 195–212.

Thompson, Paul B. 2020a. *Food and Agricultural Biotechnology in Ethical Perspective*. 3rd ed. New York: Springer.

Thompson, Paul B. 2020b. "Philosophical ethics and the improvement of farmed animal lives." *Animal Frontiers* 10: 21–28.

Thompson, Paul B. 2021. "The vanishing ethics of husbandry." In *The Animals in Our Midst: The Challenges of Co-Existing with Animals in the Anthropocene*, B. Bovenkerk and J. Keulartz, eds. Cham: Springer, 203–221.

Thompson, Paul B., and Patricia A. Norris. 2021. *Sustainability: What Everyone Needs to Know*. New York: Oxford University Press.

Timmer, C. Peter. 1986. *Getting Prices Right: The Scope and Limits of Agricultural Price Policy*. Ithaca, NY: Cornell University Press.

Timmerman, Travis. 2018. "Save (some of) the children." *Philosophia* 46: 465–472.

Trewavas, Anthony. 2002. "Malthus foiled again and again." *Nature* 418: 668–670.

Tsu, Cecilia M. 2013. *Garden of the World: Asian Immigrants and the Making of Agriculture in California's Santa Clara Valley*. New York: Oxford University Press.

Tyler, Shakara S., and Eddie A. Moore. 2013. "Plight of black farmers in the context of USDA farm loan programs: A research agenda for the future." *Professional Agricultural Workers Journal* 1(1): 6.

Tynauer, Matt. 2008. "Industrial Revolution, take two." *Vanity Fair*, June 10, 2008. Accessed August 13, 2021, at https://www.vanityfair.com/culture/2008/05/mcdonough200805

Urban, Jessica Leann. 2007. "Interrogating privilege/challenging the 'greening of hate.'" *International Feminist Journal of Politics* 9: 251–264.

Valles, Sean. 2018. *Philosophy of Population Health: Philosophy for a New Public Health Era*. New York: Routledge.

van der Weele, Cor. 2021. "How to save cultured meat from eco-modernism? Selective attention and the art of dealing with ambivalence." In *Animals in Our Midst: The Challenges of Co existing with Animals in the Anthropocene*, B. Bovenkerk and J. Keulartz, eds. New York: Springer, 545–557.

Veit, Helen Zoe. 2013. *Modern Food, Moral Food: Self-Control, Science, and the Rise of Modern Eating in the Early Twentieth Century*. Chapel Hill: University of North Carolina Press.

Veracini, Lorenzo. 2010. *Settler Colonialism: A Theoretical Overview*. London: Palgrave Macmillan.

Vileisis, Ann. 2008. *Kitchen Literacy: How We Lost the Knowledge of Where Our Food Comes From, and Why We Need to Get It Back*. Washington DC: Island Press.

Vogeler, C. S. 2019. "Why do farm animal welfare regulations vary between EU member states? A comparative analysis of societal and party political determinants in France, Germany, Italy, Spain and the UK." *Journal of Common Market Studies* 57: 317–335.

Vogt, D. U., and M. Parrish. 1999. *Food Biotechnology in the United States: Science, Regulation, and Issues.* Washington, DC: Government Printing Office.

Waldmueller, Johannes M., and Laura Rodriguez. 2019. "Buen Vivir and the rights of nature: Alternative visions of development." In *Routledge Handbook of Development Ethics*, J. Drydyk and L. Keleher, eds. New York: Routledge, 234–247.

Weber, Christopher L., and H. Scott Matthews. 2008. "Food-miles and the relative climate impact of food choices in the United States." *Environmental Science and Toxicology* 42: 3508–3513.

Weirich, Paul, ed. 2007. *Labeling Genetically Modified Food: The Philosophical and Legal Debate.* New York: Oxford University Press.

Welin, Stelin. 2013. "Introducing the new meat: Problems and prospects." *Etikk i praksis-Nordic Journal of Applied Ethics* 1: 24–37.

Wellman, Christopher Heath. 2005. "Famine relief: The duties we have to others." In *Contemporary Debates in Applied Ethics*, A. I. Cohen and C. H. Wellman, eds. New York: Blackwell, 313–325.

Werkheiser, Ian. 2015. "Community epistemic capacity." *Social Epistemology* 30: 25–44.

Werkheiser, Ian, and Zachary Piso. 2015. "People work to sustain systems: A framework for understanding sustainability." *Journal of Water Resources Planning and Management* 141: A4015002.

White, Monica M. 2019. *Freedom Farmers: Agricultural Resistance and the Black Freedom Movement.* Chapel Hill: University of North Carolina Press.

Whyte, Kyle P. 2016. "Indigenous food sovereignty, renewal and U.S. settler colonialism." In *The Routledge Handbook of Food Ethics*, M. Rawlinson and C. Ward, eds. New York: Routledge, 354–365.

Whyte, Kyle P. 2018. "Food sovereignty, justice, and indigenous peoples: An essay on settler colonialism and collective continuance." In *The Oxford Handbook of Food Ethics*, A. Barnhill, M. Budolfson, and T. Doggett, eds. New York: Oxford University Press, 345–366.

Wiencek, Henry. 2012. *Master of the Mountain: Thomas Jefferson and His Slaves.* New York: Farrar, Straus and Giroux.

Wikipedia. 2023. "The concert for Bangladesh." Accessed January 19, 2023, at https://en.wikipedia.org/wiki/The_Concert_for_Bangladesh

Wills, Garry. 1979. *Inventing America: Jefferson's Declaration of Independence.* New York: Vintage Books.

Wills, Garry. 1997. "American Adam." *New York Review of Books,* March 6, 1997. Accessed September 9, 2021, at https://www.nybooks.com/articles/1997/03/06/american-adam/

Winders, Bill. 2009. *The Politics of Food Supply: U.S. Agricultural Policy in the World Economy.* New Haven, CT: Yale University Press.

Wirzba, Norman. 2019. *Food and Faith: A Theology of Eating,* 2nd ed. New York: Cambridge University Press.

World Commission on Environment and Development. 1987. *Our Common Future.* New York: Oxford University Press.

Yakini. Malik. 2018. "Visions of a new economy from Detroit: A conversation with Malik Yakini." *Non Profits Quarterly,* July 11, 2018. Accessed February 23, 2022, at https://non

profitquarterly.org/visions-of-a-new-economy-from-detroit-a-conversation-with-malik-yakini/

Yakini, Malik. 2022. "Building black food sovereignty: An update." Zoom lecture delivered March 15, 2022. Accessed May 5, 2022, at https://www.youtube.com/watch?v=Daez RQDgHDg

Yang Jisheng. 2008. *Tombstone: The Great Chinese Famine, 1958–1962,* S. Moser and J. Guo, Tr.; E. Friedman, S. Moser, and J. Guo, eds. New York: Farrar, Straus and Giroux.

Young, Carson. 2022. "Should you buy local?" *Journal of Business Ethics* 176: 265–281.

Zerbe, Noah. 2004. "Feeding the famine? American food aid and the GMO debate in southern Africa." *Food Policy* 29: 593–608.

Zeina Nakat and Christelle Bou-Mitri. 2021. "COVID 19 and the food industry: Readiness assessment," *Food Control* 121. https://doi.org/10.1016/j.foodcont.2020.107661.

Ziff, Bruce. 2005. "Travels with my plant: *Monstanto vs. Schmeiser* revisited." *University of Ottawa Law and Technology Journal* 2: 493–510.

Index